Innovations in Health and Medicine

Innovations in Health and Medicine brings together cutting-edge research by medical historians from Britain, Germany, France, the USA, Japan, and New Zealand. Innovative in its approach to innovation, it focuses on diffusion and resistance, and organization as well as technology.

The collection features issues such as control and compliance, professional power and economic constraint, cultural divides, 'configured users' and ingenuity. The Introduction relates the collection to history and sociology of innovation and technology, asking what is distinctive about medicine and health. The book brings comparative perspectives to bear in three ways:

- Micro-studies look at close neighbours using ultrasound scanners in Scotland, and chronic disease clinics in Manchester.
- Cross-national studies show how innovations fared as they migrated: Western nursing in Japan; Eastern acupuncture in the UK; and Swiss bone surgery in the former East Germany and the USA.
- A section on re-innovation includes new media representation of medicine, and an alternative form of kidney dialysis in the UK; reinvention of the midwife in New Zealand; and living donor transplants in France.

Explorations of recent cases, along with deeper probing of the past century, call into question how the past relates to the future. Health policy-makers and analysts, practitioners, users, and historians will find the editor's claims for the uses of history provocative. With its emphasis on clarity of writing, mix of empirical details and analysis, and rich bibliography, this volume offers rewards to academic and health service readers alike.

Jennifer Stanton works with the History Group at the London School of Hygiene and Tropical Medicine. She has published on the history of medical technologies, infectious disease research and policy, and African child health.

Routledge Studies in the Social History of Medicine

Edited by Bernard Harris,
Department of Sociology and Social Policy, University of Southampton, UK

The Society for the Social History of Medicine was founded in 1969, and exists to promote research into all aspects of the field, without regard to limitations of either time or place. In addition to this book series, the Society also organizes a regular programme of conferences, and publishes an internationally recognized journal, *Social History of Medicine*. The Society offers a range of benefits, including reduced-price admission to conferences and discounts on SSHM books, to its members. Individuals wishing to learn more about the Society are invited to contact the series editor through the publisher.

The Society took the decision to launch 'Studies in the Social History of Medicine', in association with Routledge, in 1989, in order to provide an outlet for some of the latest research in the field. Since then, the series has expanded significantly under a number of series of editors, and now includes both edited collections and monographs. Individuals wishing to submit proposals are invited to contact the series editor in the first instance.

1. Nutrition in Britain
Science, Scientists and Politics in the Twentieth Century
Edited by David F. Smith

2. Migrants, Minorities and Health
Historical and Contemporary Studies
Edited by Lara Marks and Michael Worboys

3. From Idiocy to Mental Deficiency
Historical Perspectives on People with Learning Disabilities
Edited by David Wright and Anne Digby

4. Midwives, Society and Childbirth
Debates and Controversies in the Modern Period
Edited by Hilary Marland and Anne Marie Rafferty

5. Illness and Healing Alternatives in Western Europe
Edited by Marijke Gijswit-Hofstra, Hilary Marland and Hans de Waardt

Innovations in Health and Medicine

Diffusion and resistance in the twentieth century

Edited by Jennifer Stanton

London and New York

First published 2002
by Routledge
11 New Fetter Lane, London EC4P 4EE

Simultaneously published in the USA and Canada
by Routledge
29 West 35th Street, New York, NY 10001

Routledge is an imprint of the Taylor & Francis Group

Typeset in Baskerville by Taylor & Francis Books Ltd
Printed and bound in Great Britain by TJ International Ltd, Padstow,
Cornwall

British Library Cataloguing in Publication Data
A catalogue record for this book is available from the British Library

Library of Congress Cataloging in Publication Data
Stanton, Jennifer
Innovations in health and medicine : diffusion and resistance in the
twentieth century / Jennifer Stanton.
p. cm.
Includes bibliographical references and index.
1. Medicine–History–20th century. 2. Medical innovations–History–20th
century. 3. Medical technology–History–20th century. I. Title.

R855.3 .S735 2002
610'.904–dc21   2001048592

ISBN 0–415–24385–8

Contents

Introduction: on theory and practice   1

JENNIFER STANTON

Innovation studies and history of health and medicine: explaining a shortfall 1
Aims and perspectives of this book 2
Overview of the book 7
Final pointers 12
Notes 15

PART I
Close neighbours   19

1 The effects of local context on the development of
obstetric ultrasound scanning in two Scottish hospitals   21

DEBBIE NICHOLSON

The changing nature of obstetric ultrasound in the 1970s 23
Reconfiguring a medical hierarchy 24
Scanning the periphery: real-time ultrasound in a remote island community 28
Conclusion 33
Notes 34

2 Organization, ethnicity and the British National
Health Service   37

HELEN VALIER AND ROBERTA BIVINS

Introduction: chronicity, ethnicity and the role of the patient in late
*   twentieth-century medicine 37*

PART II
Across nations   65

3   The Western mode of nursing evangelized?: nursing
professionalism in twentieth-century Japan   67
AYA TAKAHASHI

4   Acupuncture and innovation: 'New Age' medicine
in the NHS   84
ROBERTA BIVINS

5   Degrees of control: the spread of operative fracture
treatment with metal implants: a comparative perspective
on Switzerland, East Germany and the USA, 1950s–1990s   106
THOMAS SCHLICH

Illustrations

Figures

Tables

Contributors

Roberta Bivins is an Assistant Professor at the Department of History, University of Houston, Texas, USA. Her interests include the cross-cultural transmission of expert knowledge, and the diverse intersections of medicine and migration. She has published *Acupuncture, Expertise and Cross-Cultural Medicine* (2000), a study of acupuncture use in Britain since 1683.

Martine Gabolde is a medical doctor working in public hospitals in Paris. She has worked at the Bioethics Division of the Council of Europe and has published on living donor transplantation. She is now completing a PhD thesis on this topic at the University of Paris – René Descartes.

Kelly Loughlin holds a Wellcome Research Fellowship at the London School of Hygiene and Tropical Medicine. She has published on medicine and the mass media and is currently researching the history of health education in post-war Britain.

Anne Marie Moulin trained both as a philosopher and a physician. She is head of the Health and Societies Department at IRD (Institute of Research for Development), Paris, France. She has published *Le dernier langage de la médicine: histoire de l'immunologie de Pasteur au Sida* (1991), *L'aventure de la vaccination* (1996), and co-edited (with Alberto Cambrosio) *Singular Selves: Historical Issues and Contemporary Debates in Immunology* (2001). Her forthcoming comprehensive book on medical history has a special emphasis on cross-cultural practices. She is a member of the National Ethics Committee of the French Transplantation Agency.

Philippa Mein Smith is Senior Lecturer in History at the University of Canterbury, Christchurch, New Zealand. She is the author of *Maternity in Dispute: New Zealand 1920–1939* (1986), *Mothers and King Baby: Infant Survival and Welfare in an Imperial World: Australia 1880–1950* (1997), and (with Donald Denoon) *A History of Australia, New Zealand and the Pacific* (2000).

Debbie Nicholson is Lecturer in Sociology at the University of Paisley, Scotland, where she teaches Sociology of Science and Technology. She has an MPhil in History of Medicine and is completing her PhD at Glasgow University, on the history of ultrasound in Scotland.

Thomas Schlich is Heisenberg Research Fellow of the German Research Council and teaches medical history at the University of Freiburg, Germany. His book *Surgery, Science and Industry: A Revolution in Fracture Care, 1950s–1990s* is published in 2002.

Jennifer Stanton is a member of the History Group at the London School of Hygiene and Tropical Medicine. She has published on the history of anaesthetics (as Beinart, *A History of the Nuffield Department of Anaesthetics, Oxford, 1937–1987*), hepatitis B, and medical technologies; also on child health in colonial Africa. She co-edited (with Virginia Berridge) a special issue of *Social Science and Medicine: 'Science Speaks to Policy'* (1999).

Aya Takahashi is based at the College of Humanities, Iwaki Meisei University, Fukushima, Japan. She completed her PhD on nursing professionalism in modern Japan at the University of London. Her main research interest is women and public health in twentieth-century society from both Japanese and international perspectives.

Helen Valier is a Lecturer in the Division of the History and Philosophy of Science at the University of Leeds, UK. Her PhD thesis looked at the development of scientific medicine in twentieth-century Manchester. She works chiefly on laboratory and academic medicine in the twentieth century.

Acknowledgements

We are grateful to *Media History* (a journal based in London) for permission to reproduce substantially the article by Kelly Loughlin, '"Your Life In Their Hands": the context of a medical-media controversy', *Media History*, 2000, vol. 6, no. 2, pp. 177–88; details of this journal can be viewed on the following website: http://www.tandf.co.uk. For Dr Takahashi's chapter, we are grateful to the Rockefeller Archive Center in New York for permission to quote from documents in Record Group 1.1, Series 609, 609A, and 609E; and to the International Council of Nurses in Geneva, Switzerland, for permission to cite material from their archives, which remains copyright of the International Council of Nurses. We are also enormously grateful to all informants who granted interviews, whether these are cited anonymously or by name.

This volume was prepared while the editor was supported by the Wellcome Trust as part of the 'Science Speaks to Policy' History Programme at the London School of Hygiene and Tropical Medicine. Several chapters grew out of papers presented at the Society for the Social History of Medicine autumn 1998 conference, organized by Jennifer Stanton, and hosted at Blythe House with the co-operation of Tim Boon and Robert Bud of the Science Museum London. Special thanks are due to Series Editor Bernard Harris, for support and commentary on the manuscript; responsibility for errors remains with the editor.

Acknowledgments

Abbreviations

AFP	alpha-feto protein
AIDS	Acquired Immune Deficiency Syndrome
AO	Arbeitsgemeinschaft für Osteosynthesefragen
ASIF	Association for Internal Fixation
BBC	British Broadcasting Corporation
BDA	British Diabetic Association
BKPA	British Kidney Patients Association
BMA	British Medical Association
BMAS	British Medical Acupuncture Society
BMJ	*British Medical Journal*
BMUS	British Medical Ultrasound Society
BPD	bi-parietal diameter
BSE	bovine spongiform encephalopathy
CAP	consumer active paradigm
CAPD	continuous ambulatory peritoneal dialysis
CHC	Community Health Council
CRL	crown-rump length
CT	computed tomography
CTC	Complementary Therapy Centre
DSN	diabetes specialist nurse
EBM	evidence-based medicine
EDTA	European Dialysis and Transplant Association
EFG	Etablissement Français des Greffes (French Transplantation Agency)
ESRD	end-stage renal disease
FAC	Family Advice Centre
GDR	German Democratic Republic
GP	general practitioner
GPO	general practitioner obstetrician
HFA	Health Funding Authority
HIV	Human Immunodeficiency Virus
HLA	Human Leucocyte Antigen(s)
ICN	International Council of Nurses

ICW	International Council of Women
IDDM	insulin dependent diabetes mellitus
IT	information technology
JBJS	*Journal of Bone and Joint Surgery*
JNA	Japanese Nurses' Association
JRCS	Japanese Red Cross Society
LMC	Lead Maternity Carer
MACHEM	Manchester Action Committee for the Health Care of Ethnic Minorities
MAP	manufacturer active paradigm
MDC	Manchester Diabetes Centre
MP	Member of Parliament
MRC	Medical Research Council
MRI	Manchester Royal Infirmary
MTA	medical technology assessment
NAJE	Nurses' Association of the Japanese Empire
NCW	National Council of Women
NHS	National Health Service
NIDDM	non-insulin dependent diabetes mellitus
NIH	National Institute of Health
NKRF	National Kidney Research Fund
NZ	New Zealand
OB	outside broadcasting
PR	public relations
PRO	public relations officer
RCOG	Royal College of Obstetricians and Gynaecologists
RCS	Royal College of Surgeons
RCT	randomized control trial
RF	Rockefeller Foundation
RT	real time
SCC	Sickle Cell Centre
SCOT	social construction of technology
SCTC	Sickle Cell and Thalassaemia Centre
SSK	sociology of scientific knowledge
UKTS	United Kingdom Thalassaemia Society
UNOS	United Network for Organ Sharing
YLITH	Your Life In Their Hands

Introduction

On theory and practice

Jennifer Stanton

Innovation studies and history of health and medicine: explaining a shortfall

Consider these two observations. History – the writing of history – is all about change and continuity, and often focuses particularly on explaining change. Quite apart from academic studies, medical 'breakthrough' is a constant topic of fascination in the media, among the public, and in museums and popular litera-ture. Given these two observations, it seems rather odd that there have not been more studies of the history of medical innovation. Indeed, two collections of essays on medical innovation that emerged ten years ago – from Pickstone in Manchester and Löwy in Paris – were themselves innovative. As the editors pointed out, most writing on medical innovation up to that point had been from the tradition that assumed innovations in medicine were adopted because they were superior, and spread with resistance merely from the unenlightened.[1] The newer work sought to situate medical innovations in professional networks and wider social change; it also tended to find failed innovations as interesting as those that succeeded. Although the past decade has seen notable publications on medical technology, inevitably relating to innovation, there has been little specifi-cally in this field.[2] Less still has been written from a historical perspective on the post-war period, the main focus of the current volume.[3]

If innovation is about change and the excitement of new developments, then we could have expected more studies. The lack may be partly due to the newer school of social and political history of medicine casting work in moulds such as social history of professions, gender relations, and policy development. Certainly all of the chapters in this book fit other categories. Again, recent 'cutting edge' work explicitly framed as innovation studies tends to draw on a dauntingly wide range of theoretical approaches and to look outside the history of medicine, to the history and sociology of science, and the history of technology. This implies a lot of new groundwork for historians of medicine who want to venture into innovation studies, and its appeal may be lessened if the sociological writing is viewed as jargon-laden.[4] However, as some of the chapters in this book will demonstrate, it is not always necessary to have a highly visible theoretical frame. Thorough empirical research itself can generate models and hypotheses.[5]

In this book, we aim to demonstrate the appeal of innovation as a theme for historians of health and medicine. Our ambitions go further than our own field; we also hope to illuminate themes that anyone interested in current controversies should find relevant. From the perspective of the present, perhaps even the very recent histories in this volume are not at first glance linked with issues of the day – currently (though this may have changed by the time the book appears) the implications of the new genetic engineering for health and medicine. We could easily stray here into conducting arguments about the uses of history, and into 'justifying' history as a quasi social science – a task I and my colleagues at a postgraduate medical school are familiar with. With discourses of risk, ethical dilemma, evidence base and audit dominating the 'production of knowledge' agenda, while 'public understanding of science' dominates the dissemination/consumption agenda, history tends to be squeezed out when studying innovation. Yet – and we will return to this point at the end of the Introduction – to forget history is always a mistake.

Aims and perspectives of this book

There are several ways in which this volume adds new perspectives. Most obviously, we concentrate on the history of quite recent innovations, mostly in the post-war period. Our work covers terrain which is recognizable in terms of current concerns, but with that historical twist which throws fresh light on the familiar. Also, we range widely, to include not only medical and health technologies (surgery, diagnostic imaging, treatment technology, transplants, and 'alternative' medicine), but also forms of organization of health services (nursing, maternity care, chronic disease clinics), as well as innovation in the representation of medicine (television). Comparative dimensions are unusually strong, with authors looking at the behaviour of innovations in different countries or localities, comparing innovations at different points in time, or a mixture of these approaches. Hence the volume is organized around these comparative perspectives.

In terms of stages of innovation we look less at initiation or invention, a focus of many past studies, and more at the spread or diffusion stages.[6] However, we do not adopt a unilinear model of how diffusion 'ought' to behave, for example, the 'S-shaped curve' prevalent in diffusion studies.[7] Although diffusion in medical and health settings can be measured as overall uptake, we are more interested in following the dynamics in particular settings. Resistance may enter the balance either to halt diffusion or as a shaping factor, in medicine as for a range of technologies.[8] In our chapters, the role of resistance is highlighted particularly – and not surprisingly – in contexts where there was greater perception of risk (Schlich, Gabolde and Moulin), or where sections of professions felt under threat (Bivins, Loughlin, Mein Smith).

History of technology and history of science have been dominated by male authors and to some extent this pattern appeared to be repeated for history of medical technologies. However, this collection, with mainly female authors and several papers on female professionals and/or patients, follows numerous contributions by women – although many of these, like the present volume, do not have a particularly feminist perspective.[9] Notable work in history of technology from women authors has varied in this respect. An American historian of technology with strong theoretical interests, Judith McGaw, offers a feminist perspective that does not allow women's contributions to be shoved into a ghetto.[10] A starting point for many of us interested in diffusion might be the survey and revision of diffusion studies by Jennifer Tann, who uses her own work on the diffusion of steam engines to illuminate diffusion across space and time.[11] Leading American historian of technology Ruth Schwartz Cowan both edited a special issue of *Technology and Culture* on medical and psychological technologies, and included the Pill in her own survey of American technology, but the majority of her work is on non-medical technologies.[12] These are female but not feminist authors, though Cowan's analysis of the Pill is informed by feminist critiques. For medical technologies, it may be too soon to say whether women writers tend to be more alert than men to questions of gender; it probably depends on the writer. Consideration of gender dimensions runs through Marjan Groen's very grounded account of intensive care nursing in The Netherlands; men as well as women become involved to varying degrees, partly depending on the technological appeal of the work.[13]

One of the 'pioneering' works on the history of medical technologies, Stanley Joel Reiser's *Medicine and the Reign of Technology*, dealt with closeness versus distance in caring for patients, an issue closely related to gender divisions of labour.[14] According to Reiser, the patient's story had been replaced by technological measurement in diagnosis. The related argument that with increasingly sophisticated technologies, the 'healing hands' of first doctors, and subsequently of nurses have been withdrawn, leading to a more impersonal style of medicine, has been challenged by voices pointing out that the more 'intuitive' side of caring creeps back in less obvious ways. [15] In any case, this whole area of patient care is one that we should note as a distinguishing feature of medical as opposed to non-medical technologies. Instead of relationships between manufacturer, consumer, and machine, normally in commercial contexts, we have manufacturer, professional, patient, and machine, within contexts of health services that have been provided by statutory, voluntary, or commercial bodies in varying mixtures.

A theoretical theme which can be imported from technology studies is that of the 'configured user', a term developed by Keith Grint and Steve Woolgar from their work on the information technology industry.[16] They used the term as an analogue to the way that the components of a computer are 'configured' or arranged so as to perform the functions required of them by the designers. Technicians in the company used language that implied consumers also had to be correctly 'configured' in order for the computer to work to its best capacity; but this was not something the designers or salespeople could influence, except at the margins, through helplines and instructions. On the whole the users were either disposed to be configured or not, even before their interaction with the computer. Those users who failed to operate the computers were deficient in some way, shown by their failure to adapt or configure themselves adequately. This makes sense intuitively, for example, young people seem on the whole better 'configured users' for computers than older people. It may be useful to think about how this might apply to medical technologies, in particular to assess whether the 'configured users' – most adapted to the technology, most likely to persist with its use – are the doctors and nurses, or the patients. Although one can think in terms of various 'end users' for computers (for example, networked office workers in a large company, as opposed to individuals working from home), we would argue that the difference is of a much greater order where medical innovations are concerned, and that the meanings of a technological or organizational innovation are likely to be quite differently constructed for patients than for nurses or doctors.

Again, comparing medical with non-medical innovations, there is a pervasive difference in where the innovation is coming from. Writers on history of technology have identified two models of origination, the 'manufacturer active paradigm' or MAP and the 'consumer active paradigm' or CAP.[17] Leaving aside the issue of whether we want to call the user a consumer (a dubious term for medical technologies), it is valid to note the historical tendency for medical innovation to be most often instituted by the users – doctors and scientists.[18] Without denying the risk involved in research and development in the commercial sector, others have pointed out the greater uncertainty surrounding technological innovation in medicine, thanks to the peculiarities of applying technology to people who are ill.[19] And in thinking about diffusion of medical innovation we have to take especial account of the limitations imposed by cost constraints, depending on policy controls at a given time and the context of the health system in the country under consideration.[20]

Running through the volume is the theme – or variations on the theme – of professional status and power, a useful analytical tool in much social history of medicine in recent years.[21] Though not unique to medicine, the particular form and strength of professionalization has been a distinctive historical feature, at least as important in relation to innovation as the others already mentioned. We argue that with medical and health technologies, techniques, or modes of service delivery, the way that innovations diffused often rested, not on some abstract notion of 'evidence' as claimed by advocates at the scene, but on assertions of authority by professional alliances which themselves fluctuated through time. A good example is the early twentieth-century fashion for 'Twilight Sleep' as an analgesic for childbirth, among middle-class women in the USA and Europe: Judith Walzer Leavitt wrote brilliantly about the alliance between obstetricians and midwives who supported this method, against general practitioners who favoured simpler concoctions which they could use unaided.[22] Whoever could capture the market of birthing women through their favoured technology, also established professional dominance, for the time being at least. Divergent national paths appeared later, with midwives in the USA losing their domiciliary role more completely than in other countries.[23]

The example of Twilight Sleep, a multitude of subsequent studies, and chapters of our book such as Nicholson's on ultrasound, Bivins's on acupuncture, Schlich's on metal implants for bone surgery, and Stanton's on renal dialysis, show people making choices; accepting or rejecting technologies; adapting themselves to the technology or adapting the technology to their circumstances. These historians' view of innovations – technologies or systems – not as given but as contingent and shaped by forces such as professional interests, fits to some extent with the 'social construction of technology' (SCOT) sociological approach. Trevor Pinch and Wiebe Bijker's paper on the twists and turns of bicycle innovation,[24] in a seminal collection on SCOT, showed how big-wheeled bicycles (such as the penny-farthing), with greater risk of spillage, appealed to young men, while the more stable smaller-wheeled bikes were first marketed as women's and older men's choice. They suggested that 'relevant social groups', as in this example, help to shape most technologies, and that seeking such groups would be more productive than simply thinking of the producer–consumer division. (We could ask, to what extent is the shaping passive as in consumer choice, or active as in Nicholson's account of doctors modifying a technology to suit different terrains?) Noting how social change produced a consensus in favour of more stable bicycles, Pinch and Bijker developed the notion of 'interpretative flexibility' to characterize social attitudes affecting technologies. Closure, or stabilization, occurs when one technological form dominates; but variants may co-exist, and as problems are redefined the dominant form can be challenged again.

Bijker later added an over-arching concept of the 'technological frame' of meaning, shared by different social groups, that helps to guide and shape the development of artefacts.[25] Presumably those elements of a culture that cut across gender and class, or which support such divisions but are commonly recognized as incontrovertible, are likely to provide such a frame. We would argue that this applies to innovations in forms of organization as well as artefacts, as in the chapters here by Valier and Bivins on clinics for diabetes and thalassaemia treatment in Manchester, Takahashi on Western nursing in Japan, and Mein Smith on the re-innovation of midwifery in New Zealand. We could speak of an 'organizational frame' as a parallel to a technological frame, and in this sense we could say that the diffusion of innovations in health care is shaped by the shared meaning possible in a given cultural and organizational setting. In different countries, of course, the health system itself provides an obvious frame, which encourages diffusion or resistance depending on time and place. Gabolde and Moulin's chapter on the varying fortunes of living donor organ transplantation in France shows the intersection of a given organizational frame with subtly shifting cultural attitudes, where transplant doctors, patients, and potential donors provided ample material for social commentators. Loughlin analyses the responses of the medical profession and media professionals to an innovation that helped to shape the way medicine would be viewed – literally – by the public, within the overall frame of the British NHS.

As these chapters demonstrate, historians tend to look at contested at least as much as shared ground, evident even within an apparently monolithic system, as sub-groups battle to promote their own position. Initiation or uptake of innovations can often be seen as one strategy in these struggles. The important role of legislation controlling contracts for childbirth professionals in the 1980s and 1990s in Mein Smith's account recalls work by Dominique Florin on contracts for health promotion work by general practitioners (GPs) in the UK in the 1990s.[26] These health checks involved technologies (for cholesterol readings, urinalysis, as well as height, weight, and blood pressure measurements), but a central issue was in a sense organizational: interpretations of trials of such health checks were affected by who does what. Though GPs held the contracts, the work was done by nurse practitioners; and they and the public health doctors valued such preventive work more than did the GPs. The society-wide bias in favour of curative, hospital care provided a frame in which (in the absence of expert advice) policy-makers interpreted the uncertain results as unfavourable to large investment in this preventive effort. An innovation in contractual relations was thus curtailed.

Historians have long used notions of interest groups and networks of social interaction around scientific, technical, and medical innovation without using the terms coined by the SCOT school, and it may be argued that these sociological framings add little to the historical ones.[27] But few would reject the influence of the German scientist Ludwik Fleck whose work, which appeared in the interwar years but was published in English much later, propounded the social genesis of scientific ideas.[28] Such work appealed immensely to the post-war school of sociology of scientific knowledge (SSK) led by Barry Barnes in Scotland and tuned to almost anthropological finesse by Bruno Latour and Steve Woolgar in France.[29] In this SSK tradition, not only the social context of science but the content of scientific discoveries are seen as socially shaped; there is no separate sphere of 'scientific truth' that has to be held sacrosanct and unquestioned. No one truth is truer than another; all are true in relation to the social group that builds and maintains them, for the time being, and therefore historically contingent. Perhaps it is slightly easier for us to envisage facts in this way, as slippery eels that wriggle out of our grasp, than to think similarly of machines, as called for by SCOT. In either case, we learn to view the creations of the people and groups we study as malleable according to criteria beyond their advertised ones of evidence, efficiency, and effectiveness.

Historians of medicine looking at innovations need to be alert to the close relation between these two domains of laboratory science and technology/techniques. Löwy, looking primarily at laboratory science, points out that the loss of a notion of 'scientific truth' is inherently unsettling:

> The new image of biomedical studies is probably less reassuring than the traditional view of the laboratory as a temple of science in which impersonal and objective observers unveil the hidden facts of nature and then attempt to apply them to the detection and cure of human disease.[30]

Although traditionalist medical historians (often doctors) still tend to search the past for the roots of true discoveries, in pragmatic terms the scientific uncertainty pinpointed by Löwy has long been recognized in the field of medicine. The attempt in post-war years to mop up the resulting untidiness through the new 'gold standard' of randomized control trials (RCTs) has only partially solved the problem, as noted by Rudolph Klein, a British health policy analyst. Raising queries about RCTs, Klein points out: 'Innovation is often a stepwise process, involving the modification of existing procedures over time, and it is not clear at what stage in the process evaluation should take place. Outcomes may, furthermore, be contingent on their setting.'[31] Such a comment, seen as challenging in the climate of fervent support for evidence-based evaluation in the NHS, chimes with a scepticism that is part of the historian's normal toolbox. And perhaps the historian's approach is confirmed rather than reshaped by SCOT and SSK. What we are saying here is that not only outcomes (mentioned by Klein), but also inputs to innovations are contingent, at whatever stage in the process you choose to look – contingent on networks, interest groups, negotiations, beliefs, economic pressures, and politics.

Of course this approach, involving deconstruction of certainties and straightforward models in order to understand social construction of ideas and meanings, leaves us with a much more complicated picture. There is a nice parallel in the literature on diffusion of technologies, where simpler models from economic theory and history of technology have been subjected to a range of critiques; but in reviewing these and moving on to her own more complex model, Tann emerges with a diagram so all-inclusive that it resembles a circuit-board or the plan of your central heating system.[32] Historians of medicine might feel comfortable with this model since we are accustomed to complexity, but we do not tend to draw models. Part of the way we deal with complexity (analogous to scientists creating artificially simplified conditions in the laboratory) is to take a case study, elaborate it, and then extrapolate to more general issues. That, after all, is what this book offers: a set of case studies that we hope together will advance our understanding of larger issues.

Overview of the book

Part I Close neighbours

Most of our case studies draw on more than one example, across space or time. We start with the section, 'Close neighbours', where local comparisons between what we might term micro-studies enable the authors to draw lessons about quite specific aspects of context and/or content. Debbie Nicholson in Chapter 1 describes the uptake of obstetric ultrasound in two Scottish hospitals in the 1970s, arguing that local context not only affected the organizational position of the technology, but led to modifications – a sort of reconfiguring of the machine by the users. She conjures up lively pictures of machines that magically change shape to fit better the demands of professionals in awkward spatial juxtapositions. She attributes differences in local 'configuring' to local factors of geography on the one hand and medical–social relations, especially distribution and redistribution of control, on the other. Nicholson shows how, from the same starting point – the first thoughts about use of ultrasound by obstetricians encountering the original models – the technology took widely differing trajectories. In one hospital, professional hierarchies were the dominant shaping force, operating in the context of a split between the site where the medical supervisors (radiologists) normally operated and the site of use where non-clinical staff (radiographers) used the machine. In the second case, outreach work among remote islands influenced the choice of technology, then led to small but significant modifications and a division of labour involving general practitioners working the machine at times. The 'relevant social groups' of SCOT are seen here as highly contextualized, both spatially and in historical time, while the practice of using the technology has itself actively shaped the groups as well as the technologies.

Valier and Bivins in Chapter 2 are not comparing like with like in different contexts, so much as two different disease models and approaches within the same context – Manchester in the 1980s and 1990s – where they examine innovations in the organization of clinics for chronic diseases which happen to have higher prevalence in immigrant communities. Innovation in the Manchester Diabetes Clinic, which had a longer history, they term 'internally driven' since diabetics specialists mobilized the organizational changes that attracted funding for the expanded hospital-based clinic from local and national sources, including industry and charities. General practitioners who had played a major role in treating diabetic patients, fearing marginalization, offered some resistance to the changes but were reassured and to some extent incorporated through further developments in community treatment spurred on by government directives. Although internally driven, the diabetic clinic innovations were linked with wider political and institutional changes in British medicine. With sickle cell and thalassaemia, on the other hand, the initiative was 'externally driven' by the South Asian and Afro-Caribbean communities, resulting in a clinic that was physically and to some extent organizationally separate from the hospital. In this case, community activists utilized the public health arena, and the clinic opened with research funds from the health authority and operated with a strong health promotion ethos. Valier and Bivins argue that understanding of these two instances of organizational innovation requires use of twin lenses: ethnicity, and medical concepts of patient compliance in chronic disease.

Part II Across nations

Ethnicity of another order forms the backdrop to Part II, where authors compare the spread of innovations across nations; either a 'transplanted' innovation in Takahashi's study of Western nursing in Japan, and in Bivin's study of acupuncture in the West; or an innovation that spreads with varying speed and efficiency in contrasting national medical cultures, in Schlich's account of an innovation in bone surgery.

Takahashi in Chapter 3 takes issue with traditional Japanese historians' interpretations of the spread of Western-style nursing along with scientific medicine in Japan, in the first half of the twentieth century. Appearances certainly suggested full adoption of the Western system, with veneration of Nightingale, growth of nurse training, and participation in international conferences. Close study of the archives reveals, however, that beneath the surface a deep resistance operated, based on Japan's militaristic and imperial culture, that curtailed the full diffusion of attitudes and activities which formed an integral part of the development of nursing professionalism in the West. Takahashi shows this through two aspects of interwar nursing history: the manoeuvres of the Japanese Red Cross Society to join the International Council of Nurses, while incorporating Korean nurses; and attempts by a few American and Japanese pioneers with Rockefeller Foundation backing to stimulate development of public health nursing in Japan. Because of a perception of nurses' services to patients as menial and intimate, the concept of a respectable female profession was not easily accepted. Nurses were welcome only as part of the military effort and as handmaidens to doctors; any moves toward a feminist professional consciousness were stifled, not deliberately, but as a function of gender relations and military dominance (which of course also existed in the West but were more pronounced in Japan). Thus Takahashi concludes that the growth of Western-style nursing in Japan was more a socio-historical than a medical–scientific development.

Bivins in Chapter 4 looks at transfer in an opposite direction, with the growth of a much older system – acupuncture – in the West, particularly in Britain. We are witnessing the cultural transplantation and diffusion of a technology that can be adopted with or without the system of beliefs which originally accompanied it, so that in some senses this case is analogous to that analysed by Takahashi. Although the historical meaning of 'Orientalism' in the West obviously differs from that of 'Westernization' in Japan, both carried a positive cultural message from the nineteenth century onwards, for at least a section of the 'importing' societies. But while the oriental/exotic connotations of acupuncture tended to attract patients and thus aid diffusion, the same connotations met with resistance from sections of the medical profession. While looking at the origins of Western fascination with Chinese medicine, Bivins concentrates on a more recent period, of 'New Age' ideology in Britain from the 1970s onwards, when acupuncture can be conceptualized either as an innovation or as 'exotically antique and alternative'. In order to tease out the layers of meaning more thoroughly, Bivins compares the coverage in the medical press of acupuncture, which was both exotic and alternative, with homeopathy as another 'alternative' therapeutic system but of Western origin, and with tamoxifen and lumpectomy as 'orthodox' medical innovations. Bivins also examines the relative roles of patients and practitioners as initiators through a detailed study of practice in an NHS centre for complementary therapies in London – a case study that provides clear resonances with that of Valier and Bivins in this volume, on the consumer-led development of a sickle cell anaemia clinic in Manchester. The mixed legacy of orientalism, together with the lack of explanation for acupuncture's mechanism of operation in terms of Western science, as we might expect from SSK, posed problems for orthodox practitioners and clinical managers; but were not a drawback for many lay consumers.

At first glance, the story outlined by Schlich in Chapter 5 for the spread of osteosynthesis, a sophisticated and risky procedure to treat bone fractures, seems to support aspects of both the conventional and SCOT approaches to history of medical innovations. There was a big gap between the origination of the method and its uptake – a common theme in more traditional history of medicine – before a professional association, the *Arbeitsgemeinschaft für Osteosynthesefragen* (AO), in Switzerland actively promoted it from the late 1950s, when it began to spread successfully. This group can be interpreted in revisionist, social history of medicine terms as exercising a profession-building strategy around a technological innovation; or in SCOT terms as a 'relevant social group'; but in any case depended largely on local notions of confraternity. By comparing the uptake of the procedure in two other countries, the German Democratic Republic (GDR) and the United States, Schlich demonstrates a relationship between diffusion and levels of control. In the communist East German state of the GDR, structural preconditions of centralized control over surgeons allowed the AO to establish the correct application of the system from the early 1960s. In the more individualistic USA, this proved to be almost impossible and very poor outcomes led to rejection by the medical community; hence osteosynthesis was not accepted as a standard therapy in the USA before the 1980s. Through his three-country comparison, Schlich underlines the importance of control in explaining the paradox of a modern technique faring better in an underfunded socialist system than in the world's wealthiest nation. He warns that we cannot predict which 'environmental' factors – cultural, political, or economic – are going to predominate in the diffusion of any given innovation, only that some aspect of these will prove crucial.

Part III Re-innovation and the state

In our third section we look at interactions between professions, publics, and the state, in the context of one country rather than across nations. In each of these cases we are looking at some sort of 're-invention' or 're-innovation' involving negotiation of choices, in which groups were either shaping, or being moulded by, new forms of technology or organization.

In the case of Loughlin's study (Chapter 6) of a British television series called *Your Life in Their Hands*, an innovative representation of medicine did not replace previous methods of representation but presented new challenges, threatening to remove some degree of control from the profession. There had been TV portrayals of medicine before, but only carefully staged, not 'actuality' footage. This created resistance, reflecting perhaps a recognition among doctors of the power of the new medium. At the same time others in the profession grasped the possibilities of television for 'selling' a preferred version of modern scientific medicine. The multiple contexts that helped shape events were medicine, the media, and a new context created at the interface between these two: the medical press and attendant public relations experts. Loughlin carefully demonstrates what was new about the series, since portrayals of hospital work had been broadcast before (it was the first to show actual operations), and how this was used in the debates and medico-political manoeuvrings around the series, as the British Medical Association worked out how this medium might reconstruct the public image of medicine.

Stanton in Chapter 7 discusses two major variants of technology for treatment of chronic renal failure which arrived at different points in time, haemodialysis in the 1960s and CAPD or continuous ambulatory peritoneal dialysis in the 1980s. Haemodialysis diffused more slowly in the UK than in countries with comparable incomes such as the USA, Germany, or France. It has been argued that there was no central policy in the UK, but a closer look confirms that policy at the centre, especially cash limitation, resulted in poorer dialysis provision in some regions. The end-users for whom innovations in renal dialysis have been designed can be discussed in terms of 'configured users', and Stanton asks which users had to adapt most: doctors, nurses and technicians, or patients. Material on haemodialysis suggests that while patients were most strongly configured in terms of adapting to fit the new technology, doctors made the choices affecting diffusion, within given financial constraints. A quantitative approach giving another perspective is supported by the importance attached to numbers by some of the historical actors. Stanton explores, through regional statistics, whether CAPD diffused most rapidly in areas with less haemodialysis, but finds this was not the case. The UK's high overall usage of this modality (on a par with poorer nations), may have resulted from a combination of economic restraint together with clinicians' preferences, with the patient entering the picture as a willing configured user for any modality.

Mein Smith in Chapter 8 examines historically the recent innovation in maternity services in New Zealand of identifying a 'lead carer' in childbirth, who may be a midwife or a doctor, required to manage a fixed budget for the total care of each patient or 'client'. This innovation itself represents a response to the reinvention or re-innovation of the midwife after her near disappearance in the 1970s and 1980s. One outcome of the new power of the midwife is that many general practitioners have withdrawn from midwifery services, and another is that midwives' incomes have increased. The chapter explores the complexities of diffusion and gender relations in childbirth management over the course of the twentieth century, during which primary responsibility for care of the birthing mother and infant has shifted from the midwife to the doctor and back again. (The time-periods covered here in detail are the interwar years, and the 1980s–90s.) In New Zealand resistance has certainly led to re-innovation in maternity care, as in the return of the midwife, but with some unexpected outcomes in terms of cost and choice.

Gabolde and Moulin in Chapter 9 turn our attention to an instance of re-innovation which captured the imagination of French medical correspondents as transplant doctors and policy-makers wrangled with the ethics and image of permitting transplants from living donors. This question was especially sharp in France where, after initially allowing the procedure, the government had discouraged living donor transplants. The authors compare French policy with that in other countries, but focus especially on variations in practice between regions of France, to try to answer questions about the nature of the medical and policy alliances that resulted in the French furore. Their work also involves questions on the meaning of organ donation for both the donor and the recipient.

Final pointers

Earlier, this Introduction asserted that it is a mistake to forget history; and said so in a manner which implied that history had something essential to contribute not only to our understanding of innovation, but also perhaps to our handling of change in the present. This should apply even when history was not dealing directly with issues of immediate concern. Additionally, after delineating ways in which our approaches are informed by linked lines of work in the history of medicine and other fields, it was suggested that our case studies should help to illuminate larger issues. This seems the right moment to review those claims.

First, for readers concerned with methodology, it is worth noting that both the topics and the very recent period covered in several of these chapters required innovative techniques. While Takahashi, dealing with an earlier period, used archives as well as nursing journals and other published sources (though she faced strict restraints on citing certain archival material), Mein Smith had to supplement such sources with draft and enacted legislative documents, for the recent period. Evidence to inquiries, and records of meetings and conferences, readily found in archives, are often much more difficult to obtain for the modern period. Nicholson, Valier and Bivins, Schlich, Loughlin, Stanton, and Gabolde and Moulin make varying use of interviews in addition to the medical press. Bivins analyses some of the medical literature in terms of citation rates, while Stanton adapts quantified data from professional sources to test a theory about patterns of diffusion.

Of course, all of us locate our studies against a background of secondary literature, the other mainstay of historical methodology – both theoretical and empirical literature. Some chapters are more overtly informed by theory than others, with the field of study affecting their slant. Loughlin, for example, is debating issues that arise in media studies as well as history of medicine, while Takahashi and Mein Smith are sharply aware of gender issues in nursing history. Our borrowings and building on other literatures were made with awareness that medicine and health are peculiar fields. While recognizing innovation and diffusion as areas where history of technology has much to offer, historians looking at medical and health innovations need to be especially alert to gender dimensions, closeness and distance in the carer–patient relationship, and the professional power of doctors. And on the sociological side we are more or less enthusiastic fellow-travellers with SCOT and SSK, insofar as they resonate with historical framings, but aim to contribute fresh insights. Encompassing in this volume organizational as well as technological changes, and active as well as passive shaping in the diffusion process, we focus (as historians tend to do) on contested ground. We are sensitive to the ways that scientific uncertainty tends to loom as an especially large shadow in medicine. And although our attention to social groups has parallels with SCOT/SSK, these chapters obviously look at innovation, diffusion, and resistance in very particular health service, political economy, and cultural settings.

We have built on previous historical work which powerfully demonstrated the importance of understanding medical innovation and change in the context of its own time and place. There are four most obvious ways the current volume offers something new. (1) Where previous work tended to consider initiation of innovations, here attention is directed to diffusion and resistance – that is, how and why changes have spread, taking into account opposing factors. (We have looked at the qualitative side of diffusion, rather than measuring how much an innovation has spread over time, except for brief statistical interventions in chapters by Bivins, Schlich, Stanton, and Gabolde and Moulin.) (2) Our case studies are all comparative, looking at diffusion of the same innovation, or two different innovations, in nearby locations; diffusion and resistance in different national settings or cross-cultural transfer; or re-innovation within short or longer time-spans. (3) Where most (though not all) predecessors have worked on innovations in technologies, concepts, and techniques in medicine, about half our work is concerned, directly or indirectly, with innovations in organization, a relatively new field. (4) We are (in all except one chapter) exploring the post-war period which has received relatively little historical attention before; and several chapters take history right up to yesterday.

The pace of change in the British NHS has been breathtaking, and those of our chapters which look at the UK should be read in that light;[33] similar changes have occurred in New Zealand and elsewhere. The wider economic picture has been post-war boom, followed by the crisis of oil price hikes in the 1970s, which impinged on health spending in most developed economies (such as we are dealing with – another book will be needed to discuss these issues in less developed countries). The 1980s saw the rise of econometric, neo-liberal approaches that changed social welfare policy at macro and micro levels in many countries. Against this background, government lack of spending on essential services may 'warp' diffusion (Stanton); private sponsors help out with experimental services (Valier and Bivins); negotiations to revise contracts tangle with the demarcation line between doctors and midwives (Mein Smith). Beyond the 'public–private partnership' in regular medicine, patients seek alternative therapies either through the NHS or privately (Bivins); this can be seen partly as a reassertion of patient choice, in a situation where market values have been forced into the public services. While the medical profession and health policy-makers may turn increasingly to evidence-based medicine (EBM) and medical technology assessment (MTA) to help judge the validity of innovation in techniques, drugs, and technologies, patients themselves perhaps remain sceptical about statistically based evidence. (Individuals tend to seek 'what works for me' rather than 'whatever is most cost-effective for the population as a whole'.)

Health systems differ greatly between countries, of course, in terms of financing and the relative autonomy of the medical and nursing professions. Very local conditions may be important in shaping diffusion of technologies, as in the case of ultrasound scanners (Nicholson). Ethnicity can affect the shaping of organizational innovations within one urban area, as in the case of Manchester chronic disease clinics (Valier and Bivins). Two of our major conceptual tools, professionalism and the social construction of meaning, operate in very particular historical and local circumstances. Thus nursing professionalism in Japan in the first half of the twentieth century actually meant something very different from in the West (Takahashi). Control and training smoothed successful diffusion of AO in Germany, in contrast to overt professional power which hampered it in the USA (Schlich). Loughlin's depiction of negotiations over images of medicine in the UK, and Gabolde and Moulin's French portrait of doctors and patients vying for control over ownership of bodies in life and death, show quite starkly the intersection of professional power, representation, and perceptions.

These variations, fascinating in their own right, also reinforce a view that present patterns are only intelligible in terms of the past. Current attempts to translate the findings of EBM and MTA into practice, or plans for reorganization and changes in contracts, may fail unless they allow for the full impact of historically determined local variations – both on the way things are now, and on the way they will change. Even beyond this, some of our accounts emphasize the role played by judgement and practical experience of individuals or teams. As Gabolde and Moulin put it, people 'do well what they have been used to do', an aspect of expertise which is difficult to incorporate in measures of efficiency and efficacy. People also perform better if they have been well trained. The history of anaesthesia indicates that improvements – or innovations – in training in the post-war period enhanced patient comfort and safety, more powerfully than (the impressive) technological innovations.

There are many excellent studies looking at the future of innovation in medicine and health policy, generally with an emphasis on genetic medicine. [34] Indeed, the new genetics has tended to dominate current health policy debates and plans for research, supplanting HIV/AIDS as a prime target.[35] The other area of innovation which excites many observers is that of computers and the Internet. Many among the medical and health research community, and among the social scientists who study them, apparently retain faith in the twin powers of molecular level interventions and information technologies. Historical studies of intensive care, for instance, confirm that computers played an important role in managing the enormous amounts of data generated by automated monitors – but nurses' expert attention was important too, and debates continue over where to place the most emphasis.[36] In either case, some countries have more intensive care units than others, and deciding what is the right level is a policy matter. Attempts to rationalize this process through research on inputs and outputs –

advanced medical audit – run up against very variable responses from the medical professionals whose co-operation is vital for the full operation of such tools. Also, all forms of rationalization, whether through audit or meta-analysis, operate within the continued constraints on health expenditure by governments. In the past as in the present, policy expediency influences what happens, as much as evidence.

Every single chapter in this book, including the whole thrust of this Introduction (and the previous historical work on which it builds), shows how historical contingencies, especially professional power and economic constraints, affect inputs and outcomes. Our social history approach (unlike 'traditional' medical history's emphasis on stages of discovery) takes account of shifts in cultural values that have tended to encourage wider participation in debates, and a multitude of factors, which require an enormous amount of detailed research. Methodological issues are not only academic; they are relevant to policy-makers as well as historians. People who are responsible for introducing new technologies or forms of organization need, but hardly ever have the time and resources for, this sort of detailed work and understanding. They may have access to the latest MTA or EBM reviews but these will not normally explain why an innovation fared so differently in one place or time compared with another. For this complex and detailed back-up work, historians (alongside sociologists, anthropologists, and other social scientists) are needed. History deals with moving pictures, not experimental conditions; but in a unique way it provides analysis alongside portrayal, with a depth of understanding that helps with predictions. For, by and large, the factors that shaped innovation, diffusion, and resistance in the recent past, will also affect these processes in the future.

Notes

1 John Pickstone (ed.), *Medical Innovations in Historical Perspective*, Basingstoke and London, Macmillan, 1992; Ilana Löwy (ed.), *Medicine and Change: Historical and Sociological Studies of Medical Innovation*, Paris, INSERM/John Libbey, 1993.
2 For a review of work in the 1990s, see Jennifer Stanton, 'Making sense of technologies in medicine', *Social History of Medicine*, 1999, vol. 12, pp. 437–48.
3 There are some institutional histories (though the first cited here would dispute such a designation) covering innovation in this period, such as Louis Galambos with Jane Eliot Sewell, *Networks of Innovation: Vaccine Development at Merck, Sharp & Dohme, and Mulford, 1895–1995*, Cambridge, New York and Melbourne, Cambridge University Press, 1995; Audrey Wood, *Magnetic Ventures. The Story of Oxford Instruments*, Oxford, Oxford University Press, 2001. An account of medical diagnostics with a completely different approach, showing a fine blend of history and sociology, is provided by Stuart Blume, *Insight and Industry: On the Dynamics of Technological Change in Medicine*, Cambridge, MA, and London, MIT Press, 1992.
4 See, for example, the complaint of 'jargon ridden socio-economic essays which promised answers which failed to emerge', in S. Webb, Review of Blume, *Insight and Industry*, *Medical History*, 1992, vol. 36, pp. 473–4.
5 For the key text on how sociologists do something similar, see B. Glaser and A. Strauss, *The Discovery of Grounded Theory: Strategies for Qualitative Research*, Chicago, Aldine, 1967.

6 Literature specifically on diffusion in medicine and health care is developing, as in J. Roth and S. Ruzek (eds), *The Adoption and Social Consequences of Medical Technologies*, Greenwich, CT, JAI Press, 1986; Ronaldo Battista, 'Innovation and diffusion of health-related technologies: a conceptual framework', *International Journal of Technology Assessment in Health Care*, 1989, vol. 5, pp. 227–48; M. Fennell and R. Warnecke, *The Diffusion of Medical Innovations: An Applied Network Analysis*, London, Plenum Press, 1989; C. Romano, 'Diffusion of technology innovation', *Advances in Nursing Science*, 1990, vol. 13, pp. 11–21. As Romano observes, the purchase of an innovation is in any case only a first step, and does not necessarily lead to 'proper' use and incorporation into practice.

7 Exemplified rather humorously in John B. McKinlay, 'From "promising report" to "standard procedure": seven stages in the career of a medical innovation', *Milbank Memorial Fund Quarterly*, 1981, vol. 59, pp. 374–411. See also David Banta and Bryan Luce, *Health Care Technology and its Assessment: An International Perspective*, Oxford and New York, Oxford University Press, 1993, showing an ideal S-shaped curve p. 34, with alternative variants pp. 37–8. 'Most innovations have an S-shaped rate of adoption' according to Everett Rogers, *Diffusion of Innovations*, 4th edition, New York and London, Free Press, 1995 (previous editions 1962, 1971, 1983), p. 23.

8 As argued in Martin Bauer (ed.), *Resistance to New Technology: Nuclear Power, Information Technology and Biotechnology*, Cambridge, Cambridge University Press, 1995; see especially Robert Bud, 'In the engine of industry: regulators of biotechnology, 1970–86', pp. 293–309, and Martin Bauer, 'Towards a functional analysis of resistance', pp. 393–417.

9 Nearly half the twenty contributors are women in Löwy (ed.), *Medicine and Change*; about a third are women in Ghislaine Lawrence (ed.), *Technologies of Modern Medicine*, London, Science Museum, 1994. See also Ilana Löwy, *Between Bench and Bedside: Science, Healing, and Interleukin-2 in a Cancer Ward*, Cambridge, MA and London, Harvard University Press, 1996 (a multidisciplinary work).

10 Judith McGaw, 'No passive victims, no separate spheres: a feminist perspective on technology's history', in Stephen Cutcliffe and Robert Post (eds), *In Context: History and the History of Technology*, Bethlehem, PA, Lehigh University Press, 1989. See also: Nina Lerman, Arwen Palmer Mohun and Ruth Oldenziel, 'Versatile tools: gender analysis and the history of technology', *Technology and Culture*, 1997, vol. 38, pp. 1–8.

11 Jennifer Tann, 'Space, time and innovation characteristics: the contribution of diffusion process theory to the history of technology', *History of Technology*, 1995, vol. 17, pp. 143–63.

12 Ruth Schwartz Cowan (ed.), *Biomedical and Behavioral Technology*, Special issue, *Technology and Culture*, 1993, vol. 34; Ruth Schwartz Cowan, *A Social History of American Technology*, New York and Oxford, Oxford University Press, 1997.

13 Marjan Groen, *Technology, Work and Organisation: A Study of the Nursing Process in Intensive Care Units*, Maastricht, University of Limburg dissertation no. 95–29, 1995.

14 Stanley Joel Reiser, *Medicine and the Reign of Technology*, Cambridge, Cambridge University Press, 1978.

15 The literature on intensive care nursing seems especially sensitive to this issue: Groen, *Technology, Work and Organisation*; Julie Fairman, 'Watchful vigilance: nursing care, technology, and the development of intensive care units', *Nursing Research*, 1992, vol. 41, pp. 56–60; Julie Fairman and Joan Lynaugh, *Critical Care Nursing: A History*, Philadelphia, PA, University of Pennsylvania Press, 1998; Jeanne Guillemin and Lynda Holstrom, *Mixed Blessings: Intensive Care for Newborns*, New York and Oxford, Oxford University Press, 1986.

16 Keith Grint and Steve Woolgar, *The Machine at Work: Technology, Work and Organization*, Cambridge, Polity Press, 1997. Note the subtitle of this book is the same as the main title of Groen's published thesis (note 13 above) – almost certainly a complete coincidence.

17 Gordon Foxall and Janet Tierney, 'From CAP1 to CAP2', *Management Decision*, 1984, vol. 22, pp. 3–15.

18 See E. von Hippel, 'The dominant role of users in the scientific instrument innovation process', *Research Policy*, 1976, vol. 5, pp. 28–39. Patients, discussed in Stanton's chapter in this book as configured users, have rarely initiated technological medical innovations.

19 A. Gelijns and N. Rosenberg, 'The dynamics of technological change in medicine', *Health Affairs*, 1994, pp. 28–46.

20 L. B. Russell, *Technology in Hospitals: Medical Advances and their Diffusion*, Washington, DC, Brookings Institution, 1979. For more recent studies, see Barbara Stocking, 'Influences on the diffusion process: government and national funding agencies', in S. Kirchberger, P. Durieux and B. Stocking, *The Diffusion of Two Technologies for Renal Stone Treatments across Europe*, London, King's Fund, 1991, pp. 121–32; B. Stocking, *Expensive Health Technologies: Regulatory and Administrative Mechanisms in Europe*, Oxford, New York and Tokyo, Oxford University Press, 1988 – although not historical, these provide an extremely valuable context for the historian of the recent past.

21 A very full (book-length) survey is provided by John Burnham, 'How the idea of profession changed the writing of medical history', *Medical History*, Supplement No. 18, London, Wellcome Institute for the History of Medicine, 1998. The use of medical ethics to support professional interests is analysed in a number of studies surveyed in Roger Cooter, 'The resistible rise of medical ethics' (Review article), *Social History of Medicine*, 1995, vol. 8, pp. 257–70.

22 Judith Walzer Leavitt, *Brought to Bed: Childbearing in America, 1750 to 1950*, New York, Oxford University Press, 1986.

23 Hilary Marland and Anne Marie Rafferty (eds), *Midwives, Society and Childbirth: Debates and Controversies in the Modern Period*, London, Routledge, 1997.

24 Trevor Pinch and Wiebe Bijker, 'The social construction of facts and artefacts: or how the sociology of science and the sociology of technology might benefit each other', in Wiebe Bijker, Thomas Hughes and Trevor Pinch (eds), *The Social Construction of Technological Systems: New Directions in the Sociology and History of Technology*, Cambridge, MA, MIT Press, 1987, pp. 17–50. See also Trevor Pinch, 'The social construction of technology: a review', in Robert Fox (ed.), *Technological Change: Methods and Themes in the History of Technology*, Reading, Harwood Academic, 1998, pp. 17–35.

25 Wiebe Bijker, *Of Bicycles, Bakelites, and Bulbs: Toward a Theory of Sociotechnical Change*, Cambridge, MA, and London, MIT Press, 1995, especially pp. 122–7.

26 Dominique Florin, 'Scientific uncertainty and the role of expert advice: the case of health checks for coronary heart disease prevention by general practitioners in the UK', *Social Science and Medicine*, 1999, vol. 49, pp. 1269–83.

27 See especially Angus Buchanan, 'Theory and narrative in the history of technology', *Technology and Culture*, 1991, vol. 32, pp. 365–76; David Edgerton, 'Tilting at paper tigers', *British Journal for the History of Science*, 1993, vol. 26, pp. 67–75. For an influential discussion of framing in medical history, see Charles Rosenberg, 'Disease in history: frames and framers', *Milbank Quarterly*, 1989, vol. 67, pp. 1–15.

28 Ludwik Fleck, *Genesis and Development of a Scientific Fact*, Chicago, University of Chicago Press, 1979, published in German, 1935; for an introduction to this work locating it in subsequent historiography, see Ilana Löwy, 'Recent historiography of biomedical research', in Lawrence, *Technologies of Modern Medicine*, pp. 99–110.

29 Bruno Latour and Steve Woolgar, *Laboratory Life: The Social Construction of Scientific Facts*, Beverly Hills and London, Sage Publications, 1979. Influences cited by Malcolm Nicholson, who participated as a student in the 'Edinburgh school' include Thomas Kuhn, *The Structure of Scientific Revolutions*, Chicago, University of Chicago Press, 1962, the later Wittgenstein, and anthropologist Mary Douglas: Malcolm Nicholson, 'Heterogeneity, emergence and resistance: recent work in the sociology of laboratory science', in Lawrence, *Technologies of Modern Medicine*, pp. 111–19.

30 Löwy, 'Recent historiography', p. 106.
31 Rudolf Klein, Patricia Day and Sharon Redmayne, *Managing Scarcity: Priority Setting and Rationing in the National Health Service*, Buckingham, Open University Press, 1996, p. 105; cites at this point: Bryan Jennett, *High Technology Medicine: Benefits and Burdens*, Oxford, Oxford University Press, 1986. Jennett, a neurosurgeon who coined the term 'vegetative state' and evolved the Glasgow Coma Score to predict likely outcomes, has written extensively on the hard choices which high technology presents to society.
32 Tann, 'Space, time and innovation characteristics', p. 159.
33 See Charles Webster, *The National Health Service: A Political History*, Oxford and New York, Oxford University Press, 1998; about one-third of the book, dealing with the 1980s and 1990s, is called 'Continuous revolution'.
34 For a broader scope, see J. Newson-Davis and D. J. Weatherall (eds), *Health Policy and Technological Innovation*, London, Chapman and Hall, 1994, which covers transplantation, the Human Genome Project, cancer, brain imaging techniques, psychopharmacology, new vaccines, health information technology, and research priorities.
35 In the UK, genetics shares top place in health policy debates together with food policy, in the light of recent food 'scares' such as that over BSE and foot-and-mouth disease.
36 Fairman, 'Watchful vigilance'; see also J. Stanton, 'Supported lives', in Roger Cooter and John Pickstone (eds), *Medicine in the Twentieth Century*, Amsterdam, Harwood Academic Publishers, 2000, pp. 601–15, for a sketch of other explanations.

Part I
Close neighbours

1 The effects of local context on the development of obstetric ultrasound scanning in two Scottish hospitals[1]

Debbie Nicholson

One of the most noteworthy features of the development of obstetric ultrasound in Scotland is the high degree of diversity involved. From hospital to hospital, differences can be detected in such areas as the organization and funding of ultrasound services, the number of scans performed and at what stages in pregnancy, the professional specialties that control and operate the technology, and so on. Furthermore, it is also possible to detect ways in which the technical elements of the technology have been reconfigured to suit different contexts: to enable it to function as the 'right tool for the job' in each specific location.[2] This is done either through careful choice of specific models and designs (selective adoption) or by 'tinkering' with existing models in use. Thus the technology develops in subtly different ways from location to location. How can this be explained?

Historians of medicine have demonstrated that the introduction of new medical tools, techniques, and practices to new users has provided opportunities for technological change.[3] Furthermore, the utility of new forms of equipment often developed during use at the level of clinical practice – technologies have not, in other words, appeared fully fledged and ready-to-use. New skills, new personnel, and new institutional arrangements create problems and opportunities in implementing technology, which have to be addressed. This can result in equipment being used in previously unimagined ways – stimulating further innovation.

In an attempt to provide a theoretical framework to explain this sociologically, the Social Construction of Technology (SCOT) approach highlights the 'interpretative flexibility' of technical artefacts.[4] The same artefact can be perceived differently by various 'relevant social groups' and it is the manner in which these differing perceptions are accommodated or overcome which drives technological change. In highlighting this, such studies have emphasized the problematic nature of a distinct linear 'stage' model of technological development.[5] Instead, the spread of new technologies is viewed as a more dynamic phenomenon – new users can form novel interpretations of a particular artefact at any point in its overall development – stimulating further change.[6]

The aim of this chapter is to make use of the SCOT concept of 'interpretative flexibility' in order to explain innovative practices and site-specific differences.

However, in doing so, two important points of divergence from the SCOT approach will be highlighted. First of all, in its conceptualization of 'relevant social groups', SCOT tends to obscure the role played by local, contextual factors in moulding actors' interpretations of technology.[7] Within SCOT, 'relevant social groups' are treated as any group of social actors who share the same view of an artefact. This characterization, however, does not pay adequate attention to the fact that actors' interpretations of technology are often shaped through their interactions with it on a practical basis. A variety of historical and contextual factors, situated in specific locations, shape actors' perceptions of technologies. The net result may well be a conglomeration of interested actors who can be identified as a 'relevant social group'. However, to rely on such groups as the sole explanatory tool of technological change eclipses the nuanced ways in which change is effected on a daily basis.

Second, the chapter will employ a broader definition of 'technology' than that used by the SCOT theorists. Common to all technologies is an interactive, performative dimension in which human actors engage with material forces and man-made structures. Thus 'obstetric ultrasound' does not simply denote a complex piece of medical equipment. Instead, the term also incorporates a form of human activity (the actual practice of ultrasound scanning with its own division of labour and social interactions) and a form of specialized knowledge (in terms of how to operate and maintain ultrasound machines and understand the images created).[8] Thus, even where the same artefact is employed, the technology itself can develop in different ways from location to location as other dimensions (such as, for example, the division of labour) develop differently.

In what follows it will be argued that a variety of material and social factors specific to individual institutions (from geography to inter-professional relations) affected the development of ultrasound in subtly different ways from location to location.[9] Ultrasound technology was, in other words, shaped by local contextual factors as much as by the interests of 'relevant social groups'. A variety of site-specific elements moulded the technology's development in ways which 'fit' the circumstances associated with each location. From choice of equipment and location of the 'scan department', to staffing decisions and routine procedures, the precise make-up and development of obstetric ultrasound were the outcome of a site-specific configuration process: matching users to machines and vice versa.

These arguments will be illustrated through examples taken from the development of obstetric ultrasound in two Scottish hospitals from the mid-1970s, using evidence drawn from interviews with the actors involved, correspondence, and official documents.[10] The chapter is organized into three broad sections: The first provides some background about the main technical features of ultrasound as an artefact, and its uses in obstetric medicine, during this period. The remaining two sections will examine what occurred when ultrasound was introduced to each of the two hospitals.

The changing nature of obstetric ultrasound in the 1970s

Ultrasound creates images on the basis of pulsed sound waves. Piezoelectric crystals emit inaudible sound waves which are transmitted into the body, via a device known as a transducer.[11] Each pulse is absorbed or reflected by the different types of tissue or structure it encounters. The resultant echoes are picked up by the transducer and then processed to create visual representations.

From its commercial introduction in 1963[12] until the mid-1970s, obstetric ultrasound machines had largely worked on the basis of creating static images. A still image was gradually built up as the transducer was swept back and forth across the abdomen. A high degree of craft skill was involved with this – too many sweeps and the image would be over-exposed, too few and structures would be difficult to identify. The only way to preserve the images created was to photograph them. Furthermore, because of the way in which these images were generated, static scanners were large and cumbersome pieces of equipment, requiring metal scanning frames which reached over a hospital trolley on which the patient would lie. At this point in the technology's development, it was not used as a routine procedure. Only women characterized as 'high risk' (such as those with suspected complications like placenta praevia or those with histories of previous miscarriage, multiple pregnancy, etc.) would be examined using ultrasound.

Around the mid-1970s, however, new scanners using different methods of image production began to appear on the market.[13] Such machines had multiple-element arrays, which were either mounted on a spinning wheel, or arranged alongside one another on a long, hand-held probe. The synchronized 'firing' of each element in turn created an image that, although considered initially to be of poorer quality than the static images of the earlier machines, enabled rapid image renewal. In other words, the image appeared in 'real time', allowing motion to be displayed. Furthermore, since there was no need with these machines for the large scanning frame which stabilized the images generated by static scanners, the new real-time (RT) machines were smaller, lighter and more portable. They were also, at least initially, less expensive.

The 1970s, however, was not only a time of technical change in obstetric ultrasound. This period also saw ultrasound increasingly being used as a routine feature of the antenatal care of all pregnant women in many centres. A number of advantages were cited, including the possibility of detecting gross foetal abnormalities early enough in pregnancy to offer selective terminations. However, the main perceived advantage of universal screening related to accurate dating of pregnancy. Many of the clinical research trajectories developed in the 1960s and 1970s were aimed at finding reliable means of dating the gestation of the foetus.[14] By the time RT scanners appeared, such methods had stabilized around two main measurements: bi-parietal diameter (BPD) – from either side of the foetal skull – and crown-rump length (CRL) – from the top of the head to the base of the spine. Such measurements could provide information for possible later diagnoses such as intrauterine growth retardation, or for procedures such as induction of labour. Furthermore, alpha-feto protein tests (AFP) – in which samples of maternal blood are analysed for indications of Down's syndrome and spina bifida – were found to have greater accuracy if they were performed between sixteen and twenty weeks' gestation. This, again, underlined the clinical utility of accurate dating of all pregnancies via ultrasound screening. Thus, the very nature of obstetric medicine was changing, as ultrasound technology and the clinical possibilities it presented became increasingly interwoven with obstetric practice.

However, greater routine use of ultrasound involved much greater workloads and thus entailed increasing use of lower-grade staff such as radiographers and midwives. In turn, the greater reliance on such non-clinical staff provoked concern over the appropriate training of ultrasound operators, and calls for standardization of training and supervision. This issue was first raised in 1979 and appropriate means of achieving such standardization were debated until well into the 1980s among the relevant professional societies (such as the Royal College of Obstetricians and Gynaecologists, the Royal College of Radiologists, the Hospital Physicists Association, and the College of Radiographers).[15] These debates were also followed closely by the most important diagnostic ultrasound interest group in the UK – the British Medical Ultrasound Society.[16]

These events – changing technological design, increasing routinization, and attempts to create standardized structures of delivery – form the general context of obstetric ultrasound from the mid-1970s. However, as will be outlined in the next two sections, the way in which these issues were played out differed from location to location.

Reconfiguring a medical hierarchy

In 1977, obstetric ultrasound was introduced for the first time to Hospital A – an average-sized maternity hospital located in a small town on the East coast of Scotland. The technology's introduction was part of a large-scale capital investment in the hospital by the local Health Board, which culminated in a new extension, housing additional ward space and an on-site radiology facility. As with most developments of this nature, the funding for the new wing covered the purchase of equipment, including an ultrasound machine with real-time capabilities.

Initially, ultrasound was conceived as part of a general obstetric imaging service alongside x-ray imaging and was thus a radiological procedure, operated and controlled by the main Radiology Department. This Department, however, was based in the main district general hospital, located a mile from the maternity hospital. Under the Health Board system and, later, the Hospital Trust system, the maternity hospital was viewed as an attachment to the district general hospital, despite the fact that they were not located on the same site. This would turn out to be an important factor in the shaping of ultrasound in this centre.

To staff the new facility, the Chief Radiologist (Dr A) advertised for, and employed, a radiographer from the district general to be based at the maternity hospital. This radiographer (Mrs Y) was given additional training in ultrasound so that she could perform both x-ray and ultrasound imaging.

In the traditional division of labour associated with x-ray imaging, non-medically qualified radiographers performed the role of image constructors, while clinically trained radiologists were solely responsible for the interpretation of those images.[17] Therefore, in addition to the radiographer, a consultant radiologist was placed in charge of the maternity x-ray imaging service on a visiting basis.

There were, however, problems associated with transporting this division of labour directly to the technology of ultrasound. With x-rays, an image can only be created from very well-defined planes and so, providing the radiographer is competent in creating those standard views, a radiologist can discern from what direction the section has been imaged.[18] For this reason, the division of labour in radiology was amenable to a structured, hierarchical separation of roles.

With ultrasound, on the other hand, there were an infinite number of planes from which an image could be created. Thus, when viewing a still image, the clinician would need to know where exactly the probe had been placed to produce the picture. This meant that, without actually watching the scan being performed, it was more difficult to translate and make sense of the resultant image.

In this sense, with ultrasound the locus of diagnosis was more intimately centred on the interactive scanning process itself, at the time in which it was performed. The person who performed the scan would simultaneously interpret the images and draw diagnostic conclusions. Thus, the technique of real-time imaging created a much more interactive relationship between the skills of image construction and interpretation – locating the latter more directly at the point of practice.

For this reason, ultrasound presented specific problems for the traditional division of labour associated with radiology. Unless radiologists carried out every single scan personally, some diagnostic authority would have to be ceded to lower grade staff. In most centres, this was accommodated by allowing radiographers to determine cases where no pathology was evident, and by limiting their role to measurements. However, in cases where suspicious indications were detected, the radiographer would have to seek assistance from a clinician.

In terms of the organization of scanning in Hospital A, this presented problems. The relatively small number of cases in which a clinical diagnosis might be required did not justify the full-time presence of a radiologist. As with all universal screening procedures, the majority of cases examined in routine ultrasound scans are 'normal'. Thus to employ a radiologist to wait around and be on-hand to examine suspicious cases was not a justifiable use of personnel.

Instead, it was the maternity hospital's obstetricians who provided clinical support. Thus the main operator of ultrasound was a radiographer employed by (and answerable to) Radiology. Nevertheless, a consultant from a different department directly supervised her. Thus, although the mismatch between the traditional medical hierarchy of radiology and the technology of ultrasound should be viewed as a generic 'problem', its accommodation, in this instance, was shaped by local factors. The small size of the radiological unit at the maternity hospital, and its geographical separation from the main Radiology Department, played their role in moulding the contours of the delivery of obstetric ultrasound.

Furthermore, in organizing the obstetric ultrasound service in this way it is clear that the Chief Radiologist felt there was a qualitative difference between obstetric scanning and other forms of ultrasound:

> I felt a sonographer[19] was all that was required because they were getting most of the things they wanted. It was a different story when you were dealing with gynaecology and abdominal scanning for surgery and things like that. As far as obstetrics were concerned I felt that the obstetrician and a sonographer were capable of doing all the scanning.[20]

Thus, the fact that the maternity hospital did not cater for gynaecology patients (who were treated at the district general hospital) led the Chief Radiologist to conclude that the radiographer's role was more straightforward than if she had been required also to examine these patients. The more simple procedures employed in routine obstetric scanning (performing basic measurements, locating the placenta, and checking foetal heart movements) were all brought into the decision-making.[21]

Therefore, to explain the shaping of this technology in this location, we must look beyond the existence of 'relevant social groups' and 'interpretative flexibility' of technical artefacts. Instead, we need to consider the role of a variety of contextual factors. In this example, a new division of labour was carved out for ultrasound to enable it to 'work' effectively. On the one hand, while the traditional division of labour associated with Radiology continued to operate for the small number of x-rays carried out at the maternity hospital, a different set of procedures, involving medical supervision by obstetricians rather than radiologists, operated for ultrasound. Furthermore, the organization of obstetric scanning was effectively split between two departments. The Department of Obstetrics was responsible for the daily running of the service, while the Department of Radiology took responsibility for staffing, budgeting, and strategic planning. Thus, obstetric ultrasound was divided into two 'spheres of influence'.

From the outset local circumstances contributed to the shaping of obstetric ultrasound in this centre. Furthermore, the particular way in which it was moulded continued to influence future developments. In 1979, for example, a new machine was purchased for the obstetric service. By this time, a number of ultrasound manufacturers and retailers competed for sales, introducing different design features to make their models more attractive. The machine eventually purchased for this particular centre (a Diagnostic Sonar 'System 185'), was chosen by the Consultant Radiologist specifically because of its suitability to the way ultrasound was organized in Hospital A:

> I had also been interested in the recording side of this – writing up the records and so on – for the obstetric cases in particular. They [Diagnostic Sonar] developed this little device that had, instead of looking up the tables and deciding what it was, it did it quickly – just like that. You put your probes on, it read out the BPD and it gave the other things right away.[22]

What is being referred to here is an electronic box which Diagnostic Sonar had designed and added to the 'System 185'. Using the equipment's on-screen callipers (referred to above as 'probes') the operator could indicate the points at which she wanted to take measurements of bi-parietal diameter or crown-rump length. The electronic unit would then not only calculate and display those measurements, but also use them to work out the weight and gestational age of the foetus. All this information was then displayed on-screen – along with the image itself – which could then be printed as a permanent record.

Thus, the radiologist's perceptions of the greatest benefit of this system related directly to the way in which scanning was organized in this hospital. Not only would this machine reduce the number of tasks performed by the radiographer during each scan, it could also be used as a technical accommodation of the hospital's medical supervision 'problem'. The clinician could oversee her scanning to some degree by examining the print-out showing where the callipers had been placed and what measurements had been taken.

Thus, both the choice of machine and the assessment of its 'qualities' were the outcome of the actual practice of scanning in this location. The 'interpretative flexibility' of this artefact was directly related to the particularities of the local context in which it was to be used. Decisions were shaped by the way in which scanning was organized in the maternity hospital; by the technological trajectory already underway in response to a variety of locational influences. Where initially social aspects of the technology were reconfigured to accommodate the need to provide clinical supervision despite the geographical separation of the main radiology department, a reconfiguration of the more technical elements of the service was now being introduced.

To conclude this section, the development of real-time scanning in this maternity hospital was shaped by social and technical factors located in a specific time and location. The geographical separation of the two hospitals, the division between gynaecology and obstetrics, and the need to provide clinical support for the radiographer who performed the scans were tied to, and helped to shape, both the choice of equipment and its practical use. Thus, an examination of the development of ultrasound in this centre demonstrates the way in which the social and technical dimensions of ultrasound were 'tuned' to accommodate one another – either through the manipulation of the social aspects of the technology or through the deliberate choice of technical features which would address this.

Scanning the periphery: real-time ultrasound in a remote island community

A characteristic feature of Scotland is its dispersed population. The most densely populated areas are concentrated in the central belt and along the East coast, while much of the rest of the country consists of remote and scattered communities. This is particularly true of the island regions, located off the North and West coasts. Such communities presented particular problems for the centralized model of specialist medical provision, which characterized much of the twentieth century. In this context, peripheral clinics attached to general hospitals played an important role in the provision of specialist medical care. The following account analyses the development of obstetric scanning in one such community and the way in which a variety of location-specific factors affected the 'interpretative flexibility' of ultrasound in this context.

In 1979, obstetric ultrasound was first introduced to Hospital B. Located in the main town of the largest of a group of islands, this centre was the main clinical provider for the entire region. Nevertheless, it was a comparatively small district general hospital, with an obstetric department staffed by only one consultant and three midwives. However, this small group of professionals dealt with a relatively low number of hospital births. Not all of the women of the Isles were delivered in the hospital (many choosing to go to mainland hospitals or to be delivered at home), while the small size of the population entailed a relatively small workload (417 live births in 1978, declining steadily to 345 by 1990).[23] Nevertheless, the absence of junior doctors and the solitary nature of the clinician's post created specific organizational features which affected the delivery of ultrasound services.

Part of the responsibilities of the Consultant Obstetrician/Gynaecologist (Dr C) was to hold a six-weekly clinic on a neighbouring island. Here he would examine women for whom it was more convenient to travel to this location than make the cumbersome journey to the main hospital.[24] On acquiring his ultrasound machine (a Diagnostic Sonar 'System 85'), the consultant made the decision to begin using it during these peripheral clinic visits. This involved transporting the ultrasound equipment by plane – with journeys to and from the airports.

Such a development would have been impossible with the original static scanner design. These earlier machines had weighed nearly a tonne, and required a huge metal scanning frame, which was installed in a fixed position. 'Portability', in other words, was not a concept that could be associated with static ultrasound scanners. It was not until the advent of real-time equipment (with smaller units and hand-held transducers) that the possibility of moving ultrasound scanners around became conceivable. Nevertheless, moving an ultrasound machine from island to island redefined the manufacturer's interpretation of portability. In their marketing strategy, portability simply entailed the ability to move the scanner between wards on its own trolley.[25]

This machine, therefore, was being used in a way that was unanticipated by the designers: it was being interpreted differently to fit this specific situation. However, this particular interpretation was the result of more than simple professional or social interest. The precise nature of the context into which this machine was placed (the travel difficulties between islands and the scattered and remote nature of the island communities) had a direct bearing on both the 'interpretative flexibility' of the artefact, and the way it was used.

However, the consultant's decision to move the scanner from location to location was formed *through* his interactions with it – he did not approach the technology with his intentions already formed:

> I didn't get the real-time scanner to go charging around the islands. I have to be honest, it was there and I was using it and these patients had to fly up to [the hospital] to get a scan and I thought, 'Now, surely, we could do something', so I started to take it down [to the peripheral clinic]. I didn't have a brilliant idea all worked out in my head beforehand, it evolved slowly over the years as being the way to do things.[26]

Thus, where portability may have been insignificant for doctors working in different areas, in this island community, characterized by the remoteness and geographical spread of its population, it emerged as an important factor in the configuration of a scanning service. In other words, the interpretation that the consultant formed of this machine was a direct result of the location in which he worked.

Aside from problems associated with the weight and bulk of the machine, there was also a concern that the flights might damage the unit. To protect the machine, a special padded case was made to order by a Scottish tent-making firm. Despite this, the first time the doctor used the machine at the peripheral clinic it stopped working after he had scanned only two patients. As it turned out, the problem and its solution were relatively straightforward. The engineer from Diagnostic Sonar found that the vibrations of the plane had loosened large pins in the electronic circuit boards at the back of the scanner and so he designed a metal plate which was screwed over these pins to keep them in place.

Although this represents a relatively minor technical modification, it nevertheless reinforces the fact that this machine was being asked to perform a role for which it had not been designed. A modification as simple as a panel screwed to the back of the unit enabled it to perform this role. However, such a modification could only be made in response to the behaviour of the machine in such circumstances. Thus the novel demands placed on the scanner provoked new responses from the machine, which then had to be accommodated. It is therefore possible to see in this example a small-scale technological development which is entirely local context-dependent. Whether or not this modification was taken up and diffused on a wider basis (and there is evidence to suggest that it was)[27] is not the issue here. What is significant is that technical modifications were being made at the level of clinical practice, and in response to local circumstances. The machine was reconfigured in a way that enabled it to function in this particular location.

Nevertheless, as the consultant was only available once every six weeks, it was only possible for him to scan women referred by their GPs with suspicious clinical indications, or who had been categorized as 'high risk'. However, the consultant was keen to extend his service in order to provide routine screening of all pregnancies. A number of circumstances made this intention problematic. As a lone consultant it was impossible to increase the frequency of the trips to the peripheral clinic in order to scan greater numbers of patients on a more regular basis. On the other hand, the same problems associated with travel between the islands for pregnant women themselves inhibited the opportunity to scan them in the hospital. Furthermore, even if this were possible, the small size of the obstetric department's staff did not make this a practical solution. Assistance could not even be sought from the Radiology Unit: this department was even smaller and had no permanent on-site radiologist (a consultant would visit once a month from the mainland).

In 1984, a new scanner was bought for the obstetric department. A local general practitioner (Dr H), based on the same island as the peripheral clinic, was employed by the Health Board to operate the new screening service.[28] Although unusual, employing a GP as sonographer did have a precedent in other remote areas of Scotland where scanners had been purchased and situated in GP-run hospitals.[29] Furthermore, in remote areas like this it was not unusual for general practitioners to undertake duties that would otherwise be considered within the remit of specialist medicine.

The GP performed two routine examinations on each pregnant woman. During the first scan (at around 16 weeks' gestation) Dr H measured BPD, confirmed foetal heart movements, and located the placenta. She would also look for signs of gross abnormalities (such as anencephaly) and identify multiple gestations. If the BPD showed the pregnancy to be within the 'window of opportunity' for AFP testing, maternal blood was drawn (otherwise an alternative appointment was made). During the second scan at 32 weeks, she checked foetal presentation and made another measurement of BPD to rule out intrauterine growth retardation. Any unusual or suspect indications from either of these scans would be brought to the attention of the Consultant Obstetrician – and the patient referred either to the local district general hospital, or to one of the larger tertiary hospitals on the mainland, for a follow-up scan.

The ultrasound and associated examinations performed by the GP were relatively simple and straightforward. The basic nature of the scans performed was a direct consequence of the way the service was organized which, in turn, was the emergent outcome of geographical factors. The GP had no on-site specialist support and was routinely scanning relatively low numbers of women (compared to sonographers located in more densely populated areas). These factors were thus taken into account in terms of the duties she performed.

Furthermore, the machine itself was chosen specifically with these issues in mind. As Dr H notes:

> A lot of machines were coming on to the market, some aimed at hospitals which were enormous things and some aimed at adventurous private obstetricians which were very flashy machines that did all sorts of print outs. But we needed something *fairly simple to use* [emphasis added], extremely robust that could go backwards and forwards.[30]

From the various models and designs available at this time, a simple-to-operate machine was required to accommodate the relatively inexperienced hands of the general practitioner. The unit eventually chosen (a Pie Data 400) was smaller and lighter than the original scanner used in this location. Weighing only 6 kilograms (compared to the 32 kilograms of the Diagnostic Sonar) this machine came with its own little carry case. Furthermore, on-screen callipers and automatically estimated gestational ages contributed to the equipment's ease of use.

Thus the equipment was chosen for qualities valued in the context of this particular location. Again, therefore, it is evident that the consultant's interpretation of this scanner was not solely the outcome of his membership of any 'relevant social group' but the result of local contingencies.

However, as well as being lighter, the new machine also had to be well enough protected to make the regular journey between the two islands. There were two principal technical ways in which this was achieved, one of which used a specific existing feature of the model itself. The Pie Data machine came with a detachable monitor and indeed was designed in such a way that the scanner could be plugged into the back of a television screen and the images displayed in this manner. Although he experimented with this, the consultant concluded that the images achieved in this way were inadequate for making accurate foetal measurements. Instead, at an additional cost of around £500, an extra monitor was purchased. Thus one single scanner had two monitors; one located in the hospital, and the other at the peripheral clinic. In this way, it was only the scanner which moved between the two centres and was plugged into the monitor on arrival, thus minimizing potential damage.

Furthermore, without the screen, the scanner could be more easily packed away and carried from place to place in its own case. The case itself was made from hard plastic and was supplied with the unit. However, while the protection and portability it afforded might be sufficient for journeys in the boot of a doctor's car,[31] previous experience with the Diagnostic Sonar machine highlighted the need for extra precautions when it came to island-hopping flights. Furthermore, the consultant no longer accompanied the scanner on its trip: the machine was taken to the airport by a member of the hospital's maintenance staff, transported in the plane's hold, and collected by a staff member from the peripheral clinic. The involvement of so many untrained 'hands' and the potentially damaging dangers of regular flights in an aircraft's hold led the consultant to have yet another case made, this time from foam-lined steel, into which the scanner, inside its manufacturer's case, could be secured.

Thus through various means the portability of this machine was extended. A model that was marketed and sold as a highly portable unit was chosen and then, through innovative modifications and practices, the manufacturer's definition of portability was again stretched to suit the requirements of this location. Thus, it is clear that the plans for this screening service were very technology-dependent; it was not simply a re-organization of personnel which was necessary but also a moulding of the technical dimensions of ultrasound to create a basis on which such a service could be constructed. Here again, it is possible to see important technological development in terms of the creation of a routine screening programme, which does not fall neatly into an explanation on the basis of 'relevant social groups'. It was the specific nature of the local context (rather than professional alliances, or shared interpretations of artefacts) which moulded the contours of this development.

The new screening service began on 13 February 1986.[32] Once a fortnight, the scanner would be packed up by the Obstetric Consultant and sent, unaccompanied, to the neighbouring island. At all other times, the scanner was based in the main hospital. The following year, the peripheral service was extended to another GP practice on a different island, and in 1988 a further GP joined the fray.

By the summer of 1988 then, the single portable Pie Data unit packed in its special metal box was being flown, ferried, and taxied between four different sites on three different islands. Such a system was highly innovative. Its devolved nature, with obstetric scanning being carried out in the community by local GPs, was facilitated by stretching the concept of portability – the scanner was travelling over 250 miles every fortnight by plane, ferry, and car. Nowhere else in the UK at that time (or subsequently) had such a system evolved to overcome the geographical and institutional barriers of a remote and scattered population such as this.

To sum up, in addition to the regular circuit of the scanner, this system was unusual in its employment of general practitioners as sonographers. Furthermore, it was developed at a time during which moves to create greater standardization in the delivery of ultrasound services were at their height.[33] Community-based obstetric scanning operated by relatively minimally trained, unsupervised general practitioners was very much against the grain of contemporary opinion. However, when this service is placed within the particular local circumstances from which it evolved, it is possible to see that its organization made sense on a practical basis.

It is, of course, possible to spot ways in which certain goals and objectives were shaped by wider professional concerns, for example, the consultant's advocacy of the benefits of ultrasound in pregnancy, and his desire to create a screening service. Nevertheless, it would be unhelpful to frame this account by explaining it in terms of 'relevant social groups' and 'interpretative flexibility'.

To do so would clearly eclipse the role played by site-specific local factors in the shaping of ultrasound in this community.

Conclusion

Ultrasound technology was reconfigured during its use in actual clinical practice – the interactions between the equipment itself and different personnel in different locations reconfigured many of the elements called into the relationship, thus mutually shaping a technology which could 'work' in each location. In the example of Hospital A, choices of equipment and the traditional hierarchy of radiology were moulded in the creation of a service which accommodated the demands of medical supervision of non-clinical staff in the context of a geographical separation between the small radiology facility and the main Radiology Department. With Hospital B, technical modifications were made to existing equipment and an elaborate division of labour developed in the creation of a universal screening service in a remote and geographically isolated region.

By examining the development of obstetric ultrasound in the context of actual practice in specific locations, it is possible to observe the variety of circumstances which helped to shape its trajectory. Such circumstances often presented resistances (or problems) for the intentions of significant social actors, which had to be accommodated. Alternatively, specific technical or social features were introduced, as a direct result of the way in which they were useful in a given situation. The net outcome is that a whole host of site-specific elements brought about a reconfiguration of ultrasound in each of these two locations. In other words, the technology was shaped by the local circumstances in which it was situated.

This observation suggests two important additions which might be made to the SCOT approach to technology. 'Relevant social groups' need to be defined not only in terms of their relationship to a particular technology at a particular historical moment, but also as contextually located. Social actors do not exist in suspended animation. The interpretations they form of different technical artefacts are often shaped by their practical interactions with them. These interactions take place in specific circumstances, and the nature of these circumstances must be taken into account. In other words, the 'interpretative flexibility' of technical artefacts is not the sole result of social interest, but is the emergent outcome of the interactions between a variety of both social and material elements, which are both historically and *spatially* located.[34]

Second, 'relevant social groups' should perhaps not be relied upon exclusively to explain technological development. While such groups do undoubtedly play a role in the shaping of technology, they are not its sole determinant. Actors within such groups may well share a common view of a particular artefact, but this is often the result of different experiences with the technology in practice, and it is perhaps these experiences which have shaped their interpretations most profoundly, rather than their membership of such groups.

Notes

1 This chapter is drawn from my PhD thesis, 'Secrets of "Success": the diffusion of obstetric ultrasound in Scotland, 1963–1990'. I am grateful to both the Wellcome Trust and the University of Glasgow for their financial support. I am also extremely indebted to Malcolm Nicolson, Raymond Stokes and Jenny Stanton, for their patience and helpful comments on earlier drafts.

2 M. J. Casper and A. E. Clarke, 'Making the pap smear into the "right tool" for the job', *Social Studies of Science*, 1998, vol. 28, pp. 255–89; A. E. Clarke and J. H. Fujimura, *The Right Tools for the Job: At Work in Twentieth Century Life Sciences*, Princeton, NJ, Princeton University Press, 1992.

3 See, for example, B. Pasveer, 'Knowledge of shadows: the introduction of x-ray images in medicine', *Sociology of Health and Illness*, 1990, vol. 11, pp. 360–81; B. Pasveer, *Shadows of Knowledge, Making a Representing Practice in Medicine: X-ray Pictures and Pulmonary Tuberculosis, 1895–1930*, Den Haag, Amsterdam, CIP-Gegevens Koninklijke Bibliotheek, 1992; Casper and Clarke, 'Making the pap smear into the "right tool" for the job'; E. Yoxen, 'Seeing with sound: a study of the development of medical images', in W. E. Bijker, T. P. Hughes and T. J. Pinch (eds), *The Social Construction of Technological Systems*, Cambridge, MA, MIT Press, 1987, pp. 281–301; S. S. Blume, *Insight and Industry: On the Dynamics of Technological Change in Medicine*, Cambridge, MA, MIT Press, 1992; J. D. Howell, *Technology in the Hospital: Transforming Patient Care in the Early Twentieth Century*, Baltimore and London, Johns Hopkins University Press, 1995; E. B. Koch 'In the image of science? Negotiating the development of diagnostic ultrasound in the cultures of surgery and radiology', *Technology and Culture*, 1993, vol. 34, pp. 858–93; J. V. Pickstone (ed.), *Medical Innovations in Historical Perspective*, New York, St Martins Press, 1992.

4 T. J. Pinch and W. E. Bijker, 'The social construction of facts and artefacts; or how the sociology of science and the sociology of technology might benefit each other', *Social Studies of Science*, 1984, vol. 14, pp. 399–441; Bijker *et al.*, *Social Construction of Technological Systems*; W. E. Bijker, *Of Bicycles, Bakelites, and Bulbs: Towards a Theory of Sociotechnical Change*, London, MIT Press, 1995. See also the debate between Pinch and Bijker, and Stewart Russell in *Social Studies of Science*, 1986, vol. 16, pp. 331–60.

5 For an example of such an approach see B. McKinlay, 'From "promising report", to "standard procedure": seven stages in the career of a medical innovation', *Milbank Memorial Fund Quarterly*, 1981, vol. 59, pp. 374–411.

6 Less dynamic studies of diffusion tend to focus on adoption rates of new technologies. See, for example, H. D. Banta, 'The diffusion of the computed tomography (CT) scanner in the United States', *International Journal of Health Services*, 1980, vol. 10, pp. 251–69.

7 Indeed, SCOT's characterization of 'relevant social groups' (especially in their earlier papers) has been criticized for a failure to properly 'locate' such groups in a wider social context with the result that they are under-theorized – see, for example, S. Russell, 'The social construction of artefacts: a response to Pinch and Bijker', *Social Studies of Science*, 1986, vol. 16, pp. 331–46; P. Rosen, 'The social construction of mountain bikes: technology and postmodernity in the cycle industry', *Social Studies of Science*, 1993, vol. 23, pp. 479–513. Such criticisms, however, focus on the relationship between a micro-level analysis of technology and wider macro-social contexts.

8 For a fuller explanation of this definition of 'technology' see the Introduction in D. MacKenzie and J. Wajcman (eds), *The Social Shaping of Technology: How the Refrigerator Got its Hum*, Milton Keynes, Open University Press, 1985.

9 A consideration of the role of material agency has been prompted by the work of Andrew Pickering. See A. Pickering, *The Mangle of Practice: Time, Agency and Science*, Chicago, Chicago University Press, 1995.

10 These centres have been drawn from a larger and more detailed comparative study, which forms the basis of my PhD thesis.

11 Strictly speaking, the piezoelectric effect relates to the way certain crystals emit electrical charges when subjected to pressure. Ultrasound waves exert such pressure and can thus be detected by monitoring the electrical charge created. Furthermore, these crystal elements can be made to produce ultrasound waves through a reversal of this procedure – i.e. by subjecting them to a fluctuating electrical voltage. See W. N. McDicken, *Diagnostic Ultrasonics: Principles and Use of Instruments*, St Albans and London, Crosby Lockwood Staples, 1976, pp. 248–52.

12 Much of the early innovation of obstetric ultrasound was undertaken in Glasgow in the late 1950s and early 1960s by Professor Ian Donald and his co-workers. In conjunction with Smith's Industries, they developed the first commercial ultrasound equipment, the Diasonograph, which went into production in 1963.

13 Much of the early development of this form of ultrasound is largely credited to Bom and his co-workers in Holland. N. Bom, C. T. Lancee, J. Honkoop and P. G. Hugenholtz, 'Ultrasonic viewer for cross-sectional analysis of moving cardiac structures', *Biomedical Engineering*, 1971, vol. 6, pp. 500–3.

14 For example, J. Willocks, 'The use of ultrasonic cephalometry', *Proceedings of the Royal Society of Medicine*, 1962, vol. 55, p. 640; J. W. Willocks, I. Donald, S. Campbell and I. R. Dunsmore, 'Intrauterine growth assessed by foetal cephalometry', *Journal of Obstetrics and Gynaecology of the British Commonwealth*, 1967, vol. 74, pp. 639–76; S. Campbell, 'An improved method of fetal cephalometry by ultrasound', *Journal of Obstetrics and Gynaecology of the British Commonwealth*, 1968, vol. 75, pp. 568–76; S. Campbell, 'The prediction of fetal maturity by ultrasonic measurement of the biparietal diameter', *Journal of Obstetrics and Gynaecology of the British Commonwealth*, 1969, vol. 76, pp. 603–9.

15 Recommendations on how this should be achieved were made in several official reports. See, for example, Scottish Home and Health Department, *Report on the Future Development of Ultrasound in Scotland*, Edinburgh, 1979; Royal College of Obstetricians and Gynaecologists, *Report of the RCOG Working Party on Routine Ultrasound Examination in Pregnancy*, London, Chameleon Press, 1984; Scottish Home and Health Department/Scottish Health Service Planning Council, *Obstetric Ultrasound in Scotland: Report of the Ad Hoc Group Appointed by the Specialty Sub-committee for Obstetrics and Gynaecology of the National Medical Consultative Committee*, Edinburgh, Her Majesty's Stationery Office, 1988.

16 British Medical Ultrasound Society (BMUS) *Bulletin of the British Medical Ultrasound Society*, no. 24, June 1979–no. 43, November 1986.

17 B. Pasveer, *Shadows of Knowledge*.

18 For a very readable scientific account of how x-ray images are created see A.B. Wolbarst, *Looking Within: How X-Ray, CT, MRI, Ultrasound and Other Medical Images Are Created and How They Help Physicians Save Lives*, London, University of California Press, 1999.

19 'Sonographer' denotes any non-medically qualified ultrasound operator. The title only came into common usage towards the end of the 1970s, and is still used alongside other professional designations, such as radiographer or midwife. Indeed, this in itself can be viewed as a sign of the still-emerging professional hierarchy of ultrasound diagnosis. For a similar account of the development of professional hierarchy in x-ray imaging see Pasveer, 'Knowledge of shadows'.

20 Interview with Dr A, former Chief Radiologist, February 1999. (Interviews cited here all by author.)

21 Ibid.

22 Ibid.

23 *Annual Report of the Registrar General for Scotland, 1978*, Edinburgh, General Register Office, 1979; *Annual Report of the Registrar General for Scotland, 1990*, Edinburgh, General Register Office, 1991.

24 Depending on which island they lived on, some of these women had to use two ferries to get to the hospital (and two on their return). This often also necessitated an overnight stay.

25 The images used in Diagnostic Sonar's advertising literature for this machine portrays a young female dressed in a nurse's outfit, pushing a trolley-mounted 'System 85' machine.

26 Interview with Dr C, former Consultant Obstetrician/Gynaecologist, February 1998.

27 The next model produced by Diagnostic Sonar (the System 185) included such a panel and it is likely that this was, in large part, a result of the company's experiences in this context.

28 Dr H was paid on an hourly rate as a clinical assistant for her ultrasound sessions. She attended two separate training courses in Glasgow and London, and was given additional practical training by the Consultant Obstetrician at the local hospital.

29 Scottish Home and Health Department/Scottish Health Service Planning Council, *Obstetric Ultrasound in Scotland*.

30 Interview with Dr H, former GP sonographer, December 1998, emphasis added.

31 Scanners were, by the late 1970s, being transported in this way by obstetricians when attending sessions at peripheral clinics; see, for example, R. P. Balfour, 'Use of a real-time ultrasound scanner in district antenatal clinics', *British Journal of Obstetrics and Gynaecology*, 1978, vol. 85, pp. 492–4. This again demonstrates that the way in which scanners were used in clinical practice filtered back to manufacturers and were built into the design of new models.

32 Correspondence, between Dr C and Dr H, 5 February 1986. Between the time of the machine's purchase and its use in the peripheral clinic, the equipment was used in the hospital by Dr C.

33 Royal College of Obstetricians and Gynaecologists, *Report of the RCOG Working Party on Routine Ultrasound Examination in Pregnancy*, London, Chameleon Press, 1984; Scottish Home and Health Department/Scottish Health Service Planning Council, *Obstetric Ultrasound in Scotland*.

34 To this end, as Joel Mokyr has noted, the sociology of technology might benefit from some of the theoretical concepts employed in evolutionary theory. In particular, the important role accorded to 'environment' in explaining the selection and survival of species, could prove useful in the analysis of technological choice, adoption and adaptation by providing a theoretical framework which includes site-specific variation. See J. Mokyr, 'Evolution and technological change: a new metaphor for economic history?', in R. Fox (ed.), *Technological Change*, Amsterdam, Harwood Academic Publishers, 1996, pp. 63–83. See also Ann Digby's employment of a Lamarkian evolutionary metaphor in her account of the development of general practice in Britain: A. Digby, *The Evolution of British General Practice, 1850–1948*, Oxford, Oxford University Press, 1999, especially pp. 8–20.

2 Organization, ethnicity and the British National Health Service

Helen Valier and Roberta Bivins

This chapter compares the development of two medical service institutions in Manchester during the 1980s and 1990s: the Manchester Diabetes Centre, and the Manchester Sickle Cell and Thalassaemia Centre. During the course of our research we have enjoyed the generous co-operation of several professionals associated with these two centres; we would like to emphasize, however, that the views expressed in this chapter, along with any conclusions drawn from the available data, relate solely to the opinions of the authors.

Introduction: chronicity, ethnicity and the role of the patient in late twentieth-century medicine

In the summer of 1995, clinicians, health managers, and a range of social scientists convened in Geneva for a major international conference (sponsored by the World Health Organization, the University of Geneva, and the Swiss Ministry of Health) to consider the status and future of patient education programmes aimed at sufferers of chronic disease.[1] Conference organizers discussed how contemporary therapies for chronic illnesses might convince patients, their families, and medical professionals of the benefits of a more active role for patients *within* conventional treatment programmes. By choosing to focus on new approaches to existing therapies, rather than on the invention of novel therapies, the Congress participants highlighted their commitment to strengthening a historically weak link in the therapeutic chain: patient education.[2]

> Treatments of almost all chronic diseases implies [sic] that patients have to learn the appropriate skills for daily management of their disease; that their family may be included in this educational process; that they may be helped to adhere day after day, to their treatment; and finally, that psychological support is available to help them cope with the burden of disease.[3]

Furthermore, in their introductory remarks to the Congress Proceedings (published in the multi-disciplinary journal *Patient Education and Counselling*), the Director of the WHO's Collaborating Centre on Diabetes Mellitus, Professor Jean-Philippe Assal, and the editor of *Patient Education*, Adriaan Visser, stated

38 *Helen Valier and Roberta Bivins*

their determination to highlight the problems of chronic diseases such as diabetes mellitus, asthma, epilepsy, and lower back pain – often 'silent' and under-examined by medical professionals – rather than those of cancer or HIV/AIDS which, while affecting lower numbers, gained a great deal more public and professional attention. The international flavour of this conference reflected widespread efforts to reform medical services for the chronically ill. The chronic patient had become an highly visible economic and social entity in the decades after 1970. By the time this conference was held – 1995 – many of the initiatives of the late 1970s and 1980s had become well established, and could be critically assessed. Historically, the 1980s and 1990s are a particularly interesting time to study innovations in service provision for chronic disease in the UK. The UK, in keeping with other Western developed countries, was grappling with the financial and social problems of an increasingly aged and chronically sick population. Furthermore, since the UK National Health Service (NHS) policy in the 1980s sought to limit hospital-based services to emergency and acute care/crisis medicine, services for the chronically ill had been increasingly shifted outside of the hospital and into more 'community-focused' environments.

In this chapter we would like to highlight three relatively 'unglamorous' chronic diseases – non-insulin dependent diabetes mellitus, sickle-cell anaemia, and thalassaemia – requiring little hi-tech medical intervention, and with fairly well-established therapies. We will assess the role that patient education, and other more broadly configured organizational innovations, have had on their treatment at two clinics based in the multi-ethnic inner-city centre of Manchester, England. Like the 'chronic disease patient', the 'ethnic patient' has remained a resolutely unglamorous and often silent figure on the stage of modern medicine. The role played by notions of race in shaping medical science and clinical practice is beyond the scope of this chapter. However, the emergence – primarily through Commonwealth immigration – of culturally, linguistically, and medically distinct populations in post-war Britain has had a substantial impact on the innovations we will describe here. South Asian and African-Caribbean immigrants and their British-born descendants are differentially susceptible to all three of the diseases we examine. Thus through examining medical provision for sickle cell, thalassaemia, and non-insulin dependent diabetes, we will also throw light on the relatively unexamined question of British medical responses to immigration and ethnic diversity.[4]

Studies in medical sociology and in the history of medicine have used the study of chronicity as a tool for reassessment of the meaning and purpose of medicine in post-World War II Western societies.[5] Work on the medical negotiation of patient compliance, especially in regard to chronic illness, has emphasized the sometimes contradictory goals of incorporating patient agency while enhancing physician control.[6] This tension between *engaging* and *controlling* patients and their social networks has also been studied as a feature of medical responses to immigration.[7] Like the chronic disease patient, the immigrant or ethnic patient 'must' be acculturated. In each case, the patient's social network must be assimilated into the culturally specific process of health maintenance.

Immigrant and ethnic communities have long been perceived (and indeed perceive themselves) as having different health care needs from the surrounding population.[8] Unsurprisingly, then, community awareness and patient education and activism in the arena of health care (whether in hospitals, general practice surgeries, or specialist clinics) have played an important role in questions of ethnic health.

The problems and challenges of immigrant and ethnic health, like those surrounding chronic disease, have focused lay and professional attention on the importance and nature of innovation in non-clinical arenas.[9] Our research has demonstrated that such innovation forms a feedback loop with investigative medicine, producing new research questions and new practice.[10] As a result, case studies of *chronic* disease and *immigrant* health offer a strong platform from which to engage with the general nature of the relationship between technical (material) innovations; innovations in the organization and delivery of medical care; and emergent user groups.

Diabetes mellitus[11] and the problem of the chronic patient

The initial discovery of insulin therapy for diabetes mellitus made in Toronto, Canada, in the early 1920s seemed at first near miraculous as sufferers, often in their teens or twenties, no longer faced the prospect of imminent death or 'treatment' involving a slow starvation.[12] Although not immediately taken up by all practitioners (for some of whom lifestyle and diet remained the key to living with diabetes), the use of insulin therapy spread quite rapidly across the Americas and Europe. It soon became apparent that insulin was not (as had initially been hoped) a *cure* for diabetes – the pancreas was not able to regenerate despite the respite offered by the insulin injections. Nonetheless, insulin was widely considered to be an innovative therapeutic agent to be used in conjunction with dietary and lifestyle regimes.

The discovery of insulin had helped to transform the once acutely (and terminally) ill diabetic into a *chronic* patient, drastically shifting the relationships between the physician, the patient, and the management of disease.[13] Part of this shift was a new emphasis on the role of patient education. For example, the eminent Boston physician and diabetologist, Eliot P. Joslin established a world-famous diabetes teaching clinic in the USA in 1929; and Robert D. Lawrence, a doctor and diabetic, founded the British Diabetic Association (BDA) in 1934, in collaboration with one of his diabetic patients, the author H.G. Wells. Chris Feudtner has argued that such programmes of education, laden as they were with the notion that the compliant patient *was* the healthy patient, further promoted acceptance of the strict *supervision* of patients by physicians.[14] Both Joslin's clinic, with its residential 'training' for patients, and 'wandering' (community-based) nursing initiatives, and the patient-oriented nature of the BDA went on to influence the organization of similar education projects for chronically ill patients world-wide.[15] Of all the chronic non-communicable conditions that increasingly affected the developed world's populations in the twentieth century, diabetes mellitus has been perhaps the most 'education-intensive'. Indeed, Charles Best, part of the original Toronto team to isolate and identify insulin, once declared, 'The diabetic who knows the most will live the longest'![16]

Aside from these early education-focused clinics and societies, diffusion of the new diabetes treatments in North American and many European countries was enabled by the changing institutional and professional structures of medicine – particularly the presence of new hospital-based clinical laboratories, and the increasing professionalization of basic medical sciences growing out of the universities. Glucose testing, integral to the new treatments, also provided clinicians with reliable, standardized data with which both to monitor an individual's disease, and to compare 'standards' of patient compliance with treatment regimes. During the 1920s and 1930s, problems of diabetic coma and gangrene served to intensify this sense of 'ideal' compliance, since patients suffering complications were considered to be those same patients with a lax approach to their dietary intake and insulin control.[17]

The 1940s and 1950s brought mounting evidence of serious iatrogenic and systemic sequelae (both 'microvascular' in the form of nerve, eye, and kidney damage, and 'macrovascular' in the form of coronary heart disease) which threatened to disable and foreshorten the lives of insulin-dependent diabetics within ten to twenty years of starting insulin therapy. Insulin technologies had altered the course and nature of diabetes and with this shift came even greater emphasis on treatment compliance. The patient's own behaviour and attitude began to be regarded by physicians as ever more crucial to an individual's long-term health and survival (and hence their own 'success'). Once again, patient education emerged as a key concept in the treatment of diabetes, in the hope that biomedical notions of 'ideal compliance' could become as much a part of public perceptions of the disorder as insulin itself.

It was also increasingly recognized during the late 1940s that there were a number of different forms of diabetes, in which insulin therapy played a greater or lesser role. These were later separated into two main types adopted by the WHO: insulin dependent diabetes mellitus (IDDM) often appearing in juveniles with the onset of severe symptoms including thirst, polyuria, weight loss, and elevated blood sugar levels; and non-insulin dependent diabetes mellitus (NIDDM) often appearing later in life, with few early symptoms and thus often diagnosed as a result of secondary complications.[18] Originally classified as a 'milder' form of diabetes, appearing mainly in the older population, NIDDM was now reconceived as a distinct and possibly preventable form of the disorder (raising a new series of medical and public health issues in relation to the treatment of diabetic populations). Pharmacological research relating to diabetes continued apace. As treatments for disorders associated with IDDM and NIDDM began to improve, so the numbers of diabetics taking up new therapies rapidly increased, substantially driving up health care costs in countries across the globe.

Treatment for both IDDM and NIDDM in Britain during the 1950s and 1960s continued to take place, occasionally in the primary care setting, but more often at special out-patient clinics held once or twice per week at large general hospitals.[19] Conditions within these clinics were far from ideal. At the Manchester Royal Infirmary (MRI) Diabetes Clinic – a classic example of an 'insulin-era' diabetic clinic – the few score users of the diabetic clinic in the 1920s, had grown to 3,500 by the early 1950s. As stated by a senior hospital consultant with a mixture of pride and despair, attempts to reduce the number of patients attending the clinic (around 90–110 at each weekly clinic) 'had been obstructed by patients who believe the MRI Clinic to be the best around'.[20] The MRI Clinic, like others, 'suffered' under a good public reputation for treatment management combined with an apparent reluctance (or lack of confidence) on the part of general practitioners to actively participate in the complicated, long-term care required by diabetics and their families.[21] As a result of the crowded conditions, and the lack of flexibility in appointment times, it was common for patients to wait for several hours to see a consultant (or perhaps a more junior, assistant doctor) for as little as a few minutes each. As patients were arbitrarily assigned to staff on duty, their care was discontinuous, and they played relatively little part in planning long-term treatment strategies.

The metabolic control of diabetes in post-war Britain was undoubtedly improved through the continued refinement of insulin, the development of more effective injection methods, and for NIDDM sufferers, the emergence of oral hypoglaecemics. Improvements in other specialties during the 1960s and 1970s enabled greater control over secondary complications. In spite of these new techniques and processes, during the early 1980s prominent doctors involved in the treatment of diabetics bemoaned the generally low standards of care.[22] One such group of doctors – the South East Thames Diabetes Physicians Group established in 1984 – conducted a survey of existing facilities and set out a strategy of care to improve standards and reduce costs.[23] This survey came to a highly significant conclusion: as a condition, diabetes was simply not taken seriously within the acute medical sector. This in turn meant that (very high) costs associated with the care of diabetic patients were not planned or focused spending, but rather the result of reactionary attempts to 'mop up' morbidities across a range of in-patient and out-patient facilities. Attention to proper staffing levels of medical and paramedical staff and dedicated, well-designed facilities would, the authors argued, prove a great deal more cost-effective.

Although the potential for high quality care of diabetes had steadily increased throughout the 1970s, the actual quality of care experienced by most diabetics and their families was perhaps most radically affected by the *organizational* innovations demanded by groups such as the the South East Thames Diabetes Physicians Group and the BDA.[24] Furthermore, studies of cost-effectiveness through patient education programmes (first conducted in the USA during the 1970s[25]) also led to the commissioning of (community-based) specialist education units for use by diabetics and the sufferers of other chronic diseases, the institution of general practitioner co-operative care schemes and the appointment of diabetes specialist nurses (DSNs).[26] All shared the aim of shifting education out of the traditional clinic, and in some cases away from the hospital entirely.

A BDA-sponsored workshop held in January 1987 at the Ipswich Hospital in the south of England brought together interested physicians, DSNs, dieticians, and government health department representatives to plan for more comprehensive diabetes care, encompassing clinical *and* educational strands.[27] In 1988 the Ipswich team published results on a feasibility study taken of their suggested 'ideal' system of integrated diabetes care and education, based on the first year of their day centre at the Ipswich Hospital.[28] In seeking to change the traditional clinic (mainly medical) model, the Ipswich team intended their purpose-built centre to increase consultation times, patient access according to social and diabetic need, and continuity of care; to minimize waiting times; and to provide objective-based learning for patients and their carers. Educational initiatives designed to improve the medical supervision and patient management of diabetes were widespread across Europe and the USA around this time.[29] However, Day's centre in Ipswich was rare in that it provided a *unified* clinical and educational system for all ambulatory patients. The importance of patient education in diabetes had of course been recognized for a century, yet it took a whole combination of circumstances to produce enduring and effective innovation in this area.

One key to change was a specific reconfiguration of the nursing and paramedical roles – roles already in the midst of profound general change. During the late 1970s and 1980s, for instance, the nursing profession in Britain underwent rapid specialization and began to undertake many more responsibilities both in the clinical and community context.[30] The Ipswich team capitalized on this change by elevating the trained diabetic nurse to a proactive role in the provision of primary consultative care and ongoing patient education. Further changes to staff organization included the rationalization of specialist sub-clinics (for heart and kidney problems, etc.), and crucially, the incorporation of paramedicals previously often excluded from decisions about patient management and treatment strategies, such as dieticians and chiropodists. Day and his colleagues reported that their focus on teamwork across disciplines and divisions had not only enabled a much more flexible service, increased staff morale, and improved 'default' rates among patients; but had done so with minimal extra spending. The Ipswich team clearly considered their experiment a success: as well as attending more regularly, with fewer cancellations and non-appearances overall, patients already demonstrated tighter glycaemic control. With this control, would, it was hoped, come a lower incidence of diabetic emergency (and therefore fewer episodes of hospitalization and rehabilitation) and so an improvement in the life of the individual diabetic and a reduction in costs for health care providers.

The model of innovation proposed by the Ipswich team could operate *within* existing budgets and other resources. In a cash-strapped NHS, such an approach generated a good deal of interest from paramedicals eager to take on greater responsibilities within the NHS, as well as physicians. For nurses, the new centres represented a chance for more advanced education and training, in addition to a bigger role; for chiropodists, on the other hand, the plans meant the first chance of any role *at all!* Encouraged by the BDA, the Ipswich team were vociferous proponents of the spread of diabetes centres across all regional health districts, arguing:

> [o]bstacles to success are largely those of ignorance of the medical and socio-economic consequences of diabetes and it has been demonstrated that they can and should be overcome by a vigorous campaign of education of professional and non-professional colleagues.[31]

One physician to heed the call was Stephen Tomlinson, Professor of Medicine at the University of Manchester. In 1988, Tomlinson founded an Ipswich-style centre at the Manchester Royal Infirmary (Manchester's oldest and most prominent – but at this point also nearly bankrupt! – teaching hospital) based upon similar considerations of cost-effectiveness and staff reorganization. Tomlinson's reforms achieved success along the lines of the Ipswich centre, but additional unforeseen effects also emerged – effects which had profound implications for Manchester's diverse ethnic populations, and for the ways in which those populations interacted with their health care providers.

The Manchester Diabetes Centre

Stephen Tomlinson arrived in Manchester in 1984 with a strong research background in clinical and laboratory endocrinology, to take up the University's Chair of Medicine.[32] Since 1947, the Manchester Chair had been held by an academic clinician–scientist, and in this respect, Tomlinson's previous laboratory-orientated research interests were not unusual. Although many academic medical professors of his generation were increasingly criticized for their intellectual and perceptual distance from both clinicians and patients, Tomlinson was active and vocal in his commitment to clinical endocrinology, and to diabetes care in particular. Despite a career spent primarily at the benchside, Tomlinson had good contacts within the larger clinical consultant community of the UK. Furthermore, when Tomlinson was made Manchester's Professor of Medicine, few other physicians interested in diabetes held such a high profile post. He therefore attracted considerable attention. Prominent doctors within the British diabetes 'establishment' – such as John Day in Ipswich and the London physician and Chair of the British Diabetic Association (BDA), Sir John Nabarro – strongly encouraged Tomlinson to reform the services in his region.[33]

Pressure for change did not emerge solely from the national clinical diabetes community. Metabolic and endocrinological clinical *research* had flourished in post-war Manchester, but patient services (especially for out-patients) had struggled (through under-funding and huge increases in patient attendance) and treatment initiatives had therefore advanced much more slowly. Tomlinson took control of the diabetic clinic soon after his appointment, and was concerned at the crowded, unpleasant conditions he found there.[34] With the help of Manchester's Director of Public Health, Peter Povey, senior NHS clinicians at the MRI, professional friends within the BDA, and particularly aided by his new colleague Jill Pooley, a DSN, Tomlinson sought to change the disorganized, 'doctor-dominated' culture of diabetes services in Manchester and the North West by establishing a new centre away from the Infirmary.

Just as the reorganization of the nursing role at Ipswich had proved so crucial to the ethos of the new centre, so at Manchester Tomlinson was keen to employ a highly capable specialist nurse. Pooley was originally appointed to a hospital in Stockport (a nearby district) as one of the first DSNs in the country where she was set the task of dealing with diabetic children. Impressed with her skills, Tomlinson poached Pooley to work at the Manchester Infirmary, planning and fundraising alongside him. The partnership enabled Pooley to escape the restrictive 'delegated task' role typical of specialist diabetic nursing at the time, but according to Tomlinson's own testimony, also changed the way he himself practised medicine. Her interest in the needs and experiences of patients shifted Tomlinson's orientation away from its narrow academic focus.[35] Tomlinson and Pooley followed their Ipswich colleagues by canvassing support not only from the BDA, the District Health Authority and the Hospital's own management, but also from national pharmaceutical companies and local industry. Individuals and patient groups, too, were active in fund-raising for the new centre. In Tomlinson's judgement, they were a key element in raising public awareness and support for increased resources for diabetics. Patient groups appeared content to work alongside medical professionals: after all, the BDA remained a joint medical-lay organization and diabetics and their carers were able to voice concerns within and through it (although as noted by Tomlinson himself, members of such groups tended to be self-selected, educated, and articulate and thus not 'representative' as such).

Lack of space within the Infirmary was not the only reason why Tomlinson sought to establish the clinic outside the hospital:

> It was the difference in concept of care between a hospital and what we were providing, which we like to think is different [from a threatening, doctor-dominated environment] … we thought it important to be slightly distanced from the hospital. To engage *directly* with the people who have the problems.[36]

This concept became embodied in the name of the centre – the *Manchester Diabetes Centre* (MDC) – which made no mention of the hospital with which it was associated, but which rather stressed the accessibility and availability of care for all. Patients did need an initial GP referral to the Centre, but after that they were able to access all its services – including specialist clinics – on demand; a radical departure from the system of the old Diabetes Clinic.

In a short article written for *Mediscope* (a magazine produced for the Manchester Medical School by its students) in February 1988, Stephen

Tomlinson gave a manifesto sketch of the Infirmary's soon-to-be-unveiled diabetes centre.[37] In this sketch (covering the endocrinological research aspects of diabetes in Manchester as well as clinical considerations), Tomlinson particularly emphasized the need for comprehensive patient education of a sort which could lead to higher levels of self-care among patient groups. The style of organization commonly seen in the traditional clinic model was clearly implicated in the existing dearth of education initiatives:

> How do we currently provide education? In a busy district general hospital (or a teaching hospital) the traditional diabetic clinic is held once or twice a week. A single consultant, with perhaps clinical assistants and a [Senior House Officer] might be expected to see well over a hundred patients in a three-hour session. People wait for periods of up to four hours to see a doctor for five minutes or even less. It is quite likely that they will see a different doctor each time they come. Such an environment is not conducive to education![38]

Effective patient education and increased standards of self-care would, he argued, only come about if medical professionals *and patients* altered their views of what diabetes care ought to be, and who ought to participate in it:

> In surveys done at the MRI, knowledge scores amongst patients have been found to be appallingly low. People have little idea *why* they attend the clinic. Their major anxieties revolve around such issues as missing their turn, and yet despite all this, when asked whether they are satisfied with the medical services provided, over two-thirds are satisfied or very satisfied. Thus, knowledge is poor and expectations are low ... The solution lies in *teamwork* with its objective being *prevention* and *self care* through education. One way of promoting this philosophy is to *abandon the traditonal diabetic clinic* which provides a *problem finding* environment but not a *problem preventing* environment.[39]

Thus, Tomlinson led the way in abandoning the old MRI Diabetes Clinic and forging its replacement: the MDC, open five days a week, and a focus for clinical expertise throughout the area. Along with dedicated sessions for chiropodists, dicticians and other paramedicals, the system was dependent upon the expansion of the role of the diabetic nurse both to take over consultation appointments from the doctors, and to run and maintain patient education programmes.

Much like the Ipswich team, Tomlinson also underpinned his plans for diabetic reform with an appeal to economics. For the 15,000 annual diabetic admissions to the MRI, the average length of stay was 11 days per patient, as compared to an average of 8 days for the non-diabetic patient. Such a discrepancy cost the Hospital's health authority something of the order of £2,000,000 per year – coincidentally almost exactly the amount of the authority's average overspend.[40] Tomlinson specifically highlighted how facilities like the MDC could prevent occurrence of problems like the 'diabetic foot' – the commonest cause of in-patient admission, and (if amputation was required) the most likely reason for a lengthy stay – cheaply and with enormous beneficial effects for patients and hospital resources. Some 50 to 80 per cent of all diabetic amputations were, as reported by Tomlinson, preventable, and so the choice of this 'syndrome' as a rationale for the organization of the MDC offered a particularly compelling constellation of moral, economic, and clinical interests.

The MDC could identify the 'foot at risk' through a more thorough examination of the patient; integrated provision of specialist chiropody services; and the deployment of DSNs to educate patients and to assess specific obstacles to self-care as experienced by the patient. The vast majority of these clinics were held *in* the MDC – patients no longer queued for a sequence of (often quite disjointed) care. For Tomlinson, the multidisciplinary approach included 'doctors, nurses, dieticians, chiropodists, opthalmists, obstetricians, nephrologists, vascular surgeons, orthopaedic surgeons, and perhaps most importantly of all the diabetic'.[41] In addition to foot specialists, Tomlinson's team also worked with kidney and dialysis experts, eye doctors, obstetricians, and a range of other medical and surgical specialists.

Many patients suffering diabetic complications experienced a fully integrated response to their disorder perhaps for the first time. Tomlinson's determination to reconfigure the role of paramedicals as a means to improve access and education, did not stop with the Centre itself. With the help of Pooley, he established a series of general practice mini-clinics supported by the main Centre and its sub-clinics. These clinics were also intended to educate and reassure general practitioners that the treatment and monitoring of diabetic patients did not have to be a hospital activity. Thus Tomlinson speaks of targeting 'leaders' and 'opinion formers' amongst local GPs to get the message across. Conversely, he was also keen to allay the fears of those GPs opposed to the MDC, who saw the Centre as a straightforward 'hospital innovation' diverting funds from the primary care of diabetics.

Through these clinics, the visibility of the MDC was raised, and more patients began to be referred *earlier* following diagnosis.[42] The MDC's sponsorship (in collaboration with the local health authority) of GP mini-clinics in diabetes helped to stem criticism by local practitioners, as did the establishment of a diabetes centre at the smaller town of Bolton, some distance away from the larger city's cluster of elite hospitals. Until the founding of the new centre, the Bolton area had had some of the worst resourced diabetes care in the North West; it was also a focus for GP resistance to (what they saw as) additional support for development at the Manchester Royal Infirmary (MRI). In supporting the Bolton Centre, therefore, Tomlinson and his allies were able to improve services in the local area, reassure local GPs, and enhance the outreach abilities of the MDC.

The cost expenditure on diabetes centres so contested by GPs was justified by Tomlinson and fellow advocates through clinical audit studies (such as that published by the Ipswich team in 1988). The 1980s saw an explosion of statistical performance assessment exercises within NHS management. Reports issued by the Central Manchester Health Authority during the early 1980s, for instance, linked an economic need to reduce the total number of beds in Central Manchester to the need to reduce the average length of stay of all patients.[43] Detailed statistical analysis could, it was argued, reveal 'problem areas' within specialty disciplines and between types of patient. Although these studies mainly focused on disciplines in anesthesiology and surgery, Tomlinson's positive emphasis on the importance of clinical audit and his use of these studies to predict (accurately as it turned out) likely future reductions in patient admissions, length of stay, etc. almost certainly eased the path and *political* acceptance of this innovation at a time of great financial strain in the NHS. The process of clinical audit also revealed another unpredicted series of problems in diabetes services, this time specifically related to the lower rates of attendance among working-class adults and members of Manchester's South Asian communities. While the majority population responded well to various standard initiatives to improve rates of attendance, these outreach tactics proved ineffective in tackling the high incidences of 'Did Not Attend' among South Asian patients.

A number of studies within the UK have shown that Asian patients respond poorly to standard clinical outreach measures, from written appointment reminders to standard information and education leafleting.[44] In the case of the MDC, Asian patients had particularly high 'Did Not Attend' rates, and failed to respond to the reminder letters which had proven successful for other high 'Did Not Attend' groups. Instead of writing off this (relatively small, but expanding) group of patients, however, the MDC team regarded this problem as an impetus to examine and improve services across the board, with more tailored clinics – not only Friday clinics with an Asian nurse and scheduled linkworkers in attendance for Asian populations, but clinics targeting particular complications: diabetic foot, male impotence, or questions of fertility. In addition, the MDC actively addressed the specific linguistic and environmental needs of its South Asian patients through the use of linkworkers and DSNs, enrolling the Manchester Action Committee for the Health Care of Ethnic Minorities in its efforts. Indeed, the support of this community group proved vital to the MDC's successful bid for linkworker funding. Moreover, Tomlinson initiated research into how South Asian patients' uptake of medical and health information might be improved, through flash cards and images, for example of healthy foods on saffron backgrounds. The results of such studies were used to improve patient education across the spectrum of patient groups.[45]

While South Asians at the MDC were important as one under-served sub-population among several, at the Manchester Sickle Cell and Thalassaemia clinic, they were a primary client group, alongside Manchester's strong African-Caribbean community. Their status as primary users has significantly affected the nature, trajectory and extent of innovations in sickle-cell and thalassaemia service provision in the city and region. As members of marginalized, but self-aware and self-identifying communities, the responses of Manchester's South

Asian and African-Caribbean populations to sickle-cell and thalassaemia service provision illustrate the importance of community, rather than professional pressure in the instigation and shaping of innovations in medical care. As Keith Wailoo has noted for the US case: 'The existence and political identity of self-conscious racial and ethnic groups … demanded that these diseases [sickle cell and thalassaemia] be treated separately yet equally.'[46]

Sickle-cell anaemia

Sickle-cell anaemia was formally identified by Chicago physician James Herrick, in a 1910 case report presented to the Association of American Physicians' annual meeting.[47] As a rare disease found solely in members of an underprivileged minority population, sickle-cell anaemia did not initially trigger much clinical or biological interest in the USA, and still less in Britain, with its tiny black population. Nonetheless, by the 1930s, sickle-cell anaemia was recognized as a genetically linked condition in which the red blood cells would (when deoxygenated) assume a pronounced crescent shape, with both immediate and long-term pathological effects. By 1932, US clinicians had also drawn a distinction between sickle-cell disease and sickle-cell trait, although the medical – and political – implications of this difference did not become apparent until much later.[48] Although Herrick's discovery of sickle-cell anaemia was triggered by his patient's clinical manifestations – severe anaemia and painful crises – clinicians almost immediately came to identify the disease with its cellular phenomena, rather than the complex of symptoms with which sufferers presented.[49] In the USA, sickle cell was regarded as a disease solely of African Americans, and stigmatized as a sign of their 'racial degeneration'.[50] Meanwhile, the 1925 discovery of sickle-cell cases in colonial Africa stimulated British interest in the disease. By 1944, it was clear that sickle cell was common in Africa. Such evidence did not shake the persistent belief that sickle-cell anaemia was more common in the USA, perhaps due to 'some factor imported by marriage with white persons'.[51] This explanation, of course, fitted in well with anxieties in the USA (and to a lesser degree the UK) about the 'dangers' of miscegenation and racial mixing. Studies of sickle-cell trait in Africa also suggested associations between sickle-cell trait and malaria.[52] In Britain, this malaria connection was to become crucial in identifying other affected populations across the emerging Commonwealth.

As Wailoo and others have demonstrated, the strong linkage between sickle cell and race, through notions of 'Negro blood', reduced and deflected US clinical interest; biological interest, however, was stimulated by the hypothesis that haemoglobin was implicated in the sickling process.[53] In 1945, chemist Linus Pauling and his new medically-trained graduate student Harvey Itano took up the problem of sickling in red blood cells as a tool through which to explore the chemical nature of haemoglobin. It is perhaps indicative of the degree to which African Americans (and their diseases) were marginalized in US medical research that Pauling learned of the sickling phenomenon through the 'chance remark' of a colleague, William Castle. Castle, a Professor of

Medicine at Harvard University Medical School, had himself become interested in sickle cell only through the rare case of an afflicted white woman, the subject of a report on sickle-cell anaemia in the 'white race'.[54] Pauling and Itano confirmed the genetic basis of sickle-cell anaemia, and elucidated 'a direct link between defective hemoglobin molecules and their pathological consequences, providing a firm basis for the concept of "molecular disease"'.[55] However, little collaboration took place between biomedical researchers (often at elite universities or teaching hospitals far from centres of African-American or African-Caribbean population) and those clinicians dealing with sickle-cell anaemia on the ground (often at less prestigious institutions). Moreover, while sickle cell was an interesting biochemical conundrum, it was of marginal clinical interest: recommending bed rest and a healthy diet was unlikely to make a clinical reputation!

It is interesting to contrast the case of sickle cell with that of pernicious anaemia. Both were rare conditions of the blood and, in the early years of the twentieth century, both were inexplicable and untreatable – yet pernicious anaemia was the subject of much clinical investigation, while sickle-cell anaemia was disregarded. The link between sickle-cell anaemia and race offers a partial explanation of this difference. Both pernicious and sickle-cell anaemia were non-infectious and had periods of remission in which the patient was apparently 'cured' (thus making their sufferers appropriate candidates for charity hospitals which would not accept either infectious or incurable cases), and both presented 'interesting' clinical pictures, with readily identifiable blood changes. But while pernicious anaemics were predominantly white, sickle-cell sufferers were almost inevitably black. Race was nonetheless only one factor shaping the professional response to each of these diseases. The difference between their levels of visibility also reflects, among other things, the markedly different levels of involvement by the pharmaceutical industry, particularly after the emergence of liver therapy – and therefore marketable products like liver extracts – for pernicious anaemia.[56] Sickle-cell research in the same period produced no such commodifiable results.

Although clinical–scientific knowledge about the nature and course of sickle-cell anaemia continued to increase, between 1940 and 1970 neither academic researchers nor their clinical colleagues could report a consistently reliable means to effectively intervene in the disease. Herrick's regime of rest, good food, and the local treatment of ulcers and infection had, since 1910, been supplemented variously with splenectomy, the liver diet, iron, arsenic, and transfusions, but these therapies *du jour* produced few successes. Transfusions emerged as helpful in managing sickle-cell disease, particularly for patients under stress or undergoing surgery; splenectomy was useful in cases of enlarged spleen. Attempts to discover a magic bullet, in the form of chemical anti-sickling agents – particularly around the time of the 1970–2 spike of US public concern about the disease, during which sickle-cell was the subject of four crucial television editorials, a presidential health message, and a highly controversial Act of Congress – produced no more encouraging results.[57] As individuals with sickle-cell anaemia began to live

longer (primarily because of improved living conditions for the affected populations), it became clear that the ischaemia (reduced blood flow) and infarction
(necrosis of blood-starved tissues) characteristic of sickle cell resulted in permanent organ damage. Long-term care for the condition therefore involved many
medical and paramedical specialties, in comparatively routine, non-curative –
but expensive and time-consuming – ways. By the 1980s, sickle-cell anemia was
among the most comprehensively understood diseases at the molecular level, but
remained clinically and pharmaceutically intransigent. Instead, health care
professionals (initially in the USA) turned towards patient education, screening,
and prevention as the means by which to address the disease.

Thalassaemia

Thalassaemia (or Cooley's anaemia), like sickle-cell anaemia, was first identified
as a specific disease in the USA in the early years of the twentieth century. In
1925, Detroit paediatric physicians Thomas Cooley and Pearl Lee observed and
reported on two Italian children suffering from severe anaemia, enlarged spleens
and livers, discoloured skin, and bone alterations. Like sickle cell, thalassaemia
rapidly came to be identified with a community initially marginalized in the
USA: individuals of Mediterranean ancestry. However, the biomedical response
to Cooley and Lee's initial paper was far more lively, and included both
European and North American reports on the condition. Any explanation for
this difference must draw upon a wide range of factors: the existing (if somewhat
inchoate) biomedical awareness of the condition in Southern Europe; the high
visibility of at-risk individuals and communities in the urban (and research)
centres of the USA; the severity of the condition in affected children; and of
course the role played by racial discrimination and prejudice in responses to
sickle cell – its labelling as a 'Negro disease'.

The first definitive evidence that thalassaemia was genetically determined
emerged from clinics in Greece and Italy between 1936 and 1938. Similar
conclusions were drawn independently by US researcher-clinicians, and by 1949
thalassaemia had emerged as a heterogeneous collection of hereditary blood
disorders, resulting from the interaction of several genetic loci involved in
haemoglobin production.[58] By 1954, biomedical researchers knew that beta-
thalassaemia was not restricted to the Mediterranean region, but was also
prevalent to varying degrees on the Indian subcontinent, South East Asia,
China, and specific parts of the Middle East.[59]

Although beta-thalassaemia, like sickle cell, is extraordinarily well understood
at the molecular and genetic levels, no cure for the condition has yet been found.
Unlike sickle-cell anaemia, untreated thalassaemia major is a fatal disease even
in good environmental conditions. However, homozygous beta-thalassaemia has
been rendered a life-long chronic, rather than an acute, condition by therapeutic, technological, and pharmaceutical developments since 1960. The first
consistently successful therapeutic intervention for thalassaemics was the 'hypertransfusion' regime of the early 1960s; however, soon after its introduction it

became apparent that while allowing patients to survive, hypertransfusion also produced iatrogenic disease, in the form of transfusional iron loading. Human bodies cannot excrete excess iron; thalassaemics undergoing regular transfusion built up deposits of iron in major organs, thus facing death in their mid-twenties, rather than childhood. The introduction of intravenous and subsequently subcutaneous desferrioxamine administration in the late 1960s and 1970s 'solved' the problem of iron loading and consequent organ damage and morbidity.[60] However, the arduous regimen of nightly subcutaneous transfusion has proven difficult for patients to accept and comply with. And of course, the transfusion and chelation regime is costly – in 1987, the WHO estimated the annual clinical cost of a thalassaemia patient at £5,500.[61] Meanwhile, failure to catch the disease early – or patient resistance to the therapeutic burden – results in chronic illness, organ damage, frequent hospitalization, and premature death. Even highly compliant patients whose condition was recognized at birth or in early childhood are nonetheless prone to developmental problems, chronic disease, and early death.

Thus like diabetes, thalassaemia's transition from acute to chronic condition has proven a major public health problem for nations in which it is common – and this group now includes the UK and USA, with large 'at-risk' immigrant and ethnic populations.[62] In the UK, recognition of this expanding problem led to the introduction of second trimester prenatal diagnosis of the thalassaemias in 1974. First trimester screening for all pregnancies at risk of sickle cell or alpha-thalassaemia, and most pregnancies at risk of beta-thalassaemia was introduced in 1982; and simpler and less-invasive (pcr-based) first trimester screening for at-risk pregnancies of all haemoglobinopathies arrived in 1990. Three diagnostic centres (two in London and one in Oxford) handle the analysis of such prenatal tests. Notably, despite being much more common in the UK population, prenatal testing for sickle-cell trait started eight years later than testing for thalassaemia – and three years after the foundation of the Sickle Cell Society, an active support group with both patient and professional members.[63] Although the emergence of new screening technologies certainly facilitated the extension of screening to sickle-cell anaemia, it seems likely that this delay was also influenced by the low rates of diagnosis and absence of specific (and therefore auditable) therapies for sickle-cell anaemia. Without specific, costed, therapeutic interventions, and with unpredictable clinical sequelae, sickle-cell anaemia was relatively invisible to the clinical audit, and consequently suffered from reduced fiscal pressure for prevention.

Marked regional and ethnic variations exist in service provision and uptake for sickle-cell disease and thalassaemia in Britain. For historical reasons, both provision and uptake remain higher in the South East (where all three of the large diagnostic centres are based) and among individuals of Cypriot descent; 87 per cent of affected British Cypriots seek prenatal screening.[64] This impressive rate of uptake is related both to thalassaemia awareness and prevention initiatives in Greek Cyprus and to the fact that 80 per cent of British Cypriots live in London, where screening facilities are most accessible.[65] Moreover, the UK

Thalassaemia Society was founded by Cypriot immigrant parents of affected children in 1976; its early activities were primarily aimed at other Cypriots in Britain, although it is now reaching out to thalassaemics from all ethnic backgrounds.[66] The decline in the incidence of thalassaemia within the Cypriot communities has justifiably been celebrated as exemplary of the positive effects of community-based (but medically driven) initiatives in reducing rates of hereditary disease.[67] However, a similar programme among affected South Asian communities – even in London – has produced more ambiguous results.

The very different pattern of immigration followed by African-Caribbeans and South Asians, has resulted in more scattered populations, with major communities established in the Midlands and North-West. The public health impact of such Commonwealth immigration was recognized by the medical profession in the mid-1960s, when Commonwealth immigrants comprised less than 2 per cent of the total population.[68] Early studies of the 'immigrant problem' in British medicine focused on these groups in relation to the potential importation of infectious diseases and parasites. By 1966, however, the medical profession was becoming aware of chronic diseases – including the 'exotic' haemoglobinopathies – found more commonly among the new Britons than in the native British population.[69] At the same time, medical professionals were coming to realize that cultural differences could have a profound impact on the uptake of medical services and the doctor–patient relationship.

Sickle cell and beta-thalassaemia: service provision in Manchester

The rise of Community Health Councils (CHCs), established in 1974, offered a new channel for consumer involvement in the NHS. In Manchester, a major destination for commonwealth immigration, defining the needs of these new users was an issue of immediate concern. The Central Manchester CHC raised the question of 'The NHS and the Immigrant Community' in its second annual report, focusing on difficulties – primarily linguistic – faced by minorities in gaining access to health service facilities, concerns about 'the noted vitamin deficiencies in Asian diets', and the need for psychiatric services to address the effects of 'migration from a peasant to an industrialized society'.[70] By 1982, *HealthLink*, the magazine of the Manchester CHCs could proclaim 'Asian healthcare receives a boost': local Asian groups had employed community workers to provide translation and support at local hospitals.[71] Clearly, the active involvement of the ethnic communities themselves played a crucial role in such developments.

In 1984, the Manchester Sickle Cell Centre (SCC) opened; based in multi-ethnic Moss Side, the new Centre offered screening, advice, and counselling on a walk-in basis. Its initial target population was the large African-Caribbean community living in Manchester, who had been very active both in calling for improved sickle-cell services and in shaping the form those services would take. Their campaign had begun in the late 1970s with the voluntary efforts of a young black haematologist (now working in Trinidad) and the Moss Side Family Advice Centre (FAC), a local and highly activist organization rooted in the Moss Side African-Caribbean community.[72] Drawing upon her findings, workers at the FAC initiated consultation meetings within the community, and discovered widespread lack of awareness of and misconceptions about sickle-cell anaemia, and worse, that patients were receiving few, if any, sickle-cell services at all.[73] This discovery prompted the establishment of a support group for patients and their families, again through the efforts of the FAC and community activists, but with the enthusiastic involvement of a scattering of interested medical professionals, including a consultant paediatrician at the Royal Manchester Children's Hospital, and a dental officer who had already been doing *ad hoc* screening among her clientele. The support group in turn submitted a report to the Director of Public Health in Manchester, Dr Povey. A working party was formed, incorporating members of the support group, Povey himself, the other medical professionals already concerned with sickle cell in Manchester, members of the Community Health Group for Ethnic Minorities, the Central Manchester CHC, and a new recruit drawn from the city centre Regional Health Promotion Unit, Verna Davis.

In response to the support group and working party's continuing pressure, the Regional Health Authority finally earmarked funds to explore the need for sickle-cell services. Initially, this money took the form of a two-year action research project, headed by Davis, to quantify the number of sickle-cell sufferers in Greater Manchester, and identify issues related to their care through providing sickle cell-specific services – but also to audit *ad hoc* services already being offered. The form assumed by the sickle-cell services and investigation, and the location where they were based, reflected intense community involvement:

> One of the things that the working group – sickle cell working group – and the support group made very clear was that they wanted the service to be community based, and they felt that was more central to the highest at risk population; and they didn't want it hospital based at all. They wanted somewhere that was accessible, that could have a walk-in, drop-in kind of basis. So that was made very clear, and that was the reason why [the SCC] was situated there.[74]

At the end of the two-year research period, it was recommended that the SCC should become a mainstream funded service (under public health management) while maintaining its community-based open access structure. In its first two years, the largest group of service-users were those who had self-referred; this fact played a major role in determining the shape taken by service provision. When NHS services were reorganized in the early 1990s, the Centre was moved from public health management to an umbrella primary care and acute services trust. A subsequent reorganization separated acute (hospital) and primary care services, and resulted in the transfer of all haemoglobinopathy services – including the SCC – from primary care to acute services. This transfer was supported by staff at the Centre as a way to maintain an integrated service for patients, and to reduce the impact of any subsequent 'internal market' on the availability of diagnostic and screening tests for haemoglobinopathies. However, the transfer of the SCC to acute services management did render the community desire for a non-hospital-based, local service somewhat problematic.

Because the SCC was to be integrated into the acute services Trust at the Manchester Royal Infirmary (MRI), hospital management suggested moving the service onto the main MRI campus. This provoked protests from the African-Caribbean community, concerned with the potential of a creeping standardizing of its day-to-day running arrangements, and loss of its community-centred approach: '[T]he community made it very clear ... that they didn't want the service to be hospital-based, ... they've always maintained that and they still maintain that.'[75] Indeed, in this case, the patient groups played a valued role in mediating between the groups of medical and management professionals, and communicating users' concerns directly to managers from other parts of the NHS. Davis recalled:

> at times when it has been difficult to illustrate to the acute service the issues ... the patients' groups illustrated it themselves much better than I could put it across. It has actually been very beneficial ... to let them express their concerns themselves, and it's actually been taken on board better – it's a two way process.[76]

Patients were (and are) encouraged to express their concerns; the Centre's steering group is comprised of health professionals, CHC members, and patient representatives. Centre patients have historically also written directly to management at the Manchester Royal Infirmary and have occasionally met with the CHC, who then represented their views to the Health Authority. In the end a 'happy compromise' was found, by moving the Centre to a building opposite the main MRI site, easily accessible to hospital staff and near the laboratory and specialist treatment facilities, but not embedded in the MRI complex itself, and only a few minutes' walk from its former site.[77]

Although they had a representative on the working group which first proposed the development of the SCC, the CHC only became active in supporting the Centre after its establishment as a community-based service. Indeed, although the CHC newsletter, *HealthLink*, noted the opening of the SCC in 1984, the annual report of that year (reporting on the CHC's own activities) made no mention of it, stressing instead its work to secure funding for interpreters. However, CHC input was crucial in forcefully representing the needs of the Centre to the Health Authority after it was established. In particular, the CHC played an important role in expanding the SCC's mandate to include thalassaemia.

SCC staff became aware of the need among Manchester's South Asian communities for genetic counselling services quite early in the Centre's history.

Members of the local South Asian community began to attend the SCC almost immediately after it opened in 1984, and Davis had soon found some thalassaemia among them.[78] Davis rapidly came to believe that they needed dedicated support and counselling:

> I felt that to do it badly was better than not doing it at all …[genetic counselling] is a very emotive subject; it's one that affects reproductive choices, there are cultural issues, religious issues … There's a dearth of knowledge in the Asian community about genetic disorders anyhow, and I didn't think it was adequate trying to interpret though a younger member of the family, a husband, … or whatever. So we campaigned vigorously to get an Asian worker involved, a health worker, who could counsel in their own mother tongue.[79]

As crucial to Davis, as the Centre's director, was the need to get feedback from the Asian community about what they wanted and needed from their counselling sessions and the SCC in general. Davis contacted the Manchester Action Committee for the Health Care of Ethnic Minorities (MACHEM – a multiethnic and multidisciplinary group of community leaders from around Manchester) who, with the CHC, strongly supported the Centre's bid for a counselling post to address the needs of the Asian community. This post was established and filled in 1991, with the appointment of Dr Rafeya Rahman, and the SCC became the Sickle Cell and Thalassaemia Centre (SCTC).[80]

Immediately upon taking up her appointment, Rahman approached established community groups across the Greater Manchester area, and arranged to meet with their members: 'Everybody was so enthusiastic about the service, and that something was happening for Asian people, so they, in their capacity [as community leaders] arranged a lot of talks and seminars' at which Rahman spoke to raise awareness both of the Centre and of thalassaemia itself. At the end of Rahman's initial contract, MACHEM and other community members arranged a public meeting at Manchester's Central Library to 'discuss' funding for thalassaemia services; community input at this meeting 'proved to the community Health Authorities that the service was needed and had to go on'.[81] Rahman's contract was extended for an additional three years. During this period, the Standing Medical Advisory Committee advised the government that thalassaemia services should be supported across the United Kingdom, giving the Health Authority little choice but to continue funding for thalassaemia services at the Centre.[82]

Like the Manchester Diabetes Centre, the SCTC saw raising awareness as a major part of its mission, but it started from a much lower baseline both in terms of the community and among medical and non-medical professionals. Unlike the MDC, the Centre had an extremely warm reception from local GPs, as well as from specialists in the haematology department at the Manchester Royal Infirmary. Collaboration with clinical haematology was particularly close, in part due to the structure of service provision – all of the SCTC's laboratory work was done in the MRI's Department of Haematology – and in part due to a mutual interest in sharing patient databases (once confidentiality was ensured).

As the Centre grew, it extended its range of services, despite chronic lack of funding – and consequent difficulties in creating secure career paths for medical and paramedical professionals. The influence of one medical member of the first working group secured for the Centre the services of a psychologist, to whom patients (and particularly young patients) had 'prophylactic' access. With this patron's retirement, those services have been compromised, and the SCTC is eager to restore them, regarding them as extremely valuable in supporting patients' self-caring and self-esteem. Professionally trained patients have also provided the Centre with educational resources it would not otherwise be able to afford. Local businessmen and community leaders have also played a role in raising funds for the Centre, which has been unable to secure the support of the pharmaceutical industry to the degree achieved by the MDC. More formally, changes in the medical curriculum have raised the profile of sickle-cell anaemia and thalassaemia among the next generation of practitioners, although without established career paths, even interested professionals are reluctant to specialize in these diseases.[83] Also, Centre staff are keen to attract more social support for their patients, particularly in the form of a dedicated social worker. Support groups for all patient groups at the Centre have flourished, and SCTC staff are justifiably proud of the relationship they have established and maintained with their patients. It is a model that Davis sees as highly compatible with the NHS's current emphasis on primary care trusts and groups.

As genetic diseases have moved up the list of national priorities, the Centre's mission has also expanded. The SCTC is now very involved in the National Screening Programme, and has received additional funds to enhance its screening provision. A major goal of Centre staff is to see the introduction of universal screening, and to provide a more equitable and standardized service across the city and the region. To achieve these goals, once again, they will seek to mobilize the support and input of the communities they serve.

Conclusion

In the previous sections we have given a brief history of the emergence of three chronic diseases – non-insulin dependent diabetes mellitus, sickle-cell anaemia, and thalassaemia, discussed patterns of treatment for each, and detailed the innovative ways in which services have been provided to their sufferers in Manchester. But what do these innovations reveal more broadly? We have used a model of internally and externally driven innovation to provide a first gloss on the Manchester Diabetes Centre (MDC) and the Sickle Cell and Thalassaemia Centre (SCTC). Internally driven innovation, as illustrated by the MDC, involved a reorganization of staff and resources that both inspired a new professional commitment on the part of medical and especially paramedical personnel, and made the Centre a magnet for local and national funds – from pharmaceutical companies to research charities; local authorities to medical and lay fundraisers.

Upon (Latourian?!) reflection, Tomlinson himself credits his success to an ability to enroll and persuade several different key groups as to the benefit of change – reflecting pastoral, economic, and ideological considerations beyond the simply scientific.[84] Thus the MDC was a successful innovation for a variety of reasons, not least of which was the powerful, and persuasive personality of its clinical head and chief fundraiser, Stephen Tomlinson, and the relatively weak opposition to the reorganization – mainly presented by a handful of general practitioners in the area.[85] General practitioners resisted the Centre on the grounds that it represented another example of NHS money being spent on hospitals rather than on primary care institutions. Tomlinson and his allies responded to this by establishing a network of mini-clinics, and a separate satellite centre initially supported by the MDC and later staffed by many professionals trained at the MDC. The Bolton Centre, interestingly, is purpose-built and in the town centre rather than on the hospital site, providing easy access especially for the local Asian communities. More generally, in supporting the consolidation of other diabetes clinics and centres, the MDC team conformed to late 1980s' NHS policy ordinances which demanded more community-based initiatives, thus easing the pressures upon hospital-based resources.

The founding and persistence of the SCTC, on the other hand, were driven by forces external to hospital medicine – demand for a dedicated sickle-cell service began in the affected patient community. This nascent activism was focused first by the work of the community-based and community-funded Moss Side Family Advice Centre. Supported and encouraged by the Family Advice Centre's opportunistic study of community awareness, a support group coalesced. Collaborating with public health and health promotion workers, and with a few interested individuals from within the hospital system – for example, a consultant paediatrician who worked with affected children – this support group was able to make its needs known, and to assist public health workers in securing Health Authority funding for a research-driven centre. This initial focus on research as the justification for public funding (perhaps related to the new national drive towards 'evidence-based medicine') was shared with the MDC. However, while the MDC was to do research around the nature of diabetes as a disease (and especially the pathological and physiological nature of its expensive complications), the SCC was funded primarily to research the community in which it was based, to assess the extent of need for the services it would simultaneously provide.[86] In turn, the community focus of the Centre's service provision produced a visibly productive 'self-caring' response among the affected community, whose co-operation and support ensured the financial survival and expansion of the Centre.

It is unsurprising that the research programmes of the MDC and the SCTC were different, given the marked differences in their respective institutional structures and alliances. The MDC was firmly rooted in academic and hospital medicine (though benefiting also from a supportive Public Health Authority and active community members). The SCTC drew its primary support from public health and from the marginalized community it was to research and treat – it is probably not coincidental that Davis came to the Centre from a health promotion background, in which this configuration of support is common. It is in this regard that the role of ethnicity in prompting innovation is most clear. Moreover, in other cases of clinics dedicated to ethnically-linked disease – for example, the thalassaemia centres in London – community activism (this time of the Cypriot community) has played a strong role.[87]

More generally, our study demonstrates that innovations and organization cannot be considered as discrete from the larger institutions and agencies of which they are a part. Nor can innovations in medicine – whether in treatment of disease or in service provision – be considered separately from the patient populations whom they are intended to benefit. In our research, ethnicity has proven a valuable lens through which to study the impact of a highly visible and distinct patient population on both internally and externally driven innovation. Indeed, one of the objectives of this study has been to emphasize the interrelated yet distinctive nature of different types of 'medical' and social action, whether in the academic unit, the hospital, the laboratory, the public health arena, the primary care setting, or within the wider community.

Ethnicity is one predictor of externally driven innovation in medicine and medical service provision. However, it is not the case that internally driven innovation necessarily fails to respond to ethnic patients – in the MDC, as we have seen, the opposite is clearly true. Rather, motivated professionals may actively seek to improve access to medical services among local disadvantaged communities, and in a setting (such as the MDC) that promotes innovation, this process of change is bolstered and encouraged by the potential for career enhancement. Moreover, the role of ethnicity in internal innovation seems also to depend on the nature of the disease itself. In the case of diabetes, where patient compliance – and therefore patient support networks and culture – has historically been recognized as central to therapeutic success, recognition of an alternative or minority patient culture is much more likely. In a sense, then, finding innovative responses to the needs of ethnic patients in such a disease is less about their particular cultural differences, than about being responsive to patients and patient needs at all.

Notes

1 See J.-P. Assal and A. Visser (eds), 'Patient Education 2000: Proceedings of the Patient Education 2000 Congress, Geneva, 1–4 June, 1994', in *Patient Education and Counselling*, 1995, vol. 26.
2 J.-P. Assal and A. Visser, 'Introduction', *Patient Education and Counselling*, 1995, vol. 26, pp. 1–4, p. 3.
3 Ibid., p. 1.
4 Other studies examining medical responses to immigration in Britain include those collected in L. Marks and M. Worboys, *Migrants, Minorities and Health: Historical and Contemporary Studies*, London, Routledge, 1997; J. Donovan, 'Ethnicity and health: a

research review', *Social Science and Medicine*, 1984, vol. 19, pp. 663–70; and many in the medical literature itself. Of particular relevance are the following: K. Hawthorne, 'Overcoming cross-cultural difficulties in diabetes management – making diabetes health education relevant to a British South Asian community', unpublished MD thesis, University of Manchester, 1997; K. Hawthorne *et al.*, 'Cultural and religious influences in diabetes care in Great Britain', *Diabetic Medicine*, 1993, vol. 10, pp. 8–12; M. Kadkhodaei *et al.*, 'Ethnicity study and non-selective screening for haemoglobinopathies in the antenatal population of central Manchester', *Clinical and Laboratory Haematology*, 1998, vol. 20, pp. 207–11; C. Smaje, *Health, Race and Ethnicity: Making Sense of the Evidence*, London, King's Fund Institute, 1995.

5   I. Baszanger, *Inventing Pain Medicine*, London, Rutgers University Press, 1998; J. Hasler and T. Schofield (eds), *Continuing Care: The Management of Chronic Disease*, 2nd edn, Oxford, Oxford University Press, 1990; P. Pinell, 'Cancer policy and the health system in France: "Big Medicine" challenges to the concept and organization of medical practice', *Social History of Medicine*, 1991, vol. 4, pp. 75–101.

6   D. Armstrong, *Outline of Sociology as Applied to Medicine*, 4th edn, Oxford, Butterworth-Heinemann, 1994.

7   L. Marks and L. Hilder, 'Ethnic advantage: infant survival among Jewish and Bangladeshi immigrants in East London, 1870–1990', in Marks and Worboys, *Migrants, Minorities and Health*, pp. 179–209.

8   Marks and Worboys, *Migrants, Minorities and Health*; J. Eade, 'The power of the experts: the plurality of beliefs and practices concerning health and illness among Bangladeshis in contemporary Tower Hamlets, London', in Marks and Worboys, *Migrants, Minorities and Health*, pp. 250–71.

9   Hawthorne *et al.*, 'Cultural and religious influences'; M. Petrou and B. Modell, 'Prenatal screening for haemoglobin disorders', *Prenatal Diagnosis*, 1995, vol. 13, pp. 1275–85; P. Coventry and J. Pickstone, 'From what and why did genetics emerge as a medical specialism in the 1970s in the UK? A case history of research, policy and services in the Manchester region of the NHS', *Social Science and Medicine*, 1999, vol. 49, pp. 1227–38.

10   B. Modell *et al.*, 'A multidisciplinary approach for improving services in primary care: randomised controlled trial of screening for haemoglobin disorders', *British Medical Journal [BMJ]*, 1998, vol. 317, pp. 788–91.

11   The term diabetes mellitus describes a state of chronic hyperglycaemia (elevated blood sugar), accompanied by certain other metabolic abnormalities, and it is characterized by a variety of clinical features. Treatments for diabetes vary depending upon the type of disorder causing the hyperglycaemia (e.g. lack of insulin production, or a decrease in the peripheral uptake of glucose) but all act to lower blood sugar and to control the elevation of other metabolites.

12   The dietary restriction or 'starvation' therapy for diabetes was introduced by the US physician, Frederick M. Allen, in the late nineteenth century. Seen as the only really effective form of diabetic control available, the therapy was in common use across Europe and North America. See F. Allen, 'Diabetes before and after insulin', *Medical History*, 1972, vol. 16, p. 266. For an account of the discovery of insulin therapy and its subsequent impact on diabetic treatments and research programmes, see M. Bliss, *The Discovery of Insulin*, Chicago, Chicago University Press, 1982; and C. Feudtner, 'The want of control: ideas, innovations and ideals in the modern management of diabetes mellitus', *Bulletin of the History of Medicine*, 1995, vol. 69, pp. 66–90.

13   For a discussion of how modern medical intervention has 'transmuted' human biology and disease (particularly in relation to diabetes mellitus) so diverting the natural history of many diseases onto other, more chronic courses, see C. Feudtner 'A disease in motion: diabetes history and the new paradigm of transmuted disease', *Perspectives in Biology and Medicine*, 1996, vol. 39, pp. 158–70.

14   Feudtner, 'The want of control'.

15 L. Krall, 'The history of diabetes lay associations', *Patient Education and Counselling*, 1995, vol. 26, p. 289.

16 Cited in ibid., p. 285.

17 See Feudtner, 'The want of control' for a discussion of the notion of 'ideal compliance' across the twentieth century. Few clinicians relied on this laboratory data *exclusively* – to a greater or lesser extent many preferred to take their cue to action from the clinical rather than chemical signs of the disease. See M. Barfoot, C. Lawrence, and S. Sturdy, 'The Trojan horse: the Biochemical Laboratory of the Royal Infirmary of Edinburgh 1921–1939', *Wellcome Trust Review*, 1999, vol. 8, pp. 58–61.

18 There are several other subcategories of diabetes mellitus and further subdivisions within NIDDM, but the vast majority of cases fall into IDDM and NIDDM types, of which straightforward NIDDM accounts for some 75–80 per cent of all cases of diabetes mellitus. See W. Laing and R. Williams, *Diabetes: A Model for Health Care Management*, London, Office of Health Economics, 1989, pp. 8–12.

19 Patients admitted as in-patients (due to a diverse range of complications) were spread across medical and surgical wards, and thus received little diabetes-specific care, or recognition as a particular patient-group.

20 H. Howatt, 'Memorandum on the diabetic clinic' (*c.*1952), contained in Manchester Royal Infirmary Memoranda, etc., 1932–1952, MRI Archive.

21 Some physicians in charge of diabetic clinics strongly criticized local general practitioners for overloading the hospital services. General practitioners could be reluctant to take on diabetic patients because they lacked confidence in the administration of insulin and other therapies. Moreover, by leaving the hospital clinics to take over not only the specialist care but also the *routine* (i.e. the 'non-diabetic') care of patients, post-war general practitioners were sometimes regarded by hospital doctors as needlessly overloading specialist facilities. See T. Stewart, 'Diabetes mellitus', in Hasler and Schofield, *Continuing Care*, p. 138.

22 Recognition of these deficiencies led to the publication of a co-authored report: Royal College of Physicians of London and British Diabetic Association, *Provision of Medical Care for Adult Diabetic Patients in the United Kingdom*, London, RCP/BDA, 1985.

23 W. Alexander and South East Thames Diabetes Physicians Group, 'Diabetes care in a UK health region: activity, facilities and costs' *Diabetic Medicine*, 1988, vol. 5, pp. 577–81.

24 Changes in organization and delivery had been suggested before the 1980s. During the 1950s, for instance, physicians working at the Leicester Hospital in the UK attempted to improve the health and quality of life of diabetics by combining traditional forms of out-patient care with home visits and consistent record-keeping. See J. Stanton, 'Supported lives', in R. Cooter and J. Pickstone, *Medicine in the Twentieth Century*, Amsterdam, Harwood Academic, 2000, pp. 601–15. Such experiments were not widespread, however.

25 Several influential studies from US hospitals published at this time emphasized the importance of patient education in reducing the incidence of acute complications requiring hospitalization, and thus improving quality of life for individual diabetics, while greatly reducing costs and the pressure on resources. See, e.g., L. Miller and J. Goldstein, 'More efficient care of diabetic patients in a county-hospital setting', *New England Journal of Medicine*, 1972, vol. 286, pp. 1388–90.

26 See J. Day and M. Spathis, '"District diabetes centres in the United Kingdom". A report on a workshop held by the Diabetes Education Study Group on behalf of the British Diabetic Association', *Diabetic Medicine*, 1988, vol. 5, pp. 372–80, for a review of some of these initiatives.

27 This workshop was also sponsored by the pharmaceutical company *Servier*, a company with a significant stake in the manufacture of oral hypoglycaemic agents for the use of

NIDDM individuals. See R. Bivins and H. Valier interview with S. Tomlinson, 11 August 2000.

28 J. Day, P. Johnson, G. Rayman and R. Walker, 'The feasibility of a potentially "ideal" system of integrated diabetes care and education based on a day centre', *Diabetic Medicine*, 1988, vol. 5, pp. 70–5.

29 See for example P. Ling *et al.*, 'The diabetic clinic dinosaur is dying: will diabetic day units evolve?', *Diabetic Medicine*, 1985, vol. 2, pp. 163–5; J. Dudley, 'The diabetes educator's role in teaching the diabetic patient', *Diabetes Care*, 1980, vol. 3, pp. 127–33; I. Malhauser *et al.*, 'Bicentric evaluation of a teaching and treatment programme for Type I (insulin dependent) diabetic patients: improvement of metabolic control and other measures of diabetic care for up to 22 months', *Diabetologia*, 1983, vol. 25, pp. 470–6; M. Beggan *et al.*, 'Assessment of the outcome of an educational programme of diabetes self-care', *Diabetologia*, 1982, vol. 23, pp. 246–51.

30 See, for example: B. Jarman, 'Developing primary health care' *BMJ*, 1987, vol. 294, pp. 1005–8.

31 Day and Spathis, 'District diabetes centres', p. 379.

32 Tomlinson had held posts as a Wellcome Trust Research Fellow, and, later, Wellcome Trust Lecturer at the University of Sheffield before his appointment to Manchester. He had also undertaken research work at the Massachusetts Institute of Technology, Boston, USA: Tomlinson, interview, 2000.

33 Ibid.

34 Ibid.

35 Ibid. Pooley's influence on the Manchester scene can perhaps also be seen in the fact that the new facility pioneered distance learning packages for diabetes nurses as well as a nursing diploma course in diabetes (in conjunction with the University of Manchester) set up in 1990. See H. Siddons, 'Diabetes specialist nurse', *Diabetic Medicine*, 1992, vol. 9, pp. 790–1.

36 Ibid.

37 S. Tomlinson, 'Diabetes mellitus – the pissing evile. Science and medicine, molluscs and man', *Mediscope*, 1988, vol. 66, pp. 58–60.

38 Ibid., p. 59.

39 Ibid., our emphasis.

40 Ibid., p. 58.

41 Ibid., p. 59.

42 Tomlinson, interview, 2000. The idea of mini-clinics was not new and had first been piloted in the early 1970s, see P. Thorn and P. Russell, 'Diabetic clinics today and tomorrow: mini-clinics in general practice' *BMJ*, 1973, vol. 2, pp. 534–6. However, once again the idea underlying the concept of the diabetes *centre* was that it would redefine the organizational relationships between existing and new services.

43 See MRI Medical Executive Committee Minutes, 14 March 1983, MRI Archive.

44 Hawthorne, 'Overcoming cross-cultural difficulties in diabetes management', pp. 22–3. See also S. Bradley and E. Friedman, 'Cervical cytology screening: a comparison of uptake among "Asian" and "non-Asian" women in Oldham', *Journal of Public Health Medicine*, 1993, vol. 15, pp. 46–51; K. Hawthorne, 'Asian diabetics attending a British hospital clinic: a pilot study to evaluate their care', *British Journal of General Practice*, 1990, vol. 40, pp. 243–7; A. Vyas, 'Knowledge awareness and self management among South Asians with diabetes in Manchester; a pilot randomised trial to investigate a primary care based education package', unpublished MPhil in Medicine, University of Manchester, 1999.

45 S. Tomlinson and K. Hawthorne, 'Pakistani Moslems with Type-II diabetes mellitus: effect of sex, literacy skills, known diabetic complications and place of care on diabetic knowledge, reported self-monitoring management and glycaemic control', *Diabetic Medicine*, 1999, vol. 16, pp. 591–7; S. Tomlinson and K. Hawthorne, 'One-to-

one teaching with pictures – flashcard health education for British Asians with diabetes', *British Journal of General Practice*, 1997, vol. 47, pp. 301–4.

46 K. Wailoo, *Drawing Blood: Technology and Disease Identity in Twentieth Century America*, Baltimore, Johns Hopkins University Press, 1997, p. 186.

47 For a history of sickle cell's biomedical discovery and elucidation, see C. Conley, 'Sickle-cell anaemia – the first molecular disease', in M. Wintrobe, *Blood, Pure and Eloquent: A Story of Discovery, of People and of Ideas*, New York, McGraw-Hill, 1980, pp. 319–37. A full discussion of sickle cell, and particularly its somewhat contested status as 'the first molecular disease' is beyond the scope of this chapter. See also K. Wailoo, 'A "disease sui generis": the origins of sickle cell anemia and the emergence of modern clinical research, 1904–1924', *Bulletin of the History of Medicine*, 1991, vol. 65, pp. 185–208.

48 Sickle-cell anaemia is now recognized as the homozygous form of a balanced genetic polymorphism (practically speaking, a trait that exists in multiple forms in a population, each form of which confers some selective advantage). People who are heterozygous for at the sickle-cell locus have no symptoms of the disease, but can pass the trait to their children.

49 The symptoms of sickle-cell anaemia, as well as the anaemia itself and the painful crises, include capillary engorgement, leg ulcers, infections, thrombosis, and a range of long-term sequelae including organ damage.

50 Wailoo, *Drawing Blood*, pp. 134–61; M. Tapper, 'An "anthropathology" of the "American Negro": anthropology, genetics and the new racial science, 1940–1952', *Social History of Medicine*, 1997, vol. 10, pp. 263–89.

51 A. Raper, 'Sickle-cell disease in Africa and America – a comparison', *Journal of Tropical Medicine and Hygiene*, 1950, vol. 53, pp. 49–53. Of course sickle-cell anaemia was no less lethal in Africans; few babies born homozygous for sickle cell lived past childhood under the harsh conditions of colonial Africa.

52 See, for example, the Oxford-trained biochemist and geneticist (and subsequently head of the MRC's London Clinical Research Centre's Cell Pathology Division) A. Allison, 'Protection afforded by sickle-cell trait against subtertial malarial infection', *BMJ*, 1954, vol. 1, pp. 290–4; and H. Power, 'A model of how the sickle cell gene produces malaria resistance', *Journal of Theoretical Biology*, 1975, vol. 50, pp. 121–7.

53 Wailoo, 'A "disease sui generis"', and K. Wailoo, 'Genetic marker of segregation: sickle cell anemia, thalassemia and racial ideology in American medical writing 1920–1950', *History and Philosophy of the Life Sciences*, 1996, vol. 18, pp. 305–20.

54 Conley, 'Sickle-cell anaemia', pp. 338–9.

55 Ibid., p. 341.

56 See H. K. Valier, 'The politics of scientific medicine in Manchester 1900–1960', unpublished PhD dissertation, Manchester University, 2001, Chapter 4; Wailoo, *Drawing Blood*, pp. 99–133.

57 B. Culliton, 'Sickle cell anaemia: the route from obscurity to prominence', *Science*, 1972, vol. 178, pp. 138–42. The sudden burst of US interest in sickle cell is closely related to the rise of patient advocacy groups within the broader context of the Civil Rights and Black Power movements – but also to the increased public understanding of sickle cell as conferring evolutionary advantage in the face of malaria, and the emergence of electrophoresis as a diagnostic tool capable of readily distinguishing between heterozygous and homozygous bearers of the sickle-cell trait. See also Wailoo, *Drawing Blood*, pp. 180–6.

58 There are many known forms of thalassaemia, including alpha-thalassaemia, thalassaemia-sickle-cell, and beta-thalassaemia. Beta-thalassaemia is the most common thalassaemia among South Asians, and therefore has been a focus of concern in the UK, with its population of 2.1 million citizens with origins in Pakistan, India, Bangladesh, and Sri Lanka. Alpha-plus thalassaemia is also found in these populations, but is 'harmless'.

59 D. Weatherall, 'Towards an understanding of the molecular biology of some common inherited anemias: the story of thalassemia', in M. Wintrobe, *Blood, Pure and Eloquent*, pp. 372–414.

60 Desferrioxamine or Desferal is an iron chelator which binds excess iron and is readily excreted from the body.

61 S. Dyson, *Beta-thalassaemia: current carrier and community awareness in Manchester*, Leicester, De Montfort University Press, 1994, p. 11.

62 See N. Heer, J. Choy and E. Vichinsky, 'The social impact of migration in disease: Cooley's anemia, thalassaemia and new Asian immigrants', in A. Cohen (ed.), 'Cooley's Anemia, Seventh Symposium', *Annals of the New York Academy of Sciences*, 1998, vol. 850, pp. 509–11. One in seven Cypriots, one in ten Sindis, Gujeratis, and South Italians, one in twenty Turks and East Asians, one in twenty-five Pakistanis and one in fifteen to thirty Punjabis and Bangladeshis is heterozygous for thalassaemia. The rate among Britons of northern European origin is approximately one in 1000. Thalassaemia trait is increasing in Britain.

63 B. Modell *et al.*, 'Audit of prenatal diagnosis for hemoglobin disorders in the United Kingdom: the first 20 years', in A. Cohen, 'Cooley's Anemia, Seventh Symposium', pp. 420–2.

64 Ibid.

65 M. Petrou *et al.*, 'Antenatal diagnosis: how to deliver a comprehensive service in the United Kingdom', in A. Bank (ed.), 'Cooley's Anemia, Sixth Symposium', *Annals of the New York Academy of Sciences*, 1990, vol. 612, pp. 251–63; Ruth Schwartz Cowan, 'Annual Cardwell Lecture: Can eugenic policies be morally right and politically correct? Thalassemia treatment and prevention in Cyprus', University of Manchester, 24 May 2000.

66 'Who is the UKTS', at http://www.ukts.org/pages/office.html (5 September 2000).

67 M. Angastiniotis and B. Modell, 'Global epidemiology of hemoglobin disorders' in Cohen, 'Cooley's Anemia, Seventh Symposium', pp. 251–69; B. Modell, 'Effect of introducing antenatal diagnosis on the reproductive behaviour of families at risk for thalassaemia major', *BMJ*, 1980, vol. I, p. 737.

68 N. Peppard, 'General review', in G. Wolstenholme and M. O'Connor (eds), *Immigration: Medical and Social Aspects*, London, CIBA Foundation, 1966, pp. 1–8.

69 B. Gans, 'Health problems and the immigrant child', in Wolstenholme and O'Connor, *Immigration*, pp. 87–8.

70 'Services for Minority Groups', Manchester Central Community Health Council Annual Report 1975–6, p. 12, MRI Archive.

71 'Asian health care receives a boost', *HealthLink, Newsletter of Manchester's Community Health Councils*, November 1982.

72 The Moss Side Family Advice Centre (FAC) was founded in 1973 on the ashes of a controversial project (funded by the Youth Development Trust) intended to alleviate racial tension and address the problems faced by young black and Asian immigrants to Manchester's Moss Side. The FAC is also known by the name of one of the earlier project's successful offshoots, the George Jackson House Trust, and by the name of the FAC's successor organization, the Moss Side Advice and Community Resource Centre. See http://webgate.poptel.org.uk/family-advice-c/Origins.htm (accessed 20 March 2001).

73 R. Bivins and H. Valier, interview with Verna Angus Davis, 14 August 2000.

74 Ibid.

75 Ibid.

76 Ibid.

77 Ibid.

78 H. Valier and R. Bivins, interview with Rafeya Rahman, 23 August 2000.

79 Davis, interview, 2000.

80 Rahman, interview, 2000. Rahman's training and previous career were in psychiatry, but after experience volunteering with a community project serving recent immigrants – particularly women – from the villages of Sylhet in Bangladesh, she decided not to return to standard NHS practice and applied instead to the newly advertised post as 'Thalassaemia counsellor' at the Sickle Cell Centre.

81 Ibid.

82 Ibid; see also Working Party of the Standing Medical Advisory Committee, *Report on Sickle Cell, Thalassaemia and other Haemoglobinopathies*, London, HMSO, 1993.

83 Personal communication with former SCC consultant, 1999.

84 Tomlinson, interview, 2000.

85 When interviewed, Tomlinson described the early resentment built up toward the Centre by some GPs as one of his few regrets about the venture. Ibid.

86 Biomedical research on the nature of the haemoglobinopathies occurred instead within academic medicine and at a national reference laboratory.

87 B. Modell, 'Delivering genetic screening to the community,' *Annals of Medicine*, 1997, vol. 29, pp. 591–9; P. Gill and B. Modell, 'Thalassaemia in Britain: a tale of two communities', *BMJ*, 1998, vol. 317, pp. 761–2; 'UKTS Funded Research', at http://www.ukts.org/pages/research.html and related pages (accessed 5 September 2000).

Part II

Across nations

3   The Western mode of nursing evangelized?

Nursing professionalism in twentieth-century Japan

Aya Takahashi

The existing medical historiography often presents nursing developments in the context of the scientific advance of medicine. It is particularly true in Japan where the history of medicine itself has often been described as a triumphant history of successful absorption of Western medical science, focusing on its rapid transfer from Japanese traditional medicine to modern, or Western, medicine.

Nursing professionalism in Japan, however, shows that the advance of nursing is more a socio-historical than a medico-scientific development. As pioneer nursing schools, which adopted the 'Nightingale System' for training nurses, were founded one after another in the mid-1880s and 1890s, a Western-style profession of nursing for women was developed to conform to Western-standard medical care. With the rapid development of modern hospitals, nurses were increasingly trained and employed at medical institutions. A series of cholera epidemics also prompted the training of nurses and provided a large number of domiciliary nurses.[1] Thus, by 1910, there were already 11,574 nurses working as hospital and domiciliary nurses all over the country, only about two decades after the emergence of professional nursing. In 1919, the number of nurses, recorded by the government, was 35,581, and increased to 68,675 in 1929, and 103,126 in 1934.[2]

The Japanese encounter with the Western profession of nursing, however, meant something more than the advance of a Western mode of medical care. Professional nursing was an alien concept to traditional Japanese culture, nor did any kind of health visiting, or voluntary care as in women's philanthropic activities in Britain, exist. Traditional sexual taboos and women's expected roles at home were sources of discrimination against nursing as a low-paid job outside the home. Moreover, since there was no status of nurses prescribed nationally by the 1915 Nurses Act, standards of nursing varied enormously, often causing criticism and prejudice towards nurses, particularly non-hospital-based domiciliary nurses. Japanese doctors, most of whom were trained in 'German medicine' with emphasis on the research side, regarded the nurses as their handmaidens, rarely as an independent profession.

The Japanese Red Cross Society (JRCS), the biggest training agency at the turn of the century, modified this picture. Through the Sino-Japanese War of 1894–5 and Russo-Japanese War of 1904–5, Red Cross nurses made a significant contribution to the war effort. As a result, military nursing won public recognition as an indispensable and critical part of advanced medical care.[3] The achievement of the Japanese Red Cross nurses in war relief also changed, if partly, the negative public view of the nurse as a low-grade occupation. The Red Cross nurses were now seen as patriotic women serving the state by helping soldiers, and attracted a number of respectable women, who came under the JRCS. This, however, elevated the social position of the Red Cross nurses only, and did not raise the position of nurses in general. Moreover, in the JRCS where its personnel were placed in quasi-military settings, the nurses were subordinate to male doctors under strict rules. In this situation, it was very unlikely that their autonomy was encouraged.

Military influences were also significant factors in nursing developments in the West, but there was a difference between the Western and Japanese cases. In the West, women's raised consciousness worked as a driving force for military nursing developments. As seen in the establishment of Clara Barton's American Red Cross and the formation of the British Voluntary Aid Detachments, grassroots developments of voluntary and patriotic nursing encouraged their nurses to have some kind of autonomy and professional identity, which occasionally caused problems in the organizations.[4]

In the twentieth century, Japanese nurses were exposed to two significant foreign influences through nurses' participation in the International Council of Nurses (ICN) and the Rockefeller Foundation's public health project in Japan. However, the Japanese encounter with Western nurses' leadership, ideologically supported by feminism, in the ICN, did not simply lead to the Westernization of nursing professionalism in Japan in the fullest sense. Inter-war public health developments, aided by the Rockefeller Foundation (RF) also, only revealed the difficulties and problems which worked to prevent nurses from exercising their influence on the new branch of health care work under military dominance. The two encounters suggest that there was inherent, if not deliberate, Japanese resistance to the social and political dimensions of Western nursing professionalism. Gender relations and military dominance over the female profession of nursing in Japan were behind its resistance. These factors of course also existed in the West but functioned differently in Japan.

This chapter attempts to analyse the implications of the importing of the Western model of the nursing profession to another culture, through the example of the Japanese development of nursing professionalism. The chapter consists of two sections. The first section looks at Japanese nurses' contact with the ICN, analysing how the combination of gender, Westernization, and nationalism supported the subordinate position of Japanese nurses. Japanese–Korean conflict over their membership will be indicated to reveal a Japanese imperialistic purpose in joining the ICN. Imperialism and militarism were indeed significant factors in the development of the nursing profession in Japan. The second section finds military incentives to the introduction of public health nursing shown in the RF's involvement in the government-led project, which confined nurses' or women's roles in the masculine system of the state.

Japanese nurses and the International Council of Nurses

The ICN was founded in 1899 in the flowering of Western feminist movements. It was almost a 'club' of British, American, and German nurses, who shared common interests in nursing developments and women's causes.[5] The ICN advocated mutual help and aimed at representing an international current of nursing ideas, raising nursing standards, and consolidating nurses' professional standing. Since none of these aims could be unrelated to contemporary women's social positions, the ICN grounded its mission in feminism, particularly a flourishing feminist movement to achieve women's equal status to men's.[6]

The founder and core figure of the ICN, Mrs Ethel Bedford Fenwick, was an influential member of the International Council of Women (ICW), and the predecessor of the ICN began as a Nursing Section at an international feminist gathering – the Second Congress of the ICW in 1899.[7] The first meeting of a provisional committee of the ICN was held in London just after the ICW Congress. The ICW proposed international unity to acquire the highest good of knowledge accumulated and synthesized through feminist movements fought for by the women of the West. The members of the provisional committee were leading nurses from Britain, the USA, Canada, New Zealand, Australia, Holland, Cape Colony, and Denmark, of whom most were participants in the ICW Congress. They created the ethical as well as administrative foundation of the ICN emulating the ICW.

Not only was the organizational origin of the ICN influenced by women's movements, but it consisted of feminist members. For instance, Mrs Bedford Fenwick and one of the most influential members, Miss Lavinia Dock, an American nurse leader, were tough suffragists, and believed that nurses' demands, such as state registration for nurses and systematic nursing education, would not be recognized and accepted until women gained citizenship.[8] Thus the proposed international professional 'unity' of nurses was the Western, feminist-centred institutionalization of nursing, in which the members who shared this psychological and socio-historical background felt, in Anne Marie Rafferty's terms, membership of 'invisible colleges'.[9]

The Japanese experience illustrates the unreality of the alleged 'universality' of the international nursing body. Japanese nurses were organizationally, socially, and psychologically remote from a Western mode of nursing professionalism conflated with feminism. Japanese nurses participated in the ICN general meetings from 1909 and officially joined the ICN in 1933. Eight ICN general meetings were held between the foundation of the ICN in 1899 and the outbreak of World War II.[10] Japanese nurses attended six of those, apart from the 1915 meeting, which was held on a small scale because of World War I. Before World War II, Japanese nurse delegates to the ICN were almost exclusively sent by the JRCS, which also played an important role in founding a national association for Japanese nurses in order to qualify for membership of the ICN.

The JRCS was a voluntary society, established in 1887 under the aegis of the royal family, and developed through the wars with China in 1894–5 and Russia in 1904–5 in close relationship with the military authority. Japanese Red Cross nurses helped Japan prove its degree of civilization to the West and succeeded in showing an example of a womanly, respectable contribution to the state for the first time.[11] Thus, in spite of the unpopularity of and discrimination towards the nursing profession in general, the JRCS succeeded in recruiting a large number of women.

Since the JRCS was the only organization which had the financial and administrative resources to contact the international body and send nurses abroad, it virtually dominated and determined the form of Japanese participation in the ICN. While the JRCS gave rare opportunities for ordinary Japanese women to attend international gatherings for the first time, it psychologically blocked its delegates from playing a full part in an international professional community with feminist political ideologies. The JRCS did not actually constrain the thoughts and actions of its nurse delegates, but the ideology of the JRCS – male, medical, military – was an invisible obstacle to any progressive thoughts that they could possibly have. Above all, the JRCS did not allow its nursing personnel, including the delegates, to be 'new women', who were at that time often labelled 'dangerous' socialists agitating Japanese society.

A few incidents are indicative of this constraint. The JRCS's relationship with the ICN suggests that the JRCS did not realize, or chose to ignore, Mrs Bedford Fenwick's serious involvement in a women's movement, which was not introduced in major JRCS publications. In the 1909 general meeting, two Japanese participants were, as Mrs Bedford Fenwick remarked, chaperoned by two medical men in the middle of a hall packed with enthusiastic feminists.[12] Notably the Japanese delegates did not share the general assumptions of the feminist-inspired gathering. There was a characteristic incident in the 1909 meeting, in that when the British Minister of War, Mr Haldane, made a speech on nurses as patriots, he was heckled by suffragettes; however, the JRCS did not mention this in its published report.[13]

The aim of the JRCS was to use the opportunities to let its nurses gain experience of modern nursing developments. It was true that the JRCS hoped that its nurses would learn from them. However, this was, more significantly, an important symbolic action for one of the rising world powers to prove its high standard of 'civilization'. In Japan 'trained nurses' did not emerge as part of women's raised consciousness as in Britain, but as a necessary element of an adopted 'civilization', which was important to conform to Western standards of medical care. Japanese delegates to the ICN always stressed, in their talks and reports presented at the meetings, the JRCS's successful relief work and efficient nursing personnel in the wars,[14] which had already been the envy of the Red Cross world.[15] However, interestingly, in the international meetings, Japanese participants wore perfect Western costumes and were careful to follow sophisticated Western manners. As epitomized by their behaviour, for the Japanese, 'international' was synonymous with 'civilized' and 'modern', which were equivalent to 'Western'.

The JRCS seemed to be interested in learning about nursing developments in Western countries in order to adopt better administration models and further improvement in its nursing and medical services. It is widely recognized that the JRCS was always keen on collecting information about Western medical developments, especially those conducted by Red Cross societies. Japanese delegates to the ICN followed this tradition: they visited numerous hospitals in European and American cities when they were abroad for the meetings.[16] Their findings, from the advanced arts of nursing to wider nursing practice, might have affected the several amendments of training schemes for nurses in the inter-war period, but we do not know if such amendments and nursing practices in the JRCS were influenced by their investigations. However, the overwhelming balance of the material, and the fact that Japan was happy with its non-affiliated membership status for more than two decades, suggest that the JRCS did not seem to be interested in the ideological and political significance to the women's cause of those issues much discussed within the ICN, such as state registration for nurses, higher education for nurses, and public health nursing (except for tuberculosis nursing).[17]

The symbolic nature of Japanese participation in the ICN became explicit when Korea, which had been placed under a Japanese military regime since 1910, applied for membership. Before the Helsingfors meeting in 1925, Korea had applied for membership, but the ICN deferred its acceptance because Korea's qualifications for membership had not reached the required standard.[18] Korea again attempted to join the ICN before the Montreal meeting in 1929 under the name of Korean Nurses' Association, established in April 1923 with sixteen Korean graduate nurses and more than thirty occidental nurses as its charter members.[19] Korea's application was deferred again, allegedly because its qualifications did not reach the required standard. Yet the real reason was that Japan, which had heard from the ICN that Korean nurses had applied for membership, claimed that the Korean application did not fall in line with the constitution. It insisted that Korea was not an independent country and the Association was therefore not a national one.[20]

After the Japanese occupation of Korea in 1910, nursing education came under the control of the Governor-General, appointed by the Japanese government, and was formed along Japanese lines. It is no more than speculation that the JRCS was prompted by Korea's application to change its policies towards the ICN, and to apply for full membership, after its twenty years of associated status but we know that Japan's application was suddenly considered when Korean nurses were making a move.

In Japan, the Dōhō Nurses' Association had been founded in April 1928. It proposed to confirm the unity of 9,000 JRCS nurses, either graduates or probationers of the Red Cross Nursing Schools all over Japan, under the initiative of the headquarters of the JRCS. 'Dōhō' signifies compatriots looking in the same direction, as described in Chinese classic literature. Although the association was founded essentially as a friendly association, aimed at socializing individual members and furthering nursing developments by the exchange of knowledge, it was expected to be the core of nursing developments in the country.[21] The existing materials do not show if the foundation of the Dōhō was a decisive step towards joining the ICN. Yet at the opening ceremony of the Dōhō Association, President Hirayama of the JRCS stated that the need for a kind of national association of nurses had certainly been felt by the JRCS when sending delegates to the ICN.[22] Japan submitted its application for membership before the Montreal meeting in 1929 after considerable advice from the ICN.

If the JRCS had been able to acquire membership in 1929 by claiming that the body of Japanese Red Cross nurses, the Dōhō, founded in the previous April, was fully representative, there would not have been any difficulties. The Dōhō was, however, not an association representing the whole nursing profession in the country. Miss Take Hagiwara, who was the vice-president of the Dōhō and was the first Japanese participant in the 1909 ICN meeting, might have hoped at one point that they would be able to meet the requirements for membership. However, according to ICN rules, a national association should be made up not only of graduates of the Red Cross schools, but also of graduates of other schools of nursing in the country, and it should be a self-governing body. The rather hasty move towards Japan's application was clearly without a solid base of Japanese nurses' professional unity in a true sense.

The best way forward seemed to be to found a league consisting of several bodies of nurses instead of a national association made up of individual members. This way of organizing a league had been adopted by the Americans and the Belgians. Wishing to join the ICN, nurses from influential medical institutions in Tokyo met in December 1928. After a couple of such meetings, the Japanese Nurses' Association (JNA) was founded in March 1929 with nurses from not only the Red Cross hospitals but also some leading hospitals and a few influential domiciliary nursing groups located in the capital. It must be mentioned that some male members of the JRCS worked for the foundation of the national association.[23] The newly established JNA could not at first unite nurses outside Tokyo, but it ostensibly formed a self-governing federation of nurses from various institutions. Therefore, in theory it fulfilled the requirements for ICN membership, although it had been so hastily founded.

As mentioned above, Japan's membership issue involved, however, more than Japan's domestic problem in forming a national nurses' association. The question as to whether the annexed Korea was to apply independently or through a Japanese association of nurses provoked enormous discussions within the ICN, while the Japanese blocked Korea's attempt. If the Japanese had failed either to join the ICN before Korea, or to compel Korean nurses to join a hastily founded Japanese national association, it would have meant that Japan would have lost face as an independent state, since the ICN constitution prescribed that only a 'national' association was permitted to apply. As the allegedly apolitical ICN had at one time considered Britain's dominions and colonies not to be independent, but had later granted them autonomous member status, 'international' as a term, was clearly subject to the interpretation placed upon it within the existing world order.

The president of the JNA advised the ICN that Korea was 'simply a province of Japan' and that although the nurses of Korea had been organized before those of Japan, they could only be dealt with through the Japanese association.[24] Both applications submitted by Korea and Japan had fallen in line with the constitutions of the ICN, although Japan's application perhaps looked slightly inferior to Korea's in terms of making an impression on the executive after a representative of Korean nurses spoke before the committee. Within Korea, there had been intense resentment towards Japanese political and economic control since the Sino-Japanese War, and the Koreans insisted on the injustice of Japan's invasion. However, the West was indifferent to Japan's control over Korea, and its colonization of Korea in 1910 was tacitly given international legitimization. One of the ICN directors, Miss Noyes, therefore thought that it was appropriate that Korea should have applied through Japan, and the ICN took no final action.[25]

In order to verify the Korean nurses' claims, the ICN secretary, Miss Reimann, had been to the League of Nations to secure complete information. Extracts of her investigation, which included the reports of government officials and missionaries, were read before the members. However, there was no decisive material which would prove Korean self-government. The ICN was supposed to be apolitical, but the Japanese–Korean membership issue was a political issue, as was the definition of an independent nation and what were considered to be 'national' associations. Other examples were cited: the Philippines were under the protection of the USA when they applied for membership, but were accepted on the ground that they would be free and independent when they could adjust to conditions under a mandate; Finland was under the Russian Empire and had a Governor-General from Russia, but had a parliament of its own when it applied. However, there was no persuasive or comparable example to determine whether or not Japan and Korea were separate countries.[26]

One way round the difficulties would have been to rely on the interpretation of the League of Nations, which did not admit Korea as an independent country. The directors of the ICN had perhaps realized that the League of Nations itself was a highly political organization: it oversaw mandates established after World War I. In the period of imperialism, any occupied country claiming its independence might have won the sympathy of the ICN. However, some ICN representatives had witnessed an international event hosted by the JRCS, the Second Oriental Red Cross Conference (Tokyo) in November 1926. Japan was certainly a leader in the Red Cross world in the Orient as well as a militaristic power in the region. Eventually, before the Meeting of the Grand Council on 6 July 1926, the Membership Committee met the representatives of the two associations and arranged that during the next four years they should organize a federation, that is, the formation of an independent federation of associations.[27]

At the Montreal meeting a luncheon was given by the Japanese delegate, Take Hagiwara. She was, however, embarrassed at the ceremony when Miss Seki Hora, attending independently from Japan, suddenly announced in the presence of Hagiwara that she was not a true representative of Japanese nurses. Hora implied that Hagiwara could only represent Japanese Red Cross nurses, not the whole nursing population in Japan. Hora had graduated from a private nursing school in 1918 and had stayed in the USA to study nursing further. Being impressed by nurses' settlement activities in the USA, in which nurses with philanthropic minds helped the poor by providing various welfare services, including nursing care, Hora later founded in 1930 the Visiting Nurses' Association – an independent body to promote such nursing for social improvement in Japan. The association was, as she declared, a self-governing body and a 'nucleus for a larger or national organization of nurses in the true sense of the word'.[28] She was clearly against the JRCS-centred national nursing association. After the membership problem and the embarrassing incident at the luncheon, the JRCS worked to form a better national association which would be admitted. The Nurses' Association of the Japanese Empire (NAJE) was founded in 1929, and its first general meeting was held in May 1931.[29]

In 1933, the NAJE contained 1,500 active members. There were 20,000 trained nurses who fulfilled the admission requirements of the association – potential members – in the country.[30] In 1933, the ICN executive committee therefore recommended acceptance, as the Korean Nurses' Association had became part of the NAJE, and had been given representation on its Board of Directors. The Committee therefore decided that Korea would no longer be entitled to separate representation in the ICN. Japan was thus officially affiliated to the ICN after twenty-four years of its relationship with the organization.

Japanese nurses' experiences in an international community in the twentieth century suggest that nursing had undergone significant modification in the process of importation from the West. Nursing professionalism was formulated as an instrument of a modern state importing Western scientific knowledge, but it was problematic in a society that was reluctant to see the imported female occupation, nursing, as suitable for respectable women. Nursing was socially recognized when a group of women, Japanese Red Cross nurses, made their womanly contribution to the state in war relief, displaying Japan's level of civilization to the world. Professional consciousness was not nurtured by feminism or women's empowerment as in the UK and the USA, but restricted by the military and imperialistic characteristics of that state. Above all, internationalism was based on imperialism in this period, and Japan was attempting to conform to international standards and requirements to join civilized and imperialist circles. Nursing professionalism in Japan, which was elsewhere nurtured by women's raised consciousness, was thus stifled by the contemporary social and international circumstances for the sake of the apparent technical as well as organizational developments of nursing.

The public health project and Japanese nursing

Stifled Japanese professionalism can also be seen in Japan's pioneer national-scale public health project in the 1920s and 1930s in association with the

American Rockefeller Foundation. As in the USA and other countries, the RF funded the establishment of a national institute of public health, which was to promote medical research in this area and help to establish a systematic provision of public health work.[31] It granted fellowships to dozens of doctors and several nurses for their study of public health in the USA to initiate this project, and also funded the establishment of one urban and one rural demonstration zone as the models for the practical fieldwork. The negotiations between the Japanese government and the RF were, however, long and laborious: an initial offer was abandoned in 1927 because of Japan's political instability and, more importantly, Japanese lack of enthusiasm for and understanding of public health. Meanwhile, a fellowship programme was independently advanced to educate Japanese associates.

New negotiations were resumed in 1930 after these problems had been sorted out. An urban demonstration zone was established in 1935, a rural demonstration zone in 1938, and the National Institute of Public Health in the same year. These were designed to be the models and centre for 550 proposed health centres which would be built all over the country within ten years under the 1937 Health Centre Law. This progressive project was designed, on the Japanese if not the American side, to support national preparedness for war. The slogan 'healthy soldiers and healthy nations' was increasingly heard in the years before World War II. This project largely determined the degree and form of Japanese nurses' involvement in public health.

Until the late 1920s, there was hardly any national concept of health promotion and maintenance in Japan. Various public health measures took a censorious form of regulating and policing to prevent infectious diseases, such as cholera, smallpox, tuberculosis, syphilis, and leprosy.[32] Although the high mortality rate had already been noticed in the early 1920s, the government scarcely paid it serious attention until around 1930, when the expanding war in China required a greater supply of healthy soldiers. There were, however, some local initiatives: from around 1920 onwards local authorities, which began to focus on their welfare policies, sporadically established clinics for infants, maternal welfare centres, and health counselling centres, and schools, particularly in large cities, and such institutions employed nurses.[33] The aim of the RF's aid was to improve such emerging, non-coercive, forms of health machinery by training public health personnel and establishing a systematic national-scale provision. One might have expected golden opportunities for nurses to emerge as leaders of this new branch of health care.

The Japanese concept of public health was based on a healthy population as part of the wealth of the state. Public health nursing developed with the state's interest and intervention in the health of the nation. In contrast, socialist-inspired, grass-roots public health movements did not continue and expand, because socialist political ideologies opposed the state policies, as feminist political ideologies were repudiated by central authorities. As discussed in the first section, the Red Cross nurses won their social recognition in war relief in the prestigious institution close to the military forces, the JRCS. Public health nursing also developed under the wartime mobilization policy. This defined the militaristic and 'public' characteristics of public health nursing developments in Japan, in which Japanese nurses signally failed to acquire an autonomous standing.

However, while public health nurses were expected to support the wealth of the state heading towards war, public health nursing was given only a marginalized place in the RF's project. Nor did Japanese nurses take part in any of the negotiating and planning processes. The prompt initiation of the demonstration centres, where nursing was most relevant, was emphasized. But, from the initial stage of choosing one urban and one rural test area for the establishment of the proposed centres, Japanese nurses were absent from discussions, as far as available material can tell.[34] The RF did not seem to be interested in inviting Japanese women to the negotiations. This was despite the fact that there were already seven nurses who had studied nursing in the USA on the RF fellowships by 1930, of whom at least one St Luke's nurse, Miss Masae Andō, had specialized in public health nursing, and the others had some experience of visiting nursing in the USA. There were certainly a few 'informed women', if not many.

Although the training of health officers and subordinate personnel, including nurses, was a significant part of the plan, and it was basically supposed to introduce American-style medical care, the project itself, paradoxically, gave nursing only a marginalized position. But the RF expected the proposed institute to train the nurses, not independently, but in association with a private medical institution, St Luke's Hospital,[35] while health officers, or male medical men, would be trained by the National Institute of Public Health. St Luke's Hospital was founded in Tokyo by the American Episcopal Church at the beginning of the twentieth century. Its founder and missionary doctor, Dr Rudolf B. Teusler was the first to introduce American-standard medical services in Japan and had developed a close relationship with the RF since 1921. The hospital had been granted a large amount of money for its building and nursing education by the RF a few times.[36]

The Institute of Public Health proposed training public health nurses, but that was not the institute's main function, but a peripheral one. St Luke's Hospital was one of the only two institutions training public health nurses, admittedly on a small scale, by adding an extra course to the ordinary nurse training course. The hospital was then expected to be a 'department of public health nursing' in the institute without any funding arrangements. This was, practically, a result of some administrative confusion between the three parties, the Japanese government, the RF, and St Luke's. Overall, however, it can be assumed that the RF's preferences in the policies of international public health projects, which emphasized the research side, caused much of this turmoil.

The RF's lack of interest in the nursing aspect of public health was, in some sense, understandable, since it was basically more interested in the research side in its international public health projects.[37] As Paul Weindling has shown in his study of the RF's aid in Central and Eastern Europe, the RF's aid was an expansion of US programmes of public health based on scientific research, and to keep the recipient countries out of German and communist influences.[38] There is no evidence of aid overtly intended to deflect communist influences in Japan. However, the RF's concern for the predominant German influence in medicine in the Far East shown in a Rockefeller officer's report in 1921, became the ideological foundation for this project in Japan.[39] This would support Weindling's arguments.

However, there was an American woman in the Japanese project, who was the leading figure in public health nursing development in her country, and she was an enthusiastic supporter of the nursing part of this project. Miss Mary Beard, a clergyman's daughter born in 1876, began her nursing career in 1904 and concentrated on the development of visiting nursing. Through her administration of the Visiting Nurse Association and her revolutionary work as Superintendent of the Instructive District Nursing Association of Boston, she became a representative figure in American public health nursing. Beard's views of autonomous nursing developments led to her extensive involvement with the National Organization for Public Health Nursing, where she served as Vice-President from 1915 to 1916. Subsequently, she was appointed a member of the Rockefeller's Committee for the Study of Public Health Nursing Education (later, the Committee on Nursing Education) in 1919.[40] Among the members of the Committee, there were distinguished nurses, whose names were internationally acknowledged, such as M. A. Nutting, Lillian Wald, and Annie W. Goodrich. Beard later served the RF as its officer between 1924 and 1938.

In 1923, the Committee on Nursing Education had produced the 'Goldmark Report', which established the hallmark of American nursing professionalism, based on the completion of high-standard nursing education and nurses' wider social influence. The report also became a basis for the RF's public health projects in the USA, and, subsequently, its international aid for nursing. This lengthy report was prepared after careful analysis made by the investigators, almost all of whom were nurses and 'lay' women, including woman professors and deans, who were working in the area of nursing and public health.[41] The report succeeded in showing that mature female leadership already existed in the area of public health and that much had already been achieved with regard to such reformers' concerns, particularly in public health nursing; and the RF recognized the problems in nursing education which they discussed. However, in practice, the RF failed to implement in its projects what the report recommended, and its international public health projects failed to promote the American nurses' leadership in public health.[42] Beard, a contributor to the 'Goldmark Report' was, perhaps, aware of the RF's reluctant attitude to the actual improvement of nursing education and funding limits for this area, before she was involved in its Japanese project as a RF officer.

Nevertheless, Beard encouraged nursing leadership in public health in Japan. St Luke's had individuals with the potential to realize her ideal. The following ideas as to nursing leadership in public health emerged from discussions between the RF, the Japanese government, and St Luke's in Tokyo in 1933: a position should be created for 'a nursing administrator in the official group' which was to operate the demonstration centres and 'a central department of nursing administration and organization' should be established in the proposed project.[43] St Luke's-trained public health nurses were of course expected to fill the post and to lead such an organization, since, apart from the JRCS, almost all properly trained public health nurses came from St Luke's at that time. However, the lack of improvement of public health nursing education in the USA after the 'Goldmark Report' was repeated in Japan – great advocacy for improvements but no decisive action. It was further discouraged by the project's political and financial confusion over the funding of public health nursing education.

My analysis of historical material of the project also reveals two other concrete pieces of evidence that the RF was less interested in the nursing aspect of public health in terms both of training nurse leaders and administrating nursing's work in this area. First of all, although the RF granted fellowships to doctors in the area of public health from 1922 onwards – when the first negotiations began – only one public health nursing fellowship (Miss Masae Andō) was granted before 1931, after the second negotiation was resumed.[44] This resulted in a lack of suitably qualified public health nursing associates who could have taken a leading role at the initial stage of the Rockefeller project.

Second, the organizational structure of the National Institute of Public Health did not give so much weight to nursing: the inclusion of a department of nursing in the institute was even considered at one point on a par with the inclusion of a department of veterinary hygiene.[45] In fact the RF almost surrendered its responsibility for public health nursing to St Luke's Hospital.

While, as we have seen, American nurses also experienced professional setbacks, the secondary role of Japanese nurses was further emphasized by the gender structure of Japanese society. Women were almost entirely excluded from 'public' activities; and nurses, as already mentioned, occupied an inferior position in a hierarchy of medical care, dominated by German-style laboratory medicine, in which they were seen as doctors' handmaidens. Since the RF had a policy to aid only government-led projects, the nursing profession in Japan, of which the majority of members were female, was unlikely to play a major role. In fact, there were no female high officials or doctors in the government and influential medical institutions. Moreover, because the main purpose of the project was to administer the existing public health machinery and to provide supervisors and administrators, priority was given to male doctors and officials who would lead public health work in local communities.[46] In other words, the RF was here supporting the status quo.

It is nevertheless true that nurses became the main health care force in the project. The urban demonstration centre, in a densely populated part of Tokyo, was staffed by thirty-four nurses, together with medical practitioners, who specialized in the prevention of infectious diseases, maternity care, childcare, and general hygiene. They visited families and schools to give instruction in preventive methods and the proper care of infants and children, and to impart general sanitary knowledge. Health centres, which followed the example of the

Rockefeller-funded model demonstration, were also staffed by three public health nurses and two doctors on average. Nurses were certainly becoming teachers for health promotion through the development of public health machinery.

However, this did not lead to expansion of the nursing profession but a divergence. Many early public health nurses from the JRCS and St Luke's, who had completed an ordinary nursing course plus a year or six-month public health nursing course, were in practice more educated than ordinary nurses, and were seen as a rank higher than them. One would have expected them to form a new and senior tier within the profession. But the nurse working in the health centres was called '*hokenfu*' in Japanese – which literally means 'a woman protecting health' and this word does not include a syllable indicating 'nurse' – in the 1937 Health Centre Law; and when the status of such workers was subsequently confirmed under the 1941 Hokenfu Act, they became a different profession. The Act required one-year nurse or midwifery training to apply for a *hokenfu* qualifying examination; applications would be accepted from, for example, less-educated nurses, as well as well-educated and well-trained nurses who graduated from government-recognized nursing schools, such as St Luke's and the JRCS, which also offered a *hokenfu* course as an optional nursing course. Furthermore, the school nurse became the '*yōgokundō*', indicating 'health teacher', but not including a syllable indicating 'nurse'; under the 1942 Yōgokundō Act, she was required to have completed tertiary education. Thus the new branch of health care work, which was supposed to give nurses more autonomous roles in health care provision and instructing roles in the diffusion of health knowledge, did not necessarily contribute to expanding the base of the nursing profession. As far as nurses belonged to hospitals and organizations, they were unlikely to be sufficiently autonomous and united to make their own ideologies and strategies.

In some Western countries, such as Britain and the USA, public health nursing had its roots in 'women's mission to women' for social improvements which subsequently gave them political and social influence. It would also be no exaggeration to say that the emergence and development of nursing professionalism in the West owed a great deal to women's raised consciousness and their wider social and political activities in the late nineteenth century.[47] Japanese nurses' involvement in public health nursing could have demonstrated the same phenomena, though in a reversed sequence – wider political influence and better social recognition arising from nursing's work. However, the nursing profession did not gain benefits from its expanded and more independent roles in health care; instead, it diverged into two different professions, if not completely, which were developed mainly in connection with military-inspired concerns for 'national health'. The first government appointment of a female public health official was that of a *hokenfu* (who was, however, also a nurse) in the Department of Population of the Japanese Central Sanitary Bureau in 1941, under the vigorous promotion of the 'healthy soldiers and healthy nations' policies.

Conclusion

Stifled nursing professionalism in Japan shows that the nature of the imported, scientific profession was never thoroughly understood, but only the style of the Western profession was successfully copied by the Japanese. Although Japanese nurses 'venerated' Florence Nightingale, following a Western model of nurse training, were keen on joining international nursing circles (which were considered to be a club of the 'civilized' societies), attended international conferences in Western costumes; and wished to forge links with the USA through the RF's project, they were not truly 'Westernized'. In fact, the development of nursing in Japan, which was given enormous influence by the JRCS, was engaged in an almost paradoxical project. It certainly created a 'Western profession' for women while avoiding or eliminating all the social factors, such as female leadership, nurses' self-governance, and some form of feminist consciousness, which were an inseparable part of the background to the advance of nursing in the West.

Japanese historiography usually refers to Westernization from 1868 to the early twentieth century, but the impacts of Japanese interaction with the West in a broadest sense, in my view, continued to the outbreak of World War II. It is the period during which Japan experienced complex pragmatic as well as psychological relationships with the West, which was the arbiter of international standards, a model of modernity, and the operator of a system that was very different from the Japanese way. Japan admired, envied, despised, and detested the West, while attempting to conform in appearance to Western medical, scientific, and technological standards.

'Western nursing' was adopted and adapted to the contemporary Japanese culture. The social gap between the two medical cultures had to be filled by an extended Japanese interpretation of 'woman's place' with the ideological assistance of nationalism. The nation at war assisted nursing developments and justified the roles of female, professional nurses. By the beginning of World War I, Japanese nurses appeared to have technically confirmed Western standards of nursing, but their professional development was limited within the framework of imperialism, in which they were expected to contribute to the state as a cog of the imperial machinery. Above all, Japanese nursing was stifled by military dominance.

Japan's military influence over nursing extended further. Korean nurses also lost their organizational and networking opportunities through the ICN membership conflict as the result of Japanese colonization of Korea. It can be assumed that Korean nursing developments were thus also stifled, though less immediately, by Japan's military machine, and were distorted by the imperial world order.

This restricted professionalism presumably created the psychological basis for Japanese nurses' passive role in health care work. This early history also seems partly to account for their relatively ill-prepared voicing of demands for better pay and better working conditions, and their limited participation in wider professional issues, under the political dominance of the Japanese Medical Association in the latter part of the twentieth century.

Acknowledgements

I am grateful to the staff of the International Council of Nurses and Rockefeller Archive Center, who have been unfailingly kind. I wish to thank Jennifer Stanton and Anne Summers for their help and advice.

Archival sources

Citations or quotes from International Council of Nurses Archives (ICNA) are copyright, the International Council of Nurses, Geneva. Citations or quotes from the Rockefeller Foundation Archives (RFA) are by permission of the Rockefeller Archive Center, New York.

Notes

1 For the general history of nursing in Japan, see M. Kameyama's representative work, *Kindai nihon kangoshi*, vols I–IV, Tokyo, Domes, 1983–5.
2 Kōseishō imukyoku, *Iseihyakunenshi: shiryōhen*, Tokyo, Gyōsei, 1976, p. 47.
3 See A. Takahashi, 'Western influences on the development of the nursing profession in Japan, 1868–1938', unpublished PhD thesis, University of London, 1999, pp. 186–263.
4 J. F. Hutchinson, *Champions of Charity: War and the Rise of the Red Cross*, Boulder, CO, Westview Press, 1996, pp. 224–36; A. Summers, *Angels and Citizens: British Women as Military Nurses, 1854–1914*, London, Routledge and Kegan Paul, 1988.
5 B. L. Brush and M. Stuart, 'Unity amidst difference: the ICN project and writing international nursing history', *Nursing History Review*, vol. 2, 1994, pp. 191–203.
6 See M. Breay and E. G. Fenwick (eds), *The History of the International Council of Nurses 1899–1925*, Geneva, ICN, 1930, pp. 7–30; D. C. Bridges, *A History of the International Council of Nurses, 1899–1964: The First Sixty-Five Years*, London, Pitman Medical Publishing, 1967, pp. 1–3.
7 Bridges, *History of the International Council of Nurses*, pp. 3–4.
8 Bedford Fenwick was 'a born fighter' in feminist and nursing activities. W. Hector, *The Work of Mrs Bedford Fenwick and the Rise of Professional Nursing*, London, Royal College of Nursing, 1973, pp. 1–6. As for Dock's involvement in feminist activities, see J. I. Roberts and T. M. Group, *Feminism and Nursing: An Historical Perspective on Power, Status, and Political Activism in the Nursing Profession*, Connecticut, Praeger, 1995, pp. 80–4.
9 A. M. Rafferty, 'Travel and travail: founders of international nursing', in *Past is Present*, The Canadian Association for the History of Nursing Keynote Presentations, 1988–96, Vancouver, 1997, pp. 189–214.
10 The eight general meetings were held in Berlin in 1904, London in 1909, Cologne in 1912, San Francisco in 1915, Helsingfors in 1925, Montreal in 1929, Paris and Brussels in 1933, and London in 1937.
11 Japan's formidable medical services in the Russo-Japanese War and the efficient Japanese Red Cross nurses were reported by N. Ariga, *The Japanese Red Cross and the Russo-Japanese War*, London, Bradbury, *c.*1907.
12 International Council of Nurses Archives (ICNA) (Copyright, the International Council of Nurses), Highlights of Meetings, *c.*1909, p. 2.
13 A report which shows Mr Haldane's speech without mentioning the incident appears in 'Bankoku Sōgō Kangofutaikai jōkyō (zoku)', *Nihon sekijūji*, no. 265, 1909, pp. 11–18.
14 See, for instance, report adopted in L. Dock's *A History of Nursing*, vol. IV, New York, G.P. Putnam's, 1912, pp. 256–77.
15 Hutchinson, *Champions of Charity*, pp. 202–11.

16 *Dōhō, Hagiwara Take kinengō*, 1973, pp. 24, 33, 36, 52.
17 As Kameyama finds, Japanese Red Cross nurses were interested in the issue of state registration for nurses because they were worried about the low quality of the nursing profession in general, but it is unlikely that they gave weight to it based on their feminist political concern. Kameyama, *Kindai*, vol. I, pp. 141–2.
18 ICNA, *Fifth Regular Meeting of the International Council of Nurses*, 1925, pp. 50–1.
19 ICNA, E. L. Shields, 'A Sketch of Nursing in Korea', *Bulletin*, no. 3, July 1924, p. 43.
20 ICNA, Membership Committee Report, 4 July 1929, p. 41.
21 *Dōhō, Hagiwara Take kinengō*, pp. 86–7; see Kameyama, *Kindai*, vol. I, pp. 195–216 for the details of the foundation of the Dōhō, leading to Japan's official affiliation with the ICN.
22 *Dōhō, Hagiwara Take kinengō*, p. 87.
23 Ibid., p. 57.
24 ICNA, Membership Committee Report, 4 July 1929, p. 33.
25 Ibid., p. 41.
26 Ibid., pp. 42–4.
27 ICNA, Membership Committee Report, 6 July 1929, pp. 64–5.
28 *International Nursing Review*, vol. 7, 1932, pp. 594–600.
29 *International Nursing Review*, vol. 6, 1931, p. 296.
30 ICNA, Report of Membership Committee, 4 July 1933, p. 14.
31 For instance, the London School of Hygiene in the UK, the School of Hygiene and Public Health at Johns Hopkins University and the School of Public Health at Harvard University, both in the USA, the Institute of Hygiene on a smaller scale in Prague and Warsaw, and a Department of Hygiene in São Paulo Medical School were funded by the Rockefeller Foundation, *Rockefeller Foundation Annual Report*, New York, 1922, p. 43.
32 See M. H. Fukuda, 'Public health in modern Japan: from regimen to hygiene', in D. Porter (ed.), *The History of Public Health in the Modern State*, Amsterdam, Rodopi, 1994, pp. 385–402.
33 For public health in pre-war Japan, see K. Shimizu, *Shōwa senzenki nihon kōshūeiseishi*, Tokyo, Fuji shuppan, 1991.
34 However, an American nurse, Miss Christine Nuno, who supervised St Luke's nurses, was involved in the discussions.
35 Rockefeller Foundation Archives (RFA), J. B. Grant to V. G. Heiser, 16 December 1930, folder 8, box 1, series 609, RF1.1.
36 Ibid.
37 S. E. Abrams, 'Brilliance and bureaucracy: nursing and changes in the Rockefeller Foundation, 1915–30', *Nursing History Review*, vol. 1, 1993, pp. 119–37.
38 P. Weindling, 'Public health and political stabilisation: the Rockefeller Foundation in central and eastern Europe between the two world wars', *Minerva*, vol. 31, 1993, pp. 253–67.
39 German influences on medicine in the Far East are well documented in a RF officer's report: RFA, 'Medical education in Japan' by Dr Pearce, 1921, folder 33, box 5, series 609A, RF 1.1.
40 M. Kaufman *et al.* (eds), *Dictionary of American Nursing Biography*, New York, Greenwood Press, 1988, pp. 21–3.
41 Committee for the Study of Nursing Education, *Nursing and Nursing Education in the United States*, New York, Macmillan, 1923, pp. 1–4.
42 S. E. Abrams, ' "Dreams and awakenings": the Rockefeller Foundation and public health nursing education, 1913–30', unpublished PhD thesis, University of California, 1992, p. 300.
43 RFA, V. G. Heiser's memo on his conference with M. Beard and C. Nuno, 2 August 1933, folder 12, box 2, series 609, RF1.1.

44 Between 1923 and 1931, seven St Luke's nurses and two nurses of Keio Hospital were granted fellowships in general nursing and paediatric nursing, but after 1931 the RF gave fellowships only to public health nursing. RFA, Japanese nursing fellowships, 1923 to 1934, September 1934, folder 64, box 9, series 609E, RF1.1.
45 RFA, V. G. Heiser to J. B. Grant, 13 January 1931, folder 9, box 1, series 609, RF1.1.
46 RFA, conference between the Director of the Central Sanitary Bureau and Mr S. M. Gunn, Vice-President of the RF, 25 February 1933, folder 12, box 2, series 609, RF1.1.
47 See C. M. Prelinger, 'The female deaconate in the Anglican church: what kind of ministry for women?', in G. Malmgreen (ed.) *Religion in the Lives of English Women, 1760–1930*, London, Croom Helm, 1986, pp. 161–92; F. K. Prochaska, 'Body and soul: Bible nurses and the poor in Victorian London', *Historical Research*, vol. 60, 1987, pp. 336–48; A. Summers, 'Nurses and ancillaries in the Christian era', in I. Loudon (ed.), *Western Medicine: An Illustrated History*, Oxford, Oxford University Press, 1997, pp. 192–205.

4 Acupuncture and innovation

'New Age' medicine in the NHS

Roberta Bivins

In early 1972, a small group of startled British medical observers watched a Chinese woman undergo a caesarian section. During the operation, she spoke to her doctors; and while the surgeons closed her abdomen, she could gaze at her newborn son with obvious delight. Minutes later, she introduced the newborn to his father and sister, and left the operating theatre with her family. Her emergency operation had been performed without chemical anaesthetic; the only analgesia had come from a set of steel needles inserted into her body at specific points. Conscious throughout the operation, she seemed to suffer neither pain nor ill-effects, not even the nausea recognized as the almost inevitable side-effect of more orthodox sedation. These medical witnesses (like a group of similarly astonished American medics who had preceded them) had been invited by the China Medical Association to tour state-of-the-art medical facilities in the newly opened People's Republic of China.[1] Unsurprisingly, their subsequent reports (published initially as letters to the *British Medical Journal*) on medicine in China particularly emphasized this use of needles – acupuncture – to produce anaesthesia in major surgery. But this dramatic intercultural encounter was not acupuncture's first appearance on the Western medical stage. The earliest detailed European medical report of acupuncture was published in London and the Netherlands over 300 years before, in 1683. In this chapter, I will draw upon comparisons first between historical and contemporary British responses to acupuncture; and then between reactions to acupuncture and other modern medical innovations (orthodox and heterodox) to explore the technique as it is perceived and practised in Britain today: as *both* an innovation *and* an example of exotic cross-cultural healing. Finally, I will describe an example of contemporary acupuncture practice in the National Health Service (NHS) to illustrate how it is positioned as an innovation within orthodox medicine – and how this configuration is rendered unstable by public (and professional) understanding of the technique as an 'alternative' or 'complement' to (rather than a potential component of) orthodox care.

There is, of course, a paradox inherent to positioning acupuncture as an 'innovation' when practised within the NHS and orthodox medicine, while it continues to be treated as exotically antique and alternative in the media and popular opinion (and by a majority of orthodox medical professionals). How appropriate or accurate is it to present an established therapeutic technique like acupuncture as an innovation, if it is simply being used in a new location? And if acupuncture remains exotic and orientalized, can it be compared with innovations whose origins are orthodox?[2] Scholars and practitioners of medicine alike have begun to acknowledge that medical practices and therapies are culturally specific. What historians of medicine are now coming to realize is that this cultural specificity has never precluded the complete or partial appropriation of medical practices from one culture by another, given the right combination of circumstances, networks, and balances of power. Acupuncture offers a case study of the processes by which non-Western and unconventional medical practices have been appropriated as 'innovations' *and* simultaneously as 'alternatives' by both orthodox practitioners and medical consumers in the West. Moreover, acupuncture's long history in Britain illustrates that this two-stranded process of appropriation and adaptation is not specific to the late twentieth-century context, but reiterates (with almost uncanny faithfulness) British responses to the technique since the eighteenth century.

Acupuncture and innovation, 1683–1901

Although popular, scholarly, and medical accounts of acupuncture circulated in Britain from the late seventeenth century (with the first extended medical description of the practice published in London in 1683[3]), acupuncture was not practised in Britain until the early nineteenth century. Information about acupuncture had been transmitted to Europe through two largely separate channels: via the small and relatively inaccessible medical literature, comprising detailed observations by medical men in Japan and (to a lesser extent) China; and via the larger and readily available scholarly and popular literatures on China, which often included general (if often inaccurate) descriptions of Chinese medical theory and practices. Over the course of the eighteenth century, popular and scholarly treatments of medicine in China had focused on the exotic Chinese theory and models of the body, examining actual medical practice in China only to demonstrate its outlandishness. A frequently repeated portrayal of acupuncture included tantalizing hints of ancient lore and esoteric ritual:

> the principal remedy for most diseases consisted in making deep punctures in the body, upon which small balls of the down of [mugwort] were burnt. These punctures were made with needles of gold or steel, without drawing blood; ... [A]s every kind of fire was not proper for lighting these salutory balls, they employed mirrors made of ice or metal. 'They caused the water to freeze,' says the ancient text, 'in a round convex vessel; and the ice, being presented to the sun, collected its rays, and set fire to the down of the plant.'[4]

Medical discussions of acupuncture had similarly highlighted exotica, particularly in the material culture of acupuncture. Acupuncture's complex of medical knowledge, expert practice, and technology was gradually reduced to a box of needles, a hammer (used to assist insertion of the needles), and variously credulous, ignorant, or culturally susceptible Asian practitioners and patients.[5] When – prompted by French experimental investigation of acupuncture, and in the wake of a chinoiserie craze – British surgeons and physicians first took up the needle, it was to this reductionist medical literature that they turned for guidance.[6] By the time acupuncture entered British practice in the 1820s, it had been completely divorced from its theoretical origins and justifications, even if it had not entirely lost its exotic flavour.

Although not the first British practitioner of acupuncture, a surgeon named James Morss Churchill was its most prolific, publishing two influential monographs and several articles on 'acupuncturation'. His first book, *A Treatise on Acupuncturation* (published in 1822) hinted at acupuncture's exotic origins, but firmly severed them – and all the theoretical knowledge and expertise embedded therein – from what he depicted as the needle's promising future as a medical innovation in Britain.[7] Instead of Chinese sources, Churchill leaned heavily on 'naturally' more authoritative European – and particularly French – experiments and clinical practice of acupuncture to legitimate and direct its use. Churchill also refused to speculate on the mechanism by which acupuncture's therapeutic effects were achieved, arguing that the effects themselves offered sufficient pragmatic justification for its use.[8]

Churchill's *Treatise* triggered two decades of highly conspicuous British experimentation with acupuncture, and laid the foundation for a century of persistent (if only sporadically visible) use of the technique. Acupuncture practice in nineteenth-century Britain, though recognizably foreign, was not represented as quackery. It was practised by moderate medical reformers, and was admired by them – and by the patients who demanded needling – for its 'simplicity, celerity and efficacy' in intransigent chronic conditions and the relief of non-specific pain.[9] Like the stethoscope, the acupuncture needle was presented by its advocates as a simple stand-alone innovation, a tool, rather than the material face of a whole new way of accessing and interpreting the body.[10] No consensus explanation for acupuncture's effects ever emerged, despite extensive experimentation and numerous attempts to find an acceptable anatomical or physiological *modus operandi*. Lacking either its original body-map and rationale or an explanation binding the practice of needling to emerging biomedical understandings of the body and disease, acupuncture use was sustained by consumer demand and empirical success. These forces proved inadequate to ensure the transmission of acupuncture usage to the next medical generation.[11] By the 1910s, evidence for the continued use of acupuncture in Britain more or less disappears. The technique did not regain its early nineteenth-century levels of visibility until the 1970s.

The conditions under which acupuncture did re-emerge were, however, remarkably similar to those under which it became fashionable in the 1830s (despite the striking differences between early nineteenth- and late twentieth-century medical practice and institutions in Britain). First, there was a wave of

interest in all things Chinese after the re-opening of China in the early 1970s –
as had been the case in the first decades of the nineteenth century, following the
return of Britain's first official embassy to China.[12] Second, there was
widespread dissatisfaction among both patients and practitioners with the shape
of contemporary medicine, and particularly with its inability to treat chronic
pain and disease. Finally, the wider context was one of political upheaval. In the
nineteenth century this transformation was evidenced by campaigns for electoral
reform, the emergence of new voices for social change, and in medicine particularly by the calls for medical reform and regulation. The late twentieth-century
context, meanwhile, comprised environmentalism, anti-nuclear activism, the
struggle for equal rights, and in medicine the drive for holism, preventative
medicine, and patient rights.

Seen in the light of these similarities, can it be argued that acupuncture was
simply ripe for a Western revival, and for some degree of assimilation into
orthodox medicine as an innovation? Of course, the reality on the ground is
never that simple. Dr Felix Mann – co-founder of the Medical Acupuncture
Society in 1959 – lectured on the technique to the British Medical Association's
1968 annual clinical meeting. The report of this session described Mann as
having '*admitted* to being unorthodox in using [acupuncture] without knowing
how it worked'. Even more revealingly, Mann himself implicitly acknowledged
acupuncture's seeming link with 'witchdoctoring': 'He added that if snakes'
blood and crocodiles' teeth produced cures, he would use them.'[13] Once again,
exactly as in the nineteenth century, the mysteriousness of acupuncture's *modus
operandi*, and its inaccessibility to the accepted methods of clinical and experimental scrutiny were at the heart of medical suspicion of the technique. And
once again, even acupuncture's orthodox proponents publicly supported its
adoption (or at least the adoption of a form of analgesic surface needling) only
as a pragmatic clinical choice – an example of medicine as an art, rather than
medicine as a science.

Orthodoxy and acupuncture anaesthesia, 1968–78

Despite the efforts of Felix Mann and other early acupuncture converts in the
1950s and 1960s, the modern British resurgence of the technique only began in
earnest with the lay and professional reports on acupuncture anaesthesia
published in the early 1970s. The *British Medical Journal*'s first printed account of
the story appeared in early 1972.[14] Its authors, four medically qualified first-
hand observers of acupuncture anaesthesia in China, described operations on
cerebral tumours, ovarian cysts, and lobectomies as well as the caesarian birth.
They noted that 'in all cases the patients were conscious, fully co-operative, and
appeared to suffer no pain … alternative methods of anaesthesia were available
but not used'. The British medics described themselves as 'astounded' by
acupuncture anaesthesia, and suggested that, '[c]onsidering the great advantages
to the patient and surgeon', British investigations should immediately begin.
However, they concluded their communication with a highly suggestive caveat:

'It is important to warn readers that acupuncture for anaesthesia must not be confused with its possible use and abuse for treating all and sundry medical conditions.'[15] Clearly, despite its low medical profile, acupuncture, either as an alternative or an adjunct to orthodox care in various conditions had already achieved at least sufficient prominence to raise medical eyebrows.[16]

Just over a month later, the *BMJ* published a query from a consultant anaesthesiologist, M. E. Ramsay, asking for confirmation that acupuncture anaesthesia had overcome 'the basic problems of an open chest and collapsed lungs' and for more detailed information on its use in chest operations.[17] This query highlighted a claim implicit in the reports from China: that the Chinese had managed to solve problems still plaguing even elite biomedicine through the use of an 'unscientific', indigenous, and traditional technique. It elicited a stream of letters, revealing an array of reactions to the earlier encouraging reports about acupuncture anaesthesia, to the parallel media presentations both of the technique and of medical evaluations of it – and indeed, to the idea of Chinese expertise in medicine. Negative responses focused on two aspects: first, that patients receiving acupuncture anaesthesia were often carefully selected, given some preparation for their operations, and occasionally received some other forms of analgesia – and that therefore acupuncture was only an adjunct analgesic; and second, that the Chinese were likely to be uniquely 'susceptible' to acupuncture either because of cultural familiarity with, or political commitment to, the technique.[18] When Ramsay responded to his interlocutors (after four months of letters addressing the subject) his sarcastic rejection of the technique bore overtones of relief:

> The Chinese report that they initially had to place needles into forty different points on the body. Over the years, this number has been slowly reduced … one wonders whether this technique would still be successful if the final reduction were made and no needles were used.[19]

Ramsay's tone prompted an exasperated reply from the original correspondents:

> There is obviously room for the whole spectrum [of responses to acupuncture] from complete scepticism to total acceptance. The essential points are that the patients are *fully conscious*, not even drowsy and that the *phenomenon works* in most cases … many patients who could not otherwise undergo major operations are able to have them with minimal physiological disturbance.[20]

However, no other *BMJ* readers responded. Their silence, after so much debate in the Letters columns, suggests a degree of concord with Ramsay's rejection both of acupuncture and the idea that the Chinese had independently solved a major problem in thoracic surgery – and still worse, had done so through an innovative use of traditional medicine.

After this outbreak of controversy and in the light of increasing

Parliamentary and popular interest in acupuncture, it is unsurprising that in June 1973 the *BMJ* ran a lead editorial article on 'Tests of acupuncture'. Echoing the popular press and acupuncture's medical supporters, the *BMJ* mused: 'Scoffing is giving place to astonished incredulity at some of the demonstrations of acupuncture anaesthesia. How many English patients sip China tea, exchange pleasantries with the bystanders, and then climb off the table unaided after a thoracotomy?'[21] But as the author turned to a description of acupuncture's long history and the Chinese model of the body underlying even such 'modern' practices as acupuncture anaesthesia, the article's tone became sarcastic. The author derided traditional Chinese medical expertise, describing acupuncture meridians in terms of their failure to relate neuroanatomically to 'any particular viscus', and dismissing the location and use of acupuncture points as irrelevant to treatment and 'an esoteric and far-fetched exercise especially when the diagnostic evidence of disease is so unconvincing'. Although the writer claimed to have resisted the temptation 'to dismiss the technique along with the intuitive nonsense that formed the basis of mediaeval medicine in Europe', this restraint only extended to recommending that acupuncture anaesthesia be studied by neurophysiologists and anaesthetists, despite its 'unorthodoxy'. Acupuncturists meanwhile were damned with faint praise: 'Doubtless the acupuncturist is as skilled at exploiting the credulity and suggestibility of his patients as many orthodox medical practitioners.' By implication, suggestion and mental influence were at the heart of the therapeutic successes exemplified by the article's dramatic opening vignette.

Responses to this editorial contribution were mixed; one reader congratulated the *BMJ* for insisting on a neurophysiological explanation for acupuncture anaesthesia.[22] However, its hostile tone proved too much for others. J. David Watts was outraged by the statement that traditional acupuncture was 'esoteric and far-fetched'. His response, like those of acupuncture's critics, resonated with earlier historical debates and emphasized the empirical success of the treatment: 'The basis of acupuncture is a large body of observed fact.' Nor would his comments on China's medical expertise have disturbed his eighteenth-century counterparts, or the late nineteenth-century medical orientalists:

> It is unfortunate that those responsible for the formulation of the traditional theory had no knowledge of occidental medical sciences and therefore expressed themselves in the terminology of oriental philosophy. The observation that the traditional theory is an absolute failure in that it does not explain the mechanism of acupuncture in scientific terms does not mean that it is completely without value in the treatment of patients on a more or less empirical basis and should not be allowed to detract from its basis in observed fact.[23]

This impression of continuity is only strengthened by two subsequent leading articles, one comparing acupuncture to hypnotism and counter-irritation (exactly as nineteenth-century sceptics had done), and the other in fact listing nineteenth-century publications on the technique – and factors implicated in its historical failure to thrive.[24] Letters meanwhile further supported the hypnotism hypothesis, or decried the whole phenomenon as 'voodoo'.[25]

It is worthy of note that a final area of concern particularly for critics of acupuncture and acupuncture anaesthesia involved the professional role and standing of those providing the technique. One physician-witness implied that the acupuncture anaesthesiologist's primary contribution was to 'calm' the patients and through 'exhortations' to remind them of their previous training in breath control – and implicitly of their 'faith in the politicians and politics of the country'.[26] Another reported in tones of some horror that the 'anaesthetist' was not 'a medical graduate as we know them, or a nurse, but a young girl who had undergone a course in acupuncture at the School of Traditional Medicine' who lacked 'rapport' with the surgeon and the operation.[27] Such questions of professional status and boundary-marking have been crucial in structuring acupuncture use and delivery within orthodox British medicine since the 1970s. In particular they have structured the process of innovation which has led to the emergence of 'medical acupuncture' – by definition, restricted to medically qualified personnel. Again, there is a striking parallel with Churchill's nineteenth-century attempts to reserve acupuncture for those trained in anatomy.[28]

The medical reports of acupuncture anaesthesia, and the responses they elicited, though revealing, were neither the first nor necessarily the most influential descriptions of acupuncture to emerge from China in this period. The British and American broadsheets had beaten them to it by several months, with sensational and widely circulated accounts of a foreign correspondent treated under acupuncture anesthesia while covering the Sino-American negotiations in Beijing.[29] In this regard, medical and popular press responses to this high-profile example of an intercultural medical encounter exemplify a persistent pattern in the history of both exotic and indigenous medical alternatives in Britain. Popular accounts of acupuncture preceded professional reports, focused on cultural content as well as physical manifestations of acupuncture, and stimulated demand by defining the technique in relation to and as a part of other social trends. Professional accounts were narrower, and far more interested in the material practices than their cultural underpinnings. Moreover, they defined acupuncture's practice and results strictly in relation to biomedical models and criteria. As the next section will document, the success of acupuncture as an innovation and as an example of cross-cultural expertise depended (and still depends) on *interaction* between popular and professional perceptions, cultural and material content.

Innovation or alternative? Acupuncture, homeopathy and tamoxifen

As both a non-Western and an alternative therapy, acupuncture was and is doubly marked. It is not only visibly exogenous – and thus marked as 'foreign' or 'other' – but also labelled as contrapositional to orthodox medicine. Have lay and professional responses to acupuncture been shaped differentially by one of these marks, or by the concatenation of these two distinguishing features? To address these questions, it is worthwhile to assess whether and how the patterns of response to acupuncture differed from responses to orthodox innovations, or to heterodox practices originating within Europe. In the following section I illustrate broad trends in the response and diffusion patterns of this non-Western alternative medicine, and briefly compare them to those of two orthodox biomedical innovations, and to homeopathy, a European alternative therapy. Because acupuncture can be analogized to and used as either a surgical procedure or a drug, I have compared it to one surgical intervention (lumpectomy) and one drug therapy (tamoxifen). Both tamoxifen and lumpectomy are therapies for breast cancer and were first reported upon in the medical press during the early 1970s. They were therefore caught up in many of the same highly politicized debates over the nature of biomedicine which formed the context for acupuncture's return to the European medical stage. I do not argue that tamoxifen and lumpectomy are necessarily representative of all Western medical innovations, any more than that acupuncture is representative of all non-Western medical imports or that homeopathy models all 'Western' alternative medicines.[30] Rather, comparing these techniques offers the opportunity to assess responses to 'innovations' which share certain crucially important traits. Acupuncture, tamoxifen, and lumpectomy, as I have suggested, share a historical moment and political context and were represented in similar ways by their medical proponents. Meanwhile, as 'alternative medicines' both acupuncture and homeopathy represent medical *systems* (by which I mean they comprise integrated theory, knowledge, and practices) with deep historical roots, positioned by their lay or heterodox advocates as both distinct from and in opposition to orthodox medicine.

Much of the rapidly expanding literature on medical innovation addresses individual techniques and specific technologies. However, large-scale and organizational innovation in medicine has not been ignored, for example, scholars have looked at the emergence of hospital medicine, medical informatics and computing, specialization and the rise of paramedical professions, and changes in funding and care management.[31] Less attention has been paid to medical innovations emerging from contexts other than those of the conventional laboratory, clinic, or hospital, despite widespread rejection of the traditional model of medical diffusion as a rigidly unidirectional flow of information from laboratory to practitioner, mediated by formal publication.[32] Explanations based on this kind of 'central dogma' have proven inadequate to capture the phenomena of innovation in healthcare. For example, Barbara Stocking's study of the NHS suggests that innovations in patient care – whether based on changes in knowledge, technology, or structure – often arise on the periphery, 'where the need is seen', and are initiated by 'service providers' rather than central policy-makers.[33] Such peripheral initiatives, she argues, must resonate with policy mandates from the centre – calls for 'budgetary restraint', 'efficiency savings', or 'a focus on primary care'. This model leaves little room in which to consider non-medical initiators; indeed, patient input was ignored even in the case of innovations in the 'patient-day' which emerged as a response to persistent and nationwide patient complaints about the scheduling of their days in hospital.[34] The uptake of acupuncture by the British medical profession in the nineteenth century does resonate with Stocking's model of innovation in the health service over a century later – orthodox medical practitioners responded positively to acupuncture once it had been redefined by its initial popularizers as *simply* a novel technique/technology. The emergence of highly reductionist and materialist models of acupuncture clearly eased its initial adoption into orthodox British medical practice. Moreover, as the previous section demonstrated, such models are actively and enthusiastically sought by current medical advocates of acupuncture.

Much social and qualitative analysis of contemporary alternative and complementary medicine (an area in which patient input is more frequently addressed) has been embedded in the US context. James Harvey Young, in his recent article examining the NIH's Office of Alternative Medicine, documents the power of consumer demand in moving medical alternatives onto the mainstream agenda.[35] However, his article also displays a common shortcoming of current work in this area: he describes advocates of alternative medicine as susceptible 'true-believers', portrays seasoned politicians as gullible, and presents non-clinical arguments supporting alternative therapies as quackery. Objections from within the scientific community are valorized, and that community as a whole is presented as reasonable and bias-free (despite his own attention to comments likening the Office of Alternative Medicine to 'An Office of Astrology'). While drawing heavily upon the popular press to make his analysis, Young portrays its coverage of alternative medicine and its practitioners as almost uniformly critical, a depiction contradicted by my own research. He concludes with a doom-and-gloom scenario of 'unrestrained access' to 'unproven therapies' episodically threatening the health of the nation: 'Whether sound science can master the challenge of hazardous alternatives and reveal what utility they may possess looms as a major public health challenge of the new millennium.' This approach does not simply demonstrate the continuing cultural authority of science. It also illustrates the persistence of a sort of medical mercantilism, in which the medical expertise of other cultures – and even Western popular culture – is treated as raw material to be refined, developed, and made marketable through 'sound science'.[36]

Not all authors so readily reinforce biomedical claims and assumptions. Ursula Sharma, a social anthropologist, examined the 'social aspects' of the subject by studying users and practitioners of non-orthodox medicine in Britain.[37] Through survey data and demographics, Sharma sought to establish who users were, and where they lived, what therapies they used and for what conditions. In interviews and case studies, Sharma also investigated the more vexed questions of why and how both patients and practitioners came to their non-orthodox therapies of choice. Of less importance to her research were questions about the relationship between 'non-orthodox' and orthodox medicine. One approach to this problem is through sociology and the responses of professional bodies, as exemplified by Mike Saks.[38] However, few have examined the interrelationship of popular and professional reactions.

Obviously, the UK and US medical contexts differ substantially – indeed since the introduction of the NHS in 1948, the economic polarity of orthodox and alternative treatment in the UK has been the reverse of that in the USA: conventional medicine has been freely (if perhaps not readily) available in Britain, while British consumers have borne the cost of alternative medicine directly. In the USA, on the other hand, the vast majority of medical care has been provided on either a fee-for-service, or third-party-payer basis; in each case, the cost of alternative/complementary medicine has compared favourably with that of orthodox medical care. Despite this fairly substantial disincentive, British medical consumers, like their American counterparts, have turned to alternative medicines in numbers which have steadily increased since at least the 1970s. A 1995 *WHICH* report put British consumer spending on alternative medicine at £60 million a year.[39] Interest is also increasing among General Practitioners – 80 per cent of whom were already willing to refer their patients to complementary practitioners by 1991 – and Health Authorities. Indeed, 65 per cent of District Health Authorities indicated that they supported the availability of at least some complementary therapies on the NHS in a 1993 survey.[40] This demand is reflected in – and is almost certainly reflective of – the increased coverage of unconventional therapies, including acupuncture, in the popular and medical press since the 1970s (see Figure 4.1). Before 1969, I found no regular coverage of acupuncture, or any other alternative medicine; as Figure 4.1 illustrates, since 1969, acupuncture has at no point disappeared from the periodical press, although coverage rapidly declined from its peak in the first years of the 1970s.

Only articles in which the designated topics are the primary subject are represented in Figure 4.1.[41] Thus only a fraction of British media coverage of

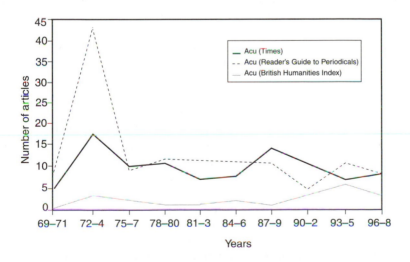

Figure 4.1   Acupuncture in UK and US periodicals, 1969–98

acupuncture is visible.[42] This fraction nonetheless demonstrates the impact of public events (such as the acupuncture anaesthesia demonstrations in the early 1970s, or a positive speech by Prince Charles in 1989) on acupuncture's visibility. The degree to which acupuncture has been normalized is also evident: by June 1998, the number of articles mentioning acupuncture in *The Times* rose to fifty-three, but only one had acupuncture as its primary subject. Acupuncture and its use in Britain were entering the fabric of daily life and were increasingly covered as such. Homeopathy shows a similar pattern, but more sporadically and on a lower level – only ten articles, for example, mention homeopathy in 1998 – suggesting that acupuncture's continued media visibility was not simply due to its status as an 'alternative' or 'complementary' medicine.

In the case of acupuncture, media interest was initially catalysed by the re-opening of Mao's China, and especially by the Chinese government's decision to showcase its integrated use of Western and traditional Chinese medicine. Both medical and popular presses immediately responded to the novel healing narratives and images – but where journalistic and medical witness accounts were generally positive, medical commentators in the UK (as demonstrated by the *BMJ* articles in the previous section) were dubious at best and often actively hostile. Politics and race played clear roles, but professional and scientific criteria underpinned most medical objections. Medically trained advocates of acupuncture responded by seeking an anatomical or physiological basis for acupuncture, creating in the process a 'science of acupuncture' which in turn sparked further reports by the popular press – a prominent scientific article validating acupuncture's principles or empirical efficacy, or 'proving' its placebo status would be almost guaranteed popular press coverage. Other factors also constrained or encouraged the media to report on unconventional therapies, whether a royal speech mentioning acupuncture in 1989, or a furious debate in the scientific press over Benveniste's 1988 hypothesis that water had a 'memory' (which might explain the apparent efficacy of homeopathic dilutions).

The most noticeable difference between acupuncture and either the orthodox therapies or homeopathy is that acupuncture never drops out of the headlines in the popular press (see Figure 4.2). Although decreasing in number, articles focusing on acupuncture either alone or as a principal subject continue to appear, while stories about 'Western' techniques – whether biomedical or complementary – become banal and disappear from the popular press.

The medical press, on the other hand, offers a slightly different picture (see Figure 4.3). Although professional interest in acupuncture did not completely disappear, it rapidly declined from its post-Nixonian spike, only to rebound gently as growing consumer interest stimulated a low but constant level of research into the technique – much of it aimed at debunking acupuncture's claims to efficacy. References to tamoxifen, on the other hand, increase steadily as it is incorporated into medical practice and research programmes. So why has acupuncture provoked such prolonged interest in the popular press, and such persistent and vociferous scepticism in the medical journals? I would argue

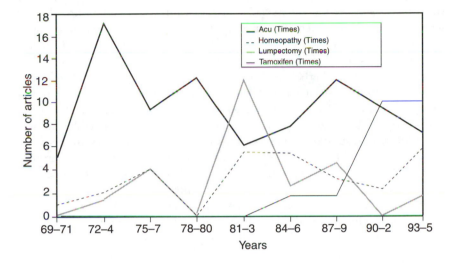

Figure 4.2   Appearance of therapies in *The Times*, 1969–95

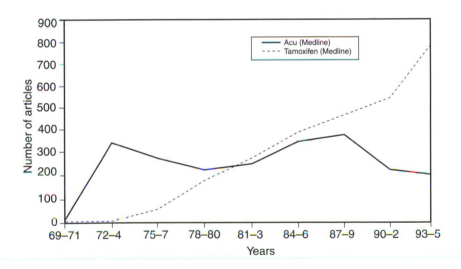

Figure 4.3   Acupuncture vs. tamoxifen (Medline), 1969–95

that both of these phenomena are related to the continuing power of orientalism as an interpretive framework.

In Britain, popular notions of acupuncture are embedded in images of 'the Orient', notions of East Asian mysticism and exoticism. Advertisements for acupuncture or other traditionally Chinese therapies habitually incorporate stereotypically 'Asian' imagery (see Figures 4.4 and 4.5). Note that the brochures which most explicitly present medicine as a consumer commodity are also the richest in prominent orientalist imagery. Compare, for example, the leaflet advertising the fee-for-service London 'Orientation Clinic' – the 'Oriental' emphasis suggested by its name further illustrated by chinoiserie representing acupuncture, Chinese herbal medicine and the Japanese practice of shiatsu – with the education-oriented leaflet from the Register of Traditional Chinese Medicine. There is, of course, a very good reason for this commercial deployment of orientalism: not only is the exotic appealing; it is also visibly distinct from orthodox Western medicine, and thus well suited to attract consumers who must pay for alternative therapies, often through desperation or frustration with the orthodox Western medicine that (in Britain) they receive free at the point of delivery. However, the historic pattern of dichotomies associating west with science and east with mysticism remains a potent one, and proponents of acupuncture within the medical establishment in Britain actively separate their use of acupuncture from traditional Chinese practice – even when the administration of the technique is done by traditional acupuncturists hired as consultants or paramedicals.

The image used by the British Medical Acupuncture Society (not illustrated) – a society of orthodox medical practitioners who use acupuncture in their NHS practices, and promote research into its *modus operandi* and efficacy – offers an enlightening contrast to those used by the 'Orientation Clinic' and the Register of Traditional Chinese Medicine. Its central motif is an image of a serpent, winding round an acupuncture needle. In the background is a map of Britain. The BMAS has simply adapted an image central to the institutions of modern biomedicine, the staff of Aesculapius, to include what is, for them, the crucial element of acupuncture: its needle. There are no reminders in this emblem that acupuncture originated in China, much less that it consists of more than its material face. Similarly, as will be discussed further in the final section of this chapter, when acupuncture was brought into a district general hospital in Greater London, the images used to promote it were carefully neutral. Publicity and other published material for the NHS clinic, unlike its fee-for-service lay competitors, made little reference to acupuncture's Chinese origins and long history and used no recognizably Chinese imagery.

In essence, media (both general and professional) treatments of acupuncture suggest that responses to acupuncture incorporate two opposed interpretive stances. Those who wish to incorporate acupuncture into orthodox Western medicine choose to present it as simply another innovation – 'medical acupuncture' – ignoring its exotic status, and the alternative view of the body and healing implicit in the daily practices of therapeutic needling. These users represent acupuncture as *complementary* to more common Western practices, and as subordinate to them. In sharp contrast, many popularizations of the technique rely heavily on exactly its exotic qualities, its difference from orthodox Western medicine. In this case, it is represented as an *alternative* to biomedicine, and as in many ways superior to it. In either case, British responses to acupuncture

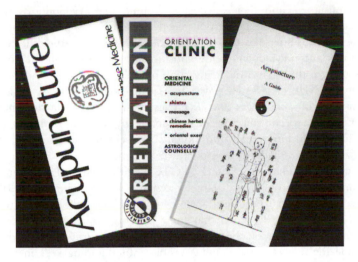

Figure 4.4 Brochures from a professional body representing traditional acupuncture practitioners; from a popular alternative medicine clinic focusing on holistic 'Oriental' medicine; and from an independent acupuncture practice in London

Figure 4.5 Illustrations from the Orientation Clinic's brochure, denoting East Asian herbal medicine, acupuncture, Japanese shiatsu and massage

demonstrate the continued power of orientalism to shape interpretations and evaluations of cross-cultural expertise and expert knowledge.

Complement or component? Acupuncture in the NHS

So how do these general trends play out in a specific case? Research suggests that for unconventional medicine, and particularly for cross-cultural practices, the process of innovation and diffusion often begins with an alliance between medical consumers and their advocates. Bonnie Blair O'Connor's work on vernacular medicine in the US response to HIV/AIDS powerfully demonstrates the impact of consumer networks on medical provision. Her study indicates that economically and educationally elite consumers can, at least in the context of fee-for-service or third-payer medicine, span boundaries.[43]

Within the NHS (as a single payer, free-at-the-point-of-delivery nationalized healthcare system) consumers have been less powerful as individual initiators. However, consumers can still drive change indirectly. The innovation of offering acupuncture – and intriguingly, traditional Chinese acupuncture rather than its Westernized form 'medical acupuncture' – among other therapies in a 'Complementary Therapy Centre' (CTC) within the Lewisham NHS Healthcare Trust Hospital was largely demand-driven. The local GPs who comprised the financial base and socio-economic justification for Lewisham's proposed centre explicitly noted that their patients requested complementary therapy for certain types of chronic conditions.[44] Structural changes within the NHS made the role of these patients visible – fundholding GPs in particular were able (and indeed structurally encouraged) to respond to their clients' requests for (inexpensive) alternatives to orthodox medicine. Their new financial clout enabled sympathetic parties within the local district hospital to make a case for investigating the provision and efficacy of complementary therapies. Finally, the lure of cheaper care for chronic conditions encouraged the local Health Authority to add its backing in the form of a block contract for referrals from non-fundholders.

Despite such (mediated) consumer involvement, the emergence and final shape of the CTC share much with the medical innovations described by scholars in this volume and elsewhere. Its existence depended on specific initiatives on the part of the hospital's medical director (a consultant) and a nurse in its research assessment unit. Much like his nineteenth-century counterparts at Leeds General Infirmary and the Sheffield Eye Hospital, the medical director's interest in acupuncture had been triggered in part by media attention to the technique and in part by personal contact with medical colleagues who had witnessed acupuncture's efficacy at first hand.[45] When a researcher trained in nursing but based in the hospital's Research Assessment Unit brought forward a proposal to assess acupuncture's clinical efficacy and economic viability within the hospital, he responded enthusiastically. The nurse herself regarded the proposed project as both intellectually and clinically valid, but also as a way of enhancing the status of nursing by incorporating research and therapeutic elements into nursing practice, and by creating 'an innovative nursing role': that of the 'nurse-practitioner'.[46] Her interest in acupuncture in particular was directly linked to the centrality of the therapeutic encounter in acupuncture treatment – ironically the aspect viewed most sceptically by clinicians and research scientists.

As Stocking's model of NHS innovation would predict, both parties supporting the introduction of acupuncture services and research also cited the new policy-drive for 'evidence-based medicine'. Similarly, in the context of the

Thatcherite push for 'free-market medicine', both repeatedly referred to rising consumer demand for alternative therapies. But similarities with other innovations and fit with central initiatives should not be seen as reducing the CTC's significance as a innovation within its local context. The Complementary Therapy Centre was set apart from other research projects conducted at the hospital in part by its clear acknowledgement of consumer demand and the fact that such demands were cited as a justification for change at the clinical as well as the organizational level of the study. Thus where the initial working paper, written in January 1993, indicated an interest in assessing the role of placebo effects and 'therapeutic interaction', and focused exclusively on acupuncture, the actual proposal submitted that autumn incorporated osteopathy and home-opathy as well – explicitly because, with acupuncture, they were the most popular options among the hospital's client GPs. As part of its focus on interaction, the original working paper stressed a holistic approach, and allowing its 'complementary' practitioners to treat as they would in traditional 'alternative' practice. Indeed, it castigated the 'cookbook acupuncture' approach of looking for scientifically proven needle sites for treating particular conditions as 'reductionist'. This was the radical innovation in the project, as previous studies conducted within the confines of orthodoxy had focused on explaining and reconstructing acupuncture in biomedical terms, as 'medical acupuncture'. The final proposal couched this choice carefully in the language of 'good science', and linked it securely to central policy initiatives, noting: 'unevaluated forms of care paid for by the NHS should only be offered as part of research designed to assess their effects.'

Perhaps to balance this bold step, the proposal stipulated a high level of professionalization for the therapists who would work in the CTC. This was defined in terms identical to those delineating orthodox practitioners, including membership of the professional organization 'currently working towards regulation and the development of standards' for its members.[47] It also spelled out a strictly subordinate position for its 'complementary' practitioners, in which decisions made about patient care were ultimately subject to approval by the patient's referring GP. The authors respected the BMA's firm distinction between referring and delegating patient care, and noted without comment its rather invidious comments about the 'difficulties in inculcating a culture that recognizes research as an essential activity', among heterodox practitioners.[48]

The CTC's 1995 annual report saw complementary medicine expanding much like innovations emerging from within orthodox medicine, and called for full integration into other departments of the hospital:

> The nature of the referrals suggests that a number of patients may also be receiving treatment from other departments within [the hospital] ... the service should begin to consider how an integrated service, based on packages of care, can be provided for the full benefit of patients. For example, patients attending the pain clinic might benefit from acupuncture.[49]

Centre staff argued strongly for more collaboration with medical colleagues. Moreover, the authors noted that the research model set up for complementary medicines could usefully be extended to orthodox units, where random controlled trials had rarely been carried out to evaluate procedures as demanded by 'evidence-based medicine' directives. Here an innovative mode of assessment for unconventional medicine was to be imposed upon orthodox departments and therapies. In addition, they suggested that the CTC's services could offer genuine 'alternatives' to orthodox treatments – steroid creams could be replaced by osteopathy, for example – thus creating savings for the hospital.

In this report, no distinction was made between acupuncture and the other therapies offered by the CTC. All were treated simply as components of a service innovation, and no further mention was made of the therapeutic interaction or the traditional cultures of medicine from which the different complementary medicines were drawn. However, the patient leaflets explaining each therapy did retain a subtle distinction between acupuncture and its Western counterparts. Acupuncture was the only therapy described in terms of its history, and reference to its 2,000 years of use in China and its system of correspondence between the body's surface and the internal organs constituted the bulk of information about the treatment provided. Homeopathy, meanwhile, was characterized by its holistic approach and 'gentleness', and osteopathy by its focus on structure and function in the body. Thus acupuncture was presented as coming from a distinct cultural context, while the other therapies were apparently universal.

The CTC proved successful and popular with local GPs and with patients; its staff attempted to expand into the mainstream of the hospital, and to export their innovative methods of assessment and treatment – much as would be expected of any successful innovation. Whether or not these ambitions played a role in the sudden demise of the CTC shortly after the publication of its 1996 research report is unknown. It is clear that in this case acupuncture's marked 'alternative' – but not its 'exotic' – status proved ineradicable among both patients and practitioners: patient feedback regularly opposed acupuncture to the orthodox treatments they had received elsewhere, but made no comments about its non-Western origins or body model.[50] Acupuncture's popularity (like the CTC's) remained undiminished by this contrapositioning, and in the end, may prove the decisive factor in determining the success or failure of this wave of acupuncture-transmission to the West. As the authors of the report themselves note:

> The move to consumerism signals a new phenomena in medicine, and could have a major impact on the provision of non-conventional therapies in the NHS. … [T]he provision of health care has been 'profession driven'. There is however, a growing recognition that patients are in fact 'partners' in healthcare, that their participation in the process of treatment can influence compliance and outcome, and that ultimately, 'their views are the ones that matter'.[51]

Conclusion

Acupuncture has, in the three centuries since it was first described to a European audience, made regular appearances on the increasingly elevated stage of orthodox medicine. Advocates, usually drawn from the mid- and outer circles of medical orthodoxy, have proposed its Western adoption in each of the intervening centuries. These serial attempts to engraft East Asian therapeutic needling onto the stock of orthodox Western medicine have consistently portrayed acupuncture as an innovation, one drawn perhaps from a different and ancient tradition but both renewed and rendered available by Westernization.

What has enabled the repeated return of this technique and, conversely, what has hampered its permanent assimilation into the mainstream of orthodox medical practice? In part, the force underlying both acupuncture's recurrent popularity and its failure to thrive is the exoticism which its medical proponents have consistently downplayed and its lay supporters have emphasized; orientalism clearly remains a powerful force in Western culture. Both the medical press and the broadsheets reporting on acupuncture anaesthesia, for example, emphasized the contrast between the biomedical context – a 'modern' hospital and operating theatre – and the exotic needles. As we have seen, in this they reiterate eighteenth- and nineteenth-century descriptions of acupuncture.

But acupuncture's exotic origins cannot completely explain its fragility within orthodox Western medicine. Rhinoplastic surgery too has its roots in non-Western practice, having originated in India as a response to the punishment of facial mutilation.[52] Witnessed by Europeans in the late eighteenth century, the technique was immediately exported back to Britain, and rapidly integrated into orthodox surgical practice. Rhinoplasty was a new procedure, in competition with no established surgical method; it was moreover, readily explicable in Western terms; and unlikely either to be assimilable by competing medical systems or adopted by lay healers. Acupuncture, in contrast, has competed with established (if imperfect) therapies; remains inexplicable except in its own terms; exemplifies an alternative medical system; and has proven readily available for adoption by heterodox lay as well as orthodox professional practitioners. Unsurprisingly, then, the integrative strand of the professional response to acupuncture has tried to explain it in Western terms, and to exclude lay practitioners.

In the wave of discussion which followed acupuncture's re-emergence in the 1970s (and which continues today), much play has been made of the distinction between 'complementary' and 'alternative' medicine. In the case of acupuncture, the difference between these two stances is marked less by the nature of the 'acupuncture' provided, than by the position taken by the acupuncture provider (and consumer) in relation to orthodox medicine. A practitioner who offers absolutely traditional acupuncture (or a patient who seeks such treatment), but does so either under the direction of, or in co-operation with an orthodox physician can be regarded as practising (or partaking of) 'complementary' medicine; a practitioner who uses electrical point-locators and anatomical maps but opposes his or her practice to biomedical norms (or a patient seeking such a polarity) is offering 'alternative' medicine. The complexity and impact of the relationship between social, professional, and self-designation in the case of acupuncture practice are illustrated by the CTC's difficulties in positioning traditional acupuncture as an orthodox innovation.

Publications produced by the CTC stressed its innovations in assessment and service delivery, but were reticent about the innovativeness of offering those services at all. In the case of the acupuncture delivered at the CTC, the novelty in Lewisham did not inhere in the therapy itself – the form of treatment the patients received was standard practice within traditional Chinese medicine, from its therapeutic encounter, to the diagnostic procedure, to the acupuncture provided. As staff at the clinic realized, one innovative aspect of the clinic was its use of clinical audit and outcome assessment to investigate not acupuncture's *objective*, but its *subjective* outcomes, through patient self-assessment of feelings of health or illness, and of social function. The second novel aspect, of course, was the (carefully unheralded) use of traditional Chinese acupuncture – rather than the fusion technique 'medical acupuncture' – within the NHS. This positioning of traditional acupuncture as an orthodox innovation was unstable because of the slippage between acupuncture's external labelling as 'alternative' (in its sense of heterodox and oppositional) medicine and the normal process by which medical innovations diffuse precisely *because* they offer orthodox 'alternatives' to other established therapies or structures. The striking popularity of this second innovation is the more remarkable since acupuncture as practised at the CTC exhibited few of the usual hallmarks of the exotic, yet also lacked the scientific gloss bestowed on 'medical acupuncture' by its professional proponents.

In the nineteenth century, British proponents constructed an innovative 'acupuncture', comprised of the needle itself, and the idea that shallow needling could be therapeutic, but stripped of acupuncture's original interpretive system and cultural markers. Although empirically successful, acupuncture thus construed proved incoherent, and disappeared from British practice. The CTC modelled a new innovative 'acupuncture', practised in accordance with another culture's models of health, disease, and especially the therapeutic encounter – but practised without obvious markers of its exogenous status and within the bureaucratic structures of late twentieth-century medicine. The popularity of this therapy among patients – and its failure nevertheless to integrate into the hospital's mainstream – suggest that models both of cultural specificity and of innovation in medicine must more seriously consider the complex relationship between popular and professional cultures of medicine.

Notes

1 S. Hamilton, P. Brown, M. Hallington and K. Rutherford, 'Anaesthesia by acupuncture', *British Medical Journal* (henceforth *BMJ*), 1972, vol. 3, p. 352.
2 Of course, one group of acupuncture practitioners in Britain has actively fought to eradicate the 'cloak of witchcraft' which they see as inherent in traditional Chinese acupuncture; they instead propose a fusion technique – 'medical acupuncture' –

which requires medical training, and uses needling only within the biomedical model. See W. Stephens, 'Personal view', *BMJ*, vol. 287, p. 906.

3   W. Ten Rhyne, *Dissertatio de Arthritide: Mantissa Schematica: De Acupunctura: Et Orationes Tres*, London, Royal Society, 1683.

4   Grosier, *A General Description of China*, London, G. G. J. and J. Robinson, 1787, vol. 1, pp. 497–8.

5   Note that the third pamphlet in Figure 4.4 uses an eighteenth-century image of the East Asian body-map which (unlike Ten Rhyne's illustrations of the same maps) tellingly lacked acu-channels or any translation of the Japanese text identifying and describing each point and its uses. I argue elsewhere that these differences indicate changes in the permeability of Western medicine to cross-cultural understandings of the body and disease. See R. Bivins, *Acupuncture, Expertise and Cross-Cultural Medicine*, Basingstoke, Palgrave, 2000.

6   For a more detailed account of acupuncture's transmission to Europe, see Bivins, *Acupuncture*, pp. 46–94.

7   J. Churchill, *A Treatise on Acupuncturation*, London, Simpkin and Marshall, 1822, p. 5.

8   Churchill, *Treatise*, p. 85.

9   'Art. XIV. [Review of recent work on Acupuncture]', *Edinburgh Medical and Surgical Journal*, 1827, vol. 27, p. 339. For more on historical British responses to acupuncture, see Bivins, *Acupuncture*, pp. 95–181.

10   While this claim provoked controversy in relation to the stethoscope, it proved more acceptable when made about acupuncture, perhaps because acupuncture was already separated from medical debate by its extrinsic status.

11   Bivins, *Acupuncture*, pp. 95–181.

12   Many members of the Macartney Embassy published accounts of that journey; every account included details of Chinese medicine and natural science.

13   'Report of the BMA Annual Clinical Meeting, Cheltenham 24–27 October: Retropubic Prostatectomy', *BMJ*, 1968, vol. 4, p. 320. Emphasis added.

14   Here I will focus on the *BMJ*, as the organ of the BMA and both the voice and journal of record for British GPs. Other medical journals, including the *Lancet* published correspondence and articles on acupuncture during this period.

15   Hamilton *et al.*, 'Anaesthesia by acupuncture', p. 352.

16   Early popularizations include F. Mann, *Acupuncture: The Ancient Chinese Art of Healing*, London, Heinemann, 1962; L. Moss, *Acupuncture and You*, London, Paul Alek Books, 1964; and for a sociological analysis, M. Saks, 'The paradox of incorporation: acupuncture and the medical profession in modern Britain', in M. Saks (ed.), *Alternative Medicine in Britain*, Oxford, Clarendon Press, 1992, pp. 183–98.

17   M. Ramsay, 'Anaesthesia by acupuncture', *BMJ*, 1972, vol. 3, p. 703.

18   See e.g. R. Macintosh, 'Tests of acupuncture', *BMJ*, 1973, vol. 3, pp. 454–5; and more explicitly, P. Skrabunck, 'Acupuncture in an age of unreason', *Lancet*, 1984, vol. 1, pp. 116–17; D. Bond, 'Acupuncture: from ancient art to modern medicine', *Lancet*, 1983, vol. 1, p. 32.

19   M. Ramsay, 'Anaesthesia by acupuncture', *BMJ*, 1973, vol. 1, p. 233.

20   S. Hamilton, 'Anaesthesia by acupuncture', *BMJ*, 1973, vol. 1, p. 420. Emphasis in original.

21   This and all subsequent quotations in this paragraph: 'Tests of acupuncture', *BMJ*, 1973, vol. 2, p. 502.

22   P. Brown, 'Tests of acupuncture', *BMJ*, 1973, vol. 3, p. 780.

23   J. Watts, 'Tests of acupuncture', *BMJ*, 1973, vol. 3, p. 780. Compare to J. Floyer, *The Physician's Pulse Watch*, London, Smith and Walford, 1701; J. Davis, *The Chinese: A General Description*, London, Charles Knight, 1837.

24   'More tests of acupuncture', *BMJ*, 1973, vol. 3, p. 190; 'When acupuncture came to Britain', *BMJ*, 1973, vol. 4, pp. 687–8.

25   C. Hewer, 'Tests of acupuncture', *BMJ*, 1973, vol. 3, p. 592.

26 I. Copperauld, 'Anaesthesia by acupuncture', *BMJ*, 1972, vol. 4, pp. 232–3.

27 D. Sharland, 'Anaesthesia by acupuncture', *BMJ*, 1972, vol. 4, p. 612.

28 Churchill, *Treatise*, pp. 13–14. At the time, anatomical knowledge was virtually exclusive to medical practitioners.

29 See Snow, *The New Republic*, 1 May 1971; Reston, *New York Times*, 22 August 1971; British broadsheets were slower, but by 30 April 1972, *The Observer Review* reported on acupuncture anaesthesia, p. 29. B. Inglis, *Fringe Medicine*, London, Faber and Faber, 1964, pp. 123–8 cites earlier popular reporting on acupuncture; however, such accounts triggered no mirroring response in the medical profession.

30 Although other parts of East Asian medicine have been imported to Europe, acupuncture is (with the possible exception of the analgesic ointment Tiger Balm) by far the most widespread, well recognized, and most discussed both within and outside the medical community.

31 See S. Blume, *Insight and Industry: On the Dynamics of Technological Change in Medicine*, Cambridge, MA, MIT Press, 1992; J. Roth and S. Ruzek (eds), *The Adoption and Social Consequences of Medical Technologies*, Greenwich, CT, JAI Press, 1986; J. Howell, *Technology in the Hospital: Transforming Patient Care in the Early Twentieth Century*, Baltimore, Johns Hopkins Press, 1995; C. Rosenberg, *The Care of Strangers: The Rise of America's Hospital System*, New York, Basic Books, 1987; W. Bynum, C. Lawrence and V. Nutton (eds), *The Emergence of Modern Cardiology*, London, Wellcome Institute for the History of Medicine, 1985. For a broader perspective, see J. Pickstone (ed.), *Medical Innovations in Historical Perspective*, Basingstoke, Macmillan, 1992.

32 M. Fennell and R. Warnecke, *The Diffusion of Medical Innovations: An Applied Network Analysis*, London, Plenum Press, 1989, p. 2.

33 B. Stocking, *Initiative and Inertia: Case Studies in the NHS*, London, Nuffield Provincial Hospitals Trust, 1985, pp. 22–9.

34 Patients complained bitterly about a daily schedule designed to fit nurse, orderly, and cleaning-staff shift patterns rather than their own therapeutic needs and preferences, or scheduled visiting hours. Subsequent efforts to reorganize the patient-day were driven by these complaints. Stocking, *Initiative and Inertia*, pp. 139–66.

35 J. Young, 'The development of the Office of Alternative Medicine in the National Institutes of Health, 1991–1996', *Bulletin of the History of Medicine*, 1999, vol. 72, pp. 279–98.

36 For 'medical mercantilism', see Bivins, *Acupuncture*, pp. 3–5.

37 U. Sharma, *Complementary Medicine Today: Practitioners and Patients*, London, Routledge, 1992, p. 3.

38 See Saks, 'Paradox of incorporation', 1992.

39 Consumer's Association, *WHICH*, November 1995.

40 National Association of Health Authorities and Trusts, *Complementary Therapies in the NHS*, Report Number 10, 1993.

41 The data illustrated here are drawn from both international (often US-weighted) and UK specific sources, including the Times Citation Index, British Humanities Index, Medline, and the Readers' Guide to Periodicals. *The Times* was chosen largely because it is the only fully indexed newspaper and is therefore conventionally taken as a standard reference point.

42 For example, in 1995, the Times Citation Index lists only four articles under the heading 'acupuncture', but a computer search by keyword finds twenty-four separate articles discussing the subject.

43 B. O'Connor, *Healing Traditions: Alternative Medicine and the Health Professions*, Philadelphia, PA, University of Pennsylvania Press, 1995. The role of organized consumers in negotiating between policy-makers, medical bureaucrats, and practitioners is also an important and under-studied one. See also Valier and Bivins, Chapter 2, this volume.

44 In the late 1980s, as part of their 'internal market' restructuring of the NHS, the Tory government offered GPs the option of becoming 'fundholders'. 'Fundholders' were given control of their practice's annual budget (which was, at least initially, set at a level above those of non-fundholding practices) and given substantial freedom to negotiate contracts with NHS and non-NHS providers for services required. In essence, they were given a profit motive. They were also allowed to spend their budgets on alternative as well as orthodox medicine.

45 Personal communication, January 1993, with medical director (who also had experience with African traditional medicine). Informal networks were crucial to the persistence of acupuncture use as its visibility declined in the mid- to late nineteenth century. See Bivins, *Acupuncture*; 'When acupuncture came to Britain'.

46 J. Richardson and A. Brennan, 'Complementary therapy in the NHS: service development in a local district general hospital', *Complementary Therapies in Nursing and Midwifery*, 1995, vol. 1, pp. 89–92. The nurse practitioner is defined (p. 89) as possessing 'expert knowledge in a special branch of practice' acquired through specialist training.

47 Complementary Therapy Unit Proposal, September 1993, p. 5.

48 British Medical Association, *Report of the Board of Science and Education on Alternative Therapy*, London, BMA, 1986, pp. 61–75.

49 J. Richardson, *CTC Annual Report*, Lewisham Hospital NHS Trust, 1995, p. 7.

50 J. Richardson, *Complementary Therapy in the NHS: A Service Evaluation of the First Year of an Outpatient Service in a Local District Hospital*, Lewisham Hospital NHS Trust, 1995.

51 Richardson, *CTC Annual Report*, p. 15.

52 D. Wujastyk, 'Medicine in India', in J. van Alphen and A. Aris (eds), *Oriental Medicine: An Illustrated Guide to the Asian Arts of Healing*, London, Serindia Publications, 1995, pp. 19–37.

5 Degrees of control: the spread of operative fracture treatment with metal implants

A comparative perspective on Switzerland, East Germany and the USA, 1950s–1990s

Thomas Schlich

Operative treatment of broken bones with metal implants such as screws and plates, called 'osteosynthesis' or 'internal fixation', is standard therapy in trauma surgery. In the 1950s, however, this kind of treatment was rejected by most surgeons. As osteosynthesis eventually started becoming a widespread procedure worldwide, both proponents and critics attributed its successful introduction to the activities of the AO/ASIF (Arbeitsgemeinschaft für Osteosynthesefragen/Association for Internal Fixation).[1] The AO was founded in 1958 in Switzerland by thirteen young surgeons who wanted to introduce the then rather exotic approach of operative fracture treatment on a broad scale. Within two decades the association had developed into a multinational enterprise with thousands of members and associates worldwide. Simultaneously, the AO's specific osteosynthesis procedures have become the standard technique throughout the world; the AO training courses are now a must for any aspiring traumatologist, the AO textbooks are bestsellers available in all major languages, and the sale of AO instruments and implants yields a substantial economic profit.

In 1960 the four leading AO surgeons also founded a company called Synthes Ltd at Chur in Switzerland to market special AO equipment. They arranged for all copyrights on instruments and implants developed by AO surgeons to be transferred to Synthes in order to redirect all subsequent profits gained from the licensing of their products. For the industrial production of this equipment, Synthes co-operated with two, later three, small manufacturing companies, which rapidly grew into the leading instrument and implant makers in the field. In exchange for the input from AO research and development and the licence to make and sell the AO devices, the manufacturers committed themselves to paying royalties to Synthes. This money was used exclusively to support the AO's scientific activities, for example, by constructing a laboratory for basic research and a documentation centre to collect and evaluate the results of the therapeutic methods introduced by the AO. The results of these activities enabled the AO to dominate the discussions on the scientific foundations of osteosynthesis as well as on its clinical outcomes, first in Europe, and later in North America. When the AO started its activities it was not at all clear that it would be successful; and the question is how it was possible for a difficult and rather risky technique to become a standard procedure throughout the world.

Part of the answer can be gained by comparing the spread of the AO technique within different contexts. In Switzerland the use of osteosynthesis became widespread from the early 1960s onwards. Operative fracture care in keeping with the AO method became an accepted therapeutic option. Before long, surgeons in the neighbouring countries, especially in West Germany, Austria, and Italy joined forces with the Swiss and contributed to the spread of the technique in their own countries. However, the success of the AO surgeons' efforts at introducing their method varied considerably depending on where it was introduced. In some countries the AO rapidly gained high prestige, its technique came to be widely adopted and its equipment sold very well. In others, it met with indifference or rejection.

Judging from the history of osteosynthesis in general, the extent of control that the AO group exerted over the use of its technique and materials seems to be a crucial factor for the success of the AO technique in different contexts. Before the 1960s, osteosynthesis had never been accepted on a large scale, even though a number of surgeons had attempted to introduce it as standard practice. The main problem was the lack of quality control regarding the materials as well as the skill of the individual surgeons who used them. Typically, an outstanding surgeon managed to master a particular method of osteosynthesis and was able to achieve at least acceptable results. But as soon as others took up the technique, they usually produced poor results and a high rate of complications. The most dreaded complication was bone infection which often led to protracted illness or amputation of the affected limb. As a consequence, the medical community rejected osteosynthesis altogether.[2]

This situation was fundamentally changed when the AO introduced a new extent of control over the technique it propagated. Control here means the power to influence others in their activities and to ensure that techniques are performed in the proper way, devices are produced of a reliable quality, and theories are understood in a certain way. For instance, in an act of self-control, the surgeons committed themselves to the exclusive use of the strictly standardized equipment; the success of each surgeon's efforts in applying the technique was monitored by the AO documentation centre; the production and marketing of the AO equipment by the manufacturers were supervised by a technical commission; the same commission decided on the development and introduction of new devices; and control over conveying skills and imparting knowledge to the individual surgeons was enhanced by standardized instruction courses and textbooks.

In the Swiss context control was achieved by organizing those surgeons who first used the AO technique in a close-knit group, forming a network of mutual surveillance. The members' relationship to the group followed the specific cultural pattern of the fraternity, a very widespread and significant form of organization in Switzerland. Within the fraternity context, individual surgeons were prepared to subject themselves to control by the group. The creation of a network-like organization was further facilitated by the peculiar structure of Swiss health care provision with its numerous small to medium-sized local hospitals scattered all over the country. Qualified across a broad spectrum and mostly very experienced, the head surgeons at these hospitals were well respected and proud autocrats in their realm. Most of them knew each other, many of them, especially within the Berne region, where the AO started, were even friends. This class of surgeons kept their distance from the professors of the university hospitals, forming their own professional network alongside academic surgery. It was this milieu in which AO emerged and achieved an unprecedented degree of control over the application of the technique of osteosynthesis.[3]

To further assess the significance of control for the spread of the AO technique I chose to look at two countries, the United States of America and the former East German communist state, the German Democratic Republic. In both countries the extent of control varied in comparison with each other as well as with Switzerland. These two countries also differed significantly with regard to the AO's success. In the USA, the AO method was initially rejected and it took a long time before the AO could gain a foothold. In the GDR the AO technique was accepted early on and has sometimes been deemed more successful than even in Switzerland.[4]

GDR: optimized control

In the GDR,[5] health care was organized and funded by the state, most institutions were run by the government, and the majority of health care providers were state employees. Free and equal availability of quality health care services was the basic goal, and centralized rational planning the method to achieve it. Scientists were expected to subordinate their personal ambitions and interests to tasks of importance to society; health care resources were to be allocated in a methodical and rational way from the top down – if necessary, against the will of those concerned.

The whole health care system was organized in a strictly hierarchical manner; the Minister of Health at the top received his directives directly from the Central Committee of the SED, the East German Communist Party; the employees at the hospitals and clinics were situated at the bottom of the hierarchy. An intermediate level was formed by the different specialist associations, such as the Surgeons Association. Each was assigned its special task by a co-ordinating council which was itself responsible to the minister. The specialist associations were in charge of health care planning and research management. They decided which research topics were to be pursued, assigned them to particular institutions, allocated the necessary funds, and evaluated the research work done. They also organized specialist training, selected those doctors who were allowed to attend conferences abroad, supervised the publishing activities of their members, and decided on the appointment of senior officials of the health care system. In addition, the associations served as umbrella organizations for the particular divisions (*Sektionen*) for special subdisciplines, such as the Traumatology Division (*Sektion für Traumatologie*), and also for the work groups (*Arbeitsgruppen*) established for studying specific problems. Even though the associations, divisions, and work groups did not form the top of the hierarchy, their influence and power were considerable: in practice, supervision from above was necessarily limited and there was much scope for decision-making on each of the administrative levels.

Introduction of the AO technology in the GDR

Because of the growing numbers of accident victims through 'increasing traffic density, growing industrialization, and the rise of popular and competitive sports'[6] in the GDR, as in other industrialized countries, fracture care was ascribed an important function. As in other countries, osteosynthesis was recommended as an economically sensible way of treating fractures; and GDR surgeons had started to work on the technique in the early 1950s.[7] But until the 1960s no-one in the GDR knew that anything like the AO existed. Then, in 1964, the foremost representative of East German traumatology Franz Mörl was invited to attend the AO course in Davos in southeast Switzerland where the AO had started its regular programme of hands-on instruction courses in 1960.[8] Mörl, who was in his sixties, passed on the invitation to his young colleague Eberhard Sander. Sander was then a senior surgeon (*Oberarzt*) in Halle specializing in traumatology. In his post-doctoral *Habilitation* thesis Sander had dealt with the electrogenetic effect of metal osteosynthesis. His experience in the field made him the obvious candidate to attend such a course.[9]

The journey to Davos was the young surgeon's first educational trip abroad and he was as much impressed by the teaching methods he experienced at the AO course as he was by the technique of compression osteosynthesis itself.[10] Back home, Sander maintained and reinforced his Swiss contacts[11] and in 1968 founded a work group for operative fracture treatment. The group comprised twenty-two members and was part of the Traumatology Division of the GDR Surgeons Association.[12]

On 13 December 1968 the statutes for the 'Work Group for Operative Fracture Treatment of the GDR' (*Arbeitsgemeinschaft für operative Knochenbruchbehandlung der DDR*) were instituted, modelled on the statutes of the other GDR work groups.[13] The Work Group for Operative Fracture Treatment was one of many similar groups. As opposed to the Swiss AO, which was a completely private organization, the East German work groups were firmly integrated into the official health care hierarchy. Starting in the 1960s, they had been established for relevant areas of study. They either had an autonomous status within the respective specialist association or were subordinate to a specific division in the way the Work Group for Operative Fracture Treatment was part of the Traumatology Division. Though, coincidentally, these work groups bore the same German name, *Arbeitsgemeinschaft*, as the AO (*Arbeitsgemeinschaft für Osteosynthesefragen*), they were fundamentally different in status.[14]

Analogous to the Swiss AO, the Work Group's list of tasks encompassed research, instruction, documentation, and exchange of experience. But the group was also assigned responsibilities within the organization of the GDR health care system: prediction and planning of the development of their field, nationwide management of operative fracture care, promulgation of guidelines for using different methods of fracture treatment, and publication of outcome studies. Remarkably, their official assignments explicitly granted them a say in the appointment of surgeons in the relevant departments, and, what is even more noteworthy, put them in charge of the distribution of the osteosynthesis equipment. This authorized the Work Group to select the surgeons who would be given access to the AO instruments.[15] Whereas in other countries, such as Switzerland or West Germany, the AO exerted influence through informal networking, in the GDR, the AO surgeons as members of an *Arbeitsgemeinschaft* in the East German sense were part of the official health care administration, vested with the power to decide on relevant questions of health care policy and appointments to positions in their field.

Scarcity and control: allocation of the hardware

After his 1964 visit to Davos, Sander made every effort to get a complete set of AO equipment imported. This proved to be very difficult. The AO instruments were simply too expensive. It took several attempts and the support of influential officials including the president of the Surgeons Association to gain permission to buy the AO material. In 1966 Sander's department in Halle became the first East German institution to be furnished with a complete set of instruments.[16] Subsequently Sander went to the Foreign Ministry and proposed the importation of AO equipment on a regular basis. As it was supported by some high-ranking colleagues within the health care hierarchy, the proposal was successful. In 1967 Sander ordered ten sets of instruments from Switzerland which were shipped to the GDR Foreign Ministry. The Ministry passed them on to Sander and gave him a free hand to distribute the material as he saw fit. As Sander later recalled, the low number of available instruments forced him to make a strict selection. In order to secure the equal access to health care facilities that was guaranteed by the GDR constitution, geographically uniform distribution of the AO material was attempted. In addition, the instruments were allocated according to the degree of traumatological specialization of the respective institutions. The first to be supplied were medical schools at the universities and academies and some larger district hospitals. Slowly, more and more equipment was bought. In 1968, 10 institutions were in possession of the equipment; in 1974 the number was 41; and by 1979, 74 traumatological institutions had been supplied with AO material. In total, 157 complete sets of equipment were delivered.[17]

Regarding the method of distribution, Sander later wrote: 'Such a procedure would have been unthinkable under free-market conditions! But what else could we do, considering the restricted number [of instruments and implants]?'[18] The quality control that was in fact achieved by the selective distribution of instruments was thus rather a side-effect of scarcity and not the result of deliberate policy but there certainly was an effect, as Sander acknowledged: 'What was definitely positive and offered considerable advantages in terms of cooperation was that we had a proper grasp of the situation! And we tried to do the allocation in a sensible way!'[19] As proven by similar examples in other fields of medicine, shortage of material makes it much easier to supervise and regulate its use.[20] Sander's allocation policy fitted in well with the general concept of health care in the GDR. A 1985 memorandum by the SED gives evidence of this. It is an appeal to party organizations within the health care institutions to make sure that resources be used in an appropriate way and in accordance with official health care policy; more specifically, new technical devices should be provided only if indispensable for high-quality and effective medical care, and only to institutions with the physical and human resources needed to achieve the technology's full effectiveness within a short time. The equipment should only be entrusted to surgeons who knew how to use it.[21] This was part of a conscious effort to concentrate resources within a few centres of expertise.[22]

Recognizing the benefit of controlled allocation, the East German AO surgeons worried whenever distribution slipped from their control. This was the case with surgeons employed by sports clubs. As was typical for socialist countries, competitive athletics had a very high standing in official GDR politics. This gave the sport clubs access to their own sources of foreign currency – in the GDR, a rare privilege that was essential for buying products from abroad. Also, in some highly industrialized areas such as Bitterfeld or the Berlin region, the industrial health care institutions had enough foreign currency to buy instruments directly from the manufacturers and circumvent the central distribution. Sander learned of these irregular channels for obtaining AO material when these surgeons turned up at the AO courses he had started to organize in his country in 1968. According to the East German AO surgeons' estimate, the rise of complication rates after the introduction of the AO equipment was largely attributable to 'institutions that had not been equipped officially and completely' with the AO instruments.[23] So even within the East German context, it was not always easy to oversee the use of the technology, and any lack of control seemed to have obvious negative effects. As a remedy, the surgeons suggested expanding the course programme and improving the documentation system.[24]

'An extraordinarily fertile soil for the AO principles': success of AO technology in the GDR

The AO was very successful in the GDR. The very name 'AO' soon came to stand for excellent quality, Sander wrote in retrospect, and even small district hospitals in the countryside made every effort to be able to work according to the AO principles.[25] From the late 1960s, the AO technology enjoyed an excellent reputation among GDR surgeons; osteosynthesis was regarded as an enormous step forward in the treatment of bone fractures.[26] Demand for AO courses was enormous; the number of applicants invariably exceeded the number of available spaces in the regular courses.[27] As another sign of success, those surgeons associated with the AO started being appointed to important positions, even if they were not active in the SED. One of these was Sander, who in 1973 was appointed chair of general surgery in Halle.[28] Official recognition is also evident by the fact that the promotion of traumatology and osteosynthesis was included in the official plans of health care development.[29]

East German AO surgeons knew that they fared very well in international comparison.[30] But commentators from outside the East German AO also found their work outstanding. As the Swiss AO surgeon Urs Heim declared after a visit to the GDR in 1972, '*never* before have we seen such a precise application [of the technique]; the systematic approach is admirable'.[31] In his annual report of 1972/73, AO secretary Robert Schneider stated that the GDR seemed to provide an extraordinarily fertile soil for the AO principles, especially viewed in contrast to the AO's difficult situation in the USA.[32] Hans Willenegger, who at that time organized the AO education programme, repeatedly stressed the GDR's high standards of organization and competence in traumatology.[33] In 1990, Urs Heim confirmed in a letter to Sander the particularly high quality of the work done in the GDR. This, Heim supposed, was due to the scarcity of instruments which had forced the East German AO surgeons to take particular care to equip only qualified colleagues with AO material.[34]

Obviously, the beneficial effects of facilitated control in the GDR outweighed the negative effects of scarcity. Because of the lack of materials, the number of osteosynthesis operations performed there was lower than in other countries.[35] But at the same time the results were better and complications occurred less frequently so that the AO was able to maintain an excellent reputation. The AO story in communist East Germany shows that the principle of control was integral to the successful spread of the AO, and that control in this case could arise from precisely those conditions which constrained the power of surgeons as individuals or as a profession.

USA: failed control

The initial conditions for a successful spread of the AO technique to the United States of America seemed to be favourable. From the outset, the AO was in close contact with American surgeons.[36] Starting in 1960, Maurice Müller, as one of the AO's founders, made several journeys to the USA to demonstrate his compression plate. As a consequence, the Campbell Clinic in Memphis, Tennessee and groups of surgeons in Boston, New York, and Los Angeles bought AO instrument sets and started using them.[37] In 1963 the *Journal of Bone and Joint Surgery* (*JBJS*), the top American journal in orthopaedic surgery, presented a detailed description of the AO equipment and technique (but gave no assessment of its usefulness).[38] Thus, by the mid-1960s, quite a few American surgeons had heard of the AO method. If the AO method failed to spread, it was not for lack of availability.

There are additional reasons why one might have expected the AO technique to spread swiftly in the USA. From the 1950s to the late 1970s the medical sector of the world's leading economic power underwent an unprecedented expansion. Paramount in the expansion of medical care was the growth of medical technology. This included the building of new hospitals and clinics but also the introduction of new therapeutic and diagnostic techniques and devices. The general growth of the medical sector facilitated the establishment of specialist and subspecialist disciplines, such as traumatology and orthopaedic surgery. For the most part, health care providers were privately run institutions; the organization and financing of health care followed market principles. In sum, conditions for technical innovation in medicine were favourable in the USA at the time.[39]

Furthermore, fracture care was considered an important issue. The 'modern monstrous disease of trauma'[40] aroused the attention of the the the medical profession as well as the general public of the United States. At the same time, the emphasis of surgical attention shifted away from merely avoiding accidental death to preventing subsequent disability of the survivors.[41] All this was very much in accord with the AO's aims. It is thus surprising to see that the AO technique did not become widespread in the USA before the mid-1980s. For an explanation one must go back to the time before the AO surgeons started to get in touch with their American colleagues.

'Keep the closed fracture closed': the rejection of operative fracture treatment in the USA

Like their European colleagues before the AO, the leading US surgeons had been very reluctant to take up techniques of operative fracture care.[42] Up until the 1960s the conservative 'English system' was standard and the popular textbook by the osteosynthesis opponent Reginald Watson-Jones was the bible of fracture treatment.[43] In 1960 the President of the American Orthopaedic[44] Association gave a passionate speech against operating on fractures which he concluded by saying: 'Keep the closed fracture closed.' In his speech he explained that the 'very satisfactory concept of the closed fracture and its treatment was rudely shattered by the sudden realization that the trend, since World War II, had been decided toward open reduction', producing a 'slow but steady stream of tragedies secondary to open reduction of closed fractures of the long bones;' he had witnessed at his clinic.[45] It was thus only logical that textbooks usually advised against the use of osteosynthesis. The 1963 edition of the leading American textbook *Campbell's Operative Orthopaedics* recommended using internal fixation 'reservedly' and related a widely shared opinion in stating that the 'early enthusiastic use' of osteosynthesis 'for too many fractures' had 'reflected discredit upon the method'.[46]

The reservations about osteosynthesis in general also applied to the AO technique in particular. The AO was seen as advocating an aggressive approach, its acronym standing for 'Always Operate'.[47] When in 1965 the English translation of the AO textbook *Technique of Internal Fixation of Fractures* came out, it received a friendly but cautious review in the American edition of the *JBJS*:

In the hands of the superb technicians who have developed and repeatedly used this system of ingeniously devised precision implants, remarkable results can be achieved. ... However, for the surgeon who by choice or chance does not use this system frequently and who cannot be assured of the technical perfection in reduction and fixation that is required, the technique should be applied with caution.[48]

It was thus not the technique *per se* that was questioned but its overenthusiastic and incorrect application. Similarly, in the following years, a number of American papers identified misapplication of osteosynthesis as one of the main reasons for disastrous complications in fracture treatment in general. Poor surgical technique and the failure to achieve stability at the fracture site are cited as the principal problems; infections, delayed healing, and permanent loss of function as the most frequent consequences. Since only very few surgeons had mastered the technique, these papers concluded, operative treatment could not be recommended as standard procedure.[49]

'The dark side of Davos': criticism of the AO technique in the US

American traumatologists discussed the AO compression plate extensively at their association's Annual Session in 1966. Even though they valued the AO technique very highly in principle, they also underlined the dangers of its widespread use in the USA: 'This form of treatment is invading our country and we have to use it with great care', one surgeon warned in the discussion, thus emphasizing that the AO technique was alien to the American surgical environment. The problem was to secure accurate replication of the procedure within the new context: if the American surgeons failed to follow 'the principles of what the originators of the technique really would do and really have described', another discussant pointed out, the technique would not be successful.[50] In 1970 (a time when the AO technique was already standard treatment in Europe) a special editorial appeared in the *Journal of Trauma* on the 'fad' of AO osteosynthesis. In the author's view, the high quality of the AO technology made it all the more dangerous; the AO had created:

> a serious problem in the development of their technique, due primarily to the excellency of their surgery and the precision of their instruments. They are master surgeons who have spent years in developing their technique. They have perfected a beautiful set of instruments, and use them with great skill. As a result, every young surgeon interested in fracture treatment becomes intrigued with the instruments and wishes to try them out immediately in his own hospital. This, then, is the problem. The beginner can no more hope quickly to emulate the work of these surgeons than a week-end skier can successfully duplicate the efforts of a champion Olympic skier.

And he concluded: 'The ASIF has created a problem, and if indiscriminate use of the method should develop, then the inevitable tragic results will give them a bad name.'[51]

Throughout the 1970s influential surgeons in the USA continued to warn against the AO.[52] The chapter on fracture treatment in the 1971 edition of *Campbell's Operative Orthopaedics* was in keeping with other publications of that time warning that the excellent results reported by the Swiss AO may not be reproducible in the USA because of the American surgeons' lack of training and experience.[53] Some of the published papers indicate how, lacking a supporting network, some American surgeons slowly and through experience learned to apply the AO implants in the correct way. Only after a certain number of incorrectly treated patients, did these surgeons dare to use the AO technique as intended: they initially combined internal fixation with a plaster cast, and only gradually gained enough confidence in the AO method to rely on the implants alone.[54] This was very different from the process of adopting the method in Switzerland, where the surgeons worked within a network of surveillance which put them under pressure, but also gave them the confidence, to apply the technique according to the principles established by the AO.

The AO was again attacked at the Chicago Orthopaedic Society meeting in 1976. A paper entitled 'The dark side of Davos' presented the retrospective assessment of 122 cases of diaphysial tibia fracture (the diaphysis is the shaft or middle part of a long bone) treated during a period of four years. Of thirty-six patients treated with the AO technique, bone infection had frequently occurred, and 11 per cent of them had remained permanently disabled.[55] On these grounds, the authors strongly advised against the AO treatment method. And again it was the incorrect application of the technique that had caused the poor outcomes. In many cases the AO's central tenet of producing rigid fixation that allowed the patient post-operative exercise had been ignored. 'Contrary to Swiss teaching', as the authors pointed out, the patients treated with the AO technique had spent an average period of 164.5 days with a plaster cast on. And in only twenty-one of the thirty-six cases was interfragmentary compression attempted at all. Since the American surgeons often failed to master the AO technique, they had modified it by using additional external plaster fixation in ways that counteracted the original intentions. According to the authors, 'the Swiss system of instrumentation, particularly the aura surrounding the pre-tapped screws,[56] gives the surgeon a false sense of security in his ability to reduce and rigidly fix complicated fractures.' The AO courses even strengthened this false sense of security: all the serious mistakes described in the paper had been made by surgeons 'trained in the Swiss technique', which means that they had at least attended a course. Accordingly, the paper was not meant as 'an indictment of the Swiss technique' *per se*, the authors wrote, but 'in certain ways … as an indictment of the Swiss educational methods'.[57] These critics thus explicitly accused the AO of failing to build up an effective network of instruction, quality control, and surveillance.

Network building

The Swiss AO was well aware that the spread of AO equipment without the simultaneous extension of the AO network of control and surveillance caused serious problems. In 1973 AO secretary Robert Schneider criticized the unrestricted sale of their instruments in the USA. Contrary to the usual strategy of the AO, the material had been made widely available before a small group of selected and well-trained surgeons had established a local culture of controlled and standardized use of the technique. The reason was that no such group existed in the USA. The Swiss surgeons could not get their American colleagues to organize themselves after their model. As a consequence, Schneider complained, the AO instruments were often simply added to the existing surgical equipment, which made their systematic application nearly impossible. This undermined the AO's central principle of standardized use. The resulting failures had so damaged the AO's reputation, the AO secretary emphasized, that even those American surgeons who were in principle sympathetic of the AO had turned against it.[58]

The general conditions for introducing a sophisticated surgical technique were not favourable in the American context. According to Hans Willenegger, American surgeons tended to over-estimate their own capabilities; many of them bought the equipment but failed to obtain adequate education; at the courses they focused on practical instruction and disregarded the theoretical basis of the method.[59] As Willenegger was told, because of the lack of systematic operative training young surgeons frequently performed difficult bone operations such as osteosynthesis completely on their own, with no more preparation than having attended a course and read a book on the operation.[60]

Adapting the kind of network-building that had worked so well in central Europe to the American context proved to be very difficult. Robert Schneider suggested replicating the Swiss success by constituting a small, closely knit, and easily controllable group of surgeons. This group would then function as a catalyst by handing down the technique to increasingly greater numbers of surgeons. But the Swiss AO surgeons did not know how to set up such a group since they felt incapable of assessing the American situation; the sheer size of the country made it difficult to gain a comprehensive view and they did not know who among the American surgeons were trustworthy and strong enough to represent the AO's interest. Müller doubted that the approach that had been successful in Switzerland could be transferred to the US context. The country was 'slightly larger than Switzerland', he quipped at a 1970 AO meeting, and in the large urban centres the impact of a small course to start the sort of spreading Schneider had proposed would be zero.[61]

Also, a formal American section of the AO never came to be established. There were two reasons for this: first, the general concept of creating national AO sections had failed, most sections that had been founded did not work as intended. The second reason had to do with differences in mentality: the American surgeons insisted on their freedom not to obey instructions from

Switzerland; even American AO supporters were very reluctant to subject themselves to surveillance by their Swiss colleagues.[62] The American AO surgeons
considered the Swiss AO dogmatic and domineering, and they especially
resented the Swiss stance of making the assignment of funds contingent on their
controllability. In their view, a formal constitution and an official agreement with
the Swiss AO would be too rigid. They would rather continue their activities in
'a loose system of teaching', believing that the 'common goal of teaching and
loving AO' was all that was neccessary to keep them together. This attitude made
them resist the Swiss attempts at establishing a 'close-knit group' after the Swiss
example with strong ties to the Swiss headquarters.[63]

The growing popularity of the AO in the USA: 'The dominoes begin to fall'

Majority opinion among American surgeons did not swing in favour of the AO
technique before the 1980s. But the process of acceptance had started earlier.
The reason why the AO and its technique had come to be the target of so much
criticism in the 1960s and 1970s was its obvious attractiveness and its gradually
increasing popularity among American surgeons. Many of the early users of the
AO technique had built a reputation on the feats they could accomplish with the
equipment.[64] And though American surgeons often warned against a more
widespread application of the AO technique because it required so much
surgical skill, they did not fail to report their own successful use of it.[65]

During the 1970s the earlier efforts by the AO surgeons to persuade their US
colleagues to accept the technique and the control began to pay off and, as
James Hughes, one of the early American collaborators of the AO, describes it
in retrospect, 'the dominoes began to fall and everybody lined up in a proper
way'.[66] One of the AO's main assets for winning their American colleagues'
respect was the high quality of its equipment. Critics and supporters alike
praised the 'fine engineering of the instruments, the rigidity of the plates, the
firm seating of the screws, and the intimate approximation of fragments after
compression'.[67] Like their European colleagues, American surgeons were
impressed by the AO's systematic approach, encompassing the technical and
biological basis as well as the technique, post-operative care, and outcome documentation. Before that time, 'everybody had picked out individual fractures and
operated on them'; the AO had 'the first complete view of the problem of fractures in a holistic way,' Hughes recalls.[68]

The 1971 edition of *Campbell's Operative Orthopaedics* declared that the use of
plates and screws in fractures of the shaft of long bone had become common-
place, and in the chapter on fracture treatment gave a detailed and almost
enthusiastic description of the AO technique and the 'well designed and beauti-
fully machined' AO equipment.[69] And even though, according to Maurice
Müller's estimate, the *JBJS* was normally not very sympathetic to the AO,[70] in
1972 the important journal gave the AO's research group the opportunity to

present their laboratory evidence for primary bone healing[71] and published a number of favourable clinical studies on the AO techniques.[72]

Another reason for satisfaction was that studies now distinguished between the technique as such and the quality of its application by the individual surgeon in their assessments. Failures were now attributable to the incompetence of the surgeons instead of the imperfection of the technique. The general thrust of the argument was that if surgeons attempted osteosynthesis, they should use the best available materials and technique – the AO's – and apply it in the appropriate way – according to the AO's instructions.[73]

In 1979 a whole issue of the American journal *Clinical Orthopaedics and Related Research* was devoted to the AO technique, marking a milestone in the reception of the AO in the USA. It provided the Swiss AO surgeons and their American followers with a forum to present the AO's aims and principles in detail and gave them opportunity to reiterate their warning of incorrect application of their technique.[74] The 1980 edition of *Campbell's Operative Orthopaedics* presented the AO's principles as authoritative knowledge. The description is more detailed than in 1971, even adopting a number of pictures and diagrams from the AO Manual. The chapter conveys the overall impression that, though the AO technique requires considerable skill and knowledge, it has definitely become state of the art.[75] A similar stance was taken in a number of American papers published in the early 1980s. Their authors tried to follow the AO's instructions strictly and adopted the AO's view that only properly executed osteosynthesis operations must be counted when evaluating the method.[76] The use of the AO technique by the US Army is additional evidence of its status as standard treatment.[77] According to a 1982 report, the initial debates 'by rabid proponents and opponents of the method' were now seen as largely irrational. A growing number of hospitals possessed 'the medical staff and equipment necessary to offer this alternative', and increasingly patients expressed 'satisfaction with the AO approach toward fracture treatment'.[78]

In 1983 the head of the American manufacturer of AO equipment Hansjörg Wyss gave the Swiss AO surgeons an idea of the potential market in the USA, with its 230 million inhabitants, 15,000 orthopaedic surgeons, and 8,000 hospitals active in the fields of orthopaedics and trauma. He also told the Swiss surgeons that by that time osteosynthesis operations were frequently being performed in the USA. And while many specialist groups and university departments were still sceptical about osteosynthesis, an appreciable shift in opinion had occurred during the past five years; doctors were 'hungry' to learn good techniques and keen to attend courses, and many of the conservative chief surgeons were either retiring, or abandoning their unfavourable judgements.[79] According to James Hughes, who as an early AO proponent had experienced the technique's difficult reception process in America, by the late 1990s the AO system was the undisputed 'standard of care for fractures' in the United States.[80]

Thus the AO finally managed to convince the majority of American surgeons of their system. In the 1980s and 1990s an increasing number of surgeons had gained sufficient competence in using the AO technique and helped to spread it among their colleagues. In other countries the AO had been able to build up a network for the controlled transmission of skill and knowledge very rapidly. Under the specific cultural and economic conditions of the USA it took them more than two decades.

Conclusion

Both the USA and the GDR seemed to offer favourable initial conditions for introducing the AO technique: on a general level, in both countries the rising number of accident victims provided good reasons for demanding high quality fracture care; regarding its starting position in both countries, the AO contacted with young innovative surgeons early on, affording the Swiss surgeons the opportunity to win over a new generation of colleagues. Despite these similarities, the AO surgeons met very different challenges in the USA and the GDR when propagating their technique.

In the GDR, against considerable economic obstacles, the AO method was rapidly introduced, though in limited quantities, and was applied very successfully. Against the background of the East German state pursuing a policy of tight centralized control of the health care system, the East German AO section was part of the official health care administration and as such it was endowed with the means to oversee the application of the AO technique by individual surgeons. Paradoxically, scarcity further facilitated control. Since the AO equipment was very expensive, the economic conditions of state socialism restricted access to it. The instruments were not freely available, but were bought and distributed by central agencies. Effectively, one surgeon was in charge of the distribution of almost all the AO equipment in the country. He was able to select those colleagues he knew would make good use of the material and who were prepared to undergo prior intensive training. Certainly, the socialist system posed a number of problems to the extension of the AO network: travelling was quite restricted, foreign books and journals were hardly available, and the rationale of communist politics often threatened to prevail over the rationality of surgery, for instance when important positions within the health care system were assigned according to political loyalty instead of expert competence. But in the end the beneficial effects of scarcity and the central concentration of power apparently outweighed the negative effects of the communist system.

The opposite was the case in the USA. In the USA the AO equipment was freely available and it was used by surgeons who were not familiar with the technique. The application of the AO system of osteosynthesis by incompetent surgeons led to poor results in bone healing and a high rate of complications. As a consequence, osteosynthesis in general, and the AO technology in particular, acquired a bad reputation and was largely rejected by the scientific authorities in the field. The critical point was that in the US context it was very difficult for the AO to oversee the application of its technology. As opposed to their European colleagues, US surgeons were not willing to subject themselves voluntarily to surveillance. Even those American surgeons who did become foreign members of the AO did not tolerate the attempts of the Swiss AO surgeons to monitor their use of the technique. Other factors impeding the acceptance of the AO in the USA include the language barrier, the distrust of the surgical public towards doctors who co-operated with industry, the fear of malpractice suits in case of complications, and the much fiercer competition among manufacturers in the field of medical devices.[81]

Comparative examination thus underlines my general thesis that control of the materials and their application was the key to the successful introduction of osteosynthesis by the AO as opposed to previous less successful efforts. The AO introduced a new measure of control in different respects and on a number of different levels and this was the crucial factor for the AO's success in general.

This fits in with the view that, from a more general viewpoint, exercising control is one of the main thrusts of modern medical science and surgery. The scientific laboratory is specifically designed to subject life phenomena to the control of the experimenter. According to the rationale of experimentalism, under the controlled conditions of the laboratory scientists can affect the workings of the living organism at their discretion. The same type of power over processes of life is also being used by doctors in the clinical setting. Surgeons try to control structures of the patient's body with their hands and their instruments. Osteosynthesis, for instance, aims at controlling the position of bone fragments. Typically, innovative surgeons would first acquire this sort of control in laboratory animals and then extend it to their patients in the operating room.

From this perspective, what the AO did, was to extend the same principle of control to include not only body structures, such as bones, and life processes, such as bone healing, but also instrument manufacturers, patients, and other surgeons in the GDR and the USA. Extending control was the only way to successfully introduce the new technique. Comparison draws attention to the importance of power and control for understanding why certain innovations spread successfully in certain contexts or not.

This is not to say that all modern science and medicine depends as much on control as bone surgery. Nor does it mean that control is always the crucial factor for success. The GDR was obviously not the world's leading nation in science and medicine in general, nor was the USA a country in which medical techniques generally failed. But the paradoxical case of a modern, highly sophisticated technique that worked well in a relatively poor socialist country but failed to work in the world's wealthiest and scientifically most advanced nation directs attention to the more general fact that even such an apparently mechanical and culture-independent technique like osteosynthesis is highly culture-sensitive. In the three countries examined here, the very same technique fared very differently: in Switzerland the cultural pattern of the fraternity provided the opportunity for its controlled application, thus keeping the numbers of failures relatively low; in the GDR, the policy of tight centralized state control over health care providers accomplished the same objective with even more efficiency; by contrast, the free market conditions of the American health care system made control, and thus consistent success, extremely difficult. As comparative studies can show, the successful introduction of any medical technology depends utterly on the cultural, political, and economic environment in which it is being performed. But it is not clear in advance which environmental factors are beneficial or detrimental for a particular technique to succeed.

Notes

1 I am grateful to the AO Foundation for having funded the first three years of the research project, of which this chapter is one outcome. For the history of the AO see: T. Schlich, *Surgery, Science and Industry: A Revolution in Fracture Care, 1950s–1990s*, Basingstoke, Palgrave, 2002. For some data on the history of the AO, see R. Schneider, *25 Jahre AO-Schweiz. Arbeitsgemeinschaft für Osteosynthesefragen 1958–1983*, Biel, AO, 1983.
2 Cf. T. Schlich, 'Osteosynthese: Geschichte einer schwierigen Therapiemethode', *Jahrbuch des Deutschen Orthopädischen Geschichts- und Forschungsmuseums*, 2000. vol. 2, pp. 55–72.
3 For a detailed analysis of the Swiss context, see my forthcoming book (see note 1).
4 On comparison as an approach to research in the history of medicine in general, see L. Sauerteig, 'Vergleich: Ein Königsweg auch für die Medizingeschichte? Methodologische Fragen komparativen Forschens', in N. Paul and T. Schlich (eds), *Medizingeschichte: Aufgaben, Probleme, Perspektiven*, Frankfurt/Main, Campus, 1998, pp. 266–91.
5 My account of the GDR health care system is based on: *Sozialismus, wissenschaftlich-technische Revolution und Medizin. Rat für Planung und Koordinierung der medizinischen Wissenschaft beim Ministerium für Gesundheitswesen*, Berlin, VEB Verlag Volk und Gesundheit, 1968, pp. 76–80; L. Rohland and H. Spaar, *Die medizinisch-wissenschaftlichen Gesellschaften der DDR. Geschichte – Funktionen und Aufgaben*, Berlin, VEB Verlag Volk und Gesundheit, 1973, pp. 181–94, 205–10; K. Winter, *Das Gesundheitswesen in der Deutschen Demokratischen Republik*, Berlin, VEB Verlag Volk und Gesundheit, 1974, pp. 13–24; K. Pritzel, *Gesundheitswesen und Gesundheitspolitik der Deutschen Demokratischen Republik*, Berlin, Osteuropa-Institut 1977, pp. 29–34, 102–4; M. E. Ruban, *Gesundheitswesen in der DDR*, Berlin, Verlag Gebr. Holzapfel, 1981, pp. 177–90; L. Mecklinger, 'Das Gesundheitswesen der DDR – Konzept und Realität', in *Das Gesundheitswesen der DDR – zwischen Konzept und Realität*, Berlin, Wissenschaftliche Arbeitstagung der Interessengemeinschaft Medizin und Gesellschaft e.V. 26.11.1994, pp. 61–7, see p. 63; A.-S. Ernst, *'Die beste Prophylaxe ist der Sozialismus'. Ärzte und medizinische Hochschullehrer in der SBZ/DDR 1945–1961*, Münster, Waxmann, 1997, p. 334.
6 H. Brückner, *Frakturen und Luxationen*, Berlin, VEB Verlag Volk und Gesundheit, 1969, Preface (no page numbers given). For figures, see Winter, *Das Gesundheitswesen*, pp. 112–18. See also letter H. Willenegger to E. Sander, 24 April 1979. If not stated otherwise, the archival material located at the AO archives, Davos, files 'DDR 1975–1980', 'DDR 1981–1987' and 'DDR 1988–1992'.
7 H. Uebermuth, 'Wandlungen der Knochenbruchbehandlung im 20. Jahrhundert', *Beiträge zur Orthopädie und Traumatologie*, 1975, vol. 22, pp. 202–8, see p. 206. On economic considerations and the loss of working capacity due to illness and disability in the GDR health care system in general, see K.-D. Müller, 'Die Ärzteschaft im staatlichen Gesundheitswesen der SBZ und der DDR 1945–1989', in R. Jütte (ed.), *Geschichte der deutschen Ärzteschaft. Organisierte Berufs- und Gesundheitspolitik im 19. und 20. Jahrhundert*, Cologne, Deutscher Ärzte-Verlag, 1997, pp. 243–73, see p. 247. For the rise of interest in fracture care in the earlier English context, see R. Cooter, *Surgery and Society in Peace and War: Orthopaedics and the Organization of Modern Medicine, 1880–1948*, Basingstoke, Macmillan Press, 1993, pp. 147–51.

   The general growth of interest in improved fracture care is dealt with in detail in my book (cf. note 1).

8 G. Hildebrandt, Sektion der AO-International, Entwicklung und aktueller Stand, typewritten manuscript for a speech given in Halle on 21 December 1987, p. 2, from the personal papers E. Sander generously made available to me. The personal papers will subsequently be quoted as ES, the paper as 'Hildebrandt 1987'.

9 Autobiographical report by E. Sander 1999, ES, subsequently quoted as 'Sander 1999'. E. Sander, 'Concluding report on my term of office as chairman of the GDR section of the AO International', 26 September 1990, AO archives, in the following quoted as 'Sander 1990'. I also used information from my interview with Sander, 8 April 1999, in Halle and from subsequent letters.

10 Sander 1999, p. 2.

11 Hans Willenegger/Robert Schneider, 'On the occasion of Professor Sander's 65th birthday', typewritten manuscript, 1987.

12 E. Sander, 'Reasons for the usefulness of the acceptance of our work group for operative fracture care into the AO International', typewritten manuscript, 17 October 1974, in the following quoted as 'Sander 1974'. Willenegger/Schneider 1987; Sander 1990; Sander 1999, p. 2.

13 'Arbeitsordnung der Arbeitsgemeinschaft für operative Knochenbruchbehandlung in der Sektion Traumatologie der Gesellschaft für Chirurgie der DDR', 13 December 1968 (ES).

14 Rohland/Spaar, *Die medizinisch-wissenschaftlichen Gesellschaften*, pp. 108, 123, 303. Winter, *Das Gesundheitswesen*, p. 196.

15 Arbeitsordnung 1968; Hildebrandt 1987; Sander 1999.

16 Hildebrandt 1987, p. 1.

17 Domestic production of osteosynthesis materials was difficult. By 1972, the AO manufacturers considered the GDR incapable of producing instruments and implants of an acceptable quality. They also ruled out co-operation with East German producers (something that in other countries was often arranged on the basis of a licensing agreement) because of the poor quality of the steel available in the GDR. (Letter M. Madl to H. Willenegger, 14 September 1972.) In the early 1980s the Ministry obliged the surgeons to buy osteosynthesis instruments from a factory in Thuringia (Report by Werner Christenat on his conversation with E. Sander on 6 June 1982; Report by H. Willenegger on the II. Symposium of the GDR Section of the AOI in Potsdam, 4–6 October 1983), but the inferior quality of the East German products was so obvious that even the most fervent Party members wished to carry on working with the AO equipment (Reports by H. Willenegger on conversations with H. Sander and W. Senst on 14 December 1982, on his GDR trip on 8–15 September 1983, and on the II. Symposium of the GDR section of the AOI in Potsdam, 4–6 October 1983); for more details, see the GDR chapter of my book (note 1 above).

18 Sander 1999, pp. 4–5.

19 Sander 1999, pp. 5–6. Sander explained his policy also in the interview with T. S. on 8 April 1999.

20 Other examples include the introduction of the antibiotic drug streptomycin in the 1940s in the USA, see H. M. Marks, *The Progress of Experiment: Science and Therapeutic Reform in the United States, 1900–1990*, Cambridge and New York, Cambridge University Press, 1997, pp. 121–6.

21 *Aktuelle Probleme der Gesundheitspolitik und Aufgaben der Parteiorganisationen*, Berlin, Dietz Verlag, 1985, p. 33.

22 Uebermuth, 'Wandlungen', pp. 207–8.

23 Hildebrandt 1987, pp. 2–3. See also my interview with E. Sander, Halle, 8 April 1999.

24 Hildebrandt 1987, p. 3.

25 Sander 1990. Sander 1999, p. 8.

26 Brückner, *Frakturen und Luxationen*, p. 60. Uebermuth, 'Wandlungen', pp. 206–7. F. Mörl, *Lehrbuch der Unfallchirurgie*, Berlin, VEB Verlag Volk und Gesundheit, 1968, pp. 155, 161.
27 Sander 1999, p. 8.
28 Sander 1974. Willenegger/Schneider 1987.
29 'Further measures to carry out the socio-political programme of the VIIIth SED Party Conference. Joint decision of the "Politbüro des ZK der SED", the council of GDR ministers and the FDGB committee', 25 September 1973. Copy sent to H. Willenegger by W. Wehner in 1974. E. Fischer, L. Rohland and D. Tutzke, *Für das Wohl des Menschen. Dokumente zur Gesundheitspolitik der sozialistischen Einheitspartei Deutschlands*, Berlin, VEB Verlag Volk und Gesundheit, 1979, pp. 189, 191.
30 Hildebrandt 1987, p. 4.
31 Minutes of the Technical Commission (TK), 24 November 1972, p. 14. 'Wir haben noch *nie* eine so präzise Anwendung gesehen; die Systematik ist bewundernswert.'
32 Minutes of the AO meeting (AO), 6 April 1974, adm. Session, annex 1: annual report 1972/73, p. 8.
33 Letter H. Willenegger to E. Sander, 1 July 1975.
34 Letter U. Heim to E. Sander, 3 October 1990. Willenegger proposed to keep up the East German AO's status as an autonomous AO section, letter to E. Sander, 10 April 1990.
35 Despite the East German surgeons' eagerness to use the new technique, decisions to apply osteosynthesis were made rather restrictively, as Sander stated in retrospect. Sander 1999, p. 4.
36 R. Schneider, *10 Jahre AO. Jubiläumsbericht herausgegeben aus Anlaß des zehnjährigen Bestehens der 'Schweizerischen Arbeitsgemeinschaft für Osteosynthesefragen'*, AO-Dokumentationszentrale, Bern, 1969, pp. 8, 52; Schneider, *25 Jahre*, p. 141. List of participants for the first AO course; see also my interview with Howard Rosen, 16 December 1997.
37 Schneider, *10 Jahre*, pp. 9–10. J. P. Harvey Jr., 'Experto Credite. Editorial Comment', *Contemporary Orthopaedics*, 1984, vol. 8, no. 6, p. 13.
38 A. H. Crenshaw (ed.), *Campbell's Operative Orthopaedics*, 2 vols, 4th edn, St Louis, The C. V. Mosby Company, 1963, pp. 34–5.
39 P. Starr, *The Social Transformation of American Medicine: The Rise of a Sovereign Profession and the Making of a Vast Industry*, New York, Basic Books, 1982, pp. 337–51, 374–8.
40 S. R. Gaston, 'The role of leadership in the quality of fracture care', *Bulletin of the American College of Surgeons*, November 1975 (reprint).
41 D. D. Trunkey, 'Trauma', *Scientific American*, August 1983, vol. 249, no. 2, pp. 20–7; T. G. Shires, 'Care of the injured in America: organizational and physiological considerations', in R. Maulitz (ed.), *Unnatural Causes: The Three Leading Killer Diseases in America*, New Brunswick, NJ, Rutgers University Press, 1989, pp. 20–7.
42 O. P Hampton and W. T. Fitts, *Open Reduction of Common Fractures*, New York and London, Grune and Stratton, 1959, p. vi; retrospectively, M. Allgöwer, 'Cinderella of surgery – Fractures?', *Surgical Clinics of North America*, 1978, vol. 58, pp. 1071–93, see p. 1071.
43 Interview T. S. with James Hughes, 15 December 1998. Interview T. S. with Joseph Schatzker, 16 December 1998.
44 As opposed to Switzerland and the GDR, in the USA acute fractures were mostly treated by orthopaedic surgeons.
45 J. R. Moore, 'The closed fracture of the long bones', *JBJS*, 1960, vol. 42-A, pp. 869–74, quotations from pp. 872 and 874.
46 Crenshaw, 4th edition, 1963, pp. 48, 374 (quotation).
47 Retrospectively: Anon., 'Cast banishment? The AO method of internal fixation', *Lynn Magazine*, Winter–Spring 1982, pp. 1–3, H. Willenegger, report on a conversation

with Dr Lawson, 14 October 1983, AO archives, Davos, file 'Synthes USA Allgemeines 1981–1983', subsequently quoted as 'USA 1'; Letter Prof. Dr B. Friedrich, Bremen, to H. Willenegger, 6 April 1982, USA 1. Interview T. S. with Marvin Tile, 16 December 1998.

48 R. G. Eaton, 'Book review. The Technique of Internal Fixation of Fractures. M. E. Müller, M. Allgöwer, and H. Willenegger, New York, Springer-Verlag 1965', *JBJS*, vol. 47-A (1965), p. 1293.

49 Though these studies worked with exact quantitative data, the causes of failure could not easily be documented and quantified and are more or less based on the personal impressions of the authors. M. J. Stewart, D. T. Sisk and S. L. Wallace, 'Fractures of the distal third of the femur', *JBJS*, 1966, vol. 48-A, pp. 799–800; C. S. Neer, S. A. Grantham and M. L. Shelton, 'Supracondylar fracture of the adult femur: a study of one hundred and ten cases', *JBJS*, 1967, vol. 49-A, pp. 591–613, especially pp. 600–12.

50 J. Wickstrom, L. Hamilton and R. P. Rodriguez, 'Evaluation of the AO compression apparatus', *Journal of Trauma*, 1967, vol. 7, pp. 210–24, and the minutes of the subsequent discussion, ibid., pp. 224–7.

51 P. A. Wade, 'ASIF Compression has a problem', *Journal of Trauma*, 1979, vol. 10, pp. 513–15.

52 See e.g. E. A. Nicoll, 'Closed and open treatment of tibial fractures', *Clinical Orthopaedics and Related Research*, 1974, vol. 105, pp. 144–53, see pp. 144, 151–3; C. A. Rockwood and D. P. Green, *Fractures*, 2 vols, Philadelphia and Toronto, J. B. Lippincott Company, 1975, pp. 50–8, 66–7, 72.

53 A. H. Crenshaw (ed.) *Campbell's Operative Orthopaedics*, 5th edition, St Louis, the C. V. Mosby Company, 1971, pp. 477–691, quotation ibid., p. 477.

54 H. S. Dodge and G. W. Cady, 'Treatment of fractures of the radius and ulna with compression plates', *JBJS*, 1972, vol. 54-A, pp. 1167–76, see p. 1172.

55 B. R. Cahill and R. E. Palmer, *Dark Side of Davos*, typewritten manuscript, October 1976, AO archives, Davos, file 'USA Allgemein – 1981' subsequently quoted as 'USA 1'.

56 This refers to the cutting of screw threads into the bone prior to applying the screws which was a distinctive feature of the AO technique.

57 Cahill and Palmer, *Dark Side*; see also letter James E. Gerry to M. Allgöwer, 13 October 1976, USA 2; from 1960 to 1975, 1,116 Americans attended the Davos courses; from the mid-1970s AO courses in North America were held on a regular basis, Schneider, *25 Jahre*, p. 262; for the inception of the American course programme see the USA chapter of my book (note 1 above).

58 AO 6 April 1974, adm. session, suppl. 1: annual report 1972/73, p. 8.

59 H. Willenegger, memorandum on his experience in the USA, 12 July 1976, USA 2. See also T. S. interview with Marvin Tile, 16 December 1998.

60 H. Willenegger, report on a conversation with Dr Lawson, 14 October 1983, USA 1.

61 TK 24 April/8 May 1970, pp. 21–3.

62 Interview T. S. with Joseph Schatzker, 16 December 1998.

63 Interview T. S. with Howard Rosen, 16 December 1997.

64 Ibid. and interview T. S. with Joseph Schatzker, 16 December 1998.

65 Wickstrom *et al.*, 'Evaluation', and the minutes of the subsequent discussion. See also P. T. Naiman, A. J. Schein and R. S. Siffert, 'Use of ASIF compression lates in selected shaft fractures of the upper extremity: a preliminary report', *Clinical Orthopaedics and Related Research*, 1970, vol. 71, pp. 208–16; G. P. Crawford, 'Screw fixation for certain fractures of the phalanges and metacarpals', *JBJS*, 1976, vol. 58-A, pp. 487–92.

66 Interview T. S. with James Hughes, 15 December 1998.

67 Wickstrom *et al.*, 'Evaluation', p. 215.

68 Interview T. S. with James Hughes, 15 December 1998.

69 Crenshaw, 5th edition, 1971, pp. 45, 477, 522.

70 Interview M. E. Müller, 23 March 1999. The *JBJS* rather 'mirrored the conservative way of looking at fractures', as James Hughes put it (interview with T. S., 15 December 1998).

71 B. A. Rahn, P. Gallinaro, A. Baltensperger and S. M. Perren, 'Primary bone healing', *JBJS*, 1971, vol. 53-A, pp. 783–6.

72 S. Olerud and G. Karlström, 'Secondary intramedullary nailing of tibial fractures', *JBJS*, 1972, vol. 54-A, pp. 1419–28; S. Olerud, 'Operative treatment of supra-condylar-condylar fractures of the femur: technique and results in fifteen cases', *JBJS*, 1972, vol. 54-A, pp. 1015–32.

73 Crenshaw, 5th edition, 1971, p. 477; Olerud and Karlström, 'Secondary'; Olerud, 'Operative'; Dodge and Cady, 'Treatment'; J. Schatzker, G. Horne and J. Waddell, 'The Toronto experience with the supracondylar fracture of the femur 1966–72', *Injury*, 1974, vol. 6, pp. 113–28; L. Anderson, T. D. Sisk, R. E. Tooms and W. O. Park, 'Compression-plate fixation in acute diaphyseal fractures of the radius and ulna', *JBJS*, 1975, vol. 57-A, pp. 287–97.

74 G. S. Laros and P. G. Spiegel, 'Editorial comments: rigid internal fixation of frac-tures', *Clinical Orthopaedics and Related Research*, 1979, vol. 138, pp. 2–22, see pp. 2–3; M. Allgöwer and P. G. Spiegel, 'Internal fixation of fractures: evolution of concepts', ibid., pp. 26–9, see p. 28. J. Schatzker and D. C. Lambert, 'Supracondylar fractures of the femur', ibid., pp. 77–83. Schatzker's line of argument was obviously convincing, see R. D. Mize, R. W. Bucholz and D. P. Grogan, 'Surgical treatment of displaced, comminuted fractures of the distal end of the femur', *JBJS*, 1982, vol. 64-A, pp. 871–9, see p. 877.

75 A. S. Edmonson and A. H. Crenshaw (eds) *Campbell's Operative Orthopaedics*, 2 vols, 6th edition, St Louis and Toronto and London, the C. V. Mosby Company, 1980, pp. 508–71. The AO technique and its theoretical basis had become 'conventional wisdom' by then; interview T. S. with Marvin Tile, 16 December 1998.

76 T. G. Grace and W. W. Eversmann, 'Forearm fractures. Treatment by rigid fixation with early motion', *JBJS*, 1980, vol. 62-A, pp. 433–8.; Rand *et al.*, 'Comparison'; Mize *et al.*, 'Surgical treatment'; P. J. Stern, D. A. Mattingly, D. L. Pomeroy, E. J. Zenni and J. K. Kreig, 'Intramedullary fixation of humeral shaft fractures', *JBJS*, 1984, vol. 66-A, pp. 639–46.

77 Grace and Eversmann, 'Forearm fractures', p. 434.

78 Anon., 'Cast banishment? The AO method of internal fixation', *Lynn Magazine*, Winter–Spring 1982, pp. 1–3, USA 1.

79 Minutes of the AO meeting, 11–12 November 1983, p. 12.

80 Interview T. S. with James Hughes, 15 December 1998.

81 These are treated in detail in the USA chapter of my book (note 1 above).

Part III

Re-innovation and the state

6 Representing medicine

Innovation and resistance in 1950s Britain

Kelly Loughlin

Innovation, in the sense of 'introducing something new', whether in the sphere of medicine, policy or technology, is now a highly constructed or managed process.[1] Likewise, effective resistance to a particular innovation draws upon a range of resources, such as media advisors, specialized public relations expertise and professional campaign managers.[2] As this brief list of professionals and advisors suggests, a complex industry of image and information management has developed in the interstices of expert, state-administrative and public cultures. This development has a relatively short history, and has been the subject of sociological rather than historical enquiry.[3] Indeed, in Britain at least, the emergence of media advisors and professional public relations was primarily a post-war development. In what follows, I outline the emergence of a particularly important player in the circulation of health and medical information in post-war Britain, the British Medical Association (BMA). The development of press and public relations work within the BMA was given a particular boost in the second-half of the 1950s by controversy over the 'introduction of something new', a television documentary about the services on offer throughout Britain's hospital system.

Medicine and television

As a forum for public presentations of medical practice and medical knowledge, broadcast television is a relative newcomer. Television transmission began in Britain in 1936, was halted by World War II and re-started in 1946. The television portrayal of medicine was a development shaped by existing conventions regarding the representation of medicine *per se*, by the numerous and often conflicting agendas of post-war broadcasting, and by a medical profession adjusting to the newly implemented National Health Service (NHS) in 1948. Amidst these developments a particular event stands out, frequently recalled by contemporaries and given the significance of a touchstone in scholarly accounts of this period.[4] The event in question is the first series of *Your Life in Their Hands* (hereafter YLITH) broadcast in the spring of 1958 by the British Broadcasting Corporation (BBC). Its particularity revolves around two possibly interrelated points: YLITH offered the viewing public footage of surgical operations in progress, and it provoked fierce condemnation from leading voices in the medical profession.

Unpacking the controversy over YLITH is the chief concern of this chapter. This exercise is productive in many ways, not least for the questions it raises about the way historians approach audio-visual sources and, more substantively, for the way it begins to map out the complex territory of medical–media relations in post-war Britain. I begin by describing the first series of YLITH and move on to consider available accounts of the subsequent controversy. These accounts are then developed through a discussion of the broader context of medical–media relations, an area that has, as yet, received little scholarly attention. However, I will argue that the controversy surrounding YLITH can only be fully explained in relation to contemporary developments in the culture and organization of medical communication.

The series in question consisted of ten half-hour programmes, almost all of which were transmitted live as outside broadcasts. YLITH went out at 9.30 p.m. Tuesday evenings, 11 February–15 April 1958, with the bulk of the programmes coming from regional hospitals, although one featured the work of general practitioners attached to a cottage hospital. Bill Duncalf, a producer working within Outside Broadcasts was responsible for the series, and its driving force, although the responsibility for medical programmes as such rested with Mary Adams, head of the Talks Department, and she oversaw much of the planning (and controversy).

Titles, locations and topics for *Your Life in Their Hands*, BBC (1958)

'Breath of Life', Oxford, Churchill Hospital (poliomyelitis, iron lung)
'Ray of Hope', Manchester, Christie Hospital (cancer treatment, radium, x-ray)
'A New Lease of Life', Birmingham, Queen Elizabeth Hospital (rheumatic fever, mitral valvotomy)
'Out on a Limb', Cornwall, Cottage Hospital (general practice, cottage hospital)
'Thought is the Seed of Action', Edinburgh, Royal Infirmary (brain function)
'The Ever-Lessening Shadow', Glamorgan, Sully Hospital (tuberculosis prevalence and treatment)
'Diverting the Stream', Bristol, Royal Infirmary (malfunctioning liver)
'The Fires of Life', Glasgow, Western Infirmary (thyroid deficiency)
'Machinery for Living', Glasgow, Western Infirmary (artificial kidney machine, heart/lung machine)
'Looking to the Future', Glamorgan, Llandough Hospital (preventive medicine and pneumoconiosis)

The purpose of the series was, 'To see research and treatment in Provincial Hospitals and to demonstrate the fact that the most up-to-date Hospital treatment can be obtained outside London'.[5] Dr Charles Fletcher presented each programme from the Hammersmith Hospital, London, introducing the topic then handing over to the medical team of the respective hospital for the rest of the programme. The average audience for YLITH was approximately 8.25 million.[6] Its novelty lay in the portrayal of actual surgical procedures, a first for British television. Of the ten programmes, three included filmed inserts of stages in certain operations: the diversion of the blood supply to the liver, the removal of a blood clot and a mitral valvotomy. These inserts drew particular criticism in the controversy following the launch of the series.

The main thrust of the attack on YLITH came from the BMA, although it became the focus of heated debate at the Royal College of Surgeons, and the subject of an adjournment debate in the House of Commons.[7] A series of editorials in the *British Medical Journal* (BMJ) entitled 'Disease Education by the BBC' expressed the main tenets of the BMA's condemnation of YLITH:

> The treatment of disease is first and foremost a highly individual matter between the doctor and the patient, part and parcel of what is meant when we talk about the doctor–patient relationship. Because the hospitals are now owned by the State, and therefore the owner, the Ministry of Health, can give a national broadcasting corporation permission to enter the public wards does not justify the intervention of the television camera in the doctor–patient relationship ... What they are exhibiting on the television screens all over the country is not solely and simply Mrs. X's heart operation, or Mr. Y's cirrhotic liver. They are by this means intervening in the doctor–patient relationship of other practising doctors.[8]

The quotation brings together the BMA's main concerns over YLITH. First, as the title 'disease education' indicates, and as the editorial went on to argue, health was considered a less contentious and more seemly topic for television than disease; by 'disease education' the editorials seem to mean actual medical practice, consultations and the activities within hospitals.[9] Second, the detailed presentation of treatment and prognosis was seen to undermine medical authority, especially the authority of individual general practitioners. Complaints from individual practitioners were cited as evidence for incursions into the doctor–patient relationship:

> The first letter in our correspondence columns this week points the dilemma: as a result of a television programme the patient guessed correctly that he was suffering from cancer, a diagnosis which in the interest of the patient the practitioner had not disclosed to him.[10]

Third, as the reference to the State and the Ministry of Health indicate, broader issues of control and authority were raised by 'the fact that it [the BBC] is going to show real operations, by real doctors, on real patients'.[11] The *owner* of the hospitals (the Ministry of Health) had given permission for the cameras to enter hospitals and the only way the BMA could exercise any influence over this development, it seemed, was through its support for the ethical embargo against 'indirect advertising'; a General Medical Council rule that deterred many practitioners from appearing in the media at this time:

> Though the anonymity of the doctor is being preserved – for what that is worth in this publicity-seeking age – their colleagues may well think it is demeaning for doctors and nurses to appear as mummers on the television screen.[12]

Indeed, senior colleagues warned the presenter of YLITH, Charles Fletcher, that his involvement with television could undermine his future career.[13]

The controversy surrounding YLITH and the three concerns outlined above are touched upon in studies by Anne Karpf and Ghislaine Lawrence.[14] Karpf's account locates YLITH within her study of the development of media coverage of health and medicine from the 1930s to the 1980s. Karpf contrasts YLITH with an earlier radio tradition of 'health talks' extolling a look-after-yourself approach, and sees the series as heralding the rise of a 'medical approach' that focused on hospital-based, curative medicine. Her understanding of the BMA's response to YLITH is shaped by knowledge of what came after i.e. the second series, screened in 1961. The second series was markedly different in that it focused exclusively on the London teaching hospitals and increased the number of surgical sequences shown:

> There was another difference in the second series. This time, the programmes came with the imprimatur of the medical profession. The BMA blessed them in advance, announcing that, 'We are glad to see any attempt to extend people's knowledge of what really goes on in hospitals' … The doctors had been co-opted.[15]

This turnaround adds weight to Karpf's claim that the BMA's response to the original 1958 series was motivated largely by a sense of exclusion – had they been consulted beforehand, then the whole dispute could have been avoided. She goes on to note that in retrospect, 'what's surprising is how few doctors awoke to the potential public relations role it [television] would play for the medical profession'.[16] This lack of media savvy or public relations acumen is all the more surprising given that – according to Karpf – in the eyes of the media, the BMA and the medical profession had 'largely replaced the Ministry of Health as the pressurising body to be soothed and placated'.[17] According to this view, the medical profession had, by the second series of YLITH, become the main arbiters of what was acceptable for a lay television audience.

I shall return to Karpf's claims shortly, but here I want to outline Lawrence's account of the controversy. Lawrence's account is more tightly focused, in that it explores the particularities of the medium (television) and the form (documentary) which distinguished YLITH from other public displays of medicine. She contrasts the new representational possibilities raised by television documentary with more established static presentations of medicine in exhibitions and museums.

In her analysis Lawrence focuses on the filmed inserts of operations in progress, highlighting the fact that they offered the viewing public chunks of 'actuality footage', i.e. a sequence of action that was obviously less rehearsed and less formally structured than the ward scenes or the sequences where doctors addressed the camera directly. According to Lawrence, the use of actuality footage exacerbated established concerns about the lack of control associated with broadcasting generally. These concerns related to the distributed nature of the radio and television audience; the unique conditions of listening and viewing that broadcast technology had brought into being. Broadcasting raised the problem of how to maintain social relations of authority, or how to limit or prescribe the kinds of meanings that were imparted to an absent audience, an audience that was not co-present. The classic illustration of such concerns occurred in 1923, when the BBC were nor allowed to transmit the marriage service of the Duke of York for fear that men in public houses would listen with their hats on.[18]

This lack of control over the distributed audience contrasts sharply with Lawrence's counterpoised example, the museum:

> Television documentary provided what museums conventionally removed from their artefacts – a context of use. In doing so, it provided, almost entirely by non-verbal means, new forms of knowledge about medical practice. Museum objects taken out of their context in museums, could convey virtually any message at all.[19]

The *new forms of knowledge about medical practice* were those conveyed in the actuality footage:

> It was the element derived from documentary ... the element which rooted the activity in some form of social reality ... Gestures, tones of voice and use of language could reveal something of the surgical team's attitudes to each other, to their patients and to their instruments.[20]

As Lawrence notes, no one challenged the accuracy of what was seen in the inserts, the challenging issue was whether the public should have access to such raw and unstructured medical activity.

Lawrence's somewhat incongruous pairing (between museums and documentary) is productive, because it helps us to think about the rather awkward phrase conjured up in the *BMJ* editorials: 'disease education'. In essence, the 'actuality' footage was not framed by the accepted, didactic relations of public education – nor could it be. Public education in health, characterized by the conventions of the lecture and exhibition, lacked the problem of an absent audience, and other vehicles like the radio 'talk' and instructional film used modes of address that positioned the audience in ways that sought to reproduce accepted didactic relations of authority.[21] Looked at in this way one can begin to appreciate the impact the filmed inserts might have had, and why the curious notion of 'disease education' was invoked – commentators in the *BMJ* could not frame this footage as educational or beneficial for a lay audience.

The accounts provided by Karpf and Lawrence are valuable, although I would hesitate to place so much emphasis on the 'actuality' footage as the engine of the subsequent controversy; and the claim that the BMA response was motivated by a sense of exclusion needs considerable unpacking. In approaching the controversy over YLITH I want to highlight the problem of allowing television to stand as a metonym for the media as a whole, and the need to separate out the BMA from the medical profession as such. Unpacking these distinctions, in relation to YLITH, requires an awareness of the context of medical–media relations in 1950s' Britain. Moreover, an awareness of this context begins to pave the way for a much clearer understanding of the BMA's response. A good point of entry, and one that enables distinctions between the BMA and 'medicine' and television and 'the media' to be drawn out, is to consider the media activities of the BMA and the particularity of its relationship with the emerging medium of television.

Medicine and the media

Prior to the events of 1958 the BMA had developed a very distinct style of press and public relations (PR) work.[22] The PR activities of the BMA were defensive in origin; in as much as they were developed in relation to the Beveridge Report (1942) and the planned implementation of the NHS.[23] In 1943 the BMA's propaganda offensive was anchored around a designated committee, the public relations committee, and in 1947 a full-time public relations officer (PRO) was appointed, John Pringle. The PR section, as it developed under Pringle, fulfilled the vision laid out in the first meeting of the PR committee in 1943 by creating an effective mechanism 'for the collection and collation of medical intelligence'.[24] A short-lived publication *PR News* began in 1947, as a means of keeping honorary PR secretaries in the divisions of the BMA up-to-date with the latest posters, charts and booklets explaining the NHS.[25] Moreover, the PR 'department' introduced an information service for press enquiries in 1947, which by 1949–50 was receiving one hundred phone calls a week plus correspondence and personal enquiries. *A Medical Information Service*, the pamphlet advertising the BMA's 'clearing-house' for medical intelligence announced the availability of their free service:

> A new service is now available in the London district. It is already widely used by the National Press, by the London representatives of the World Press and by many official bodies, business firms and voluntary organisations. Information is supplied on all subjects within the general field of medicine and public health ... Articles in the medical press are indexed and a catalogued file of press cuttings on all branches of medicine is maintained.[26]

By the early 1950s Pringle was sending circulars to the national press listing forthcoming medical conferences in the UK and abroad, noting that 'these lists are maintained by my department and issued, free of charge, to selected persons and organisations ... These lists are believed to be the most complete of their kind in the country.'[27]

Pringle was instrumental in the BMA's expanding PR activities and, although it lost the propaganda war over the NHS, it had, almost by default, developed a unique and accessible news and information service. Other medical–professional organizations, such as the Royal Colleges, had nothing comparable to the BMA; and the Ministry of Health press office, headed by Stephen Heald, a civil servant, is described by Fleet Street journalists active at the time as 'helpful but not forthcoming'.[28] However, the important point to note about the BMA's press and PR function under Pringle is that it was interested primarily in 'news' management and, consequently, its focus was on the press and to a lesser extent radio. This pattern was largely an historical legacy, reflecting the development and organization of news reporting in Britain. Up until the mid-1950s 'news' was an activity firmly anchored around the print press; radio was a recent player in the field owing to its emergence as a news vehicle during the war. Television news was a relative late comer, one associated with the development of commercial television after 1955 and the pioneering efforts of Independent Television News.[29]

For much of Pringle's career, television had been a marginal medium, a poor relation of radio. The BBC hierarchy was dominated by radio personnel in the late 1940s and early 1950s, and radio's 'news function' was a jealously guarded aspect of it seniority. Pringle had no experience of television (news or otherwise) and in this respect he was very much a part of the old guard. His background was in print journalism, having worked as a leader writer at the *Manchester Guardian* in the early 1930s, and he later moved to BBC radio to produce a 'current affairs' style programme *The World Goes By*. During the war he was moved at his own request to the BBC news service of the Ministry of Information. In many ways Pringle's career was typical of the post-war expansion in PR and the emergence of the government's home information initiative, the origin of which lay in the wartime control of information. The overtly propagandist Ministry of Information was replaced in 1946 by a Central Office of Information. Indeed, Pringle's referee for the post at the BMA was none other than Sir Stephen Tallents, a Director General of the Ministry of Information.[30]

Politics and medico-politics in particular became Pringle's forte at the BMA. Moreover, 'medical news', had emerged as a specialist area of reporting alongside and in relation to the struggles surrounding the NHS, a development crystallized in the person of John Pringle.[31] Pringle cut his teeth at the Press Association and as a political and lobby correspondent at *The Times*. After the war he joined the *Daily Telegraph*, developed a particular interest in health services and the NHS, and went on to become its first Health Services correspondent in 1957. In the late 1940s and for most of the 1950s 'medical news', as such, *was* medico-politics and the NHS. Given his background and contacts within Whitehall and Fleet Street, Pringle became a key player on the medical–media interface. Indeed, I would argue that, thanks to Pringle, the BMA had become a more significant player than the Ministry of Health press office by at least 1954–5. It was the BMA's PR 'department' that negotiated a routine procedure for the release of information from hospitals at this time, arranging a meeting between representatives of the press and the profession, and drawing up guidelines that were subsequently ratified by the Ministry.[32] However, I would also argue that the BMA's position *vis-à-vis* the media at this time was based on its relationship with the press and not with television.

The YLITH controversy

With this in mind I want to return to Karpf's and Lawrence's explanations for the controversy over YLITH, i.e. the BMA's sense of exclusion from decisions surrounding the 1958 series, and the shock of the 'actuality' footage. From my reading of the debates and letters in the *BMJ* and the House of Commons Debate, the three filmed inserts used in the series were not *the* central concern, although I accept the novelty of surgery on television, and that the anticipation this created in the popular press placed YLITH under a spotlight. However, I believe that the points emphasized in the *BMJ* editorials (above) are equally representative of the kind of concerns expressed in the medical press and in Parliament. These concerns, however, were not specific to the 'actuality' footage, they had longer trajectories, especially the related issues of indirect advertising and releasing the kind of information that undermined the authority of the general practitioner.[33] Lawrence's analysis of the 'actuality' footage provides insights into the concern over what was suitable for a lay audience and what could be framed as educational. However, these concerns were not focused exclusively on the 'actuality' footage, as many practitioners could not frame the programme from Christie Hospital as beneficial or educational given contemporary reservations about 'cancer education'.[34]

Turning now to the BMA's sense of exclusion I believe it is worth asking, what exactly did they feel excluded from? Here, it should be emphasized that YLITH was part of a longer development in television portrayals of medicine. The 1958 series originated in an early set of programmes called *Thursday Clinic*, transmitted in 1954 and in 1956, which consisted of outside broadcasts from St Mary's Hospital Paddington. The work of NHS hospitals had also been seen in earlier programmes, such as *Matters of Life and Death* (1951) and *Matters of Medicine* (1952) and medical procedures (not major operations) were shown in *The Hurt Mind* (1957).[35] Initially, YLITH had the working title *Eye on Medicine*, a direct echo of the science series *Eye on Research* – an outside broadcast production that focused on medical research, produced by Aubrey Singer. Interestingly, the BMA did not respond to the forerunners of YLITH, despite the fact that NHS hospitals had been used and information that could and did inform patients over and above the authority of their general practitioners had been revealed. Moreover, the BMA had not been consulted over these programmes and, more importantly, it did not expect to be.

The process of consultation during the development of YLITH had been extensive. Bill Duncalf, who pushed for the 1958 series, arranged a meeting at the Ministry of Health on 30 July 1957:

> I met with Mrs. Mary Adams, Dr. Charles Fletcher, Mr. Stephen Heald and another representative of the Ministry of Health. Agreement was reached that such a series was desirable and the general method of presentation agreed with Dr. Fletcher. It was agreed that the general theme should be that no longer do 'all signposts lead to Harley Street for specialist treatment'.[36]

Fletcher, already a stalwart of medical broadcasting, especially through his involvement with *The Hurt Mind*, suggested several hospitals that might be included; suggestions were also put forward from the BBC regions. Directories of hospitals in England and Wales, and in Scotland were purchased and the BBC research unit identified the relevant people to be contacted. 'In every case an approach was first made to the Hospital Authorities and after agreement by the Board of Governors or the appropriate administrative officials, detailed discussion with the Medical, Surgical and Nursing Staff was begun.'[37] Advice was also sought from the Scientific Film Association, the Society for the Study of Medical Education and through the doctors who worked with the BBC on the series: Dr Charles Fletcher (presenter) and Mr A. G. Ellerker, a surgeon from Leicester General Hospital (medical advisor involved with script development).

A week before the first programme was aired a lunchtime conference was held at Lime Grove:

> The Royal College of Surgeons and the Royal College of Physicians were invited to come and in each case the Presidents nominated representatives. The College of General Practitioners and the Ministry of Health were also represented. *The BMJ was represented, not by its Editor, but by a correspondent.* The first edition of 'The Mitral Valvotomy Operation' was shown and comments invited on the propriety of showing it. Adverse opinion was not expressed.[38]

Throughout the meticulous and widespread consultation during the planning of YLITH, the idea of contacting the BMA was never an issue to the producer, or to Mary Adams, who had overall responsibility in matters medical. Moreover, eminent members of the BMA were involved in the programmes and it is unlikely that knowledge of the intended series had not reached at least some sections of the Association's central hierarchy. For example, the debate recorded in the Proceedings of Council contains the following statement from the President Elect: '[I] was one of those responsible for the televising of the mitral valvotomy', and that the discussion of the Council 'reflected closely the discussion at the medical advisory committee meeting when the project was considered'.[39] Given the fact that it was by no means routine for the BBC to approach the BMA as such, what then accounted for the Association's bluff and bluster over YLITH?

I would argue that this programme arrived at a pivotal point in the reorientation of the BMA's PR policy, a reorientation that was symptomatic of a more general acceleration in the publicity surrounding medical science in the latter half of the 1950s. What's more, it seems that John Pringle, the BMA's chief PRO, was a casualty of this reorientation. The index of this shift is discernible in the letters and debates that addressed YLITH in the medical press. On the one hand, some contributors speak of sensationalism and the ethicality of doctors appearing in such programmes; 'doctors decided just how much to tell each patient, but this was impossible with television'; more worrying still was the 'creation of television personalities within the profession'.[40] On the other hand, a more positive attitude to televising medicine is evident. One commentator noted that the profession 'had not done itself any good by suggesting that such programmes were a cheap form of public entertainment'.[41] Another stated that the BBC was 'doing something to satisfy an interest in scientific matters, and there was an era of new interest in any scientific advances'.[42] This theme was echoed elsewhere, 'It is not clear why we should call a growing desire to understand what goes on in nuclear physics as enlightenment and the same enquiry into medicine as morbid curiosity.'[43] Indeed, the preference for talk over action in television presentations of medicine was reversed by one commentator, 'doctors, as scientists, should be pleased to communicate their knowledge to others [but he wished that] there could be more demonstration and less talk on television'.[44]

A key motif in the positive response is the association with science and scientific advance, and this association was also evident in the shifting policy of the BMA's PR committee. Minutes of the PR committee record this shift from the mid-1950s. Amid discussion of whether the press should continue to be allowed into the Annual Representatives Meeting a specific dilemma was raised:

> To invite the Press to attend is merely asking the public to conclude that the profession is thinking about nothing – or scarcely anything – except its own material welfare ... If the Press were not allowed at the Annual Representatives Meeting it is highly probable that the total press 'coverage' of the Annual Meeting as a whole would be drastically curtailed.[45]

A decline in overall coverage was undesirable because:

> The fact should be plainly faced that at its present level of general appeal the Scientific Section of the meeting does not deserve much newspaper space ... the effect of excluding the Press from the Annual Representatives Meeting might mean a drastic fall in the publicity given to the Scientific Meeting.[46]

The minutes report that that year twenty-two newspapers and agencies sent representatives to cover the Annual Representatives Meeting, and although many stayed over to attend the scientific meeting, only three newspapers sent specialists to report specifically on the scientific meeting. Put briefly, the BMA and its annual meeting were first and foremost sources of medico-political news.

Since the Beveridge Report and on through their battles with the post-war Labour government, the public image of the BMA had become skewed towards issues of political conflict, remuneration and professional self-interest. Science, it seems, was a way to redress this situation. The 1955 discussion expressed this desire to increase

> the 'newsworthiness' of the Scientific Meeting so that, eventually, the interest of the BMA in medical science and medical progress would be seen by the public in its true value, whereupon the profession's legitimate concern for its own material rewards would automatically fall into correct proportion in our publicity.[47]

John Pringle urged such a policy, and his activities, such as the circular listing forthcoming medical conferences, were attempts to highlight the medical rather than the trade union side of the Association, although his focus was the press rather than television, as the circular and the 1955 discussion illustrate.

The interest in developing a public profile that associated the BMA with medical science and medical progress received a considerable boost in 1957–8 with the arrival of a new Secretary and Deputy Secretary, Derek Stevenson and John Havard. However, the new leadership pressed for a closer association with television and, I would suggest, although the minutes are circumspect on this issue, the departure of John Pringle. Pringle's position and the PR committee both came to an abrupt end in the winter of 1959–60, and the final discussion before the committee centred on the need to develop the new policy (high-lighting medical science). The minutes record the importance of developing BMA 'personalities', stating that 'television represents the most powerful medium through which the doctor can be presented to the public' and that 'what is now required is an opportunity to present the BMA to the public'. The programmes considered most suitable for this end were 'the BBC's *Panorama*, the *Brains Trust*, *Press Conference* and Independent Television's *This Week* and personal interviews'.[48] These were current affairs type programmes and it seems that what the BMA wanted was to present medical science as newsworthy and as something that was their legitimate territory. The personality who would repre-sent the BMA was not Pringle, his forte was medico-politics and Fleet Street, and it was doubted whether a lay man could push the scientific agenda. It was decided that a PRO was no longer necessary, indeed the Secretary himself would assume the Association's PR role.[49]

Interestingly, John Havard submitted a report to the PR committee in 1958–9 arguing that the BMA should be publishing reports on important public issues of the day. His provisional list of subjects included issues such as abortion, artificial insemination, euthanasia, family planning, heart disease and smoking and disease. He noted that 'it is a mistake to assume that just because the MRC or some other body has investigated a subject, there is nothing left to be said on it'. This was especially true for the issue of smoking: 'it is difficult to see how a BMA report on smoking and lung cancer could attract anything but the widest publicity ... even if it does no more than review the existing material'.[50] Producing a high impact report on a topic like smoking could and did attract the widest publicity, although it was the Royal College of Physicians, not the BMA, who took this step in their 1961 report.[51] Here, I would suggest that the BMA was not alone in developing a new style of PR, although its position as a source of medical science news had been sidelined in the immediate post-war years.

To those operating in the field of medical PR, or wanting to, in the second half of the 1950s YLITH was a golden opportunity. PR consultants Campbell-Johnson Ltd contacted Duncalf before the series went out, in the hope of arranging a dinner with Allen Duckworth, secretary of the Association of British Pharmaceutical Industries, 'to emphasise the part played by the Pharmaceutical Industry in the medical achievements you will be covering'.[52] Public Campaigners, PR consultants who handled the first International Hospital Equipment and Medical Services Exhibition also sought a tie-in with YLITH. The exhibition opened in London on 23 April 1958, and the correspondence sent to Duncalf emphasized that this was the *first* exhibition of its kind to be open to the public.[53] Moreover, the Royal College of Surgeons hosted a special PR lunch for broadcasters (not the press) because 'the need to increase the income of the College to finance the development of its work has persuaded its members to "lift the veil" on their work to the public'.[54] The BBC representative who attended the lunch reported on the address by the President of the RCS that 'we might look for full and willing co-operation in any series we in the BBC television service might be interested in doing'.

> I referred specifically to *Your Life in Their Hands*, pointing out that this type of programme was the best way to enlighten the public and interest them in the sort of work they at the College were doing. He [the appeals secretary] assured me that this was so.[55]

These events indicate that YLITH coincided with a broader reorientation in the public image of medical science. And I would suggest that a key element in the BMA's response to the series was part-and-parcel of its attempts to identify medical science and medical progress as an area in which it had a legitimate voice. The image of medical progress depicted in YLITH was *de facto* an image of a medical profession coming to grips with a National Health Service that was, by then, ten years old. In its portrayal of the profession YLITH was weighted towards hospital medicine, specialization and the consultant; one programme dealt with preventive medicine in the context of pneumoconiosis and one covered the work of general practitioners in a remote part of Cornwall. The depiction of general practice associated with a cottage hospital, entitled 'Out on a Limb', spoke of a lack of facilities and a shortage of staff. Charles Fletcher, writing to Duncalf, noted that, 'your choice of material, with the possible exception of Cornwall, was admirable'.[56] Michael Essex-Lopresti, the *Lancet*'s reviewer, noted that 'it was difficult to appreciate why it was included in the present series'.[57]

Conclusion

In the context of the 1950s YLITH was a politically fraught representation of British medicine. It many ways it could be seen as a hymn to the equitable provision of facilities throughout the NHS hospital system. After all, the Ministry of Health supported the idea of the series in a context where the lack of government expenditure on hospital building was a subject of debate and criticism about twentieth-century medicine taking place in nineteenth-century hospitals.[58] A commentator in the BMA debate also noted the role of YLITH as an advertisement for the NHS:

> The public were told that the hospitals belonged to them. They knew that they were spending £400m a year on those hospitals ... It seemed that it might be salutary from a public point of view if it was shown the elaborate care which was taken of patients *with no direct reference to the cost of it.*[59]

In its representation of hospital consultant and general practitioner, and through its presentation of the NHS as a national system of care it seems that controversy of some kind was almost a foregone conclusion, and the press interest surrounding the three filmed inserts provided a catalyst for this.

Unpacking the events surrounding the controversy over YLITH provides grist for a number of mills. Primarily it highlights the need to think of media portrayals of medicine or medical practice as the product of two interconnected spheres, medicine *and* the media. For historians, this requires a double or even a triple sense of context, i.e. the media context, the medical context and the context of a developing field of practice located at the interface between medicine and the media: medical press and PR. More specifically, for those interested in innovation, diffusion and resistance, especially in post-war medicine, this broader context of medical–media relations is particularly important. In relation to the United States, Dorothy Nelkin has drawn attention to a particular science and media relationship. For Nelkin the media is a potent vehicle for 'selling science' to various publics – garnering public support for particular research programmes and thereby helping to secure financial backing.[60] The case study presented here indicates the importance of the media and media management in constructing, contesting and negotiating the public image of hospital medicine in post-war Britain: introducing something new in medicine and in the media.

Notes

1   On the 'management of impressions' in the field of science and policy see S. Hilgartner, *Science on Stage: Expert Advice as Public Drama*, Stanford, CA, Stanford University Press, 2000.
2   There is an extensive literature concerned with information management and what sociologists describe as 'agenda setting' in the media and public policy fora. On large-scale information subsidies, especially in relation to health, see O. H. Gandy, *Beyond Agenda Setting: Information Subsidies and Public Policy*, Norwood, NJ, Ablex, 1982. For more specific UK studies, see D. W. Greenberg, 'Staging media events to achieve legitimacy: a case study of Britain's Friends of the Earth', *Political Communication and Persuasion*, 1985, vol. 2, pp. 347–62, M. McCarthy, *Campaigning for the Poor: CPAG and the Politics of Welfare*, Kent, Croom Helm, 1988. A good introduction to the issues involved in information management and media relations is contained in studies of the environment and environmentalism, A. Hansen (ed.), *The Mass Media and Environmental Issues*, Leicester, Leicester University Press, 1993, and A. Anderson, *Media, Culture and the Environment*, London, UCL Press, 1997.
3   On the development of public relations see J. Eldridge, J. Kitzinger and K. Williams, *The Mass Media and Power in Modern Britain*, Oxford, Oxford University Press, 1997, especially pp. 110–24.
4   For recollections of YLITH, by those involved in the series, see *Professor Charles Fletcher in interview with Max Blythe, Interview One*, Oxford Brookes University, Education Media Unit, 1985, and M. Essex-Lopresti, 'Medicine and television', *Journal of Audiovisual Media in Medicine*, 1997, vol. 20, no. 2, pp. 61–4. Charles Fletcher presented the programmes and Michael Essex-Lopresti was technical advisor. This series is commonly mentioned in historical studies that consider medicine in the 1950s, although the most developed accounts are A. Karpf, *Doctoring the Media: The Reporting of Health and Medicine*, London, Routledge, 1988 and G. Lawrence, 'Object lessons in the museum medium', in S. Pearce (ed.), *Objects of Knowledge*, London, Athlone, 1990, pp. 103–24.
5   Mary Adams, BBC Written Archives, Caversham (hereafter BBC) T14/1863/1 TV OB Your Life in Their Hands (hereafter YLITH) File 1. 'Your Life in Their Hands' OB Series on Provincial Hospitals, page 1. This description of the purpose of YLITH dates from after the transmission, although it is consistent with earlier descriptions.
6   *Your Life in Their Hands: An Enquiry into the Effects of the Television Series Broadcast in the Spring of 1958, Part II Additional Tables & Appendices*, London, BBC, 1958.
7   For a report of the debate by the Council of the BMA see 'Proceedings of Council', *British Medical Journal*, 1958, 1 March, pp. 89–92. For a report of the debate at the Royal College of Surgeons see *British Medical Journal*, 1958, 27 November, pp. 1351–2. For the adjournment debate see *Parliamentary Debates (Commons) Official Report, Fifth Series*, 1957–1958, vol. 583, pp. 688–700 and 1577–8.
8   *British Medical Journal*, 1958, 1 March, pp. 510–11, quote from p. 11. On 'disease education by the BBC', see also *British Medical Journal*, 1958, 15 February, pp. 388–9, 22 February, pp. 456–7, 22 February, pp. 449–50.
9   The issue of health rather than disease education was also expressed in the BMA debate on YLITH, see 'Proceedings of Council', *British Medical Journal*, 1958.
10   *British Medical Journal*, 1958, 1 March, pp. 510–11. Similar incidents were also reported in the House of Commons debate on YLITH.
11   *British Medical Journal*, 1958, 15 February, p. 388.
12   *British Medical Journal*, 1958, p. 388. On the development of the GMC's ethical guide-lines on medical advertising and self-promotion see A. Morrice, 'The medical pundits: doctors and indirect advertising in the lay press, 1922–1927', *Medical History*, 1994, vol. 38, pp. 255–80.

13 *Professor Charles Fletcher in interview with Max Blythe*, 1985.

14 Karpf, *Doctoring the Media*, Lawrence, 'Object lessons'.

15 Karpf, *Doctoring the Media*, p. 53.

16 Ibid., p. 52.

17 Ibid., pp. 53–4.

18 K. Wolfe, *The Churches and the British Broadcasting Corporation, 1922–1956*, London, SCM, 1984, p. 79.

19 Lawrence, 'Object lessons', p. 120.

20 Ibid., p. 120.

21 On public education in health see T. Boon, 'Film and the contestation of public health in interwar Britain', unpublished PhD thesis, University of London, 1990, and E. Lebas, 'When every street became a cinema: the film work of Bermondsey Borough Council's Public Health Department, 1923–1953', *History Workshop Journal*, 1995, vol. 39, pp. 42–66. A. Karpf's discussion of radio health talks is also useful.

22 On the history of the BMA, see P. Vaughan, *Doctors Commons: A Short History of the British Medical Association*, London, Heinemann, 1959; E. Grey-Turner and F. M. Sutherland, *History of the British Medical Association*, vol. II, 1932–1981, London, BMA, 1982.

23 On the publicity campaign that launched the NHS, see T. Wildy, 'From the MOI to the COI – publicity and propaganda in Britain, 1945–1951: the National Health and Insurance campaigns of 1948', *Historical Journal of Film, Radio and Television*, 1986, vol. 6, no. 1, pp. 3–16.

24 BMA archive, *Minutes of the Public Relations Committee, 1942–1943*.

25 BMA archive, *PR News*, 1 (April 1948); *Minutes of the Public Relations Committee, 1947–1948*.

26 BMA archive, 'A Medical Information Service' (leaflet); *Minutes of the Public Relations Committee, 1949–1950*.

27 BMA archive, Circular written by John Pringle, April 1951; *Minutes of the Public Relations Committee, 1950–1951*.

28 Interview by author with Ronnie Bedford, former science editor at the *Daily Mirror*, 11 September 1998.

29 For an account of the development of television news, written by a participant, see G. Cox, *Pioneering Television News: A First Hand Report of Revolution in Journalism*, London, John Libbey, 1995.

30 On the expansion of government information services, see J. Tulloch, 'Managing the press in a medium-sized European power', in M. Bromley and H. Stephenson (eds), *Sex, Lies and Democracy: The Press and the Public*, London, Longman, 1998, pp. 63–83. On the Ministry of Information and Stephen Tallents, see also M. Grant, *Propaganda and the Role of the State in Inter-War Britain*, London, Clarendon, 1994.

31 On the development of medical reporting in Fleet Street since the 1940s, see K. Loughlin 'Mediating medicine: doctors, journalists and the reporting of health and medicine in post-war Britain', paper presented at the Joint Conference of the European Association for the History of Medicine and Health and The International Network for the History of Public Health, Almuñécar, Spain, 5 September 1999.

32 On the meeting and the guidelines see *British Medical Journal*, 1955, 29 October, pp. 100–1.

33 Morrice, 'Medical pundits', 1994.

34 On 'cancer education' and the Christie programme see the debate from the Annual Representatives Meeting of the BMA in *British Medical Journal*, 1958, 19 July, pp. 54–5.

35 It is also interesting to note that birth had been shown on BBC television prior to the controversy surrounding YLITH, see *Panorama*, 4 February 1957.

36 Bill Duncalf, 'Medical Series – Your Life in Their Hands', 24 February (1958) BBC T14/1863/2 TV OB YLITH, File 2.

37 Mary Adams, 'Memo' (n/d), BBC T14/1863/2 TV OB YLITH, File 2, p. 1.
38 Mary Adams, 'Memo', (n/d) p. 2 (italics added). The editor of the *BMJ* was invited along with representatives of the medical press, and according to Michael Essex-Lopresti – a technical advisor on YLITH who attended the conference – the person sent by the *BMJ* was very junior; interview with author, 22 July 1999. Indeed, the person in question was Paul Vaughan, a press officer who worked with Pringle at the BMA; interview with author, 3 July 2000. In the controversy that ensued the BBC's process of consultation, including the conference, was dismissed by some as informal, see the statement on consultation by the Postmaster-General in *Parliamentary Debates (Commons) Official Report, Fifth Series*, 1957–58, vol. 583, pp. 1577–8.
39 Supplement to the *British Medical Journal*, 1958, 1 March, p. 91.
40 Report of the debate at the Royal Society of Medicine, *Lancet*, 1958, 29 November, p. 1171.
41 *British Medical Journal*, 1958, 19 July, p. 54.
42 *British Medical Journal*, 1958, 1 March, p. 90.
43 Letter in *British Medical Journal*, 1958, 13 December, p. 1472.
44 *Lancet*, 1958, 29 November, p. 1171.
45 BMA archive, *Minutes of the Public Relations Committee February 9th, 1955*.
46 Ibid., *Minutes of the Public Relations Committee February*.
47 Ibid., *Minutes of the Public Relations Committee February*.
48 BMA archive, *Minutes of the Public Relations Committee (1959–1960)*.
49 The documents are circumspect on Pringle's departure and the demise of the PRO role, although it has been suggested that Pringle was pushed rather than jumped; interview by author with Paul Vaughan, 3 July 2000.
50 BMA archive, *Minutes of the Public Relations Committee (1958–1959)*.
51 On the Royal College of Physicians 1961 Report, see V. Berridge, 'Passive smoking and its pre-history in Britain: policy speaks to science?', *Social Science and Medicine*, 1999, vol. 49, pp. 1183–95.
52 Letter to Duncalf, 15 January 1958, BBC T14/1863/1 TV OB YLITH.
53 Material relating to the exhibition is contained in BBC T14/1863/2 TV OB YLITH.
54 Memo to Duncalf, 19 September 1958, BBC T14/1863/2 TV OB YLITH.
55 Bill Duncalf, 'Memo', 19 September (1958) BBC T14/1863/2 TV OB YLITH. The appeals secretary at the RCS, W. F. Davis, was acting as the contact person for PR activities.
56 Bill Duncalf, Letter (n/d), BBC T14/1863/2 TV OB YLITH.
57 Michael Essex-Lopresti's review of the ten programmes was not published due to the controversy surrounding YLITH. Copies of the review and the correspondence with the *Lancet* in author's possession.
58 On debates about hospital building programmes, or the lack of them, see J. Hughes, 'The "matchbox on a muffin": the design of hospitals in the early NHS', *Medical History*, 2000, vol. 44, pp. 21–56.
59 *British Medical Journal*, 1958, 1 March, p. 91.
60 D. Nelkin, *Selling Science: How the Press Covers Science and Technology*, New York, W. H. Freeman, 1995.

7 The diffusion of two renal dialysis modalities in the UK, 1960s–1980s

Jennifer Stanton

This chapter looks at the diffusion of two technological innovations that perform essentially the same function, but which were introduced at different points in time. Successive innovations within the same field are not of course unusual. In medicine as elsewhere, quite often one innovation will be replaced by another, or they may co-exist. The 'sailing ship syndrome' is a phrase coined for the continued development of an essentially obsolete technology long after its successor comes on the scene.[1] This is not the case with the technologies discussed in this chapter; here, one innovation (haemodialysis) held sway for a couple of decades, and then another (CAPD: see below) came along, providing an alternative with different attractions and drawbacks. The second technology did not replace the first, which shows no sign of becoming obsolete. They overlap, not like steamship and sailing ship, one of which gradually took over, but as alternative modalities – that is, forms of medical technology performing the same purpose. The diffusion of each has been uneven, between regions of the UK, to an extent that could not be explained by any inherent differences in the needs of populations. There could be many ways of looking at this problem; the two that will be explored here are the role of the 'configured user', which will be introduced presently, and a more quantitative approach. Some context of policy developments will be provided. First, however, a little background on the technologies is in order.

The two innovations discussed here are treatments for kidney disease which has reached the point where the patient cannot long survive – what is often known as 'end-stage renal disease' or 'ESRD' in current terminology. Since we are thinking historically, the expression 'chronic renal failure' may be more helpful, to distinguish these conditions from (reversible) acute kidney failure. In either case, the history of the treatment technology to some extent determines our conception of the illness. As Steven Peitzman has pointed out, ESRD did not exist before dialysis.[2] Nor could the distinction between acute and chronic renal failure mean much before the time when artificial kidneys allowed people to survive short shocks that shut down the kidneys, while long-term disease still killed. In fact, the term 'treatment' is misleading with regard to chronic renal failure, since treatment implies cure, and this is not achieved by dialysis. What is achieved is maintenance of the patient, only so long as they keep coming back for dialysis. It is a classic example of what Lewis Thomas has termed a 'half-way technology' that produces an endless need for more of the same.[3] Another example, from the area of pharmaceutical technologies, would be beta-blockers for a patient with high blood pressure who may have to take them for the rest of his or her life. The big difference is that kidney dialysis is hugely expensive. Keeping a patient with chronic (as opposed to acute) renal failure alive this way imposes a great expense on the health care system.

There is another modality that is somewhat cheaper if it works: transplantation. But this was not very secure in the early period, is still not considered suitable for all patients, and above all there were not enough donor kidneys to cater for the demand. (See Chapter 9 by Gabolde and Moulin in this volume on the construction of a kidney shortage 'crisis'.) It should also be noted that patients often moved between modalities, including between dialysis and transplant (or 'graft') once or many times; but this chapter considers the diffusion of dialysis modalities *per se*, rather than patient careers.

Renal dialysis provides an alternative means to cleanse the blood of accumulated toxins that are filtered out by the normal kidney and excreted in the urine. Without some sort of filtration or dialysis, people die of uraemia (uric acid on the blood); patients in terminal renal failure in the past died as their skin became coated in crystals of 'uraemic frost'. Dialysis, like insulin in its time, must have seemed like a miracle when first introduced.[4] The two dialysis modalities discussed in this chapter are haemodialysis and continuous ambulatory peritoneal dialysis or CAPD. In haemodialysis, the patient's blood is channelled outside their body and through an artificial kidney that can take many shapes but is essentially an arrangement of semi-permeable membranes with blood on one side and a solution – dialysate – on the other, allowing concentrated molecules of unwanted substances in the blood to pass through, by osmosis, into the dialysate and be washed away.[5] In CAPD, no blood leaves the body. Instead, dialysate is poured into the patient's abdominal cavity through a tube in the belly, and a few hours later is drained away and replaced. The membranes that we all have lining the cavity act as the dialysis membranes. The tube has to be left in place and the process repeated several times a day.[6]

The essential innovation that allowed haemodialysis to be used for chronic kidney disease patients came in about 1960 in the USA and was adopted in the UK about 1964.[7] Haemodialysis remained almost the only modality of continuous dialysis (although there was some short-term peritoneal dialysis) until innovations in CAPD made this an acceptable alternative: the key 'advances' here were about 1978 and the diffusion of CAPD in the UK took off from about 1980, with acceleration in the mid-1980s. David Kerr, a leading British renal specialist, commented of CAPD: 'its expansion was phenomenal. In absolute numbers, its use expanded in Britain almost ten times as fast as haemodialysis in its early years.'[8]

Part of finding a way through the tangle of technological, policy, and clinical issues is to consider the continuum from manufacturer, developer, or innovator through to the user. Steve Woolgar and Keith Grint evolved the concept of 'configured user' in their work on the computer industry, where they felt it was an apt designation for the way the consumer, or user, was expected to adapt to the technology.[9] Designers were accustomed to thinking of the configuration, or most acceptable arrangement, of components of circuitry but they were unaware themselves (it took the sociologists infiltrating their domain to tease this out) that they expected consumers to conform to the demands of the machinery in pre-configured ways. To some extent there are different types of consumer, or user, in the world of information technology, but the differences are more marked in medicine where configured users may include doctors, nurses, technicians, and patients, or even perhaps managers.[10] Without wanting to overdo the analogy with Grint and Woolgar's computer users, it seemed productive to think about who among the potential users of dialysis was most 'configured' to adopt the technology, to adapt to it, and to turn to the alternative when it became available.

Who chooses which treatment to use? This is often presented in textbooks on renal treatment as though the doctor and patient choose in concert according to the patient's needs, with input from renal nursing staff, pharmacists, and social workers. In each individual case it may feel like this. But if we look at patterns of diffusion it is apparent that some wider forces are operating, unless we accept the unlikely proposition that patients in different regions of one country, or in different countries, are collectively more suited to one modality or another. Within the UK at the end of our period, Mersey region had 28 patients per million population (pmp) on CAPD while South East Thames had 85.[11] About the same time, as a proportion of patients undergoing treatment for ESRD, Mexico had 74 per cent on CAPD while Germany had 4 per cent; and in 1989, the USA had 17 per cent while the UK had nearly 50 per cent on CAPD.[12] Presumably something is going on besides clinical choice.

This chapter falls into three sections, starting with a brief review of shifts in policy to give a historic dimension of movement through time, together with the health service context into which the innovations in renal dialysis entered and through which they diffused. An element to bear in mind here is resistance by inertia, common in British policy history, especially in relation to the National Health Service (NHS). Then the notion of configured users is deployed in the second section to explore the question of who adapts to technology, bringing in issues of compliance and duress, and different experiences. But it also seemed necessary to consider larger economic forces that could influence uptake of a new dialysis technology, so the third section looks at counting in relation to dialysis – how estimates of numbers needing treatment shifted, costs escalated, and numbers actually receiving treatment were restricted. Supposing CAPD to have been cheaper (a debatable point), it may have 'filled in the gaps' left by under-use of haemodialysis in the initial period in some regions. This can be tested by looking at recorded levels of uptake of CAPD. The expected finding would be that CAPD diffused most in those regions which previously had the greatest shortfall in dialysis. Finally, the chapter looks at links between policy, the observed patterns of differential diffusion, and the various users. Along the way, reference will be made to other countries with different health systems, where this seems to illuminate the argument.

One further note: for brevity, 'dialysis' is often used below to stand for 'haemodialysis', where this meaning should be clear from the context.

Policy on renal dialysis

In 1971 the Department of Health ended central funding that, from 1965, had allowed the establishment of a dialysis centre for every health region, and delegated responsibility to regional bodies. Policy scientist Thomas Halper, an American writing on UK renal dialysis policy, saw this move as severely curtailing the diffusion of dialysis (although he did not put it in quite those terms).[13] Not surprisingly, some regions prioritized renal therapy sufficiently for expansion of dialysis programmes to continue, while others allowed it to stagnate. In central policy terms, Halper characterizes the long phase from 1971 to the early 1980s as one of 'what policy?', with only small, incremental growth in dialysis services.[14]

The outline of developments is clear: an early surge, making the UK one of the world leaders in dialysis in the 1960s, followed by relative retrenchment during the 1970s. Regional variations grew and patient support groups campaigned for funds to buy 'kidney machines'.[15] The national voluntary body that was most policy-oriented, the British Kidney Patients Association (BKPA), while engaging in such fund-raising, also worked to influence opinion formers in the medical profession and in Parliament. Probably through their work, there was a constant stream of parliamentary questions in the late 1970s, with the thrust of shaming successive governments over the poor record on renal treatment provision in the UK, especially in some regions. Local Members of Parliament (MPs), briefed with case details, asked repeatedly for figures which government spokespeople repeatedly denied were available centrally.[16] The shaming game must have worked to some extent; in two bursts of generosity in 1977 and 1978 the government allocated extra funds for regions to purchase dialysis machines. They earmarked the first slice for juveniles, partly in response to the awful stories of dying children that MPs had brought before the House.

The decision to expand provision for children was also, perhaps, influenced by a small group of renal specialists, or nephrologists, who were treating children in the 1970s. About a dozen in number, they formed the British Association of Paediatric Nephrology and produced a report setting out exactly how many units should treat children, where they should be located, and what catchment area they would serve. Printed with aid from the BKPA, the report had 'a major influence' on government, according to one leading doctor, who believed it was responsible for the extra funding allocated to paediatric dialysis machines in 1977.[17]

Despite some success in influencing government to provide more funding, the patients' advocates did not gain their main objective, an 'opt-out' donation policy. They pressed for legislation to make organ donation at death the norm, with only those who deliberately opted out being exempt. Politicians in the UK baulked at such a radical intervention in people's rights to dispose of their own bodies, fearing it would be unpopular. Although the motion to change to this 'opt-out' organ donation system was passed in a parliamentary debate, it was quietly dropped and never saw the statute books.[18] Yet the UK led Europe in rates of kidney transplants (perhaps exacerbating the perceived lack of donor kidneys), precisely because the shortage of kidney dialysis machines forced physicians to lean more towards other options. In similar vein, the UK led the field in home dialysis, an option that was capital-intensive at the outset but thereafter cheaper than hospital dialysis.[19]

Thus the relatively slow diffusion of haemodialysis in the UK in the 1970s produced a pattern that some doctors see in retrospect as quite healthy: a predominance of home dialysis, and above European average rates of transplantation, meaning that a higher proportion of patients led a more normal life. The drawback was that many patients were never admitted to renal treatment programmes. While the patient groups drew attention to cases of children being denied treatment, and occasionally to cases of adults, it was in the main the elderly who were denied treatment. Many commentators from the 1970s onwards observed the covert rationing that took place in the NHS, noting to greater or lesser degrees the exclusion of the elderly.[20] Others with a diminished chance of receiving dialysis included patients with diabetes or heart disease, mentally ill or less able people, and 'moral' categories such as drug addicts or alcoholic street dwellers.

The UK record was seen as increasingly diverging from that in other European countries. This comparison was consistently more meaningful than comparison with the USA, where a change in Medicare law in 1972 ensured that the majority of patients deemed in need of dialysis did receive it. The situation varied between European countries of course, depending on the system of health care organization and financing. Most West European countries had higher rates for renal therapy than most East European countries, but there were marked variations within the West. In the Federal Republic of Germany where there was health insurance to pay for any procedure deemed life-saving, dialysis centres multiplied as doctors could claim payment for each dialysis session.[21] In the Netherlands, rates were similar to those in the UK. But the UK with its comprehensive tax-funded NHS appeared increasingly anomalous as its hospital dialysis shortfall undermined its achievements in other forms of renal treatment. Nor was this a case where better prevention could avoid the need for treatment, despite the efforts of the National Kidney Research Fund.[22]

Given the shortage of dialysis machines in UK hospitals, the relative quiescence of renal specialists seems surprising. Not all were quiet, of course; but their critique was relatively muted until the early 1980s. At that point, their outcry took two forms. One was typified by a report from the Royal College of Surgeons suggesting that no patients died because of a lack of dialysis machines, that all suitably referred patients were treated, and that if anything needed to change, it was that the number of renal specialists needed to be increased. This was a strike back against those who were saying that shortage of kidney machines was leading to patient deaths.[23] Halper suggests that nephrologists had been 'incorporated' by government buying them off in the early stages, offering centres of excellence which then were strongholds which they jealously guarded. However, their caution about expansion is rather typical of the process of specialty-building, as seen in many other areas in the history of medicine: where control over resources is in the hands of specialists, constituting a symbol of their prowess, there is a tendency to welcome additional recruits only so far as they can be kept within the established bounds of the profession.[24]

The other protest can be seen as breaking ranks. Between 1981 and 1984, individual renal specialists wrote inflammatory pieces in medical journals, arguing that the UK system had definitely killed elderly patients in renal failure by denying them access to dialysis.[25] How this system actually operated was a matter of debate; dialysis doctors claimed they did not themselves refuse to treat the elderly, but that other doctors further upstream failed to refer – a view borne out by one of the few studies to address the issue.[26] When asked why they would not refer certain patients, doctors gave answers indicating that those patients would not benefit from this treatment. This notion of 'gatekeepers' had most often been used in analysing the role of the general practitioner (GP) in the UK health care system, but comments from GPs in this survey showed awareness of lack of resources, and a wish to refer patients more readily. The phrase 'gate-keeper' here could be applied mainly to hospital doctors, including other consultants, deciding not to refer to the renal specialist. In this context, the protests of Wing and colleagues were shocking, as they directed blame at other doctors as much as at government. However, they did call for expansion of services and specialist posts.

These protests may have carried more force precisely because they represented a more public airing of arguments that were in fact winning ground behind the scenes, in contacts between medical civil servants and the professional bodies, colleges, and individuals regarded as experts in the field of renal therapies. Following the contentious 1981 *British Medical Journal* article from the Royal College of Physicians mentioned above, the need for more specialists was again argued in an unpublished report in 1983 from the College and the Renal Association.[27] Both had links with senior medical civil servants who oversaw special hospital services.[28] This report compared results of surveys in 1975 and 1982, showing growth in patient numbers not backed up by growth in manpower. It also stressed that data from the European Dialysis and Transplant Association (EDTA) had:

> repeatedly shown how small is the UK renal replacement programme compared with that in many other 'developed' countries. Moreover our position in the 'league' of European countries providing this therapy is falling. Nephrology in the UK is a very small specialty compared with many other countries. For example, there are 87 NHS consultant nephrologists in the UK and the total membership of the Renal Association is under 400.

This compares with more than 2500 accredited nephrologists in Italy, while the Japanese Society of Nephrology had 3154 members in 1981.[29]

They argued for the specialty of nephrology to be built up in the UK, but admitted that it was a costly demand, with new posts beyond established units involving highly expensive technology. This was clearly a policy matter, since only the government could decide whether to allocate the funds required for expansion.

Clearly, by 1984, the overall shortage of provision as well as the huge discrepancies between regions were becoming impossible to conceal. One solution would have been the massive new investment hinted at by the specialists. Another was the preferred path of the government: delegating responsibility to regional health managers and clinicians, by issuing a target for the level of services that should be provided. This was upgrading by exhortation. Renal dialysis, which had been an obvious problem area for years, was an obvious choice for the government in its first experiment in target-setting in the NHS. The target of forty new patients pmp had become an 'often quoted incidence estimate' that had gained general circulation;[30] and there was uneven distribution, with some regions under-performing, sending patients to other regions for their dialysis. Since some regions were already ahead of the new target, everyone could achieve it by prioritizing renal services. Amazingly, it worked. There was a great leap forward so that all regions had achieved their target by 1986, a year ahead of schedule.[31]

We have seen in this section how initial innovation and diffusion via designated centres in the UK were subsequently strangled through regional delegation, with the result that poorer regions, or those without particularly strong advocates of expansion of dialysis, spent less on this expensive technology. After a long period of resisting significant policy involvement, the Conservative government in 1984 accepted professional input and set a target for dialysis provision (in general, not specific modalities), thus accelerating diffusion. We will now return to the early years of dialysis in the UK, to look at the way different users related to the technology.

Configured users and dialysis

Grint and Woolgar give a definition of configuring the user as a struggle to define, enable, and constrain the user.[32] In their study of information technology, they witnessed this happening in a number of ways: through usability studies where novice members of staff stood in for 'users'; through a telephone helpline; and through written instructions, especially the warnings on the case or shell of the computers telling users not to open them up. Just as with the components of the technology, so the user's practice is arranged, adapted, and constrained. Configured users in the case of a medical technology such as dialysis may undergo much of the struggle themselves as they, rather than the manufacturer, are at the forefront of working with the technology.[33] Who were the users, and what changes did they have to make in order to use the machine?

When innovators in the Netherlands, the USA, the Scandinavian countries, and the UK tried out repeated dialysis technologies in the 1960s, their aim was to produce an artificial kidney that would do the job of the patient's defunct kidneys; but the user they had in mind, in terms of operating the technology, was initially the doctor.[34] In their accounts of setting up the first wave of dialysis centres in the UK, doctors speak of a sense of departure, of moving out on a limb. They felt they were striving on behalf of the new technology, against opposition from the 'old guard' – a common enough experience in innovation. Some, in retrospect, framed the experience literally in terms of young versus old:

> It comes to the point about whether there was resistance to these new developments. This was technological medicine and I suspect that because there was a generation older than me, that the [renal] physicians of the day were less certain it was a good thing than the enthusiasts really.[35]

The same informant pointed out that most early renal centres, although associated with prestigious teaching hospitals, were actually located 'off piste' in nearby units, probably because the procedures of dialysis were seen as mechanical, not requiring the intellectual calibre of the academic doctor. Renal physicians occupied prestigious positions including a number of chairs of medicine; both established and rising members of the profession were often reluctant to move into the more mechanical realm of dialysis.[36]

Dialysis was also seen as a handmaiden to early attempts at kidney transplantation, although for many years dialysis remained the more secure option for patients; and this led to a 'never-ending commitment' to patients that many doctors were unwilling to contemplate.[37] As one enthusiast mused in 1966:

> the most important thing which puts many people off intermittent dialysis is that it takes up time. And most nephrologists are already fully engaged in research and existing clinical work ... they rightly surmise that once they begin [dialysis] their lives will never again be quite as free as they were before.[38]

The enthusiasts foresaw that the technology would become more streamlined, but meanwhile they sought a way of becoming involved without the massive time commitment that the technology seemed to imply.[39] Doctors who took up the innovation, therefore, rapidly recruited nurses to perform most of the time-consuming tasks around dialysis. As well as providing the hands-on care, nurses who specialized in dialysis in those early days taught more doctors, and also technicians, to handle the technology.

Even while the technology was diffusing and spaces were being set up as dialysis units, a further innovation was introduced in a few centres: patients were trained to run their own dialysis, at home. With home dialysis, the patient would seem to be the obvious 'configured user'. Whether the location of dialysis was home or hospital, it seemed that patients were the ones who had to do the most adapting; they became most rearranged. They spent hours of every week linked up to the huge machine on which their life depended, so that their schedule was rearranged. Their ingestion of food and drink was arranged to fit the dialysis sessions, and was very strictly regulated. And during each session the circulation of their blood was rearranged as it took a loop outside their body.

But home dialysis patients also had to have their house rearranged, and in the early days when they could not do dialysis single-handed, their spouse was involved and their relationship often altered. Here are a couple of illustrations, from a patient taken onto dialysis in the late 1960s:

Patient:　　The training was a funny thing because by the time my house – I mean, we got a bit ahead and we did the things that they said you had to do, like putting lino on your floors and putting lino round the edges of the floors so the water couldn't leak out if there was a flood or anything – so we did all of that, and the machine was there ready and waiting for me.

Interviewer:　How was the machine provided?

Patient:　　The hospital – I mean, they had a set of machines and they had ones that were not in use. They were just sitting in cardboard boxes down in the basement, and they were there against [the chance of] getting people onto home dialysis.[40]

There are echoes here of a story recounted to Steve Woolgar by one of his IT company informants:

> Another tale I remember hearing is that a school who had a machine up to like four months. They wouldn't unpack it or anything, they were too scared. There was no-one around they thought was able to do much with it … Yes, I mean GOOD GRIEF![41]

As with school computers, dialysis machines awaited configured users, users with the necessary skills.[42]

Motivated patients rapidly learned to dismantle and rebuild the artificial kidney. One patient recalled:

> It isn't difficult, there's no skill involved. To a large extent it's luck. You know, you get these membranes out, you wet them, in mild formaldehyde solution, and then you just lay them down one on top of the other. The only thing is that you need to check that those little nylon connecting pieces at both ends, you just need to rub something over them to make sure that they're not rough at all and, if they are, you just take a piece of fine sandpaper to clean them up.

His wife learned to connect and disconnect him, but this involvement led to stress, and on occasions he had to disconnect himself from the machine because she lost her nerve.[43] Written accounts by male patients from the early period (1970s) frequently emphasize the stress of role conflict: for the wife, having to become a nurse and perhaps also take on more paid work; and for themselves, becoming more dependent on their wives both physically and economically. Although in those days the aim was to enable all male patients to continue in work, many had periods when they could not work normally.[44]

The 'configured user' in Woolgar's terminology, the IT user, is shaped to fit the technology even while the technology is being developed, ostensibly, to fit them. People with terminal kidney failure were desperately keen to receive dialysis, and in this sense they were already configured users, but their accounts abound with the sense of struggle, of difficulty – and these accounts come from successful patients, obviously, rather than those who gave up. For the majority who were less able to adapt readily to the demands of the technology, support disciplines burgeoned. In the UK, renal social workers emerged as a sub-specialty to assist patients with the social and employment problems surrounding dialysis and transplantation.[45] In France, psychologists were appointed to help not only patients but also staff with the traumatic impact of these therapies.[46] The anxious gaze of professions around medicine turned to the issue of compliance, as doctors reported patients failing to follow the treatment regime or even discontinuing dialysis. In the USA, where selection had ceased in the early 1970s, a multi-centre study found: 'The most frequently cited reactions to chronic hemodialysis are denial, depression, suicide, dependency, sexual dysfunction, and psychosocial problems.'[47] From their data, they further reported that: 'An average of 44% of hemodialysis patients are noncompliant with some aspect of the treatment regime.'[48]

All of this was not what could be expected of the ideal configured user who has no trouble with the machine. On the other hand, it does illustrate the enormous amount of adaptation that was required of patients. In the UK, a system operating a maximum amount of selection – never openly acknowledged – had favoured the fit and those between 15 and 50 years of age in order to maximize the success rate. In this sense, the user was configured by an unwritten code (as discussed in the previous section), applied by doctors upstream of the specialists, putting forward the patients considered most suitable for the dialysis machine.[49] Patients who were excluded had of course no chance to configure themselves, except in the sense of complying with the doctors' decisions. Many of those excluded were elderly.

Over time, some criteria relaxed, but discrimination on grounds of age seemed most entrenched. Perhaps this was partly because the elderly had no vociferous advocates to parallel the outcry over children's deaths already referred to. By the early 1980s, this was beginning to shift. Among articles in the *British Medical Journal* and elsewhere by doctors protesting over shortage of provision (see previous section), a few emphasized the under-treatment of the elderly in Britain. Reports began to come in of success in treating those over 55 or even older.[50] Meanwhile the issue of selection hit British television screens in a programme called *Lottery for Life* in August 1983.[51] The focus was still on the general shortage of dialysis services, rather than the resulting exclusion of certain categories, but it helped give impetus to those advocating more treatment for those patients who were considered poor risks.

Amidst the flurry in the wake of the television programme, a British doctor working in Iowa in the USA wrote about success with treating blind diabetic patients – diabetics being a large proportion among the over-50s who would be unlikely to be offered treatment in Britain. These blind diabetics, he claimed, 'achieved exemplary self care over extended periods. No better demonstration of a strong will to live, a keen interest in their own well-being, and a wish not to burden others could be asked of any patient.' Most notably for our story the author asserted that 'these patients chose CAPD as the mode of dialysis'.[52] Wing, the leading campaigner for more resources, in the same issue of the journal, pointed out that, while CAPD may help, the staff with appropriate skills were 'already fully stretched' and that more specialist posts were needed.[53] He further emphasized the link between consultant posts and expansion of treatment with the example of experience in the UK's second largest city, Birmingham: 'the appointment of a nephrologist with training in modern techniques quickly increases the number of patients referred for treatment'.[54] The point for those advocating CAPD, however, was that it enabled expansion of dialysis with minimal expansion of hospital facil-ities, since many CAPD patients, even quite elderly ones, could use the technique at home.

Perhaps this is a key. Already, before the UK government set targets for expansion of dialysis in 1984, renal doctors who had encountered CAPD in America or elsewhere were quietly trying it out with their patients in the UK.[55] Some wrote about it, others did not. But the use of CAPD in the UK was on a fairly steady curve from 1979 to 1984 and through to 1987. The technology was not 'waiting in the wings' when the government moved to set targets, but was already on stage in a minor role. In 1983 a seven-centre study had started in the UK, to look at all new patients taken onto CAPD over a three-year period, to see how well they fared compared with patients on haemodialysis. Clearly, the policy on targets did not wait for the outcome of that study. What is not clear is whether this new policy rode on the back of the knowledge that a new dialysis modality was available to enhance provision.

We have seen in this section that while patients were in a sense the most highly 'configured users' for dialysis, they varied in their ability or willingness to adapt, often experiencing great struggle. Doctors varied in their degree of enthu-siasm for dialysis, in their advocacy of patients through a covert system of selection, and in their militancy in calling for more provision. Latterly, some doctors were more inclined than others to employ the newer modality of CAPD, often with a view to including patients previously excluded from dialysis programmes.

How, then, did we arrive at the situation outlined earlier, where by the end of

the 1980s the UK had such a high level of CAPD compared with other countries, and some regions within the country had so much higher levels than
others? Policy history shows that because of tight cost constraints imposed on
the NHS in the 1970s, the UK had developed lower levels of hospital
haemodialysis than comparable countries, and regions that were poorer or
decided to spend less on dialysis had lower levels than the national average. In
1984, when the policy decision was made centrally to improve levels of provision, perhaps the regions with lowest provision relied most heavily on CAPD to
make up their shortfall, because it was cheaper and easier to expand, requiring
less complex technology. The next section looks at acceptance and rejection onto
dialysis programmes from another dimension, remote from the configured user,
that is, calculations of numbers in need, which changed over time. Numbers
involved in the spread of CAPD are then examined to see if the newer modality
diffused (as predicted here) mainly where the older one had been most restricted.

The numbers game

In retrospect, it might seem extraordinary that the gap between Britain's provision of dialysis for renal patients, and that in comparable countries, failed to
cause more scandal. Reports in the popular press were intermittent, tending to
focus on individual stories, and rarely dealt with numbers. Academic analysis
was more quantitative but had less impact on politicians. Cumulatively, however,
commentary and campaigning did affect policy (as outlined earlier). As early as
1974, the contrast between the USA with its full treatment programme, and the
UK with only about half the coverage, raised the question of what happened to
those who were not treated.[56] Comparisons with European countries were similarly to Britain's disadvantage; policy analyst Rudolf Klein put it bluntly: 'people
in Britain are being turned away to die who, if they lived somewhere else, would
be successfully treated'.[57] Halper's whole analysis is predicated on the notion
that the UK's successful covert rationing was costing the lives of renal patients.[58]
But only the boldest commentators tried to attribute a number to the patients
dying for lack of treatment; Wing in 1983 suggested 2,000 people a year were
thus turned away, presumably to die.[59]

How did this situation arise, how was it maintained, and what was its impact
on the diffusion of the two modalities of dialysis we are looking at here? In the
early days of dialysis there was huge uncertainty about how widely the technique
should be applied, in terms of how many patients in renal failure it could assist.
When only a handful of artificial kidneys and centres were available, it was
obvious that demand outstripped supply – and this was the motivation behind
the passing of US legislation to fund dialysis – but it was unclear how great the
demand, and the cost, might become. When Senator Hartke introduced the
amendment to the Social Security Act in 1972, to afford universal access to dialysis, he suggested costs of $75 million the first year, up to $250 million four years
later. In the event, the figure was more like $1,000 million by the Senator's latter
date; that is, four times his estimate.[60] Both costs and patient numbers were

continually expanding beyond original predictions. The difference in the UK was that no universal provision was ever enacted as in the USA.

The Ministry of Health for England and Wales gathered successive conferences of 'experts' in the mid-1960s, to offer advice on a UK dialysis programme, and received widely varying estimates of need each time. In 1965, Professor Max Rosenheim, the Chairman, reckoned that possibly 7,000 people died in the UK each year of chronic renal failure; of these, anything from 400 to 1,000 per annum might be 'suitable' new patients for dialysis.[61] By December 1966 a Swedish delegate suggested 88 new patients pmp as a reasonable figure.[62] At about the same time, Professor Hugh de Wardener, a pioneer of dialysis in the UK at Charing Cross Hospital London, estimated new patients at 30 pmp, or 1,500 per year, levelling off at a total of 7,500 on dialysis as most patients might live for up to five years.[63] His estimate of total costs, in the expectation that most patients would be transferred to home dialysis, was £11.5 million per year.[64]

In the mid-1960s, renal physicians such as de Wardener based their estimates of numbers dying from renal failure on death registration data, and then used their brief experience of treating patients with dialysis, to arrive at probable demand. They realized that cause of death on the death certificate might miss many cases of kidney failure – for example, some patients might die of heart failure. More rigorous methods were needed.

At the request of the Ministry of Health's working party, Mary McGeown, a Belfast renal physician, conducted a prospective survey through general practitioners or hospital consultants in Northern Ireland, a 'province' of the UK with a population of 1.5 million and one renal unit. Between 1968 and 1970, she followed up patients with chronic renal failure, until the patients died or were given dialysis. Another type of counting is significant in this study. To be regarded as sufficiently ill to require dialysis, the patients had to have a particular concentration of urea – one of the substances excreted in the urine – in their blood. A blood urea count above 100 mg per 100 ml qualified the patient as being in chronic renal failure for the purposes of the study. McGeown calculated the numbers suitable for treatment (when patients were excluded as theoretically unsuitable for dialysis due to mental or physical disease) as 38 pmp in the age group 5–60 years, or 33.3 with age limits 5–55 years.[65] Although age was taken to be a disqualifier, the upper age limit was only discussed in McGeown's report in terms of what difference it made to the acceptance rate; the absence of discussion on whether any such limit was justified implies that it was widely accepted at the time. McGeown advocated increased use of transplantation as an economically and socially valuable modality, arguing that the kidney shortage problem could be overcome 'if clinicians can be induced to offer suitable cadaveric organs to transplantation units'.[66]

McGeown's 1972 estimate of new patients needing treatment each year, one of the few based on a prospective study, continued to be cited, for example, in a 1978 discussion of the economics of renal treatment.[67] By far the most comprehensive discussion of the economics of treating renal failure also emerged in 1978, in a report by William Laing for the Office of Health Economics.[68] Laing collated the results of three surveys, which collectively gave the figure of 40 pmp, a figure regarded by this time as fairly standard for the numbers suitable for treatment – although, as he pointed out, criteria for dialysis were 'continuously relaxing'.[69] According to Laing, what restricted the acceptance of people with diabetes, or those over a certain age, in the UK, was 'more a function of shortage of facilities for new patients than any conviction that they would be unsuitable.'[70] Clinicians in the UK were widely aware of the greater acceptance of such patients on to dialysis programmes in other countries.

Laing made full use of data collected by EDTA since its inception in 1964, on numbers of patients treated, numbers of centres, numbers of specialists, in the whole of Europe plus Turkey and Israel. The UK, with its early head-start, had more patients under treatment than the European average – which included many poorer countries – but was accepting fewer new patients annually by the time of Laing's study: 15 pmp as compared with 19 pmp European average, 30 pmp for France and Germany, and 40 pmp for Israel. Projections for future need, Laing pointed out, were extremely unstable because they depended on the survival rate of patients, which in turn depended on health care and basic health of the population. Taking the Polish example, the total stock of renal patients could end up at 90 pmp, whereas the Dutch record would result in 470 pmp on treatment at the point where adequate provision enabled all suitable patients to be taken on, merely replacing those who died. Future developments in technology could further alter the picture.[71]

By 1976, the 47 renal units in England and Wales were treating about 4,000 patients which represented a 'patient stock' of 71 pmp, but this could rise to 340 pmp if annual acceptance rates rose to 40 pmp. Costs which in 1976 were about £22 million would rise to £120 million with the higher acceptance rate, or even £170 million if the UK achieved Dutch levels of survival.[72] And if people over 60 were included, the figure would double again, to £350 million.[73] The extra kidney machines allocated by the Secretary of State for Health in 1977–8 for paediatric use, and the extra 400 machines at a cost of £3.5 million for adult dialysis announced in 1978, raised annual intake from 15 to above 20 pmp – still a low figure. In Laing's view, mainly children from middle-class homes had received dialysis in the 1970s, but the rate of provision had not been very different from that of adults; however, the refusal of dialysis for children raised emotive issues which pushed the government into making special provision.

Against unmet need, the extra machines provided in 1977–8 made little difference. By the start of the 1980s, the UK fell short of comparable European countries in terms of overall renal treatment; some regions of the UK fared far worse than others; the shortage was in hospital or 'satellite' dialysis, while home dialysis and transplant services were relatively well provided; there were fewer centres and specialists relative to the population than in comparable countries; and above all, there seemed less chance of treatment for the elderly than in similar countries. The newer modality of CAPD was just beginning to supplement haemodialysis.

When, in December 1984, the government relented to the extent of including dialysis among its targets for expansion, no guidelines instructed specialists or health managers how these targets should be achieved, but they were reached a year early in 1986. Between 1984 and 1986 the uptake of new patients increased by 24 per cent.[74] Numbers of new patients per million population rose from 25 in 1980, 36 in 1984, to 51 in 1987. The total stock of surviving patients also rose, by an outstanding 50 per cent between 1984 and 1988 (see Table 7.1).[75]

The annual acceptance rate was still below that of Germany or France, though now above Italy's; and the total patient stock, historically so limited in the UK, remained well behind those of other wealthy countries.[76] However, in this period of rapid expansion, the whole culture of renal therapy allocation in the UK underwent a mini-transformation which included the increased use of CAPD.

At first glance, the total contribution of CAPD to this increase does not appear enormous; its share of the total of patients on treatment rose from 17 per cent to 21 per cent between 1984 and 1988. However, its use nearly doubled in that time (90 per cent growth), making it by far the *fastest growing* modality.[77] If this was due to its lower cost, we could expect the growth of CAPD to be most marked in those regions that had most restricted dialysis provision before 1984. Let us look first at rates of increase in provision, without distinguishing modality. The picture is complicated: figures were distorted by the transferral of patients from one area to another – for example between South East Thames and South West Thames, inflating the latter's figures.[78] Leaving aside regions which exhibit cross-region distortion, if we take areas with the lowest and highest acceptance rates in 1984, on the whole those with the lowest rates in 1984 exhibit the greatest increase in acceptance of new patients by 1988 – exactly as might be expected (see Table 7.2).[79]

We have to treat these figures with caution; for example, data on West Midlands were incomplete. However, if we look at Northern Ireland, West Midlands, and Wessex, all with annual new patient acceptance rates below 30 pmp in 1984, we find they have achieved rates above 40 pmp by 1988, entailing fairly heroic increases between 60 and 112 per cent. By contrast, three regions

Table 7.1   Numbers of surviving patients on renal replacement therapy by modality in the UK, plus total per million population, 31 December 1984 and 31 December 1988

UK figs	Hospital HD	Home HD	IPD	CAPD	Graft	Total	Total pmp	CAPD as % of total
1984	1,744	2,006	68	1,859	5,299	10,976	195	17
1988	2,556	1,582	84	3,529	8,404	16,155	284	21
Increase	812	-424	16	1,670	3,105	5,179	89	

Notes: HD = haemodialyis; IPD = intermittent peritoneal dialysis; CAPD = continuous ambulatory peritoneal dialysis; pmp = patients per million population.

Sources: Registry Report (1986: 2); Tufveson (1989: 6).

Table 7.2   Acceptance rates for new patients for renal replacement therapy in selected UK regions, 1984 and 1988, showing increase

Regions	New patients 1984	New patients 1988	Increase 1984–8
	Numbers per million population		*%*
Low in 1984			
N. Ireland	20.0	42.5	112.5
W. Midlands	26.3	52.0	97.7
Wessex	27.9	44.8	60.6
High in 1984			
Trent	40.4	49.1	21.5
E. Anglia	40.5	65.0	60.5
Northern	40.6	58.4	43.8

Source: First two columns adopted from Mays (1990: Table 4, p. 13), using EDTA Registry data.

that already had rates above 40 pmp in 1984 – Trent, East Anglia, and Northern – while still performing reasonably well in 1988, achieved lower increases, in one case just above 20 per cent, although East Anglia's 60 per cent increase equalled that of one of the 'lower' band, Wessex. Thus, regions responded to the government targets, and those that had already reached them made less effort to expand provision, even though their annual acceptance rates left much room for improvement to reach levels equivalent to other wealthy countries.

So much for overall increase, but what of modality? Did CAPD in fact make up a higher proportion of dialysis modality in those regions that had made the largest increases? A glance at Table 7.3 shows (without any need for sophisticated statistical tools) that uptake of CAPD varied quite wildly from region to region, bearing no clear relation to rates of increase.

Table 7.3   Proportion of total patients on CAPD in selected UK regions, 1988

Regions	Total number of patients	Number on CAPD	CAPD as % of total
N. Ireland	260.6	24.4	9.4
W. Midlands	173.8*	94	54
Wessex	202.4	46.6	23
Trent	292	69.3	23.7
E. Anglia	328	31.5	9.6
Northern	301.3	54.2	18

Note: * Incomplete data.

Source: First two columns adapted from Mays (1990, Table 5, p. 13), using EDTA Registry data.

So CAPD was not taken up consistently as a recourse for poorly supplied regions that needed rapidly to plug the gap in their dialysis provision, and ignored by the better-provided regions. Yet, given the variation in uptake – the *uneven diffusion* of this newer modality – there must have been differential factors involved. As Nicholas Mays pointed out in his comprehensive review of renal therapies in the UK at the end of the 1980s, allocation of resources at regional level classically followed one of two patterns: incremental, based on historic allocation, or budgeting according to breakdown of activities and predicted costs for each unit.[80] Haemodialysis fits best the historic and incremental pattern, while CAPD entered the UK scene at a point when budgeting had begun to dominate.[81] But resource allocation is only one sort of choice, and although it appeared likely to have influenced diffusion of CAPD (given the government's emphasis on budgeting within the NHS in the 1980s), the figures discussed here do not bear this out.

Indicators from around the UK suggest rather that historical precedence and preferences of heads of renal units in each region influenced the uptake of CAPD. In Northern Ireland, with its highly successful programme of transplantation, CAPD accounted for very little of the expansion to meet the new target after 1984. Oxford used CAPD to expand its catchment area, at the same time pushing use of haemodialysis by having three shifts a day on the machines, but managed to reach a 'happy steady state' requiring no further increase in numbers on dialysis, thanks to its 'exceptional transplant programme'.[82] Manchester launched into CAPD early and fast, only to find its patients stuck with the system requiring a long tube to be left *in situ*, since switching to the new generation short-tube system was too expensive. The consultant here had previous experience of peritoneal dialysis.[83] In Charing Cross Hospital, London, where again the consultant had previous experience of peritoneal dialysis, CAPD was used especially to bring more elderly people onto the programme.[84] Birmingham's expansion relied on a 'huge' CAPD programme.[85] Not only the elderly were thus catered for; in Newcastle, for example, it was CAPD that allowed more young children to be taken on to dialysis.[86] While many patients must have accepted CAPD, the decision about which modality to use seems to have been shaped by clinicians' inclinations and experience.

Costing came into the equation, but despite its simpler technology, CAPD was apparently not much cheaper compared with haemodialysis. However, to the renal units CAPD appeared cheaper because they could expect the GP to pay for the bags of fluid, thus shunting the main running cost off the unit's budget.[87] The greater 'suitability' of the newer mode for the elderly was gradually constructed, as the risk of infection (peritonitis) was reduced; for some physicians, this had seemed a contra-indication especially for older patients. Perhaps, once CAPD had become routinized and perceived as safe, it was more often used for elderly patients precisely because it saved having to expand hospital haemodialysis facilities with concomitant rapid increase in staff numbers. The particular circumstances in the UK certainly accelerated and distorted the diffusion of CAPD – although we cannot assume any 'normal' path of diffusion, and must always see a possibility of contested ground.

Conclusion

'The technology' is the machine's relations with its users.[88]

The notion of 'configured user' is useful in moving us away from looking at 'inherent' qualities of technologies, towards looking at the interpretation of technologies (like texts) within a social context. What if there is no machine, as with CAPD – is this 'recidivism', a stepping back from the apparently inexorable route of increasing complexity and technological dependence of modern medicine?[89] In any case CAPD, though lacking machinery, constitutes a technology with definite social dimensions.

The social interpretation of the technology obviously varied, but in what way? This chapter looked at two categories of 'configured users': clinicians and patients. In the early days of haemodialysis, the few renal specialists who were attracted to this demanding and unproven approach tended to select patients who would succeed with the technology. While this also happened elsewhere, in the UK it became entrenched over time, in the face of limited resourcing. The selected patients were prepared for maximum adaptation to the technology, at great personal cost. With CAPD there was less technology to adapt to, although there was the bodily configuration of a permanently implanted tube protruding from the abdomen. The simpler technology of CAPD seems to have enabled some doctors to conceive of expanding dialysis to hitherto excluded categories of patients: the sick (for instance, diabetics), the elderly, and very young. In the latter case, configuration stretches beyond the patient to the parents. In fact, with such long-term life-maintaining technologies, it may be more appropriate to envisage a *mutual configuring* between doctors and patients, together with renal nurses, social workers, technicians, pharmacists, and auxiliaries; all in turn feeding back to the manufacturers.[90]

Haemodialysis had spread unevenly in the UK, with some regions having much lower rates of provision than others. The reasons for this require further research. The calibre and enthusiasm of the lead clinician at each regional renal therapy centre, combined with varying priorities and cost constraints imposed by each regional board, were factors suggested by interviews and by current resource allocation debates.[91] Some of the lowest provision of dialysis in the 1970s occurred in the traditionally under-resourced old industrial regions such as the West Midlands and Merseyside. Assuming that CAPD was cheaper, it could have been expected to diffuse rapidly to 'fill the gaps' especially after the government introduced targets for dialysis in 1984. This chapter looked at figures for selected regions which indicated, not surprisingly, that the regions with lowest rates of renal therapy increased their provision faster than others in the period 1984–8. However, a closer look showed that the part played by CAPD in this increase varied enormously, contrary to expectations. Why did this simpler, cheaper, technology not diffuse in such a way as to make up the shortfall in dialysis provision?

Some sources suggested that although simpler, CAPD was not much cheaper than haemodialysis in terms of running costs, although views on this varied as there were different ways of accounting for costs. It has been noted that the government introduced dialysis targets before the evidence from a significant CAPD trial in the UK would become available. Whether or not doctors tend to be influenced by such trials, without the results they were free to exercise their clinical judgement much as in the era of haemodialysis alone. Again, more research is needed, but interviews and articles in the medical literature suggest that the experience of clinicians and the culture built up in each centre – with some already more oriented towards peritoneal dialysis by the time CAPD was introduced – played a part in the highly variable uptake of the newer modality in the period after target-setting. Although the language of patient choice is increasingly apparent, it would seem that at least in the 1980s, the choices made by doctors were more influential. Patients, perhaps especially those patients on the margin who previously had little chance of being accepted onto a dialysis programme, would tend to comply with whatever was offered. As with the earlier modality, while doctors, nurses, and technicians were 'configured users' analogous to those for computers in Grint and Woolgar's study, it was the patients who were most highly 'configured users' in another sense, in having their lives most rearranged by the technology of dialysis.

Through explorations of the 'configured user' via unpicking of numbers, the story returns to the familiar territory of clinical control. The observed irregular pattern of diffusion can better be explained in terms of prior experience of clinicians in each renal centre, shaping not only their confidence with the alternative modality, but also their expectations of patients as suitably configured users for CAPD as compared with haemodialysis. Regional variations at this stage are idiosyncratic, whereas in the case of the earlier modality there does seem to have been some correlation with resources. Yet there is an overall correlation of resources and modality. If we look at the national level, we find that countries like the UK with more socially equal health services, which had fallen behind with dialysis provision by the late 1970s, had by the late 1980s expanded by achieving a much higher uptake of CAPD than other comparably wealthy countries. CAPD as the lower-tech modality appealed more in countries with more restricted use of expensive technologies overall, not necessarily because it was cheaper, but perhaps because it took up less space – less mental space as well as physical space.

Acknowledgements

Thanks are due to the Wellcome Trust for funding the research of which this chapter is one outcome; to the History Group and especially Professor Virginia Berridge at the London School of Hygiene and Tropical Medicine for support and discussion of ideas; and to Bernard Harris for valuable comments. Views and interpretations expressed here remain the author's responsibility.

Notes

All interviews referred to below were conducted by the author.

1 Jennifer Tann, 'Space, time and innovation characteristics: the contribution of diffusion process theory to the history of technology', *History of Technology*, 1995, vol. 17, pp. 143–63, note 9.
2 Steven Peitzman, 'From dropsy to Bright's Disease to end-stage renal disease', *Milbank Quarterly*, 1989, vol. 67, Suppl.1, pp. 16–32.
3 Lewis Thomas, 'Notes of a biology-watcher: the technology of medicine', *New England Journal of Medicine*, 1971, vol. 285, pp. 1366–8; for discussion of this concept in relation to ventilation therapy, see James Maxwell, 'The iron lung: halfway technology or necessary step?', *Milbank Quarterly*, 1986, vol. 64, pp. 3–29.
4 For several points of comparison between the histories of these innovations, see J. Stanton, 'Supported lives', in R. Cooter and J. Pickstone (eds), *Medicine in the Twentieth Century*, Amsterdam, Harwood Academic Publishers, 2000, pp. 601–15.
5 For an illustrated historical account, see W. Drukker, 'Haemodialysis: a historical review', in W. Drukker, J. F. Maher and F. M. Parsons (eds), *Replacement of Renal Function by Dialysis*, The Hague, Martinus Nijhoff, 1978, pp. 3–37.
6 For historical account with diagrams of function, see R. Gokal, 'Historical development and clinical use of continuous ambulatory peritoneal dialysis', in R. Gokal (ed.), *Continuous Ambulatory Peritoneal Dialysis*, Edinburgh, Churchill Livingstone, 1986, pp. 1–13.
7 This was a 'shunt' connecting artery and vein, allowing repeated connections to an artificial kidney – previously, since each session resulted in the collapse of blood vessels, only about eight treatments could be conducted on one patient. At first, plastic materials, and later, the patient's own blood vessels were used as the bridge. See Drukker, 'Haemodialysis'.
8 David Kerr, 'Foreword', in Gokal, *Continuous Ambulatory Peritoneal Dialysis*.
9 Keith Grint and Steve Woolgar, *The Machine at Work: Technology, Work and Organization*, Cambridge, Polity Press (in association with Blackwell Publishers, Oxford), 1997.
10 I would like to acknowledge the unknown colleague who raised this question at a talk by Steve Woolgar at the London School of Hygiene and Tropical Medicine in 1997.
11 Nicholas Mays, *Management and Resource Allocation in End Stage Renal Failure Units: A Review of Current Issues*, London, King Edward's Hospital Fund, 1990, Table 5, p. 13 (figures for 1988, based on data from the European Dialysis and Transplant Association); patients 'per million population' or pmp came into use as the unit of measure because numbers of ESRD patients in each country or region were too small to be measured in more conventional terms such as per cent or per thousand.
12 For latter statistics, see Jack Moncrief, Robert Popovich and Karl Nolph, 'The history and current status of continuous ambulatory peritoneal dialysis', *American Journal of Kidney Diseases*, 1990, vol. 16, pp. 579–84, at p. 582.
13 Thomas Halper, *The Misfortunes of Others: End-Stage Renal Disease in the United Kingdom*, Cambridge, Cambridge University Press, 1989.
14 Halper, *Misfortunes*, pp. 29, 61–5.
15 Later, in 1983, the children's television programme *Blue Peter* raised £2.5 million to buy kidney machines. See Elizabeth Ward, *Timbo: A Struggle for Survival*, London, Sidgwick and Jackson, 1986.
16 Jennifer Stanton, 'The cost of living: kidney dialysis, rationing and health economics in Britain, 1965–1996', *Social Science and Medicine*, 1999, vol. 49, pp. 1169–82.
17 Personal communication from renal specialist, 30 June 2000.

18 Stanton, 'Cost of living', p. 1175.
19 Stanley Shaldon from the Royal Free Hospital in London pioneered home dialysis in the early 1960s according to one informant: interview, renal specialist, north London, 8 March 1995.
20 W. Laing, *Renal Failure: A Priority in Health?*, London, Office of Health Economics, 1978; J. Aaron and W. Schwartz, *The Painful Prescription: Rationing Hospital Care*, Washington DC, Brookings Institution, 1984; Thomas Halper, 'End-stage renal failure and the aged in the United Kingdom', *International Journal of Technology Assessment in Health Care*, 1985, vol. 1, pp. 41–52; Rudolf Klein, *The Politics of the NHS*, London, Longman, 2nd edn, 1989, pp. 85–6.
21 Thanks to Soraya de Chadarevian for pointing this out in discussion following my talk in the History of Modern Medicine and Biomedical Sciences seminar series, Cambridge, 9 November 1998.
22 Interview with official of NKRF, London, 7 December 1995.
23 Royal College of Physicians Medical Services Study Group, 'Deaths from chronic renal failure under the age of 50', *British Medical Journal*, 1981, vol. 283, pp. 283–7; see editorial criticism in same issue: Editorial, 'Audit in renal failure: the wrong target?', *British Medical Journal*, 1981, vol. 283, pp. 261–2.
24 This rather provocative formulation is only one aspect, of course; for a full (book-length) survey, see John Burnham, 'How the idea of profession changed the writing of medical history', *Medical History*, Supplement 18, London, Wellcome Institute for the History of Medicine, 1998.
25 G. Berlyne, 'Over 50 and uremic = death', *Nephron*, 1982, vol. 13, pp. 189–90; A. Wing, 'Why don't the British treat more patients with kidney failure?', *British Medical Journal*, 1983, vol. 287, pp. 1157–8.
26 S. Challah, A. Wing *et al.*, 'Negative selection of patients for dialysis and transplantation in the United Kingdom', *British Medical Journal*, 1984, vol. 288, pp. 1119–22.
27 Royal College of Physicians Committee on Renal Disease and the Renal Association, *Manpower and Workload in Adult Renal Medicine*, typescript report, London, Royal College of Physicians, 1983.
28 Telephone interview with medical civil servant, between Oxford and Saudi Arabia, June 1997.
29 Royal College of Physicians, *Manpower and Workload*, no page nos.
30 Laing, *Renal Failure*, p. 16.
31 Halper, *Misfortunes*, p. 20; interview with medical civil servant, who mentioned that other intransigent problems tackled this way included hip replacements and coronary artery bypass operations.
32 Grint and Woolgar, *Machine at Work*, p. 74.
33 See references to 'MAP' and 'CAP' – manufacturer active paradigm and consumer active paradigm – in Introduction to this volume.
34 The inventors and innovators were mainly doctors; see Belding Scribner, 'A personalized history of chronic hemodialysis', *American Journal of Kidney Diseases*, 1990, vol. 16, pp. 511–19.
35 Interview with renal physician, Manchester, 1 November 1996.
36 Interview with renal physician, south London, 8 September 1995.
37 Interview with renal physician, north London, 8 March 1995; on dialysis being preferable to transplants, also: interview with dialysis nurse, south London, 5 December 1995.
38 H. de Wardener, 'Some ethical and economic problems associated with intermittent haemodialysis', in G. Wolstenholme and M. O'Connor (eds), *Ciba Foundation Symposium on Ethics in Medical Progress*, London, Churchill, 1966, pp. 104–18, at pp. 114–15.
39 In other areas, perhaps especially diagnostic technology, innovations might bring prestige and more immediately attract doctors; even so, the more mechanical side of

the operation was rapidly handed over to less qualified staff. On X-rays, see J. Howell, *Technology in the Hospital: Transforming Patient Care in the Early Twentieth Century*, Baltimore and London, Johns Hopkins University Press, 1995, pp. 103–32.

40 Interview with dialysis patient, 14 October 1995.

41 Grint and Woolgar, *Machine at Work*, p. 76.

42 Charitable donations of dialysis machines could be an embarrassment to hospitals, as running costs and staff costs were not covered, so machines remained unused for months: interview with renal physician, south London, 8 September 1995.

43 Interview with patient, 14 October 1995.

44 See, for example, James Campbell and Anne Campbell, 'The social and economic costs of end-stage renal disease', *New England Journal of Medicine*, 1978, vol. 299, pp. 386–92.

45 Interviews with renal social workers, Oxford, 18 December 1995, and Newcastle, 21 February 1996.

46 Personal communication from doctor who had worked in renal unit, Paris, May 1996.

47 Brendan Maher, Donna Lamping *et al.*, 'Psychosocial aspects of chronic hemodialysis: The National Cooperative Dialysis Study', *Kidney International*, 1983, vol. 23, Suppl. 13, p. S-50.

48 Donna Lamping and Kent Campbell, 'A methodological study of hemodialysis compliance criteria', *Journal of Compliance in Health Care*, 1989, vol. 4, p. 117.

49 Further discussion provided in J. Stanton, 'Suitable patients, sustainable lives: dialysis and intensive care compared', paper presented at Second European Social Science History Conference, Amsterdam, 5–7 March 1998.

50 For example, D. Taube, E. Winder and C. Ogg, 'Successful treatment of middle aged and elderly patients with end stage renal disease', *British Medical Journal*, 1983, vol. 286, pp. 2018–20.

51 Yorkshire Television, *Lottery for Life*, 2 August 1983, reported in: 'Medicine and the media', *British Medical Journal*, 1983, vol. 287, p.492; see letter from Julian Tudor Hart, *British Medical Journal*, 1983, vol. 287, where he complains that his interview for this programme was cut probably because he said that one Trident missile cost the same as the country's entire renal dialysis programme – 'the choice between the welfare state and warfare state', as he put it.

52 L. Flynn, 'Why blind diabetics in renal failure should be offered treatment', *British Medical Journal*, 1983, vol. 287, pp. 1177–8.

53 Wing, 'Why don't the British treat more patients?', p. 1158.

54 A. Wing, 'Treatment of renal failure in the light of increasingly limited resources', *Contributions to Nephrology*, 1985, vol. 44, pp. 260–75, at p. 263.

55 Interview with renal physician, west London, 6 July 1995.

56 Aaron and Schwartz, *Painful Prescription*.

57 Klein, *Politics of the NHS*, pp. 85–6, referring to 1975 figures.

58 Halper, *Misfortunes*.

59 Citing J. Cameron's estimate of costs of treating these 2,000 as a further £50 million a year, Wing pointed out, 'This is less than we now spend each month on fewer people in the Falklands Islands': Wing, 'Why don't the British treat more patients?', p. 1158.

60 Laing, *Renal Failure*, p. 44, note 12.

61 Ministry of Health, Minutes of conference on intermittent dialysis, typescript, 1965, p. 2.

62 Ministry of Health, Minutes of conference on intermittent dialysis, typescript, 1966, p. 4; note that this Swedish figure was only approached *as a target* for the UK in the late 1990s. For pmp, see note 11 above.

63 Hugh de Wardener report, typescript, October 1967, p. 3.

64 By 1976, about half this number of patients were being treated in England and Wales at about twice this cost, see below.

65 Mary McGeown, 'Chronic renal failure in Northern Ireland, 1968–70', *Lancet*, 1972, vol. 1, pp. 307–10, at p. 309. She noted that a Swedish colleague informally estimated 50 pmp when 60 years was the upper limit, and 90 pmp when there was no upper limit, p. 310.

66 Ibid., p. 310; on the other main problem of transplantation, rejection, Northern Ireland achieved much better results than other parts of the UK. The rejection problem was to be revolutionized by the introduction of drugs to suppress the immune response, starting with cyclosporine in 1978 (commercially available 1983); see Geoffrey Rivett, *From Cradle to Grave: Fifty Years of the NHS*, London, King's Fund, 1997, p. 314.

67 D. Parkin, 'Chronic renal failure: the economics of treatment', *Community Health*, 1978, vol. 9, pp. 134–41, at p. 135.

68 Laing, *Renal failure*, 1978.

69 Ibid., p. 17.

70 Ibid., p. 18.

71 Ibid., p. 34.

72 Ibid., p. 42.

73 Ibid., p. 44.

74 Mays, *Management and Resource Allocation*, p. 11.

75 Sources for Table 7.1: Registry Report, 'Demography of dialysis and transplantation in Europe, 1984', *Nephrology Dialysis Transplantation*, 1986, vol. 1, p. 2; G. Tufveson *et al.*, 'Combined Report on regular dialysis and transplantation in Europe, XIX, 1988', *Nephrology Dialysis Transplantation*, 1989, vol. 4, Suppl. 4 , p. 6.

76 Mays, *Management and Resource Allocation*, p. 11. By 1987, when it had doubled compared with 1980, total patient stock in the UK was still only about 270 pmp compared with 333 pmp for France, and 434 pmp for Germany.

77 It had already been expanding: from 5.2 per cent of new patients on CAPD in 1979 to 27.6 per cent in 1981, according to the Under-Secretary of State for Health, *Hansard*, 8 November 1983, quoting EDTA figures for 1982.

78 Mays, *Management and Resource Allocation*, p. 13.

79 Sources for Tables 7.2 and 7.3: Mays, *Management and Resource Allocation*, Tables 4 and 5, p. 13, using EDTA Registry data.

80 A radical third alternative – making districts act as 'purchasers' who had to 'buy' specialist services from regions – was just being introduced in the 'internal market' of the NHS at the end of this period: Mays, *Management and Resource Allocation*, p. 17; this was radical in the sense of enormously disruptive.

81 For incrementalism in dialysis policy, see Halper, *Misfortunes*, pp. 61–7.

82 Juliet Auer, 'The Oxford Renal Unit Silver Jubilee', typescript, 1993, p. 3.

83 That is, intermittent peritoneal dialysis; interview with renal physician, Manchester, 1 November 1996.

84 Interview, renal physician, west London, 6 July 1995.

85 Ibid.

86 C. Wood, 'The impact of childhood renal failure and its treatment by peritoneal dialysis (CAPD and PROD) on family life and functioning', report commissioned by the British Kidney Patients Association (BKPA) and researched in 1988 by the Paediatric Renal Unit and the Psychology Department, Royal Victoria Infirmary, Newcastle, typescript, 1989.

87 Personal communication from renal specialist, 30 June 2000.

88 Grint and Woolgar, *Machine at Work*, p. 93.

89 This idea came from discussion following my talk in Cambridge, 1998 (see note 21 above).

90 In another study, it would be worth looking at the 'reconfiguring' over time of both modalities, in the light of demands from doctors, nurses, and patients and others; for

example, the increasing miniaturization and disposability of components of the technologies as use increased and competition grew. Attention should be paid to whether such changes answered patients' preferences for portable, disposable 'machines', or rather tended to cater for the convenience of hospital practitioners.

91 For survey of approaches, see Rudolf Klein, Patricia Day and Sharon Redmayne, *Managing Scarcity: Priority Setting and Rationing in the National Health Service*, Buckingham, Open University Press, 1996. This book mentions dialysis rationing in historical context but does not refer to CAPD. See also, Stanton, 'Cost of living', especially for parliamentary questions on regional inequalities and shortfall of provision.

8 Midwifery re-innovation in New Zealand

Philippa Mein Smith

The twentieth century saw major innovations in midwifery in New Zealand, an isolated and thinly populated country which serves as an ideal case study for examining the diffusion of international trends. 'It had taken a century for the fashion to swing from the extreme conservatism of the 1820s and 1830s to the apogee of intervention in the 1920s and 1930s'[1] and New Zealand was no exception. The aim of this chapter is to extend the time frame for analysis from 1900 to 2000, in order to examine a subsequent return to the idea of birth as a normal, physiological process and the reinvention of the midwife in the 1980s and 1990s. The twentieth century proved to be a century of change in birth practices in the Western, and colonized, world: from the midwife to the doctor, and back to the midwife as the preferred health professional to deliver the baby; and from home to hospital as the officially sanctioned place of birth, followed by moves to make the hospital more homely, with a reduced length of stay. In order to examine these trends, this chapter is structured into two halves, the first covering innovations in the early twentieth century and the second re-innovations in the late twentieth century.

These changes were international in scope, including the trend to 're-creating midwifery'. An analysis of the United States and the Netherlands has identified the 'structural position of midwifery' as central to this latest re-innovation.[2] This is true also in New Zealand, with the formation of the New Zealand College of Midwives in 1989. But midwifery's structural position is only one in a kaleidoscope of reasons for this change. A local mix of ingredients created outcomes that resulted more from internal dynamics than from external pressures: a mix distinctive by place, shaped by local politics, social relations, economic constraints, and indigenous means of 'configuring' the new mother as the consumer or 'user' of maternity services.[3] Particularly important was the 'fit' between the political agendas of the professions, the state (ambiguous, never unified), and organized women's groups.[4] In this case, a 'fit' in political positions allowed space for the reinvention of the midwife. This entailed finding points of agreement among the competing views of doctors and midwives; mothers' needs and preferences; and the government and the Health Funding Authority,[5] which sought a cap on maternity care costs.

Maternity historically is contested terrain. Birth services, and the birth of new services, have provided sites for battles for control over who is the appropriate professional to catch the baby.[6] As Marland observes, changes in birth practices 'cannot simply be interpreted along gender lines'.[7] Struggles for control are not simply a matter of doctors versus midwives; nor do they engage 'women' as a category against 'doctors'. Networks of people with shared interests, expressed as identities, do not add up to a single, unified group. It is better to consider midwifery and medicine as competing discourses.[8]

Conceptualizing re-innovation

To avoid confusion because of the varied use of 'invention' as a concept by historians, this chapter is titled 'Midwifery re-innovation' rather than 'Reinventing midwifery', with re-innovation referring to who manages the delivery and who is sanctioned as the most appropriate carer to do so. Like Pickstone, it highlights the central role of prices and costs in shaping patients', professional and political choices towards the re-innovation of the midwife.[9] This case study supports the argument that power and control are central to the acceptance or rejection of innovation in health care delivery. Professional alliances themselves were not static: they changed through time, and the locus of power shifted continually, as demonstrated for the inter-war period in *Maternity in Dispute*.[10]

We can understand the history of midwifery more clearly as 'a struggle to configure (that is, to define, enable and constrain) the user', using Grint and Woolgar's concept. Doctors and midwives offer conflicting accounts of 'what the user is like', for example, of birth as a normal event, on the one hand, or as risky and dangerous, on the other. Each claims more expertise than the other.[11] The problem with this approach is that it is potentially top-down, like older social control interpretations. What place is there for agency on the part of the user of maternity services: the new mother and her baby?

Here we find assistance from the social theorist Charles Tilly, on interactions among parties, and from new work on doing interactive as well as comparative history, located in the Antipodes.[12] Tilly argues that there is more explanatory power in an interactional way of thinking, one which interprets political processes as 'strongly-patterned transactions within interlocking networks'. In his analysis of social movement theory, he outlines three points which provide a useful model for midwifery re-innovation: first, there are powerful analogies between processes which drive local social movements and 'national' and 'international' processes; second, identities people advance to make political claims consist of 'contingent relationships with people rather than inbuilt personal traits'; and third, there is incessant interaction between things 'domestic' and 'international'.[13] This last point is even more apparent in an era of globalization.[14]

Competing campaigns through time between doctors and midwives over who should preside at birth make more sense when viewed as heated 'conversations' or 'interactions among parties'.[15] It is unsurprising that Tilly sees analogies between such processes and nationalism because in these historical episodes of 'maternity in dispute', challengers and powerholders – alternatively midwifery and medicine – claimed to speak for the national good.[16] This is particularly the case in a small society like New Zealand, a former White Dominion which, historically, has liked to see itself as a model for the world and a site of social experiment. Sometimes it is; sometimes it is merely the recipient of innovation. But always ideas are adapted 'here', from 'over there'. In short, this small country's culture is distinctive not in its parts but in the way things are pieced together. Culture consists of collections, and this extends to innovations in childbirth.

From the 1920s the New Zealand way of birth came to comprise attendance by both a midwife and a doctor in hospital, on the assumption that this was progressive, modern, and would ensure 'safe maternity'. This pattern of attendance by a general practitioner assisted by a maternity nurse, rather than a midwife working autonomously, became institutionalized in 1939 under the First Labour Government's social security legislation, when childbirth became free, paid for by the taxpayer.[17] Since 1990 there has been a swing back to care by an independent midwife, but not as yet from the hospital. Thus New Zealand's experience of changes in the usual way of birth has comprised a shift from a midwife and doctor, in hospital, by the late 1930s, to a midwife in hospital or a maternity unit in the late 1990s. Papps and Olssen have traced the conditions under which childbirth became medicalized in New Zealand up to 1990, pursuing a Foucauldian approach which focuses on the control of birth, as evidenced in law which regulates midwifery. They see a three-way struggle between midwives and doctors, midwives and nurses, and doctors and consumers.[18] But this neglects the contingent nature of identities involving differences through time among midwives, among doctors, consumers and between midwives and mothers.

Cost has proved pivotal. Who pays, and who is paid has varied according to how the mother and baby are configured, and to contingent identities deployed in jostles over power relations. In 1939, the 'best' service was thought to be the most expensive one, while in 1996 the Lead Maternity Carer scheme sought to put a cap on the cost of maternity services, by preventing duplication of care by a midwife and a doctor. Why pay for both when, if birth were normal, only one was necessary?

Gender and the 'state'[19]

In her analysis of the effects of gender, culture, and class on the transition to doctor-attended birth in the United States, Borst argues that the shift from midwife to doctor is 'one of the striking examples of the relationship of gender, class, and culture' in the twentieth-century movement to increased professional authority.[20] So is the swing back to the midwife, it is argued here, amidst the increased questioning of that authority. Women served as agents in the shift from midwife to doctor, as Leavitt has shown, and in the move to medicalized birth; women made conscious choices for themselves and their babies, influenced by fears of death and pain.[21] Correspondingly, women played an active part in the re-innovation of the midwife. In New Zealand, they did so as politicians, health managers, and midwives, as well as mothers.

Historically, gender as a concept throws into sharp relief the place of mothers and babies in nation-building. New Zealand as well as France, Germany, the United Kingdom, and other New World settler societies experienced a birth rate scare in the early 1900s at a moment of consolidating national and imperial identities. If it could not do anything about the birth rate, it could about the mortality rates of babies and mothers as part of its strategies for defence and development. Patriotism for women amounted to motherhood.[22]

Such anxieties in New Zealand generated a legislative response in the form of the Midwives Act 1904, intended to provide better training of midwives, to regulate midwifery through a midwives' register, and to reduce infant and maternal mortality among respectable working-class mothers, who were potentially 'good' mothers for producing better British 'stock'. The Midwives Act was the initiative of Grace Neill, New Zealand's senior woman public servant, herself a trained nurse and midwife. Neill aimed to establish a state hospital for women run by women, which offered good care at a moderate price and at the same time provided a midwifery training school. Inevitably she met opposition from doctors worried about their incomes and about the potential threat that trained midwives posed to family practice.[23] New Zealand's population only reached one million in 1908 and the most lucrative medical practices were in the main towns, where these maternity hospitals were situated.

At Neill's shrewd behest, the St Helens hospitals established from 1905 took their name from the Premier Richard Seddon's Lancashire birthplace, in the hope that flattery would pay. It did. Seddon aimed to reduce loss of life among mothers and babies, for the colony, soon to become a nation, and for the Empire: as he told Parliament, 'reproduction is essential for the continuation of the human race', and loss of child life showed 'decadence in any nation'. Preserving life required the skill of qualified midwives who would serve as health missionaries, who 'in being qualified ... will be able to disseminate knowledge, give instruction, and drive away ... ignorance'. These would not be women of 'advanced years' but 'single girls': it is, he asserted, 'false modesty to say that only married women shall be midwives'. The government carried a 'duty to humanity', especially in the 'dark hour of maternity'.[24]

The Midwives Bill met with 'almost unanimous approval'.[25] It represents one example of innovation achieved through a transactional process. Innovation was decided through interaction, and the 'fit' that was possible between political identities and the government. The consensus over nation-building and the imperative of reducing maternal and infant mortality gave the new trained midwives opportunity for leverage against a colonial medical profession which comprised mainly general practitioners, and against community midwives who were qualified by experience. Against medical protest, the Midwives Act endorsed independent, certified midwifery. The midwife, trained and registered by the state, could attend normal birth without supervision by a doctor. The government also provided maternity care for 'respectable wives of workingmen' in the St Helens hospitals, at a modest fee.[26] Relations between the various arms of the state proved of central importance in the success of this midwifery innovation. Neill interacted personally with Seddon; and the population imperative prompted politicians to support the idea of the trained midwife.

Such thinking loomed even larger after the First World War when childbirth became central to concerns about national efficiency, the future of the new nation and the imperial world. A maternal mortality scare provided focus, made public as scandal. Statistics published by the US Children's Bureau displayed to the world a New Zealand anomaly of low infant mortality, but a high maternal death rate. This was embarrassing because New Zealand was proud of its reputation as a healthy country and as an exemplar for personal health services intended to promote a better imperial type. Population policy, influenced by eugenics, justified state involvement in policy affecting childbirth.

A jurisdictional dispute

Against this backdrop, a dispute erupted in the 1920s, extending into the 1930s, over who were to be the dominant experts with control over childbirth. This dispute resulted in a shift in the balance of power, from midwife to doctor. The role of the state was critical, as were shifting identities and power relationships within it, in deciding who enjoyed state support. In the 1920s, the state – the government and a modernizing Department of Health – backed midwives. In the 1930s, the government backed doctors.

In terms of diffusion, it was culturally appropriate for politicians and public officials to support a midwife system, because this, historically, was the British way of birth. It was endorsed by British-educated medical authorities in New Zealand, namely Dr Henry Jellett, former Master of the Rotunda Hospital in Dublin, who volunteered his services to the Department of Health as consulting obstetrician; and Dr Tom Paget, a popular rural general practitioner. Jellett's and Paget's view that a midwife service would be safer and more cost-effective appeared confirmed first by New Zealand's high maternal death rate, and second by an actual outbreak of puerperal sepsis in a private hospital in 1923, in which women died. The subsequent inquiry exposed low standards of practice and the shocking state of private hospitals. In search of a culprit, the commission of inquiry blamed the Department of Health, because it was responsible for epidemic diseases, including the major killer of women in childbirth, puerperal sepsis. The Department and its obstetrical consultant, Jellett, in turn pointed the finger at general practitioners in private practice. A class effect unsettled the public: evidently well-to-do women, who could afford a doctor and private hospital care, were more at risk.[27]

These British-trained officials, themselves skilled medical practitioners, demonstrated statistically that a midwife was safer. From the returns of New

Zealand mixed hospitals, which admitted medical and surgical as well as maternity patients, Paget showed how most cases of puerperal sepsis could be traced to an exogenous cause. He calculated that the seventy-one hospitals of this type, where women were attended by general practitioners, shared an average maternal mortality rate of 8.23 per 1,000 live births in 1929, when the seven St Helens hospitals run on a midwife system had a rate of 2.08.[28] Paget and Jellett showed the influence that key personalities could exert in a small country. Jellett the Rotunda man advocated a midwife and specialist service, based on four large teaching hospitals, one in each of the four main centres, while Paget favoured a midwife and general practitioner. Jellett's suggested innovation would take another fifty years to be fully implemented. Both medical men insisted that puerperal sepsis had an external cause, and that birth was a physiological process. Jellett hoped to banish the GP because there was no need for a doctor at normal births. Logically, the campaign for safe maternity which the two steered through in 1924 had the young, trained midwife to the forefront.

It is worth noting that nurses in New Zealand, while they did not dispute their subordinate role as the doctor's helpmeet, enjoyed a higher status than in the United Kingdom. Hester Maclean, the country's head nurse as Director of the Health Department's Division of Nursing, actively promoted the Nurses and Midwives Registration Act 1925, which upgraded midwifery to a postgraduate qualification in order to oust the community midwife whose expertise rested on age and experience, and in the process demoted most practising midwives to maternity nurses. Lobbying led by Maclean's successor, Mary Lambie, preserved the new trained midwife's autonomy in the 1930s, by keeping the St Helens hospitals, the midwifery training schools, under direct state control rather than transferring them to hospital boards which were dominated by the views of local general practitioners.[29] As a consequence of these reforms, however, midwifery was effectively subsumed into nursing.

Despite the long-term opportunity which this presented to doctors, the state campaign for safe maternity provoked an institutionalized response by the medical profession, which organized into the Obstetrical Society in 1927. This consisted mainly of general practitioners since specialization did not become a dominant trend until after the Second World War. Here indeed was a clash of discourses, a heated 'conversation' between doctors and midwives. An outspoken woman doctor with firm eugenic views, Doris Gordon, rallied the medical response. Australian-born and New Zealand-educated, she entered small town general practice with her husband, where the Gordons ran their own private hospital (purchased from Paget). Gordon led the Obstetrical Society in opposition to state control, refuted allegations of blame, and asserted that a doctor service was superior. Alert to the importance of birth to the general practitioner, she embarked on a mission to save the 'family practitioner spirit'.[30] Gordon proceeded to lead two public campaigns for professorships in obstetrics and two teaching hospitals, to raise the status of her specialty, and to write books depicting herself as a pioneer in saving the mothers of New Zealand from the primitive horrors of natural birth.[31]

Both sides in the debate used theory to justify their political positions. Against the departmental view, the Obstetrical Society argued the autogenous theory, that puerperal sepsis had an internal cause. They insisted that birth was pathological and maternity 'highly dangerous' since women had become weakened by civilization, which justified a doctor's attendance. Whereas the Department of Health used maternal death rates as a gauge of safety, or the lack of it, the Obstetrical Society employed the concept of satisfaction, as we would now term it, in promoting medicalized birth, arguing that maternity services provided by a doctor were better because they were more expensive, modern, and scientific.

Women and medicalization

While no dichotomy existed of women versus doctors, the opposite, of women in support of doctors, was closer to the truth. By the 1930s the majority of women's groups favoured 'modern' management of birth, that is, a doctor and hospital.[32] Their reasoning must be understood in the context of the fertility decline and the smaller family. Women's groups which supported medicalized birth had a wider conception of the needs of mothers and maternal citizenship than maternal mortality and birth services. For example, the National Council of Women, first established in 1896, continued to advocate freedom and justice for women, a stance which explains why women's agency does not fit the disease model: their reasoning reached beyond medicine. It was only in the 1920s and 1930s moreover that they became aware of the high maternal mortality rate through media publicity and their political and health networks.

Innovation was accepted, in the form of a doctor service and childbirth in hospital, because of a 'fit' between the aims of the Obstetrical Society and women's organizations. Gender, culture, and class played their part. Women sought relief from pain and anxiety in their 'time of trouble', relief which a doctor could provide in a hospital setting. Educated women believed that science could better nature, and that birth should be a safe and joyous experience. This is what they expected from scientific innovation. Chloroform, which New Zealand midwives were allowed to use, did not meet modern women's demands; nor did the analgesia provided by gas and air machines in the late 1930s. Women sought control of birth through control of labour pain. Doctors offered not just pain relief, but *painless* childbirth, and privacy through amnesia (as lack of memory of the event enabled women to retain their perceived sense of dignity and privacy). Ironically, birthing mothers lost control, when their aim was to retain it.[33]

Organized women and the contingent relationships which they formed with the Obstetrical Society through the mediation of women doctors – notably Doris Gordon – helped to tilt the balance of power from midwife to doctor by the 1930s. Obstetrics was professionalizing, and yet in the Depression the Department of Health was weakened by deep funding cuts. Amidst this shifting ground, mainstream women's groups affiliated to the National Council of Women – a non-party political lobby which served as an umbrella for 168 organizations comprising 40,000 women in New Zealand – campaigned with Gordon to raise the funds for the first Chair of Obstetrics at the University of Otago, then New Zealand's sole medical school, in 1930. In the middle of the Depression the women's campaign obtained its funds in just six weeks. Organized women repeated their efforts in support of a second professorship in obstetrics in Auckland in the 1940s, at the new National Women's Hospital. The most active fund-raisers were 'society women' with husbands in politics and business, targeted by Gordon because they were all 'eminently respectable ladies of the right tint of politics'.[34]

Pain relief provided a lure, while birth in a new hospital and a fortnight's rest held the attractions of a hotel service. Competing claims over how to be humane and humanitarian surfaced by the 1930s, whereby most women's organizations perceived attendance by a doctor as more humanitarian than a midwife service. As the matron of the Christchurch St Helens Hospital confided in 1938 about the move to have a doctor attend at all hospital deliveries, it would hurt the St Helens midwives, 'but from a humanitarian standpoint we could be cried down for appealing against it'.[35] Humanitarianism itself proved to be a contested and contingent concept.[36]

A rival 'Hands Off St Helens' campaign in defence of the midwifery model occurred in 1930, just four months after the successful women's campaign for a professorship in obstetrics. Labour women, who were becoming more organized, protested that to admit medical students violated the purpose of these midwifery teaching hospitals, to provide quality maternal care at a moderate cost, and to train midwives.[37] The 'political opportunity structure' was such that the National Council of Women, rather than Labour women, had economic power and political leverage in 1930. Women doctors were crucial mediators. As superintendents of the St Helens hospitals, two had secured access for medical students as early as 1918, with the aim of improving medical education. Labour women did not know this. Consequently 'Hands Off St Helens' failed. Yet this split in the women's movement over a midwife or doctor service had closed by 1937–8.

By the 1930s, the balance of power had already shifted from the Department of Health, supportive of midwives, to the medical profession. The class issue came to the fore with the election of the Labour government in 1935. Egalitarianism, a powerful myth in New Zealand, became invoked in the cause of pro-doctor innovation. Women's groups agreed with politicians on the need for equality in pain relief, and the Committee of Inquiry into Maternity Services established by the Labour government in 1937 concluded that birthing mothers should have access to the 'fullest degree of pain-relief consistent with safety to mother and child'.[38] The Committee was:

> not impressed with the arguments of those who contrast the midwife system at its best with the doctor service at its worst. It [was] more concerned to decide which system *at its best* offers the fullest advantages ... to the lying-in mother.[39]

Although the midwife system was demonstrably 'safe and efficient', the combined system of doctor and nurse was argued to be 'still more efficient', and, most tellingly, 'a more satisfying service'.[40] Clearly, successful innovation depended on power and on users' approval.

When Mrs Jennie Bean, who worked for women's and children's causes in Christchurch, declared in 1937 that 'the birth of children is a natural thing, and it is not meant that doctors should come into it', her statement was unfashionable. By contrast, the Society for the Protection of Women and Children asserted the newly prevalent view: 'We think that painless maternity is every woman's right.'[41] Half a century later, Mrs Bean's outlook once again became fashionable. From 1939, a medical model of birth became incorporated into the welfare state because of a fit between the majority of doctors', politicians', and women's aims. Childbirth was free to women, paid for with public funds from 1939, and it was this relief from the cost of having a baby which marked the most significant improvement in women's lives: a notable achievement.

The midwife returns

By the 1970s, 99 per cent of births took place in hospital. The midwife finally lost autonomy under the Nurses Act 1971, which required a doctor's presence at birth. Doctors, especially consultants, enjoyed state endorsement. Under the Nurses Amendment Act 1990, however, the independent midwife returned, and in 1996 the Lead Maternity Carer innovation was introduced to cap costs by requiring mothers to choose between a doctor and a midwife as their lead carer and budget-holder.

In the 1970s and 1980s it seemed as if the midwife might disappear. The St Helens basic midwifery course ceased when the last class graduated in 1979, and aspiring midwives moved overseas for training. The low point came in 1983 with the Nurses Amendment Bill which proposed to place maternity care in the hands of nurses who were not necessarily qualified midwives. An alliance of midwives and middle-class women consumers fought back, aided by women in the state apparatus.[42]

Consumer support proved a key asset for midwives in the 1980s. This was not simply a matter of 'configuring the user', but of the user configuring the carer. From the 1970s, second-wave feminism began to exert influence, partly through the natural birth movement which advocated patients' rights and home birth. Women continued to call for respect, control, and to oppose separation of mother and baby in hospital (originally justified by infection), and to these demands added expectations of cultural diversity and more scope for maternal choice. In the 1980s, middle-class women's organizations in tandem with a Labour government again used gendered citizenship arguments to justify midwifery reforms. Consensus across interlocking networks was vital: in the late 1930s between the medical profession, the government, and middle-class women's organizations; and in the late 1980s between midwives, the government, and middle-class women's organizations.

This time midwives developed an institutionalized response to state action, politicized by the 1983 Nurses Amendment Bill. The New Zealand College of Midwives formed in 1988–9, through interactions between midwives and women's groups, a 'save the midwives' lobby and the women's health movement. Its membership increased tenfold from 50 to 500 in just five years, from 1991–5, and by 1998 the College represented 83 per cent of practising midwives. The College established networks with the Ministry of Women's Affairs established by the Fourth Labour government, which held 'women's forums' in the 1980s just as the First Labour government had sought women's opinions in 1936–8. For midwives, as for doctors sixty years earlier, resistance in the form of an institutionalized response to government intervention which threatened to undermine their status helped to create a collective identity; and resistance as a process itself bred midwifery innovation.

This was assisted by changes in the 'political opportunity structure', to use Tilly's term. From the 1980s organized obstetrics turned on the defensive, following a cervical cancer inquiry in 1988 centred on the National Women's Hospital in Auckland, initiated by feminist health campaigners and chaired by Dame Silvia Cartwright, who subsequently became New Zealand's first woman High Court judge (and from 2001 its second woman Governor-General). The inquiry into the 'Unfortunate Experiment' at National Women's, as it became known, brought obstetrics and gynaecology into disrepute because women in the care of consultants at the country's major teaching hospital, diagnosed with cervical cancer, were not told and were treated too late. The Cartwright inquiry endorsed patients' rights and intensified public questioning of medical authority.[43] The medical profession's power and influence were under challenge, in direct contrast to the 1930s.

An opportunity opened for the midwife. Her moment came with the Nurses Amendment Act 1990, under which the midwife regained autonomy as an independent practitioner, and won the feminist demand of equal pay for work of equal value, as she was to be paid the same fee for birth services as a general practitioner. This re-innovation resulted from interactions between a Labour government and middle-class women who sought to regain control of birth. In response to middle-class women's demands, a reformist government this time backed the midwife.

The midwife's return occurred in the context of radical economic deregulation in New Zealand from 1984, under the Fourth Labour government. Known as Rogernomics after the then Minister of Finance, Roger Douglas, this local equivalent of Thatcherism unleashed revolutionary social and economic changes as the government proceeded to restructure the economy and society in an effort to make both more open to globalization. The 1990s' changes in maternity services were reinforced by larger health reforms begun by Labour but continued by a more conservative, monetarist National government. Managerialism, introduced under the State Sector Act 1988 (which required the public service to run on business ethics) reconceptualized birthing women as 'clients', which gave extra weight to the women's movement and to patients' rights. Significantly, the

Nurses Amendment Act 1990 suited both feminist and economic rationalist agendas. Helen Clark, then Minister of Health – New Zealand's first elected woman Prime Minister a decade later – revealed in her keynote speech at the first New Zealand College of Midwives conference in 1990:

> When I became Minister of Health last year I had the opportunity to do something about the injustice which I consider the loss of autonomy for midwives to be … I discovered surprising allies. Even the Treasury could see merit in increased autonomy. And if we look at the problem from the perspective of those officials who have been charged by Government with reviewing restrictions on practice which are in essence anti-competitive, there is certainly a strong argument to be mounted against the monopoly of registered medical practitioners in taking full responsibility for the supervision of childbirth.[44]

Helen Clark was influenced by the swing from intervention to natural childbirth in the 1980s, and by the 'Unfortunate Experiment' at National Women's. She expected the 1990 legal change would lead to more home births, not increased costs from women opting to choose care by both a doctor and midwife in hospital. If it had been politically possible in 1990, she would have required women to choose between a doctor and midwife. In deciding against this, she predicted that doctors would raise safety worries about mothers and babies in the hands of independent midwives.[45]

The Nurses Amendment Act 1990 which restored the midwife as an autonomous practitioner, consistent with the WHO definition of a midwife, also provided for direct-entry midwifery education, to separate midwifery from nursing. With the state on their side, midwives transformed themselves from state employees, in an unequal relationship with doctors and a subset of the nursing profession, to independent practitioners. Midwifery instantly became a profession in its own right, autonomous and self-regulating. The government and Treasury officials expected that midwifery re-innovation would increase competition and reduce costs. The outcome was indeed to increase competition between doctors and midwives. But costs soared because women opted for shared care by a doctor and midwife under the 1990 legislation and this doubled state expenditure on maternity services from 1990–4, when the birth rate stayed the same.

The result was the Lead Maternity Carer (LMC) scheme of July 1996. In what came to be known as the Section 51 Notice, issued under Section 51 of the Health and Disability Act 1993, each mother was to choose either a midwife or a doctor as her LMC who would have overall responsibility for her primary maternity care for the final six months of her pregnancy, labour, and birth, and postnatal care for mother and baby. A capped fee was paid to the LMC, who carried both clinical and financial responsibility for birth management. The scheme succeeded in capping costs: expenditure on maternity services levelled out from 1996.

While this innovation was cost-driven, it was couched as advancing a health model as opposed to a medical model for birth services, where women could choose their type of care, hold the caregiver accountable, and obtain continuity of care from a midwife as opposed to a doctor. The LMC innovation was based on six principles: (1) services were woman-centred; (2) safety was paramount; (3) the woman had a choice of carer; (4) she chose her LMC; (5) the LMC was responsible for co-ordinating her care; and (6) the scheme emphasized health and parenting education. In addition, New Zealand was to develop a national perinatal information system.[46]

This scheme cemented the changed power dynamic between doctors and midwives. It recognized midwives' independence, and the need for the midwife during birth. By the late 1990s, 61 per cent of New Zealand babies had a midwife as the lead carer assisting their mothers at delivery, compared to one-third (33 per cent) a general practitioner and 6 per cent an obstetrician.[47]

General practitioners and hospital consultants objected to the scheme because of inadequate funding and excessive paperwork. They secured changes to the scheme in 1997, assisted by hospitals which had lost 'market share' under the 1990s' health reforms, which had imposed a funder/provider split whereby hospitals competed as providers with independent midwifery practices. In response to medical protests, the system of payments changed from separate payments for each visit, service, or hour of care in labour, to modular payments for the second and third trimesters, labour and birth, and postnatal care – again with the aim of containing costs.

The College of Midwives opposed any change in the LMC scheme. It capitalized on this re-innovation by claiming to represent women generally, and invoked feminist arguments that midwives provided what women who made informed choices wanted: a woman-centred partnership which approached childbirth as a normal life event. The midwifery model, it argued, was distinguished by a partnership between midwives and women. The concept of 'partnership' had a mixed heritage: locally, in the Treaty of Waitangi of 1840, that enshrined the concept of partnership between Maori and the Crown, which was cited by the College of Midwives as a model in response to the Treaty of Waitangi negotiations in the 1980s and 1990s over indigenous rights and claims to land; and internationally, in the return to more natural birth.[48]

Problematically for the partnership concept, the interests of midwives and birthing mothers may overlap, but are not the same.[49] In an unintended outcome, former activists in the home birth movement, who had lobbied for a midwife service, felt disenfranchised.[50] New Zealand mothers had already shown that they favoured a doctor service, provided it was free, and considerate of their needs. Midwives claimed to speak for women in their attempt to strengthen the midwife's position against the medical profession, at the expense of co-operation between midwife and doctor. In this sense, the claim of midwifery to speak for women proved as potentially problematic as in an earlier era when doctors assumed to speak for women.

Professional views

Karen Guilliland, National Director of the New Zealand College of Midwives, recognized that the late twentieth-century jurisdictional dispute between midwives and doctors was not new: 'To understand the issues around shared care requires an understanding of the history of childbirth and maternity services.'[51] But the re-innovation of the midwife in 1990 removed the medical monopoly over maternity care and so reactivated competition, which was further encouraged by health reforms and budgetary constraints in the 1990s. Historically, hospital records showed that in fact most births were conducted by midwives, in hospital, while general practitioners provided back-up. Yet before 1990 the doctor was legally in control, rendering the midwife invisible. Guilliland favoured the Lead Maternity Carer scheme in its 1996 format because doctors had to negotiate with midwives as LMCs to agree on a price for the service women required, and fees began to be based on actual work. She blamed general practitioners for thwarting the potential of shared care by opting out of maternity services. Midwives felt betrayed by subsequent revisions to the scheme in response to doctors' protests, which divided maternity care into modules and set a new lower fee for hospital midwifery services, so that doctors who were lead carers could obtain cheaper support from hospital midwives.[52]

Midwifery autonomy, according to Guilliland, made a 'positive difference to women' in New Zealand. She saw the medical objective as control and supervision by doctors, and hence the undermining of midwifery, whereas the midwifery view was that the midwife served as 'gatekeeper' in birth services, not the doctor. This represented a strong challenge to the doctor's traditional role, offering a competing model of the midwife as the woman's and baby's partner in childbirth. She appealed to nurses and hospital midwives to back independent midwifery on the grounds that all benefited from the autonomous profession's increased income and status, and she expressed dismay at midwives and nurses who, in a 'women-intensive profession', supported the doctors, deploying the language of feminism to allege that they displayed 'oppressed group behaviour'.[53] She continued, '[A] continuing lack of faith in the ability of a women dominant profession to provide a quality service constantly challenges our autonomy.' [54]

Certainly, midwifery re-innovation posed problems for hospital midwifery, because the changes offered incentives for hospital-based midwives to work independently, and so to leave public hospitals for the private sector where they could earn much higher incomes than hospital salaries. Hospitals faced difficulties with retaining and recruiting midwives, while midwives who stayed faced confusion over changing ideas about their practice and the new emphases on cost and accountability.[55]

At National Women's Hospital, the retiring head of Obstetrics and Gynaecology, Professor Gillian Turner, who steered the hospital in the aftermath of the cervical cancer inquiry, expressed concern at what health reforms internationally had done to birth services: they fragmented care, reduced choice for women, and eroded doctor–midwife teamwork through competition. In particular, she criticized the new LMC scheme and its payment regime for removing women's choice of general practitioner.[56] The New Zealand Medical Association warned that New Zealand was heading for a 'doctor-free maternity system'.[57] Disillusioned by waning power and incomes, an increasing number of general practitioner obstetricians (GPOs) left maternity services, their departures covered in the media and in letters to the press.

Specialist obstetricians also expressed exasperation. From July 1999 hospitals were required to provide a 24-hour consultation service for women and babies under a LMC who needed secondary (hospital) maternity care. Specialists who worked on call provided consultations as hospital employees, as part of their contract with the hospital, and were not to claim under the Section 51 Maternity Notice. The problem was that few consultants worked as salaried specialists. Usually they divided their time between sessions in public hospitals and in the private sector. Specialists could not claim for caesarean sections performed as part of their public hospital duties under the LMC scheme, for example, because the government funded caesarean sections only through its secondary maternity contracts with hospitals. Private specialists, on the other hand, could charge women a co-payment for consultations.[58] Not only women were confused, who understood birth services to be taxpayer-funded, so were consultants.

Obstetricians and GPOs both argued that the object of choice was not attained: rather, women had less choice with midwifery re-innovation. The medical profession claimed that 80 per cent of women preferred shared care with a doctor and midwife. They invoked the old family practitioner argument that general practitioners had the most potential for long-term continuity of care from before a woman was pregnant to when her children grew up.[59] Numbers of GPOs registered as LMCs declined from 845 in July–September 1997 to 451 in July–September 1998, and GPOs attending births at National Women's Hospital dropped from 141 in August 1995 to 21 in November 1998. The government responded that midwives would fill the gap, but GPOs countered that they could not, because midwives did not deal with what goes wrong.[60] Some general practitioners claimed that intervention rates rose because of the departure of GPOs, and by inference because of midwife-attended births.[61] Rural practitioners maintained that 'the preferred option of most women' under a fee for service regime was shared care between a GPO and independent midwife, and yet the LMC scheme had allowed midwives as LMCs to exclude GPs, but not the reverse.[62]

Review of maternity services

These arguments from specialist and general practitioner obstetricians led to the setting up of the maternity services review in 1999, to inquire into access, choice, and the exit of GPOs. It found the highest levels of satisfaction among mothers with midwives as LMCs (89–93 per cent in three different surveys). During actual childbirth, the midwife, not the doctor, now attended the majority of births. About a third of women did not obtain the type of LMC they wanted, usually because their doctor no longer attended births. GPOs who claimed for maternity services in the three months ending September 1997 numbered 626, falling to 429 by March 1999. By contrast, the number of practising midwives grew from 740 in September 1997 to 789 in March 1999.

The review committee decided that there was no reason to recommend new expenditure to combat the departure of GPOs from maternity services. A higher proportion of mothers were satisfied with a midwife service rather than a doctor service; and safety was not compromised by midwife care. Rather, its findings proved consistent with the historical pattern that it was safer for a mother to have a midwife attend her in normal labour. As in 1939, the maternity services review favoured continuity of care, or what in 1999 they termed a continuum of primary health care, into which maternity services were integrated, and that professionals work in teams. What had changed in sixty years was the midwife's status; and what had not changed was the continuing rivalry between doctor and midwife. The maternity services review committee expressed concern about the 'apparent tension and lack of communication among providers',[63] which was exactly what, historically, put mothers at risk.

Conclusion

Power and control shaped midwifery re-innovation in the 1990s, as in the 1920s and 1930s, supported by user preferences. Outcomes were contingent, and depended on the political opportunity structure and spaces opened within it for interactions among parties with overlapping agendas. Cost loomed as a constraint, and there was an incentive to promote competition in the 1990s, whereas in the 1930s expense served as another gauge of scientific value. Cost imperatives assured the return of the midwife in 1990 through legislative change, supported by feminist politicians and economic rationalism promoted by Treasury officials. Ironically, this re-innovation led to soaring costs of maternity care because the government overlooked the historical pattern of New Zealand women's preference for shared care by a doctor and a midwife, a model that was itself given legislative sanction half a century earlier. Women's preferences prompted the LMC scheme to cap expenditure.

In both eras, state support was vital for professions in their jurisdictional disputes over midwifery. The source of this support varied with the contemporary pattern of power relations and whether politicians or bureaucrats were driving policy. In the 1920s power rested with the Department of Health; in the 1930s, with professionalizing doctors and a Labour government which sought their agreement to introduce state-funded medical services, supported by middle-class women's organizations. In the 1990s, power rested with a Labour government in contingent alliance with the Treasury, again supported by organized middle-class women.

Resistance to state intervention served as another shaping force which helped to create and crystallize professional identities. In the late 1920s the Obstetrical

Society formed in response to the state's campaign for safe maternity which supported the trained midwife, and in the late 1980s the College of Midwives organized in response to proposed legislative changes which would have meant the end of the trained midwife.

Wider social and cultural changes helped shape the nature of innovation, notably the tenor of feminism, which was maternalist in the 1930s, while second-wave feminism supported professionalizing midwives in 1990. The centrality of maternity persisted, and mothers remained an afterthought. Birth has always been contested, and the same applies to midwifery innovation. In the 1990s midwife care and a brief stay in hospital became the New Zealand way of birth. Though safe and cost-effective, this reduced mothers' options. General practitioners withdrew their services, and midwives' incomes increased. Cost ruled, cloaked ostensibly as choice.

Notes

1 Irvine Loudon, *Death in Childbirth: An International Study of Maternal Care and Maternal Mortality 1800–1950*, Oxford, Clarendon Press, 1992, p. 349.
2 Raymond G. DeVries and Rebeca Barroso, 'Midwives among the machines: re-creating midwifery in the late twentieth century', in Hilary Marland and Anne Marie Rafferty (eds), *Midwives, Society and Childbirth: Debates and Controversies in the Modern Period*, London and New York, Routledge, 1997, pp. 248–68.
3 The idea of 'configuring the user' is outlined in Keith Grint and Steve Woolgar, *The Machine at Work: Technology, Work and Organization*, Cambridge, Polity Press, 1997.
4 On the idea of 'fit', see Theda Skocpol, *Protecting Soldiers and Mothers: The Political Origins of Social Policy in the United States*, Cambridge, MA, Belknap Press of Harvard University Press, 1992; Philippa Mein Smith, *Mothers and King Baby: Infant Survival and Welfare in an Imperial World: Australia 1880–1950*, Basingstoke and London, Macmillan, 1997. On the ambiguity of the state's positions in the New Zealand context, see Melanie Nolan, *Breadwinning: New Zealand Women and the State*, Christchurch, Canterbury University Press, 2000.
5 The HFA ceased to exist in 2001, becoming absorbed into the Ministry of Health. It was formed in the late 1990s from an amalgamation of four Regional Health Authorities (RHAs) established as part of a radical restructuring of the health sector in 1993, which introduced a competitive model into health and a funder/provider split, where the RHAs were the funders.
6 Examples include Philippa Mein Smith, *Maternity in Dispute: New Zealand 1920–1939*, Wellington, Government Printer/Historical Branch, 1986; Charlotte G. Borst, *Catching Babies: The Professionalization of Childbirth, 1870–1920*, Cambridge, MA, Harvard University Press, 1995.
7 Hilary Marland, 'The midwife as health missionary: the reform of Dutch childbirth practices in the early twentieth century', in Marland and Rafferty (eds), *Midwives, Society and Childbirth*, p. 171.
8 These thoughts have benefited from the argument about formation of identities in Donald Denoon and Philippa Mein Smith with Marivic Wyndham, *A History of Australia, New Zealand and the Pacific*, Oxford, Blackwell, 2000, and Charles Tilly, 'Social movements and (all sorts of) other political interactions – local, national, and international – including identities', *Theory and Society*, 1998, vol. 27, pp. 453–80. They are developed in the next section. On competing discourses, see Susan Pitt, 'Midwifery and medicine: gendered knowledge in the practice of delivery', in Marland and Rafferty (eds), *Midwives, Society and Childbirth*, p. 219.

9   John V. Pickstone (ed.), *Medical Innovations in Historical Perspective*, New York, St Martin's Press, 1992, Introduction. See, in a different historiographical context, the use of 'invention' by Eric Hobsbawm and Terence Ranger, *The Invention of Tradition*, Cambridge, Cambridge University Press, 1983.

10 Mein Smith, *Maternity in Dispute*.

11 Grint and Woolgar, *The Machine at Work*, p. 74.

12 Tilly, 'Social movements'; see also the argument independently developed by Denoon and Mein Smith, *A History of Australia, New Zealand and the Pacific*.

13 Tilly, 'Social movements', p. 478.

14 Denoon and Mein Smith with Wyndham, *A History of Australia, New Zealand and the Pacific*, especially Chapters 19 and 20.

15 Tilly, 'Social movements', pp. 457, 467.

16 For a detailed analysis of the politics of birth in New Zealand between the wars and the shift to medical control, see Mein Smith, *Maternity in Dispute*.

17 In NZ 'First' has a capital 'F', such was the significance of this government's legislative reforms.

18 Elaine Papps and Mark Olssen, *Doctoring Childbirth and Regulating Midwifery in New Zealand: A Foucauldian Perspective*, Palmerston North, Dunmore Press, 1997.

19 'State' is in quotation marks in light of Melanie Nolan's argument that the state's role can be contradictory, Nolan, *Breadwinning*.

20 Borst, *Catching Babies*, p. 1.

21 Judith Walzer Leavitt, *Brought to Bed: Childbearing in America, 1750 to 1950*, New York and London, Oxford University Press, 1986.

22 Three points of entry into a large literature are Valerie Fildes, Lara Marks and Hilary Marland (eds), *Women and Children First: International Maternal and Infant Welfare, 1870–1945*, London, Routledge, 1992; Alisa Klaus, *Every Child a Lion: The Origins of Maternal and Infant Health Policy in the United States and France, 1890–1920*, Ithaca and London, Cornell University Press, 1993; and Mein Smith, *Mothers and King Baby*.

23 Margaret Tennant, 'Grace Neill', in C. Macdonald, M. Penfold and B. Williams (eds), *The Book of New Zealand Women*, Wellington, Bridget Williams Books, 1991, pp. 467–71.

24 Midwives Bill, *New Zealand Parliamentary Debates*, vol. 128, 1 July 1904, pp. 70–1.

25 *New Zealand Parliamentary Debates*, vol. 128, 1 July 1904, p. 88. Cf. Marland on 'The midwife as health missionary'.

26 This target group received further support in the form of a £6 maternity benefit for members of the National Provident Fund, a state-subsidized friendly society for workers with incomes of less than £200 a year, from 1910.

27 See Mein Smith, *Maternity in Dispute*, Chapters 1 and 2.

28 Report of Department of Health, *AJHR*, 1930, H-31, p. 54. For statistics cited internationally by Jellett in his textbooks, see Henry Jellett, *The Causes and Prevention of Maternal Mortality*, London, J. and A. Churchill, 1929, and Loudon, *Death in Childbirth*.

29 Mein Smith, *Maternity in Dispute*, p.95.

30 Ibid., pp. 41–2.

31 Doris Gordon, *Backblocks Baby-Doctor*, London, Faber and Faber, 1955, and *Doctor Down Under*, London, Faber and Faber, 1957.

32 As Paget observed during evidence of Dr H. Jellett, Christchurch, 23 June 1937, Committee of Inquiry into Maternity Services, Evidence, 1937, H 3/7, Archives NZ.

33 See also J. Beinart (Stanton), 'Obstetric analgesia and the control of childbirth in twentieth-century Britain', in J. Garcia, R. Kilpatrick and M. Richards (eds), *The Politics of Maternity Care: Services for Childbearing Women in Twentieth-Century Britain*, Oxford, Oxford University Press, 1990, pp. 116–32. There were moves in NZ for midwives to provide analgesia, as in the UK under the National Birthday Trust Fund.

Qualified midwives could use chloroform from 1926, at Jellett's instigation, and Minnitt's gas and air machine in the St Helens hospitals in the later 1930s. Cf. A. Susan Williams, *Women and Childbirth in the Twentieth Century: A History of the National Birthday Trust Fund 1928–93*, Stroud, Sutton Publishing, 1997, Chapter 6.

34 Gordon, *Backblocks Baby-Doctor*, pp. 181–95; quotations from pp. 183 and 189. On the National Council of Women, see A. Else (ed.), *Women Together: A History of Women's Organisations in New Zealand*, Wellington, Historical Branch/Daphne Brasell Associates Press, 1993.

35 E. M. Sparkes, Matron St Helens Christchurch to M. Lambie, Director Division of Nursing, 21 July 1938, H 13/39/3 20542, Archives, NZ.

36 This argument runs counter to that of Charlotte Parkes, in Linda Bryder (ed.), *A Healthy Country*, Wellington, Bridget Williams Books, 1991, p. 180.

37 *Evening Post*, 3 July 1930, Secretary, Wellington Women's Branch NZ Labour Party to Stallworthy, 8 July 1930, H 111 03020.

38 Report of Committee of Inquiry into Maternity Services, *AJHR (Appendices to the Journals of the House of Representatives)*, 1938, H-31A, p. 107.

39 *Report of Committee of Inquiry into Maternity Services*, Wellington, Government Printer, 1938, p. 98 (different pagination from *AJHR* version; quotation in n.38 is on p. 118).

40 Ibid., p. 99.

41 Evidence of Mrs Bean, Christchurch, 2 July 1937, evidence of Society for the Protection of Women and Children, Auckland, 6 September 1937, Committee of Inquiry into Maternity Services, Evidence, H3/7.

42 Joan Donley, *Save the Midwife*, Auckland, New Women's Press, 1986, pp. 103–9.

43 Silvia R. Cartwright, *The Report of the Committee of Inquiry into Allegations Concerning the Treatment of Cervical Cancer at National Women's Hospital and into Other Related Matters*, Auckland, Committee of Inquiry, 1988; Sandra Coney, *The Unfortunate Experiment*, Auckland, Penguin, 1988.

44 Helen Clark, 'Opening Address', *New Zealand College of Midwives Conference Proceedings*, Dunedin, New Zealand College of Midwives, 1990, pp. 2–3, quoted in Rea Daellenbach, 'The paradox of success and the challenge of change: home birth associations of Aotearoa/New Zealand', PhD thesis, University of Canterbury, 1999, pp. 168–9.

45 David McLoughlin, 'The politics of childbirth', *North and South*, August 1993, pp. 54–68.

46 Kim Wheeler, 'Maternity Services (1996 Advice Notice) – where to from here?', *Health Manager*, vol. 4, no. 4, 1997, pp. 5–8. Thanks to NZHTA for a search of literature since 1990.

47 National Health Committee, *Review of Maternity Services in New Zealand*, Wellington, NHC, September 1999, p. 82.

48 Valerie E. M. Fleming, 'Midwifery in New Zealand: responding to changing times', *Health Care for Women International*, 1996, vol. 17, pp. 343–59.

49 Valerie E. M. Fleming, 'Women and midwives in partnership: a problematic relationship?', *Journal of Advanced Nursing*, 1998, vol. 27, no. 1, pp. 8–14.

50 Daellenbach, 'Paradox of success', ch. 8.

51 Karen Guilliland, 'Shared care in maternity services: with whom and how?', *Health Manager*, 1999, vol. 6 no. 2, pp. 4–8.

52 Ibid.

53 Karen Guilliland, 'Learning from midwives', *Kaitiaki: Nursing New Zealand*, October 1996, p. 23.

54 Karen Guilliland, 'Current issues for New Zealand midwifery and maternity services', *Our Newsletter*, December 1998, New Zealand College of Midwives; http://www.midwives. org.nz/colnews/newsdec1.html.

55 'Hospital midwifery: where to now?', *New Zealand Health and Hospital*, March/April 1994, p. 7.

56 'Obstetrics facing crisis says retiring professor', *New Zealand Doctor*, 17 March 1999, p. 5.

57 'Medical Assoc slams maternity funding', *Press*, 8 September 2000, p. 3.

58 Health Funding Authority Consultation Document, *Specialist Maternity Services: Obstetricians, Paediatricians and Anaesthetists*, Wellington, September 1999.

59 'GPs turn away from birth work', *Press*, Christchurch, 2 November 1998, clipping courtesy of Kerri-Ann Hughes.

60 'GPOs thrown out with bathwater', *New Zealand GP*, 6 October 1999, pp. 1–2.

61 'Birth interventions on rise', *New Zealand GP*, 6 October 1999, p. 2.

62 Tim Malloy, chairman Rural GP Network political issues committee, *New Zealand Doctor*, 2 April 1997, p. 4.

63 National Health Committee, *Review of Maternity Services in New Zealand*, Wellington, September 1999, pp. 5, 7, 40, 44.

9 French response to 'innovation'

The return of the living donor in organ transplantation

Martine Gabolde and Anne Marie Moulin

A medical innovation is an important change in medical practice which is recognized by the concerned professionals and often by the public as well. This chapter attempts to explore an innovation of a specific kind. It is neither the improvement of a surgical procedure, nor the clinical trial of new drugs, it is the utilization, in a new guise, of the reservoir formed by human organs. In other words, it is a new way of tapping human potentialities in a context of scarce resources.

In France, after a pioneering period, during the 1950s and early 1960s where living donors constituted the main source of kidneys, the use of living donors had plummeted from 5 per cent in the 1980s to 2.5 per cent in the early 1990s. Recently it has re-emerged and concerns additional organs: livers in the first place but also lungs. This 'return of the living donor' is in many ways different from the practice of the early years.

Transplantation has become an autonomous field of medicine since the first successful kidney grafts in the early 1950s, then in the following years with the growing use of cadaver organs. The subsequent extension of transplantation to liver, lung and bowels has illustrated the amazing potentialities of a surgical technique assisted by growing knowledge in immunology and pharmacology. Transplantation is helping to provide a decisive support to the prolongation of human life and radically modify human destiny, in the same way as with gene selection we are about to enter 'God's council',[1] and interfere with the divine plan for human species. With potentially iterative transplantation, a kind of immortalization is indeed conceivable.

Transplantation may also be considered as one of the pillars of surgery in the future. Renée Fox, author of a pioneering study on transplantation and dialysis in 1974,[2] predicted that, in the twenty-first century, 1 in 4 surgical operations would be a transplant.[3]

Transplantation has also emerged as one of the great testing grounds of bioethics, on account of the novel moral issues involved and of the many legal problems linked to its social organization.[4] This organization was made necessary by the emergence of transplantation as a regular medical procedure founded on organ removal and in contradiction to the law punishing all voluntary damage to individuals' bodies.

With our study of transplantation with living donors, we have selected a medical therapy which bears some of the markers of innovation and allows us to unravel the multiplicity of factors which play a role in the acceptance and diffusion of new medical practices. In our chapter we will only briefly compare the French response to similar responses in other countries, but we will focus on a comparison of the French attitude in transplantation at several times in the history of organ grafts: it is not so much the history of the response to a scientific change than the complex building of a new procedure, resulting from contributions of the professionals (doctors, scientists, administratives, legislators) and public demand.

This chapter has been written by two authors who are practising doctors involved in social sciences: the first one is completing a thesis on the ethical issues linked to the practice of transplantation with living donors, the other has worked for a long time on the history of immunology, which in the past bore the label of 'philosophy of science', and is happy to rally more modestly to the empirical format of 'Science Studies'. This chapter is based on a study, carried out by one of us, of the response to the 'innovation of the living donor' conducted among transplantation professionals.

New technologies link medical instruments, scientific knowledge and patients' bodies. The development of these technologies means that we are all concerned directly or indirectly by them. Even if the medical responsibility for the extension of the life span is a controversial topic (see Illich's *Medical Nemesis!*[5]), we all owe some of our life breath to these technologies. It does not require blind gratitude or excessive devotion to science, but it is a fact. Nobel Prize winner Peter Medawar, recovering from his stroke, remembered his debt to the intensive care people who helped him while he lay unable to express his anxiety and wish to survive.[6] Surgeon Thomas Starzl, while suffering from coronary obstruction and being rushed to the operating room, considered himself a 'cousin' of the transplantees for whom for years he had tried to win additional life.[7]

Innovation has become synonymous with modernity, and the urge for medical innovation is the corollary of a growing awareness of the 'right to health'. (Whether this right to health, held as universal, is distributed equally among all humans, is another question.) Organ transplantation has moved from the realm of fantasy to reality and when it takes place in developing countries proves that they share the scientific conquests of the more advanced parts of the world.

At the start of the twenty-first century, innovation is supposed to incorporate theoretical breakthroughs and high-tech advances, bold investigations into cells, genes and tissues.[8] In contrast, transplantation with living donors is a good example of the combination of several models once active in medicine: the biographical approach or the close patient–doctor relationship (the 'royal' model, inspired by the proximity of the physician to his powerful patient[9]), the analytical approach, relying on dissection of bodies, the experimental one dealing with animal studies and laboratory devices, and the technological one with development of robots and sophisticated instruments. Transplantation obviously integrates all these models. How, in these conditions, are we to distinguish between tradition and novelty? How are we to distinguish between the experimental and the therapeutic? The picture of innovation is fascinatingly complex.

Innovation may relate to the improvement of a complex surgical act but we focus here on one of the facets, the increased use of available resources, with people providing their organs as a cure. In order to legitimize this strategy, the notion of a crisis, the crisis of 'organ shortage', had to be constructed,[10] on the basis of an assessment of both demand and supply. On the one hand, the right to health implies that people suffering from various organic failures are entitled to benefit from transplantation, at the expense of others' organs, possibly at the risk of others' lives.[11] Modernity means the recognition of these extreme, some say 'catastrophic', rights. On the other hand, organs need to be located and can be tapped from various sources: living donors as well as cadavers or animals (xenografts). As the problem was invented in the mid-1990s, so a solution had to be found.

Consequently, the area of transplantation is undergoing a period of turbulence in France. These rapid changes suggest an analogy between the medical field and the economic one. Transplantation, like any kind of market, has to improve its products, in order to fulfil the expectations of its clients whose preferences are also changing. The urge for innovative procedures is linked to the growing demands of patients, emboldened by the recognition of the new human rights to health and well-being.[12] In France, where the state has claimed total control of surgery, and where, unlike many other countries, there is no such thing as private clinics performing surgery, in the face of this growing demand, organs have been officially recognized as a limited resource – the 'crisis' mentioned above.

The history of grafting with living donors

Admittedly, the use of the living donor is not an absolute innovation. It is in fact the rediscovery of a procedure, which was once the only way of performing transplantation. The use of a living donor was the only accessible procedure at the beginning of kidney transplantation. In the early 1950s, a few surgeons decided to progress from animals to people and perform transplantation. The kidneys were taken either from cadavers or from living subjects.[13] Professor René Küss, then the young assistant of surgery at Cochin Hospital in Paris, reports in his memoirs that from 1951, when he decided, in his own words, to 'progress from animal to man', he used organs from prisoners who had agreed to donate them and the kidneys were removed during the minutes following decapitation. Nephrectomies on living subjects were performed for therapeutic reasons: tuberculosis, renal stones.[14] These organs which had been removed for therapeutic reasons without asking consent, were termed 'free organs'.[15]

The failure of these transplants was attributed to biological incompatibility between donor and recipient, bearing out Alexis Carrel's prediction, fifty years earlier.[16] The only rational transplant, it was considered, would be an exchange between monozygotic twins. In December 1952, Jean Hamburger's team in Paris grafted a young man, Marius Renard, with his mother's kidney: this première of the Necker Hospital was hailed as the 'Christmas miracle' by the popular press, but survival was brief. The first successful transplant took place in Boston in 1954 when John Murray grafted a young patient with the kidney of his identical twin, which ensured him a six-year survival.[17] It was not very encouraging since few people benefit from having a clone or an identical twin. However, this 'première' had a paradoxical effect in the sense that it fuelled research and fostered the optimistic belief in surgeons that nature could at least partially overcome the barriers between individuals, and that it was not an 'all or nothing' phenomenon.

This paved the way for the adoption of biological criteria to sort out the best donors. HLA groups (Human Leucocyte Antigens) were considered for the selection procedure.[18] HLA antigens are borne on white blood cells and tissues, they play an important role in the immune response and recognition of 'self and non-self' and allow differentiation of individuals. Jean Dausset, who was to receive the Nobel Prize for his major contribution to instituting the HLA system, has equated this selection with the use of blood groups for transfusion.[19] In spite of its complexity, the identification of HLA groups, after many workshops, came to be reasonably standardized. The HLA pairing between donor and recipient reigned for more than twenty years over transplanters (some said 'tyrannized' them), although its importance in organ survival was not equally appreciated by all teams.

Looking back to their 'heroic' attempts in the past, surgeons wondered whether it was legitimate to 'mutilate' healthy subjects, related or not, even if they were volunteers. Sociologist Herpin notes that this word is never used in countries displaying a positive attitude towards living donors.[20] During the years following the shift to cadaver organs, abandoning the use of the living donor was applauded by many teams working in transplantation. It is still easy to interview witnesses of this period in France. Many consider organ retrieval from a living donor to be laden with ethical and psychological difficulties. A difficult procedure, it implied a heavy responsibility for the team in charge of the patient. They emphasized the impossibility of assessing the free choice of the donor, subjected to pressure from the family circle and from the receiver, who was under the threat of death. They also pointed to the grief for the donor if the graft ultimately failed, or, if it was successful, the psychological burden for the receiver whose debt could not be extinguished. Donors belonged to the family circle, but the spouse competed with the sister or brother to donate. Küss evokes the family disputes between the frustrated candidates to donate and the generous donor. These disputes sometimes lasted long after the transplantee's death. The strident character of family disputes and the decision-making nexus were such that many people having worked with living donors still today express the relief they felt when the tide turned in the late 1960s and the use of cadaver organs (the explicit goal of the France-Transplant Association) came to be the standard procedure.[21]

France in the concert of nations: a comparative view

When doctors eagerly adopted cadaver organs, they tried to solve simultaneously the scientific, legal, managerial and moral problems: in short, they conducted what sociologists of science call the 'construction' of transplantation on different grounds. The legal definition of death as cerebral offered them the possibility of retrieving organs of good quality within a short period of time. In France, the legal frame was established with the definition of cerebral death, following the so-called Harvard Criteria[22] by the Jeanneney circular of 1968, the creation in 1967 of Paris-Transplant, and in 1969 of France-Transplant, private associations for the promotion and the organization of organ donation, topped by the Caillavet law on the donor's presumed consent in 1976.[23] Simultaneously, the first networks for cadaver organ exchange in the rest of the world were created, at a national or supraregional level, such as Scandia-Transplant, or Eurotransplant, or UNOS, United Network for Organ Sharing, a federal institution in the United States. These networks tried to recruit the maximum number of donors in order to broaden the selection basis and give the recipient the best chance.

Since then, grafts with kidneys from both living donors and cadavers were both available, with major variations from one country to the other. The acceptance of cadaver organ transplantation, and the criteria for donor selection, were far from uniform.[24] An extreme case is Japan, where organ retrieval on cadavers has not developed because Japan did not adopt the definition of death as cerebral, which permitted the use of cadavers in good condition.[25] Elsewhere, the proportion of living donors varies between 60 per cent and 5 per cent of all donors. In Germany, the law has long been very reluctant to admit organ donation, in remembrance and redemption of the past tragedy (of human experimentation in Nazi times).[26] A complete law was enacted only in 1997. In 1998, the rate of transplantation with living donors was around 15 per cent.[27] In Spain, thanks to an active promotion across community barriers, the donation rate has escalated, and the proportion of living donors reached 25 per cent in 1998.[28]

In 1984, in the Scandinavian countries, transplantations with living donors amounted to 8.1 per million inhabitants, compared with 2.1 in the United States and only 1.1 in France. Kidney transplantation with a living donor represents the majority in Norway.[29] In the 1970s, the majority of public health professionals acknowledged that renal haemodialysis was not the appropriate solution in a country with a population scattered in valleys with difficulties of transport due to icy roads. Doctors promoted transplantation and helped to identify donors in the family and neighbourhood. Norway is a small country with a strong Protestant tradition, and a vivid sense of community, linked to the relative isolation of the citizens in a hostile environment.

A high proportion of living donors is also notable in the United States: it is globally higher in America than in Europe. Interestingly, the explanation for the higher percentage in the United States is the opposite of the one given for the same phenomenon in Norway. In the American case, commentators put forward the reign of liberal thinking, the praise lavished on those who face risk (Young Man Go West!) and the encouragement of individual initiative, the approbation given to free enterprise, defiance of a regulatory and paternalistic state, and respect for individual privacy and liberty. To illustrate this interpretation, after the use of a potent immunosuppressive drug, cyclosporin, discovered in 1976, allowed circumvention of HLA selection, surgeon Najarian from Minneapolis, at a congress, produced a slide showing cheerful young people wearing a T-shirt 'We gave a kidney'! A gesture of bravery and challenge directed at the squeamish European teams.

These disparities between countries suggest that acceptance of surgical transplantation procedures and forms of organization are strongly shaped by cultural factors interacting with scientific and technological factors, in other words, that science is not the same everywhere. Even in France, after cadaver organ retrieval was organized, the use of living donors never completely disappeared; it was retained in some places, in Lyons, for example.

At the time of the first organ transplants in France, during the 1950s and 1960s, living donor transplantations (and cadaver organ removal as well) were being conducted in a relative legal void. Any action undermining physical integrity being forbidden, if not required for therapeutic purposes for the subject him- or herself, the removal of an organ from a healthy subject, for the sole interest of a third person, could be considered an infraction of the law, and any surgeon involved in a living donor transplantation could have been prosecuted.[30]

The Caillavet law explicitly gave priority to the development of cadaver donors in order to secure the widest variety of HLA types, and the central issue that was debated before Parliament was the one of presumed consent (since the dead person cannot proffer his or her opinion!). The law, adopted by December 1976, was the first global regulation of transplantation activities and thus included the legalization of living donor transplantation. It allowed organ removal from mentally competent adults for the benefit of any recipient (i.e. without imposing particular links, familial for example, between donor and recipient), with the specific donor's consent. As regards the very controversial question of organ removal from minors, it allowed such practice only for the benefit of the donor's sibling, and with a double protection: the authorization of a three-member committee and the consent of the minor's legal representative.

The return of the living donor

From the time (around 1970) when cadaver organs became available, France ranked among those countries having the lowest rate of grafts with living donors. Since 1994–5, however, the procedure has regained some favour, although very variably between centres. In 1995, one team performed a kidney transplant between spouses. Today the percentage of grafts with living donors ranges from 1 to 22 per cent of all grafts according to centres.[31]

The practice has allegedly been reintroduced by technological innovations such as the possibility of splitting a liver, of cutting off a pulmonary lobe and general improvement of surgical procedures. In parallel, immunosuppression has been adjusted for isotransplantation between genetically unrelated donors and recipients. In the case of the liver, the discovery has been made that, contrary to previously accepted knowledge, the liver has a capacity of regeneration. It is possible to split a cadaver liver between two recipients, but it has also become possible to remove a lobe in a living donor and reinstall it in the recipient's body. In order to avoid taking away the failing organ, surgeons have tested various locations for grafts, outside the normal site. This experimental work was reminiscent of studies at the beginning of the century, when surgeons tried (in the dog) to hang a kidney around the neck or in the upper thigh.[32] The improvement of surgical and intensive care procedures has also led a team in Chicago to perform lung transplantations with a lobe from a living donor. The use of pancreas from a living donor has also been attempted.

The long period of oblivion in France explains why the use of a living donor has to be considered as a (re-)innovation. A debate is now opening up in France over the legitimacy of this procedure, in scientific as well as human terms, the risk of its commercialization, and its impact on cadaver organ retrieval, with the two practices being presented as antagonistic rather than complementary. Analysing what we call the 'return of the living donor', we hypothesize that medical innovations do not occur in an unmodified context, with other things remaining stable. Innovation takes place in a society where values undergo continuous change in a globalizing world, although these transformations may not affect all individuals in the same way, even a rather homogeneous professional body with a strong *esprit de corps* such as the transplanters. Surgeon Gérard Benoit wonders whether transplantation has 'gone out of fashion'.[33]

Whether living donor transplantation is scientifically recommended and socially acceptable is also linked to changing representations and values attached to medical practice, the relationship between individuals and between group and individual, and the social view of the link between the living and the dead. The development of the right to health, already mentioned, is concomitant with the demand for access to emerging technologies to postpone the end of life: transplantation not only appears as a heroic act of saving life in danger but also as a means of prolonging lives otherwise doomed. Transplanters, emboldened by their successes, have seen their human venture celebrated by the media as an analogue of *Star Wars* or, in the medical field, of the Human Genome Project, itself compared to a 'Manhattan Project' for biologists.

In their zealous unceasing quest for more organs, of either good or lesser quality (organs from the ageing, steatosic livers), transplanters sometimes tend to ignore the many questions and doubts raised in society by such a choice. These queries are first of all religious, psychological and ideological, but also economic, the choice of priorities in research and therapeutics having to be debated in face of other emergencies and other medical or economical needs.[34] In the fierce competition, transplantation benefits from the persisting prestige of avant-garde surgery, on the scientific side, but also displays the symbolic value associated with the gift notion, featured by Richard Titmuss in a famous and controversial book.[35] Had he not suggested that the blood exchange system was a good marker of the moral and political choices of a society?

Transplanters today do not hesitate to use all the media armoury, shifting from mere information to proselytism: circus, interactive plays, conferences, everything is warranted in order to persuade the unfaithful, reminiscent of the time when vaccination was preached, pleaded, sung before being enforced with fines and jail sentences.

But the prestige of transplantation has also to be weighed against the negative impact of the Contaminated Blood Affair (when transfusion professionals were charged with having unduly postponed HIV testing of donated blood[36]), the Tesniere scandal (1991) where a young man's corneas were retrieved without the parents' explicit permission, and more generally, anxiety over risks related to the exchange of biological material. The public audience is increasingly concerned by the transmission of viruses or infective material, known and unknown, in natural substances, implying responsibility for future generations. A sinister counterpart of the harmonious donation scene is the development of a market of organs for sale, fuelled by the desperate desire of the well-off to acquire, at any cost, the precious organs necessary to their survival.

The coverage of the field by the media, entailed by the necessity of promoting organ donation, has turned transplantation into a very sensitive issue for public opinion. A short movie entitled *Stolen Eyes* had depicted the shameful traffic of corneas among the poor or insane in a Latin American country. It turned out later to be a fraud, but it left a stigma on the transplantation business and its advocates. Rumours spread, as described by Campion-Vincent.[37] The officials in charge of transplantation have made efforts to rehabilitate transplantation and clarify its doings, most notably with the creation of the Etablissement Français des Greffes (EFG, French Transplantation Agency) in 1994, a state institution. With the creation of the EFG, one shifted from a peer medical association promoting transplantation and encouraging scientific research, to a state agency controlling and regulating more strictly, in a typically French centralized manner, all transplantation activities. Nevertheless, the percentage of negative answers to requests to donate organs from dead relatives has slowly risen to 30 per cent. It is clear that any scandal or proof of irregularity has a sustainable negative effect on the attitudes of the public, which shifts easily from mystic adhesion to complete rejection. This versatility is observed in other public health procedures such as vaccination.[38]

Eighteen years after the Caillavet law, the 'Bioethics laws' of July 1994 increased the donor's protection.[39] The formalism of the adult donor's consent has been strengthened, organ donation has been restricted to the family circle. Organ removal is authorized for the sole benefit of the donor's parents, siblings or children, donation between spouses is restricted to emergency situations and organ removal from a minor has been forbidden, except for bone marrow. The rights of the next-of-kin over their relatives' bodies have been made official. These very careful and protective laws reflected the fact that cadaver transplantation had become in France the benchmark method for treating end-stage organ failure and was preferred to living donor transplantation, as it avoided the 'mutilation' of a healthy person. The legal framework of living donor transplantation is nevertheless destined to be modified again, as a re-examination of bioethics laws has been planned after a five-year period. The predicted evolution of the law will be discussed below.

The return of the living donor in France is still a discrete tendency: liver grafts and kidney grafts are unevenly scattered across the national territory and among the teams. But whatever its numeric importance, a real change has occurred. In March 1997, the community of transplanters acknowledged this novelty and gathered in Paris, at the initiative of the French Transplantation Agency, in order to debate the scientific, cultural and ethical issues around the living donor.[40] A notable proportion of the transplantation teams expressed the wish that the 1994 law be modified, with an extension of the procedure to unrelated donors, in first place the spouse and dedicated friends or 'emotionally-related' persons.

It seems important to describe (before assessing them) the actual practices of transplanters. It was predictable that paediatricians, nephrologists and surgeons would not display the same range of stances as kidney and liver transplanters, all heirs to different traditions, facing chronic patients or confronted with therapeutic necessity.

The heterogeneity of practices in France

The living donor (re-)innovation is far from being equally adopted and perceived throughout France. As regards the adoption of this practice by the transplantation professionals, a double heterogeneity, both quantitative and qualitative, should be emphasized. Living donor transplantation was performed in 1998 by only 69 per cent and 30 per cent of renal and liver transplantation teams respectively, and accounted for only 3.88 per cent and 4 per cent of all renal and liver transplantations performed in France during that year.[41] The percentage of living donor transplantation varied greatly among centres, some of them – usually the paediatric ones – using living donors for up to 25 per cent of all renal transplantations, whereas others had recourse to living donors exceptionally, even never.

From a qualitative point of view, there is also a marked disparity in the management of living donors in France, as revealed by a recent study carried out among the forty-six French renal transplant centres.[42] Substantial heterogeneity in practices was found in all steps of living donor transplantation, i.e. information, evaluation, selection and follow-up of living donors. As regards the information process, transplanters are divided, some of them giving an almost positive and encouraging view on organ donation, while others prefer not to raise this possibility before the patient's family has asked for it, in order to avoid any pressure on the patient's relatives. The diversity of the information provided to the potential living donor is particularly obvious when focusing on the details given concerning the risk of death associated with donation. While the majority of transplanters state this risk by giving the usual mortality rate (0.03 per cent), some hardly emphasize the reality of this risk and a minority do not mention it at all. The evaluation of potential living donors before nephrectomy occurs is unevenly performed, as regards the screening for specific short- or long-term risk factors (especially cardiovascular or thrombotic risk factors and diabetes), and the intervention either of an independent third party, usually a nephrologist acting as the donor's advocate, or a psychologist or social worker. The list of exclusion criteria also differed, in particular the cut-off age for donation, which ranged between centres from forty-five to seventy-five. This diversity probably reflected the different weight given by health professionals to the impact of various medical, psychological and social risks. The ways of selecting or excluding a potential donor, the composition of the team involved in this decision, as well as the role assigned to the potential donor in the decision-making process and the procedure of receiving his or her consent to donation, were also highly variable. Thus the centres' attitudes tended to polarize towards either the 'paternalist' or 'autonomist' stances, whose opposition is crucial in the field of living donor transplantation. The autonomist viewpoint lets the patients' autonomy and their capacity to take decisions concerning themselves prevail over an attitude of benevolence and authoritarian protection, the latter characterizing the paternalistic stance.

The last step of living donor transplantation, i.e. the follow-up of living donors, also varied in length and nature: responsibility devolved on various actors, as it might be delegated to the family doctor or be carried out by the transplant centre itself. This diversity in practices does not appear as a rare event and should be interpreted on a worldwide basis. Indeed, other surveys, performed in the United States[43] and in Europe,[44] revealed a similar variability in inter-centre practices.

The very low proportion of transplantations carried out with a living donor organ reflects the mixed feelings of the French transplant teams towards this practice. A recent survey indicated that only 17 per cent of chief renal physicians tended to prefer living donor transplantation (this percentage was even lower as regards liver and lung transplantation), 57 per cent favouring the use of cadaver organs.[45] However, although low, the percentage of medical professionals favourable to living donor transplantation was clearly higher than ten or twenty years previously. Similarly, almost half of health professionals are today in favour of a more flexible legal framework for living transplantation, namely allowing donation between spouses and even possibly between partners.

Predicting the evolution of practices?

The resurgence of interest in living donor transplantation among French transplanters[46] has been driven by various arguments, among which are the belief that living donors could compensate to some degree for the scarcity of cadaveric organs,[47] the good or even excellent results of living donor transplantation in comparison with cadaveric transplantation,[48] and the fact that both short- and long-term risks for living donors seem to be minimized by rigorous evaluation and selection of potential donors.[49] This increased interest in living donors has been reflected in France between 1993 and 1998 by an increase of 78 per cent in the use of living donors in renal transplantation.[50] It is foreseeable that this tendency will intensify over time, as and when medical technical difficulties will be overcome and mentalities evolve.

From a qualitative point of view, the disparity in living donor transplantation practices could be matter of concern, although disparity in medical diagnostic or therapeutic procedures is not exceptional. Variability in a medical practice – organ donation – which is not performed for the 'patient's' benefit (organ retrieval will benefit a third person, the recipient) raises the fundamental issue of equity in the management of all living donors. This leads to the question of whether it would be appropriate to bring these practices into line and adopt guidelines in this field. The concept of guidelines for living donor transplantation is not uncommon, as revealed by the elaboration of American[51] and British[52] guidelines a few years ago, providing a very comprehensive framework for living renal transplantation. Such guidelines are currently under discussion within the French Transplantation Agency and would certainly allow improved equity in the management of French living donors.

One should also emphasize the close links between the acceptance of the concept of living donor transplantation, on the one hand by health professionals, and on the other hand by society, as reflected, *inter alia*, by the law. The cautious tendency observed among health professionals in favour of a more flexible legal framework for living donor transplantation has been noted by several national authorities and committees, which plead for an extension of the categories of authorized living donors outside the family circle, thus putting the emotional links on an equal footing with the family ties. The bill proposed by the government by the end of 2000, as regards the re-examination of the bioethics laws, is indeed in accordance with this evolution.

The medical urgency contrasts with the cautiousness of the legislators, conservative by tradition, and with the scepticism of social science experts suspecting, beneath the moral claims, the protection of vested interest and social status by the medics. By admitting the necessity, due to scientific progress, of periodically revising the law, the jurists may have opened a new Pandora's box, or, in current sociological jargon, a black box.

Opening the black box of the living donor

Indeed, law may be perceived as the reflection of social and cultural attitudes towards living donor transplantation, and its evolution may characterize changes in perception, by the whole society, of this (re-)innovation.

Are we witnessing a change of mentality with the coming of a new generation, young transplanters having no experience of psychological complexities and ignoring the emotional impact of the living donation? In the first place, it seems that the risk of organ donation has become more acceptable, first of all, because the progress of anaesthesiology has made surgery safer. The risk of nephrectomy has been rated as lower than the risk of a traffic accident in some states of America. But, on the other hand, not to mention taking off a pulmonary lobe, hepatectomy is still a major surgical operation. We have to hypothesize that a certain kind of risk has become increasingly part of our ethos, in a society privileging mobility, tempted by liberalism and the American model,[53] dismissing the values attached to Social Security and the 'Etat-Providence',[54] the importance of civil service and economic regulations.

Professor René Küss, who had been a pioneer in the 1950s, attended the 1997 meeting on the living donor. He did not hide his satisfaction at hearing stories about the use of the living donor. He was obviously happy to witness a rehabilitation of a practice that in the past had yielded excellent results under skilful hands. The language of heroism, a language forgotten in the morose mood of 'decadent' contemporary France, was welcome to galvanize fresh energies.

The rediscovery of an earlier innovation warrants a great deal of attention be paid to the new scientific style and to the motivations of those who plead for a modification of the legal prescriptions by pointing to an evolution of scientific knowledge and practices. Which arguments are so forcibly presented in order to rehabilitate and promote the use of the living donor? Scientific arguments. The battle over survival statistics is going on. Ronald Guttmann once demonstrated the many artefacts contained in the construction of the 'survival curve'.[55] At the bottom of this controversy is a debate around the crucial character of HLA selection: whether HLA selection has made a big difference between unrelated or related donors. In the 1970s, while it was unanimously agreed that the HLA pairing made a great difference between related partners (being probably similar on other genetic loci as well), it was far from generally agreed that it made a difference between unrelated donors. A review of data suggests that the success of grafts is not exclusively based on genetic selection and may involve many other factors, including surgical experience. Teams do well what they have been used to do: experience is a crucial part of their expertise, which does not facilitate the assessment of innovations.

The return of the living donor affords the possibility of revisiting forgotten evidence and second thoughts on things that seemed to be established for ever. When death was defined as cerebral death, two things turned out to be problematic. First, it was necessary to combat the idea that cadaver organs were deteriorated and were of no use for giving life. On the other hand, when cadaver organ transplantation was organized, it was necessary to convince the public that the organs were not being robbed prematurely from patients who were not quite dead.

In the eighteenth century, concern about being buried alive was very common, perhaps because of rumours legitimately stemming from hasty burial during plague epidemics. Buffon wrote extensively on the subject.[56] The Marquess d'Aligre detailed in successive versions of his will the multiple precautions, inspired by extensive readings, to be taken before his burial to verify that he was no longer alive. The same fear prevailed among the enlightened Jews in

Berlin during this period. They opposed the burial procedures (within the twenty-four hours after death) recommended by religious law and enforced by traditional rabbis. They relied on scientific progress to argue in favour of a delay before burial, long enough to ensure that the dead person did not happen to revive. Fears of premature burial flourished again in the nineteenth century.[57]

When cadaver organ transplantation was organized, it was necessary, on the one hand, to convince the family that the dead were absolutely dead and, on the other, it was necessary to advertise the good quality of organs, collected and stored outwith the body in appropriate fluids. The quality of organs maintained in artificial life suggests that patients in a comatose state (the category of so-called *coma dépassé* was described by Mollaret and Goulon in 1965) retained some of the properties of living bodies. Dead enough to figure as deceased citizens. Alive enough to provide good organs. This was the dilemma faced in 1968 by those who established the official definition of death at Harvard, paving the way for the legal authorization of organ removal, widely accepted by nations, with some notable exceptions such as Japan or Israel, and today followed by a growing number of countries in Africa and Asia.

Clearly enough, the definition of death criteria, made more precise with the invention of sensitive procedures for testing cerebral stem activities, was greatly influenced by the will to frame transplantation activities, in spite of the remaining gaps in our understanding of mechanisms and nervous activity during coma.

One suspicion comes to mind when arguments are turned upside down that were once brought into the debate, conveying the feeling of 'reversible truth'.[58] Transplanters have reversed their former argument and reconsidered their previous assessment of cadaver organs, suggesting that the cadaver does not provide organs of such good quality, in spite of their careful perfusion (the use of Belzer's fluid and the propeller were among the technical tricks which increased the acceptable delay for the use of organs). They point to the deleterious effects of physiopathological processes intervening during removal and perfusion. On the other hand, they argue that the living (and healthy) donor can be better prepared and can undergo careful preliminary explorations. (This does not exclude the possibility that organs of a lesser quality are now offered as was previously mentioned.) In other words, once the concept of the living donor has been organized, the procedure can be reconceptualized, forgetful of the statements put forward in the past on organ quality.

Is the reserved judgement on the quality of organs in warm bodies a thoroughly scientific statement or to what extent is it influenced by changes in mentalities? Let us turn to the cultural side. Cadaver organ removal had in the past raised numerous doubts. René Küss in France had performed grafts with organs retrieved from prisoners, whose organs were removed immediately after their execution. He himself has depicted the discomfort of the operation, 'performed on the ground by torchlight'.[59]

An unforeseen difficulty faced by the use of cadaver organs for transplantation has progressively emerged. Transplantation includes two phases. The first one is the organ retrieval step, the second one is the graft itself. In order to avoid suspicion of collusion and vested interests in the pursuit of grafts, the legislators have reinforced the division of labour between the two groups. This division which did not exist in the past has created an opposition between the people of death and the people of life, darkness and radiant light, the sinister dagger and the helpful surgical blade. This labour division in hospital has created psychosociological unrest among the people belonging to the former team. The anthropologist Marie-Christine Pouchelle has described the anxiety and nightmares of the staff dedicated to the task of removing organs from corpses or bodies, who, to the staff, were still imbued with persisting life.[60] This explains the relative lack of motivation among the intensive care attendants who maintain the organs for transplanters and for whom a graft is synonymous with their own failure to resuscitate patients. Ironically, this beautiful term 'to resuscitate' has a semantic affinity with the 'resurrectionists' of the nineteenth century, a nickname applied to those who salvaged bodies at the site of execution and delivered them to academics for money.[61] The modern resuscitator does not like to act as procuror of organs for transplanters.

In France, the discussion on the extension of living donors pivots around the flexibility of the emergency definition (the so-called 'therapeutic necessity'[62]) and the extension of the category to spouses, concubines or 'Pacs' people. (Pacs is an economic association implying living together, sharing resources and benefiting from tax exemptions on heritage. Pacs has benefited gay and lesbian couples but can also be applied to other categories.) The fear is expressed that volunteer emotionally related donors might be in fact mercenaries offering their organs. The risk is not negligible, with the growing poverty in industrialized countries and the developing countries where the state has neither the capacity nor the will to regulate the traffic in organs.

In the past, some transplanters operating outside of the Western world have been critical of the Westerners' protests. A. S. Daar is a transplanter born in Tanzania and practising in Oman. He has campaigned for a reappraisal of the lack of payment and advocates a 'rewarded gifting'. He frequently intervenes in international meetings and in France to suggest a more realistic management of the issue. As soon as there is a differential between the rich and the poor, there will be space for such transactions. When the price of an organ is enough to allow a person to embark on business, the reward for organs is not that far from the small loans that experts of microfinance promote in the less advanced countries. It is impossible to prevent wealthy patients negotiating to obtain organs from their less affluent brothers. Daar, not unlike some practitioners in the United States, wants to protect transactions so that they respect minimal guarantees (such as insurance and medical follow-up) and respect codes.[63] In India, doctors have been shocked by the uproar of protest against the practice of selling and buying organs, and the role of doctors, and by the derisive attitude toward 'Kidneypolis', the Indian village where a proportion of the population displays nephrectomy scars.

Daar underlined the heterogeneity of living donor practices in the Western countries themselves. Some medical informants do not mention to the relatives the possibility of donating unless they themselves raise the question. Some others list at length the complications of the surgical operation. It is usually the head of the department who sets up the model, with possible disparities at the lower stages in the ward and the merging of differences, as younger elements join the team, who have not the same cultural background and belong to a new generation.

In some anthropologists' eyes, the contract advocated by Daar and colleagues has analogies with the legal contract through which proletarians engage their life forces. But Veena Das points to the fact that poor people are more liable to have their bodies engaged in demeaning and dangerous trade, and that it is not a reason for endorsing these shameful transactions.[64] She nevertheless admits that it is important to engage in concrete action at a local level rather than taking refuge behind mere moral condemnation.

For some French transplanters today demanding a modification of the law, the main argument for an extension of the living donor category is the shortage of available organs. The list of candidates is always longer as the criteria of admission become more flexible. (For example, AIDS seropositive subjects, who were before excluded, may be soon included, provided that their clinical state is stable under tritherapy, and patients above seventy years may be candidates.) They also argue that the structure of society has changed. The high rate of divorce shows the fragility of the traditional family while the frequency of partners living together for many years and having children together illustrates the robustness of emotional links.

The interaction between transplanters and society goes both ways. The living donor is altogether modern and traditional. A comparison is possible with the way the new modes of assisted procreation interact with representations of pregnancy and giving life. The normativity goes both ways. There is an incentive to be modern in asking for reproductive high technology (such as 'fivette') or bequeathing organs. The use of living donors can arguably be part of the postmodern ethos. Some transplanters are ready to promote transplantation with living donors by all available means, in spite of those who protest that careless publicity about living donors could curb the cadaver organ procurement since it would suggest alternatives. The opponents also mention that this could be a way of once more favouring the well-off and those who have a social and family network, while marginalized people, foreigners and illegal immigrants have no such effective network.

Few people note the relevance to democracy and civic obligation, perhaps because of the weakening of the state and global solidarity ties. (The French philosopher François Dagognet once went so far as to picture the transplantation organization as an equivalent of civic solidarity and the bodies as a collective resource guaranteed and distributed by the providential state.)

Requesting more studies

While writing this chapter, the authors waited in vain for the anticipated finale: new regulations framing (or limiting) the recourse to new categories of donors. The French Parliament has not yet examined the project of the new law of bioethics including revised dispositions for living donors. The registration by law would have been final proof of the profound change occurring in French society, with official encouragement given to living organ donation.[65]

The debate goes on, regarding many aspects of transplantation. First, economists challenge the extensive practice of grafts; they conducted studies on the cost of liver and lung transplantations and while pointing to disparities between one centre and the other, they commented that this was an enormous amount of money, suggesting that the funds could be put to better use in an era of budget cuts.

Second, just as there is a transplant lobby, there is also a resistance movement, although less vocal or less publicized. It is rather an aggregate than a lobby. People come from the ranks of the anti-vaccinationists or from the religious adherents reluctant to oppose God's decrees, or people alarmed by the social pressure exerted by associations.[66] Some compare the pressure on individual donors to the pressure exerted on soldiers going to war and having no other option than to behave heroically. The call for organs is also a rallying call to another type of war, allegedly waged for the common good, the medical fight against death. Anthropologist Maurice Godelier admitted that 'it is not certain that, in our individualist society, personal indebtedness of this kind is easily accepted. There is a cultural bias in favour of the autonomy and personal non-dependence of individuals.'[67]

This chapter was constructed on a study conducted from an ethical viewpoint to ascertain the disparities in medical behaviour and attempt to standardize practices in a code of good practices. This was a bias and also a limitation. By this ethical perspective, we did not explicitly target the differentiation between categories of professionals: nurses and doctors, surgeons and medics, nephrologists and immunologists. We only sketched the opposition between the old and the young, the provincial researchers and the Parisian stars. We did not detail the conflicts between schools of immunologists, with diverging views on the means of diagnosing rejection and taming the immunological monster.

Conclusion

We will try to conclude on the daunting task for legislators who are to examine the legal issues, in the coming years. When the bioethics laws were enacted in France in 1994 with the prospect of the revision of the Caillavet law, the decision was made to reconsider the laws after five years of an experimental stage, to decide whether they would remain unchanged or undergo modifications, resulting from medical advances. Our chapter attempts to show that not only the medical procedures have changed but also the social demand and current ideologies. Legislators will listen to the experts' advice but will also be sensitive to the opinions voiced by their constituency, with possibly a growing difficulty in reaching a consensus.

Opening the black box of innovations in transplantation meant exploring the complex knots between scientific and cultural motivations. Innovation is the intersection of the experimental and the therapeutic. All efforts tend to formalize the passage from one to the other, in order to discipline and socialize progress. But this has a social and human cost. One of these costs in transplantation is, to some extent, the commodification of human organs and a utilitarian vision of the Other's body. The ultimate goal of this chapter is, by illuminating the practices, to indicate more clearly what have been, and are (or should be?) the scientific and social choices.

Transplantation with living donors is a strange practice. Like all medical techniques, it links worlds which usually remain apart: the home and the hospital, society and the medical faculty. Although it is unceasingly celebrated as the triumph of biomedical science, it is reminiscent of ancient practices, the traffic of human bodies, here linked to modern therapeutics. In the Renaissance context, Shylock contracted with the merchant of Venice on the basis of a pound of flesh. He was dismissed by the judge on the grounds that he had not contracted to spill blood and would be prosecuted if he did. Transplanters spill blood and yet are protected by law on behalf of their altruistic motivation, but the fact remains that they mutilate and bleed somebody for the sake of another. Our society needs human flesh in order to satisfy its urgent (and in a way artificial) need for survival through organ retrieval, and implements a redistribution of its life energy: fluids and, since more recent times, organs.

The return of the living donor is not the mere re-emergence of an old practice abandoned thanks to the plentiful supply of cadaver organs, it is the result of a transformation of both society and medicine. The way both supply and demand evolve and interact is an interesting marker of historical and national specificities. Whether organ donating is a solitary gesture or results from a collective structure imposing rights and duties over its members is only one of the many issues at stake.

The aim of this chapter was to stimulate and initiate other studies (including by the authors themselves) on the socio-immunological fabric of the body. One of us claimed once that immunology was the science of boundaries.[68] As the sociologists of science claim to focus on boundary objects or transactional zones between the interests of various groups, the circulation of organs between the living is certainly a privileged target for all who follow the changes undergone in the construction of the social and individual body, the co-construction of nature and society.

Notes

1 M. Serres, 'Foreword' to Jacques Testard, *L'œuf transparent*, Paris, Flammarion, 1986, pp. 5– 19.

2 R. C. Fox and J. P. Swazey, *The Courage to Fail: A Social View of Organ Transplants and Dialysis*, Chicago, University of Chicago Press, 1974.

3 R. C. Fox and J. P. Swazey, *Spare Parts: Organ Replacement in American Society*, New York and Oxford, Oxford University Press, 1992; A. M. Moulin, 'Body parts, the modern dilemma', *Transplantation Reviews*, 1993, vol. 25, pp. 33–35.

4 I. Löwy and A. M. Moulin, 'Les institutions de transplantation: du don à l'échange', *Culture Technique*, 1985, pp. 157–63.

5 I. Illich, *Medical Nemesis: The Expropriation of Health*, New York, Pantheon, 1976.

6 P. B. Medawar, *The Threat and the Glory: Reflections on Science and Scientists*, ed. by David Pyke, Oxford, Oxford University Press, 1990.

7 T. Starzl, *Memoirs of a Transplant Surgeon: The Puzzle People*, Pittsburgh, University of Pittsburgh Press, 1992, p. 317.

8 J. V. Pickstone (ed.), *Medical Innovations in Historical Perspective*, London, Macmillan, 1992; J. V. Pickstone, 'The biographical and the analytical: towards a historical model of science and practice in modern medicine', in I. Löwy (ed.), *Medicine and Change: Historical and Sociological Studies of Medical Innovation*, Paris, INSERM Editions, 1993, pp. 23–47.

9 A. M. Moulin, 'L'équivoque médicale: interprète ou agent double', *Sciences Sociales et Santé*, 1998, vol. 16, pp. 97–106.

10 J. Prottas, *The Most Useful Gift: Altruism and the Public Policy of Organ Transplant*, San Francisco, Jossey-Bass, 1994.

11 A. M. Moulin, 'The foundations of the right to be grafted', in J. L. Touraine *et al.* (eds), *Organ Shortage: The Solutions*, Dordrecht, Kluwer, 1995, pp. 223–34.

12 A. M. Moulin, 'AIDS and the history of the right to health', *AIDS, Health and Human Rights*, Les Pensières, Fondation Marcel Mérieux, 1993, pp. 67–73.

13 R. Küss, J. Teinturier and P. Milliez, 'Quelques essais de greffe de rein chez l'homme', *Mémoires de l'Académie de Chirurgie*, 1951, vol. 77, 22–3, pp. 755–68.

14 R. Küss, 'Human renal transplantation memories, 1951 to 1981', in P. I. Terazaki (ed.), *History of Transplantation: Thirty-five Recollections*, Los Angeles, UCLA Tissue Typing Laboratory, 1991, p. 40.

15 On the availability of such derelict corporal objects, without anybody to claim them, see J. P. Baud, *L'Affaire de la main volée: une Histoire Juridique du Corps*, Paris, Seuil, 1993.

16 A. Carrel, 'Remote results', *Journal of Experimental Medicine*, 1910, vol. 12, p. 246.

17 A. M. Moulin, *Le Dernier langage de la médecine*, Paris, PUF, 1991, pp. 179–226.

18 J. Dausset, *Clin d'Œil à la vie. La grande aventure HLA*, Paris, Odile Jacob, 1998.

19 Ibid., pp. 79–108.

20 N. Herpin and F. Paterson, 'La pénurie et ses causes', in R. Carvais and M. Sasportes (eds), *La Greffe humaine, (in)certitudes ethiques: du don de soi à la tolérance de l'autre*, Paris, PUF, 2000, p. 330.

21 Interviews with Henri Kreis, Béatrice Descamps, Necker Hospital, 1995.

22 Ad Hoc Committee of Harvard Medical School, to Examine the Definition of Death, 'Definition of irreversible coma', *Journal of the American Medical Association*, 1968, vol. 205, pp. 85–8.

23 French Law no. 76–1131 of December 22, 1976, relating to organ removal, *Official Journal* (23 December 1976), p. 7635.

24 I. Löwy, 'The impact of medical practice on biomedical research: the case of human leucocyte antigen studies', *Minerva*, 1987, vol. 25, 1–2, pp. 171–200.

25 On Japan see M. Lock, 'The unnatural as ideology: contesting brain death in Japan', in P. Asquith and A. Kalland (eds), *Representing the Natural in Japan*, Cambridge, Cambridge University Press, 1997, pp. 121–44; E. Ohnuki Tierney, 'The reduction of personhood to brain and personality: Japanese contestation of medical high technology', in A. Cunningham and B. Andrews (eds), *Western Medicine as Contested Knowledge*, Manchester, Manchester University Press, 1997.

26 F. Hogle, *Recovering the Nation's Body: Cultural Memory, Medicine and the Politics of Redemption*, New Brunswick, NJ, Rutgers University Press, 1999.

27 R. Waissman, *Le Don d'organes*, Paris, PUF, 2001, p. 29.

28 Ibid., p. 33.

29 J. Elster and N. Herpin (eds), *Ethique des Choix médicaux*, Arles, Actes Sud, 1992.

30 J. Savatier, 'Les prélèvements sur le corps humain au profit d'autrui', *Les Petites Affiches*, 1994, vol. 149, pp. 8–13.

31 M. Broyer and O. Boillot, 'La transplantation d'organes avec donneur vivant', Rapport d'étude, typed manuscript, Paris, EFG, 1997; M. Broyer, 'Le paradoxe du don dans la greffe avec donneur vivant', in Carvais and Sasportes, *La Greffe humaine*, pp. 420–43.

32 Moulin, *Le Dernier langage*, p. 216.

33 G. Benoit, 'La "pénurie", une réalité quantifiable', in Carvais and Sasportes, p. 277.

34 J. P. Moatti, 'Dons d'organes: un révélateur des arbitrages entre l'efficience et l'équité dans le système de santé', in Carvais and Sasportes, *La Greffe humaine*, pp. 599–628.

35 R. Titmuss, *The Gift Relationship*, New York, Pantheon Books, 1991 (first published London, Allen and Unwin, 1970).

36 A. M. Casteret, *L'Affaire du sang*, Paris, La Découverte, 1991; A. M. Moulin, 'Reversible history: blood transfusion and the spread of AIDS in France', in C. Hannaway, V. Harden and J. Parascandola (eds), *AIDS and the Public Debate*, Amsterdam, IOS Press, 1995, pp. 170–86; M. A. Hermitte, *Le Sang et le Droit*, Paris, Seuil, 1997.

37 V. Campion-Vincent, *La Greffe, les rumeurs et les média. Les Récits de vol d'organes*, Paris, Maison des Sciences de l'Homme, 1996; V. Campion-Vincent, 'Les récits et la légende des vols d'organes', in Carvais and Sasportes, *La Greffe humaine*, pp. 356–72.

38 A. M. Moulin, *L'Aventure de la vaccination*, Paris, Fayard, 1995, introduction; A. M. Moulin, 'Les sociétés et leurs vaccins', *Comptes rendus de l'Académie des Sciences de Paris*, 1999, vol. 322, pp. 983–7.

39 French Law no. 94–653 of 29 July 1994, relating to respect for the human body, *Official Journal* (30 July 1994), pp. 11056–9, and French Law no. 94–654 of 29 July 1994, relating to gift and use of human body's elements and products, medically assisted procreation and prenatal diagnosis, *Official Journal* (30 July 1994), pp. 11060–8.

40 *Colloque Greffe et donneur vivant*, Paris, EFG, 1997.

41 Conseil médical et scientifique de l'Etablissement Français des Greffes, *Report. Le Prélèvement et la greffe en France en 1998*, Paris, Etablissement Français des Greffes, 1999, pp. 157–90.

42 M. Gabolde, C. Hervé and A. M. Moulin, 'Evaluation, selection and follow-up of live kidney donors – review of current practice in French renal transplant centres', *Nephrology Dialysis Transplantation*, in press; M. Gabolde, *La transplantation d'organes avec donneur vivant, étude contextuelle, enquête sur les pratiques, réflexions sur les aspects éthiques*, Report to the Etablissement Français des Greffes (French Transplantation Agency), 1998.

43 M. J. Bia, E. L. Ramos, G. M. Danovitch *et al.*, 'Evaluation of living renal donors: the current practice of US transplant centers', *Transplantation*, 1994, vol. 57, pp. 1722–6.

44 P. K. Donnelly and D. Price, 'Eurotold professional questionnaires', in P. K. Donnelly and D. Price (eds), *Questioning Attitudes to Living Donors Transplantation: European Multicentre*

Study, Transplantation of Organs with Living Donors, Ethical and Legal Dimensions, Leicester, The Project Management Group Eurotold, 1997, pp. 85–125.

45 M. Gabolde and C. Hervé, 'Living kidney donors: ethical considerations about the current practice of French transplant centers', *International Journal of Bioethics*, 1998, vol. 9, pp. 141–8.

46 A. M. Moulin, 'The crisis of organ transplantation: the quest for "cultural compatibility"', *Diogenes*, 1995, vol. 172, pp. 76–97.

47 R. W. Johnson, 'Shortage of organs for transplantation, living donors should be used more often', *British Medical Journal*, 1996, vol. 312, p. 1357.

48 J. Jones, W. D. Payne and A. J. Matas, 'The living-related donor – risks, benefits and related concerns', *Transplantation Review*, 1993, vol. 7, pp. 115–28.

49 J. S. Najarian, B. M. Chavers, L. E. McHugh and A. J. Matas, '20 years or more of follow-up of living kidney donors', *Lancet*, 1992, vol. 340, pp. 807–10.

50 Conseil de l'Etablissement Français des Greffes, *Report*, pp. 157–90.

51 B. L. Kasiske, M. Ravenscraft, E. L. Ramos, R. S. Gaston, M. J. Bia and G. M. Danovitch, 'The evaluation of living renal transplant donors: clinical practice guidelines', *Journal of the American Society of Nephrology*, 1996, vol. 7, pp. 2288–313.

52 Working Party of the British Transplantation Society and the Renal Association, *United Kingdom Guidelines for Living Donor Kidney Transplantation*, Access online at: http://www.jr2.ox.ac.uk/bts/index.htm (accessed January 2000).

53 E. Martin, *Flexible Bodies: Tracking Immunity in American Culture from the Days of Polio to the Age of AIDS*, Boston, Beacon Press, 1994.

54 F. Ewald, *L'Etat-providence*, Paris, Grasset, 1986.

55 R. D. Guttman, 'The graft survival curve', *Transplantation Proceedings*, 1992, vol. 24, pp. 2407–10; R. D. Guttman, 'The graft survival curve, Part II: Ideology and rhetoric', in J-L. Touraine *et al.*, *Organ Shortage: The Solutions*, Dordrecht, Kluwer, 1995, pp. 235–41.

56 Michèle Duchet (ed.), *Buffon: De l'homme* (On *Histoire Naturelle de l'Homme*, from Buffon's *Histoire Naturelle, 1749–1788*), Paris, Maspéro, 1971, pp. 159–60.

57 M. Pernick, 'Back from the grave: recurring controversies over defining and diagnosing death', in R. Zaner (ed.), *Death: Beyond the Whole-brain Criteria*, Dordrecht, Kluwer, 1988, pp. 17–74.

58 A. M. Moulin, 'Reversible history: blood transfusion and the spread of AIDS in France', in C. Hannaway, V. Harden and J. Parascandola (eds), *AIDS and the Public Debate*, Amsterdam, IOS Press, 1995, pp. 170–86.

59 Küss, 'Human renal transplantation memories', p. 39.

60 M. C. Pouchelle, 'Transports hospitaliers, extravagances de l'âme', in F. Lautman and J. Maitre (eds), *Gestion Religieuse de la Santé*, Paris, L'Harmattan, 1995, pp. 247–99.

61 R. Richardson, *Dissection, Death and the Destitute*, London, Routledge, 1988.

62 A. M. Moulin, 'Postface', in Carvais and Sasportes, *La Greffe humaine*, pp. 749–63.

63 A. Daar, 'Ethics and commerce in living donor renal transplantation, a classification of the issues', *Transplantation Proceedings*, 1990, vol. 22, p. 922; A. Daar, 'Marketing human organs, the autonomy paradox', *Theoretical Medicine*, 1996, vol. 17, pp. 1–18.

64 V. Das, 'The practice of organ transplants', in M. Lock, A. Young and A. Cambrosio (eds), *Living and Working with New Medical Technologies: Intersections of Inquiry*, Cambridge: Cambridge University Press, 2000, pp. 263–87.

65 The analysis of an important inquiry into public opinion regarding the graft will be found in an epoch-making collective book, mentioned many times in the footnotes: R. Carvais and M. Sasportes (eds), *La greffe humaine, (in)certitudes éthiques: du don de soi à la tolérance de l'autre*, Paris, PUF, 2000; see also, D. Houssin, *La greffe*, Paris, Odile Jacob, 1999.

66 On the donors' profiles, see R. Waismann, *Le Don d'organes*, Paris, PUF, 2001, pp. 94–104.

67 M. Godelier, 'Postface', in Carvais and Sasportes, *La Greffe humaine*, p. 365. [English translation by authors, modified by editor.]
68 A. M. Moulin, 'Immunology or the science of boundaries: A "science dans le siècle"', in J. Krige and D. Pestre (eds), *Science in the Twentieth Century*, Amsterdam, Harwood Academic Publishers, 1997, pp. 479–95.

Bibliography

'Art. XIV. [Review of recent work on Acupuncture]', *Edinburgh Medical and Surgical Journal*, 1827, vol. 27, pp. 334–49.

'Asian health care receives a boost', *HealthLink, Newsletter of Manchester's Community Health Councils*, 1982, November.

'Audit in renal failure: the wrong target?', Editorial, *British Medical Journal*, 1981, vol. 283, pp. 261–2.

'Birth interventions on rise', *New Zealand GP*, 6 October 1999.

'GPOs thrown out with bathwater', *New Zealand GP*, 6 October 1999.

'GPs turn away from birth work', *Press*, Christchurch, 2 November 1998.

'Hospital midwifery: where to now?', *New Zealand Health and Hospital*, March/April 1994.

'Medical Assoc slams maternity funding', *Press*, 8 September 2000.

'Medical profession and the press', *British Medical Journal*, 1955, vol. 2, pp. 100–1.

'Medicine and the media', *British Medical Journal*, 1983, vol. 287, p. 492.

'Medicine on television', *Lancet*, 1958, vol. 2, pp. 1170–1.

'More tests of acupuncture', *BMJ*, 1973, vol. 3, p. 190.

'Obstetrics facing crisis says retiring professor', *New Zealand Doctor*, 17 March 1999.

'Report of the BMA Annual Clinical Meeting, Cheltenham 24–27 October: Retropubic prostatectomy', *BMJ*, 1968, vol. 4, p. 320.

'Tests of acupuncture', *BMJ*, 1973, vol. 2, p. 502.

'When acupuncture came to Britain' *BMJ*, 1973, vol. 4, pp. 687–8.

Aaron, J. and Schwartz, W., *The Painful Prescription: Rationing Hospital Care*, Washington, DC, Brookings Institution, 1984.

Abrams, S. E., '"Dreams and awakenings": the Rockefeller Foundation and public health nursing education, 1913–30', PhD thesis, University of California, 1992.

——, 'Brilliance and bureaucracy: nursing and changes in the Rockefeller Foundation, 1915–30', *Nursing History Review*, vol. 1, 1993, pp. 119–37.

Adas, M., *Machines as the Measure of Men: Science, Technology, and Ideologies of Western Dominance*, Ithaca, NY, Cornell University Press, 1989.

Ad Hoc Committee of the Harvard Medical School, to Examine the Definition of Death, 'Definition of irreversible coma', *Journal of the American Medical Association*, 1968, vol. 205, pp. 85–8.

Aktuelle Probleme der Gesundheitspolitik und Aufgaben der Parteiorganisationen, Berlin, Dietz Verlag, 1985.

Alexander, W. and South East Thames Diabetes Physicians Group, 'Diabetes care in a UK health region: activity, facilities and costs', *Diabetic Medicine*, 1988, vol. 5, pp. 577–81.

Allen, F., 'Diabetes before and after insulin', *Medical History*, 1972, vol. 16, pp. 266–73.

Allgöwer, M., 'Cinderella of surgery – fractures?', *Surgical Clinics of North America*, 1978, vol. 58, pp. 1071–93.

Allgöwer, M. and Spiegel, P. G., 'Internal fixation of fractures: evolution of concepts', *Clinical Orthopaedics and Related Research*, 1979, vol. 138, pp. 26–9.

Allison, A., 'Protection afforded by sickle-cell trait against subtertial malarial infection', *British Medical Journal*, 1954, vol. 1, pp. 290–4.

Anderson, A., *Media, Culture and Environment*, London, UCL Press, 1997.

Anderson, L. *et al.*, 'Compression-plate fixation in acute diaphyseal fractures of the radius and ulna', *JBJS*, 1975, vol. 57-A, pp. 287–97.

Angastiniotis, M. and Modell, B.,'Global epidemiology of hemoglobin disorders' in A. Cohen (ed.), 'Cooley's Anemia, Seventh Symposium', *Annals of the New York Academy of Sciences*, 1998, vol. 850, pp. 251–69.

Anon., 'Cast banishment? The AO method of internal fixation', *Lynn Magazine*, Winter–Spring 1982, pp. 1–3.

Ariga, N., *The Japanese Red Cross and the Russo-Japanese War*, London, Bradbury, *c.*1907.

Armstrong, D., *Outline of Sociology as Applied to Medicine*, 4th edn, Oxford, Butterworth-Heinemann, 1994.

Assal, J-P. and Visser, A. (eds), 'Patient Education 2000 Proceedings of the Patient Education 2000 Congress, Geneva, 1–4 June, 1994', *Patient Education and Counselling*, 1995, vol. 26.

Auer, J., 'The Oxford Renal Unit Silver Jubilee', typescript, 1993.

Balfour, R. P., 'Use of a real-time ultrasound scanner in district antenatal clinics', *British Journal of Obstetrics and Gynaecology*, 1978, vol. 85, pp. 492–4.

Banta, H. D. and Luce, B., *Health Care Technology and its Assessment: an International Perspective*, Oxford and New York, Oxford University Press, 1993.

Banta, H. D., 'The diffusion of the computed tomography (CT) scanner in the United States', *International Journal of Health Services*, 1980, vol. 10, pp. 251–69.

Barfoot, M., Lawrence, C. and Sturdy, S., 'The Trojan horse: the Biochemical Laboratory of the Royal Infirmary of Edinburgh 1921–1939', *Wellcome Trust Review*, 1999, vol. 8, pp. 58–61.

Baszanger, I., *Inventing Pain Medicine*, London, Rutgers University Press, 1998.

Battista, R., 'Innovation and diffusion of health-related technologies: a conceptual framework', *International Journal of Technology Assessment in Health Care*, 1989, vol. 5, pp. 227–48.

Baud, J. P., *L'affaire de la main volée: une histoire juridique du corps*, Paris, Seuil, 1993.

Bauer, M. (ed.), *Resistance to New Technology: Nuclear Power, Information Technology and Biotechnology*, Cambridge, Cambridge University Press, 1995.

Beggan, M. *et al.*, 'Assessment of the outcome of an educational programme of diabetes self-care', *Diabetologia*, 1982, vol. 23, pp. 246–51.

Beinart, J. (Stanton), 'Obstetric analgesia and the control of childbirth in twentieth-century Britain', in J. Garcia, R. Kilpatrick and M. Richards (eds), *The Politics of Maternity Care: Services for Childbearing Women in Twentieth-Century Britain*, Oxford, Oxford University Press, 1990, pp. 116–32.

Bennett, M. J. and Campbell, S., *Real-time Ultrasound in Obstetrics*, Oxford, Blackwell Scientific, 1980.

Berlyne, G., 'Over 50 and uremic = death', *Nephron*, 1982, vol. 13, pp. 189–90.

Berridge, V., 'Passive smoking and its pre-history in Britain: policy speaks to science?' *Social Science and Medicine*, 1999, vol. 49, pp. 1183–95.

Bia, M. J., Ramos, E. L. and Danovitch, G. M. *et al.*, 'Evaluation of living renal donors. The current practice of US transplant centers', *Transplantation*, 1994, vol. 57, pp. 1722–6.

Bijker, W., *Of Bicycles, Bakelites, and Bulbs: Toward a Theory of Sociotechnical Change*, Cambridge, MA, and London, MIT Press, 1995.

Bijker, W. E., Hughes, T. P. and Pinch, T. J. (eds), *The Social Construction of Technological Systems*, Cambridge, MA, MIT Press, 1987.

Bijker W. E. and Law, J. (eds), *Shaping Technology/Building Society: Studies in Sociotechnical Change*, Cambridge, MA, MIT Press, 1992.

Bivins, R., *Acupuncture, Expertise and Cross-Cultural Medicine*, Basingstoke, Palgrave, 2000.

Bliss, M., *The Discovery of Insulin*, Chicago, Chicago University Press, 1982.

Blume, S., *Insight and Industry: on the Dynamics of Technological Change in Medicine*, Cambridge, MA, and London, MIT Press, 1992.

Bom, N. *et al.*, 'Ultrasonic viewer for cross-sectional analysis of moving cardiac structures', *Biomedical Engineering*, 1971, vol. 6, pp. 500–3.

Bond, D., 'Acupuncture: from ancient art to modern medicine' *Lancet*, 1983, vol. 1, p. 32.

Boon, T., 'Film and the contestation of public health in interwar Britain', PhD thesis, University of London, 1990.

Borst, C. G., *Catching Babies: The Professionalization of Childbirth, 1870–1920*, Cambridge, MA, Harvard University Press, 1995.

Bradley, S. and Friedman, E., 'Cervical cytology screening: a comparison of uptake among "Asian" and "non-Asian" women in Oldham', *Journal of Public Health Medicine*, 1993, vol. 15, pp. 46–51.

Breay, M. and Fenwick, E. G. (eds), *The History of the International Council of Nurses 1899–1925*, Geneva, ICN, 1930.

Bridges, D. C., *A History of the International Council of Nurses, 1899–1964: The First Sixty-Five Years*, London, Pitman Medical Publishing, 1967.

British Medical Association, *Report of the Board of Science and Education on Alternative Therapy*, London, BMA, 1986.

Brown, P., 'Tests of acupuncture', *BMJ*, 1973, vol. 3, p. 780.

Broyer, M. and Boillot, O., 'La transplantation d'organes avec donneur vivant', Rapport d'étude, EFG, Paris, typed manuscript, 1997.

Brückner, H., *Frakturen und Luxationen*, Berlin, VEB Verlag Volk und Gesundheit, 1969.

Brush, B. L. and Stuart, M., 'Unity amidst difference: the ICN project and writing international nursing history', *Nursing History Review*, vol. 2, 1994, pp. 191–203.

Bryder, L. (ed.), *A Healthy Country*, Wellington, Bridget Williams Books, 1991.

Buchanan, A., 'Theory and narrative in the history of technology', *Technology and Culture*, 1991, vol. 32, pp. 365–76.

Bulger, T., Howden-Chapman, P. and Stone, P., 'A cut above: the rising caesarean section rate in New Zealand', *New Zealand Medical Journal*, 1998, vol. 111, pp. 30–3.

Burnham, J., 'How the idea of profession changed the writing of medical history', *Medical History*, Supplement 18, London, Wellcome Institute for the History of Medicine, 1998.

Bynum, W., Lawrence, C. and Nutton, V. (eds), *The Emergence of Modern Cardiology*, London, Wellcome Institute for the History of Medicine, 1985.

Campbell, J. and Campbell, A., 'The social and economic costs of end-stage renal disease', *New England Journal of Medicine*, 1978, vol. 299, pp. 386–92.

Campbell, S., 'An improved method of fetal cephalometry by ultrasound', *Journal of Obstetrics and Gynaecology of the British Commonwealth*, 1968, vol. 75, pp. 568–76.

Campbell, S., 'The prediction of fetal maturity by ultrasonic measurement of the biparietal diameter', *Journal of Obstetrics and Gynaecology of the British Commonwealth*, 1969, vol. 76, pp. 603–9.

Campion-Vincent, V., *La greffe, les rumeurs et les média: les récits de vol d'organes*, Paris, Maison des Sciences de l'Homme, 1996.

Carrel, A., 'Remote results', *Journal of Experimental Medicine*, 1910, vol. 12, pp. 246.

Carrubba, R. and Bowers, J., 'The western world's first detailed treatise on acupuncture: Willem Ten Rhijne's *De Acupunctura*, *Journal of the History of Medicine*, 1974, vol. 29, pp. 371–98.

Cartwright, S. R., *The Report of the Committee of Inquiry into Allegations concerning the Treatment of Cervical Cancer at National Women's Hospital and into Other Related Matters*, Auckland, Committee of Inquiry, 1988.

Carvais, R. and Sasportes, M. (eds), *La greffe humaine, (in)certitudes ethiques: du don de soi à la tolérance de l'autre*, Paris, PUF, 2000.

Casper, M. J. and Clarke, A. E., 'Making the pap smear into the "right tool" for the job', *Social Studies of Science*, 1998, vol. 28, pp. 255–89.

Casteret, A. M., *L'affaire du sang*, Paris, La Découverte, 1991.

Challah, S., Wing, A., *et al.*, 'Negative selection of patients for dialysis and transplantation in the United Kingdom', *British Medical Journal*, 1984, vol. 288, pp. 1119–22.

Churchill, J., *A Treatise on Acupuncturation*, London, Simpkin and Marshall, 1822.

Clarke, A. E. and Fujimura, J. H., *The Right Tools for the Job: At Work in Twentieth Century Life Sciences*, Princeton, NJ, Princeton University Press, 1992.

Colloque Greffe et Donneur Vivant, Paris, EFG, 1997.

Committee for the Study of Nursing Education, *Nursing and Nursing Education in the United States*, New York, Macmillan, 1923.

Committee of Inquiry into Maternity Services, *Report*, AJHR [Appendices to the Journals of the House of Representatives, NZ, 1938, H-31A.

Coney, S., *The Unfortunate Experiment*, Auckland, Penguin, 1988.

Conley, C., 'Sickle-cell anaemia – the first molecular disease', in M. Wintrobe, *Blood, Pure and Eloquent*, New York, McGraw-Hill, 1980, pp. 319–37.

Conseil médical et scientifique de l'Etablissement Français des Greffes, *Report. Le prélèvement et la greffe en France en 1998*, Paris, Etablissement Français des Greffes, 1999.

Consumer's Association, *WHICH*, November 1995.

Cooter, R., *Surgery and Society in Peace and War. Orthopaedics and the Organization of Modern Medicine, 1880–1948*, Basingstoke, Macmillan Press, 1993.

——, 'The resistible rise of medical ethics' (Review article), *Social History of Medicine*, 1995, vol. 8, pp. 257–70.

Cooter, R. and Pickstone, J. (eds), *Medicine in the Twentieth Century*, Amsterdam, Harwood Academic Publishers, 2000.

Copperauld, I., 'Anaesthesia by acupuncture', *BMJ*, 1972, vol. 4, pp. 232–3.

Coventry, P. and Pickstone, J., 'From what and why did genetics emerge as a medical specialism in the 1970s in the UK? A case history of research, policy and services in the Manchester region of the NHS', *Social Science and Medicine*, 1999, vol. 49, pp. 1227–38.

Cowan, R. S. (ed.), *Biomedical and Behavioral Technology*, Special issue, *Technology and Culture*, 1993, vol. 34.

——, *A Social History of American Technology*, New York and Oxford, Oxford University Press, 1997.

Cox, G., *Pioneering Television News: A First Hand Report of a Revolution in Journalism*, London, John Libbey, 1995.

Crawford, G. P., 'Screw fixation for certain fractures of the phalanges and metacarpals', *JBJS*, 1976, vol. 58-A, pp. 487–92.

Crenshaw, A. H. (ed.), *Campbell's Operative Orthopaedics*, 2 vols., 4th edn, St Louis, The C.V. Mosby Company, 1963.

—— (ed.), *Campbell's Operative Orthopaedics*, 2 vols., 5th edn, St Louis, The C.V. Mosby Company, 1971.

Culliton, B., 'Sickle cell anaemia: the route from obscurity to prominence', *Science*, 1972, vol. 178, pp. 138–42.

Daar, A., 'Ethics and commerce in living donor renal transplantation, a classification of the issues', *Transplantation Proceedings*, 1990, vol. 22, p. 922.

——, 'Marketing human organs, the autonomy paradox', *Theoretical Medicine*, 1996, vol. 17, pp. 1–18.

Daellenbach, R., 'The paradox of success and the challenge of change: home birth associations of Aotearoa/New Zealand', PhD thesis, University of Canterbury, 1999.

Das, V., 'The practice of organ transplants', in M. Lock, A. Young and A. Cambrosio (eds), *New Medical Technologies: Intersections of Inquiry*, Cambridge, Cambridge University Press, pp. 263–87.

Dausset, J., *Clin d'œil à la vie. La grande aventure HLA*, Paris, Odile Jacob, 1998.

Davis, J., *The Chinese: A General Description*, London, Charles Knight, 1837.

Day, J. and Spathis, M., '"District Diabetes Centres in the United Kingdom": A report on a workshop held by the Diabetes Education Study Group on behalf of the British Diabetic Association', *Diabetic Medicine*, 1988, vol. 5, pp. 372–80.

Day, J. *et al.*, 'The feasibility of a potentially "ideal" system of integrated diabetes care and education based on a day centre', *Diabetic Medicine*, 1988, vol. 5, pp. 70–5.

Denoon, D. and Mein Smith, P. with M. Wyndham, *A History of Australia, New Zealand and the Pacific*, Oxford, Blackwell, 2000.

de Wardener, H., 'Some ethical and economic problems associated with intermittent haemodialysis', in G. Wolstenholme and M. O'Connor (eds), *Ciba Foundation Symposium on Ethics in Medical Progress*, London, Churchill, 1966, pp. 104–18.

Digby, A., *The Evolution of British General Practice, 1850–1948*, Oxford, Oxford University Press, 1999.

Dock, L., *A History of Nursing*, vol. IV, New York, G. P. Putnam's, 1912.

Dodge, H. S. and Cady, G. W., 'Treatment of fractures of the radius and ulna with compression plates', *JBJS*, 1972, vol. 54-A, pp. 1167–76.

Donley, J., *Save the Midwife*, Auckland, New Women's Press, 1986.

Donnelly, P. K. and Price, D., 'Eurotold professional questionnaires', in P. K. Donnelly and D. Price (eds), *Questioning Attitudes to Living Donor Transplantation: European Multicentre Study, Transplantation of Organs With Living Donors, Ethical and Legal Dimensions*, Leicester, The Project Management Group Eurotold, 1997, pp. 85–125.

Donovan, J., 'Ethnicity and health: a research review', *Social Science and Medicine*, 1984, vol. 19, pp. 663–70.

Drukker, W., 'Haemodialysis: a historical review', in W. Drukker, J. F. Maher and F. M. Parsons (eds), *Replacement of Renal Function by Dialysis*, The Hague, Martinus Nijhoff, 1978, pp. 3–37.

Duchet, M. (ed.), *Buffon: De l'Homme* (On *Histoire Naturelle de l'Homme*, from Buffon's *Histoire Naturelle, 1749–88*), Paris, Maspéro, 1971.

Dudley, J., 'The diabetes educator's role in teaching the diabetic patient', *Diabetes Care*, 1980, vol. 3, pp. 127–33.

Dyson, S., *Beta-thalassaemia: Current Carrier and Community Awareness in Manchester*, Leicester, De Montfort University Press, 1994.

Eade, J., 'The power of the experts: the plurality of beliefs and practices concerning health and illness among Bangladeshis in contemporary Tower Hamlets, London', in L. Marks and M. Worboys (eds), *Migrants, Minorities and Health: Historical and Contemporary Studies*, London, Routledge, 1997, pp. 250–71.

Eaton, R. G., 'Book Review. The Technique of Internal Fixation of Fractures. M. E. Müller, M. Allgöwer, and H. Willenegger, New York, Springer-Verlag 1965', *JBJS*, 1965, vol. 47-A, p. 1293.

Edgerton, D., 'Tilting at paper tigers', *British Journal for the History of Science*, 1993, vol. 26, pp. 67–75.

Edmonson, A. S. and Crenshaw, A. H. (eds), *Campbell's Operative Orthopaedics*, 2 vols., 6th edition, St Louis, Toronto and London, The C.V. Mosby Company, 1980.

Eldridge, J., Kitzinger, J. and Williams, K., *The Mass Media and Power in Modern Britain*, Oxford, Oxford University Press, 1997.

Else, A. (ed.), *Women Together: A History of Women's Organisations in New Zealand*, Wellington, Historical Branch/Daphne Brasell Associates Press, 1993.

Elster, J. and Herpin, N. (eds), *Ethique des choix médicaux*, Arles, Actes Sud, 1992.

Ernst, A.-S., *'Die beste Prophylaxe ist der Sozialismus': Ärzte und medizinische Hochschullehrer in der SBZ/DDR 1945–61*, Münster, Waxmann, 1997.

Essex-Lopresti, M., 'Medicine and Television', *Journal of Audio-Visual Media in Medicine*, 1997, vol. 20, pp. 61–4.

Ewald, F., *L'Etat-providence*, Paris, Grasset, 1986.

Fairman, J., 'Watchful vigilance: nursing care, technology, and the development of intensive care units', *Nursing Research*, 1992, vol. 41, pp. 56–60.

Fairman, J. and Lynaugh, J., *Critical Care Nursing: A History*, Philadephia, University of Pennsylvania Press, 1998.

Fennell, M. and Warnecke, R., *The Diffusion of Medical Innovations: An Applied Network Analysis*, London, Plenum Press, 1989.

Feudtner, C., 'The want of control: ideas, innovations and ideals in the modern management of diabetes mellitus', *Bulletin of the History of Medicine*, 1995, vol. 69, pp. 66–90.

——, 'A disease in motion: diabetes history and the new paradigm of transmuted disease', *Perspectives in Biology and Medicine*, 1996, vol. 39, pp. 158–70.

Fildes, V., Marks, L. and Marland, H. (eds), *Women and Children First: International Maternal and Infant Welfare, 1870–1945*, London, Routledge, 1992.

Fischer, E., Rohland, L. and Tutzke, D., *Für das Wohl des Menschen. Dokumente zur Gesundheitspolitik der sozialistischen Einheitspartei Deutschlands*, Berlin, VEB Verlag Volk und Gesundheit, 1979.

Fleck, L., *Genesis and Development of a Scientific Fact*, Chicago, University of Chicago Press, 1979 (published in German, 1935).

Fleming, V. E. M., 'Midwifery in New Zealand: responding to changing times', *Health Care for Women International*, 1996, vol. 17, pp. 343–59.

——, 'Women and midwives in partnership: a problematic relationship?', *Journal of Advanced Nursing*, 1998, vol. 27, pp. 8–14.

Florin, D., 'Scientific uncertainty and the role of expert advice: the case of health checks for coronary heart disease prevention by general practitioners in the UK', *Social Science and Medicine*, 1999, vol. 49, pp. 1269–83.

Floyer, J., *The Physician's Pulse Watch*, London, Smith and Walford, 1701.

Flynn, L., 'Why blind diabetics in renal failure should be offered treatment', *British Medical Journal*, 1983, vol. 287, 1177–8.

Fox, R. C. and Swazey, J. P., *The Courage to Fail: A Social View of Organ Transplants and Dialysis*, Chicago, University of Chicago Press, 1974.

——, *Spare Parts. Organ Replacement in American Society*, Oxford, Oxford University Press, 1992.

Foxall, G. and Tierney, J., 'From CAP1 to CAP2', *Management Decision*, 1984, vol. 22, pp. 3–15.

Fukuda, M. H., 'Public health in modern Japan: from regimen to hygiene', in D. Porter (ed.), *The History of Public Health in the Modern State*, Amsterdam, Rodopi, 1994, pp. 385–402.

Gabolde, M., *La transplantation d'organes avec donneur vivant, etude contextuelle, enquête sur les pratiques, réflexions sur les aspects ethiques*, Report to the Établissement Français des Greffes (French Transplantation Agency), 1998.

Gabolde, M. and Hervé, C., 'Living kidney donors: ethical considerations about the current practice of French transplant centers', *International Journal of Bioethics*, 1998, vol. 9, pp. 141–8.

Gabolde, M., Hervé, C. and Moulin, A. M., 'Evaluation, selection and follow-up of live kidney donors – Review of current practice in French renal transplant centres', *Nephrology Dialysis Transplantation*, in press.

Galambos, L. with Sewell, J. E., *Networks of Innovation: Vaccine Development at Merck, Sharp & Dohme, and Mulford, 1895–1995*, Cambridge, New York and Melbourne, Cambridge University Press, 1995.

Gandy, O. H., *Beyond Agenda Setting: Information Subsidies and Public Policy*, Norwood, NJ, Ablex, 1982.

Gans, B., 'Health problems and the immigrant child', in G. Wolstenholme and M. O'Connor (eds), *Immigration: Medical and Social Aspects*, London, CIBA Foundation, 1966, pp. 85–93.

Gelijns, A. and Rosenberg, N., 'The dynamics of technological change in medicine', *Health Affairs*, 1994, pp. 28–46.

Gill, P. and Modell, B., 'Thalassaemia in Britain: a tale of two communities', *British Medical Journal*, 1998, vol. 317, pp. 761–2.

Glaser, B. and Strauss, A., *The Discovery of Grounded Theory: Strategies for Qualitative Research*, Chicago, Aldine, 1967.

Gokal, R., 'Historical development and clinical use of continuous ambulatory peritoneal dialysis', in R. Gokal (ed.), *Continuous Ambulatory Peritoneal Dialysis*, Edinburgh, Churchill Livingstone, 1986, pp. 1–13.

Gordon, D., *Backblocks Baby-Doctor*, London, Faber and Faber, 1955.

——, *Doctor Down Under*, London, Faber and Faber, 1957.

Grace, T. G. and Eversmann, W. W., 'Forearm fractures. Treatment by rigid fixation with early motion', *JBJS*, 1980, vol. 62-A, pp. 433–8.

Grant, M., *Propaganda and the Role of the State in Inter-war Britain*, London, Clarendon, 1994.

Greenberg, D. W., 'Staging media events to achieve legitimacy: a case study of Britain's Friends of the Earth', *Public Communication and Persuasion*, 1985, vol. 2, pp. 347–62.

Grey-Turner, E. and Sutherland, F. M., *History of the British Medical Association, Volume II, 1932–1981*, London, BMA, 1982.

Grint, K. and Woolgar, S., *The Machine at Work: Technology, Work and Organization*, Cambridge, Polity Press, 1997.

Groen, M., *Technology, Work and Organisation: A Study of the Nursing Process in Intensive Care Units*, Maastricht, University of Limburg dissertation no. 95–29, 1995.

Grosier, *A General Description of China*, London, G. G. J. and J. Robinson, 1787.

Guillemin, J. and Holstrom, L. *Mixed Blessings: Intensive Care for Newborns*, New York and Oxford, Oxford University Press, 1986.

Guilliland, K., 'Learning from midwives', *Kaitiaki: Nursing New Zealand*, October 1996, p. 23.

——, 'Current issues for New Zealand midwifery and maternity services', *Our Newsletter*, December 1998, New Zealand College of Midwives. Access online at: http://www.midwives.org.nz/colnews/newsdec1.html.

——, 'Shared care in maternity services: with whom and how?' *Health Manager*, 1999, vol. 6, no. 2, pp. 4–8.

Guttmann, R. D., 'The graft survival curve', *Transplantation Proceedings*, 1992, vol. 24, pp. 2407–10.

——, 'The graft survival curve, Part II: Ideology and rhetoric', in J-L. Touraine *et al.*, *Organ Shortage: The Solutions*, Dordrecht, Kluwer, 1995, pp. 235–41.

Halper, T., 'End-stage renal failure and the aged in the United Kingdom', *International Journal of Technology Assessment in Health Care*, 1985, vol. 1, pp. 41–52.

——, *The Misfortunes of Others: End-Stage Renal Disease in the United Kingdom*, Cambridge, Cambridge University Press, 1989.

Hamilton, S. *et al.*, 'Anaesthesia by acupuncture', *British Medical Journal*, 1972, vol. 3, p. 352.

——, 'Anaesthesia by acupuncture', *BMJ*, 1973, vol. 1, p. 420.

Hampton, O. P. and Fitts, W. T., *Open Reduction of Common Fractures*, New York and London, Grune and Stratton, 1959.

Hansen, A. (ed.), *The Mass Media and Environmental Issues*, Leicester, Leicester University Press, 1993.

Harvey, J. P. Jr., 'Experto Credite'. Editorial Comment, *Contemporary Orthopaedics*, 1984, vol. 8, p. 13.

Hasler, J. and Schofield, T. (eds), *Continuing Care: The Management of Chronic Disease*, 2nd edn, Oxford, Oxford University Press, 1990.

Hawthorne, K., 'Asian diabetics attending a British hospital clinic: a pilot study to evaluate their care', *British Journal of General Practice*, 1990, vol. 40, pp. 243–7.

——, 'Overcoming cross-cultural difficulties in diabetes management – making diabetes health education relevant to a British South Asian community', MD thesis, University of Manchester, 1997.

Hawthorne, K. *et al.*, 'Cultural and religious influences in diabetes care in Great Britain', *Diabetic Medicine*, 1993, vol. 10, pp. 8–12.

Health Funding Authority Consultation Document, *Specialist Maternity Services: Obstetricians, Paediatricians and Anaesthetists*, Wellington, September 1999.

Hector, W., *The Work of Mrs Bedford Fenwick and the Rise of Professional Nursing*, London, Royal College of Nursing, 1973.

Heer, N., Choy, J. and Vichinsky, E., 'The social impact of migration in disease: Cooley's anemia, thalassaemia and new Asian immigrants', in A. Cohen (ed.), 'Cooley's Anemia, Seventh Symposium', *Annals of the New York Academy of Sciences*, 1998, vol. 850, pp. 509–11.

Hermitte, M. A., *Le Sang et le droit*, Paris, Seuil, 1997.

Hewer, C., 'Tests of acupuncture', *BMJ*, 1973, vol. 3, p. 592.

Hilgartner, S., *Science on Stage: Expert Advice as Public Drama*, Stanford, CA, Stanford University Press, 2000.

Hobsbawm, E. and Ranger, T., *The Invention of Tradition*, Cambridge, Cambridge University Press, 1983.

Hogle, F., *Recovering the Nation's Body. Cultural Memory, Medicine and the Politics of Redemption*, New Brunswick, NJ, Rutgers University Press, 1999.

Houssin, D., *La Greffe*, Paris, Odile Jacob, 1999.

Howell, J. D., *Technology in the Hospital: Transforming Patient Care in the Early Twentieth Century*, Baltimore and London, Johns Hopkins University Press, 1995.

Hughes, J., 'The "Matchbox on a Muffin": the design of hospitals in the early NHS', *Medical History*, 2000, vol 44, pp. 21–56.

Hutchinson, J. F., *Champions of Charity: War and the Rise of the Red Cross*, Boulder, CO, Westview Press, 1996.

Illich, I., *Medical Nemesis: The Expropriation of Health*, New York, Pantheon, 1976.

Inglis, B., *Fringe Medicine*, London, Faber and Faber, 1964.

Jarman, B., 'Developing primary health care', *British Medical Journal*, 1987, vol. 294, pp. 1005–8.

Jellett, H., *The Causes and Prevention of Maternal Mortality*, London, J. and A. Churchill, 1929.

Jennett, B., *High Technology Medicine: Benefits and Burdens*, Oxford, Oxford University Press, 1986.

Johnson. R. W., 'Shortage of organs for transplantation, living donors should be used more often', *British Medical Journal*, 1996, vol. 312, p. 1357.

Jones, J., Payne, W. D. and Matas, A. J., 'The living-related donor – risks, benefits and related concerns', *Transplantation Review*, 1993, vol. 7, pp. 115–28.

Kadkhodaei, M. *et al.*, 'Ethnicity study and non-selective screening for haemoglobinopathies in the antenatal population of central Manchester', *Clinical and Laboratory Haematology*, 1998, vol. 20, pp. 207–11.

Kameyama, M., *Kindai nihon kangoshi*, vols I–IV, Tokyo, Domes, 1983–5.

Karpf, A., *Doctoring the Media: The Reporting of Health and Medicine*, London, Routledge, 1988.

Kasiske, B. L., Ravenscraft, M., Ramos, E. L., Gaston, R. S., Bia, M. J. and Danovitch, G. M., 'The evaluation of living renal transplant donors: clinical practice guidelines', *Journal of the American Society of Nephrology*, 1996, vol. 7, pp. 2288–313.

Kaufman, M. *et al.* (eds), *Dictionary of American Nursing Biography*, New York, Greenwood Press, 1988.

Klaus, A., *Every Child a Lion: The Origins of Maternal and Infant Health Policy in the United States and France, 1890–1920*, Ithaca and London, Cornell University Press, 1993.

Klein, R., *The Politics of the NHS*, 2nd edition, London, Longman, 1989.

Klein, R., Day, P. and Redmayne, S., *Managing Scarcity. Priority Setting and Rationing in the National Health Service*, Buckingham, Open University Press, 1996.

Koch E. B., 'In the image of science? Negotiating the development of diagnostic ultrasound in the cultures of surgery and radiology', *Technology and Culture*, 1993, vol. 34, pp. 858–93.

Kōseishō imukyoku, *Iseihyakunenshi: shiryōhen*, Tokyo, Gyōsei, 1976.

Krall, L., 'The history of diabetes lay associations', *Patient Education and Counseling*, 1995, vol. 26, pp. 285–91.

Küss, R., 'Human renal transplantation memories, 1951 to 1981', in P. I. Terazaki (ed.), *History of Transplantation: Thirty-five Recollections*, Los Angeles, UCLA Tissue Typing Laboratory, 1991, p. 40.

Küss, R., Teinturier, J. and Milliez, P., 'Quelques essais de greffe de rein chez l'homme', *Mémoires de l'Académie de Chirurgie*, 1951, vol. 77, pp. 755–68.

Laing, W., *Renal Failure: A Priority in Health?*, London, Office of Health Economics, 1978.

Laing, W. and Williams, R., *Diabetes: A Model for Health Care Management*, London, Office of Health Economics, 1989.

Lamping, D. and Campbell, K., 'A methodological study of hemodialysis compliance criteria', *Journal of Compliance in Health Care*, 1989, vol. 4, pp. 117–34.

Laros, G. S. and Spiegel, P. G., 'Editorial comments: rigid internal fixation of fractures', *Clinical Orthopaedics and Related Research*, 1979, vol. 138, pp. 2–22.

Latour, B. and Woolgar, S., *Laboratory Life: The Social Construction of Scientific Facts*, Beverly Hills and London, Sage Publications, 1979.

Lawrence, G., 'Object lessons in the museum medium', in S. Pearce (ed.), *Objects of Knowledge*, London, Athlone, 1990.

—— (ed.), *Technologies of Modern Medicine*, London, Science Museum, 1994.

Leavitt, J. W., *Brought to Bed: Childbearing in America, 1750 to 1950*, New York and London, Oxford University Press, 1986.

Lebas, E., 'When every street became a cinema: the film work of Bermondsey Borough Council's Public Health Department, 1923–1953', *History Workshop Journal*, 1995, vol. 39, pp. 42–66.

Lerman, N., Mohun, A. P. and Oldenziel, R., 'Versatile tools: gender analysis and the history of technology', *Technology and Culture*, 1997, vol. 38, pp. 1–8.

Ling, P. *et al.*, 'The diabetic clinic dinosaur is dying: will diabetic day units evolve?', *Diabetic Medicine*, 1985, vol. 2, pp. 163–5.

Lock, M., 'The unnatural as ideology: contesting brain death in Japan', in P. Asquith and A. Kalland (eds), *Representing the Natural in Japan*, Cambridge, Cambridge University Press, 1997, pp. 121–44.

Loudon, I., *Death in Childbirth: An International Study of Maternal Care and Maternal Mortality 1800–1950*, Oxford, Clarendon Press, 1992.

Löwy, I., 'The impact of medical practice on biomedical research. The case of human leucocyte antigen studies', *Minerva*, 1987, vol. 25, pp. 171–200.

—— (ed.), *Medicine and Change: Historical and Sociological Studies of Medical Innovation*, Paris, INSERM/John Libbey, 1993.

——, 'Recent historiography of biomedical research' in G. Lawrence (ed.), *Technologies of Modern Medicine*, London, Science Museum, 1994, pp. 99–110.

——, *Between Bench and Bedside: Science, Healing, and Interleukin-2 in a Cancer Ward*, Cambridge, MA, and London, Harvard University Press, 1996.

Löwy, I. and Moulin, A. M., 'Les institutions de transplantation: du don à l'échange', *Culture Technique*, 1985, pp. 157–63.

Lu, G. and Needham, J., *Celestial Lancets: A History and Rationale of Acupuncture and Moxa*, Cambridge, Cambridge University Press, 1980.

McCarthy, M., *Campaigning for the Poor: CPAG and the Politics of Welfare*, Kent, Croom Helm, 1988.

McDicken, W. N., *Diagnostic Ultrasonics: Principles and Use of Instruments*, St Albans and London, Crosby Lockwood Staples, 1976.

Macdonald, C., Penfold, M. and Williams, B. (eds), *The Book of New Zealand Women*, Wellington, Bridget Williams Books, 1991.

McGaw, J., 'No passive victims, no separate spheres: a feminist perspective on technology's history', in S. Cutcliffe and R. Post (eds), *In Context: History and the History of Technology*, Bethlehem, PA, Lehigh University Press, 1989.

McGeown, M., 'Chronic renal failure in Northern Ireland, 1968–70', *Lancet*, 1972, vol. 1, pp. 307–10.

Macintosh, R., 'Tests of acupuncture', *BMJ*, 1973, vol. 3, pp. 454–5.

MacKenzie D. and Wajcman, J. (eds), *The Social Shaping of Technology: How the Refrigerator Got its Hum*, Milton Keynes, Open University Press, 1985.

McKinlay, J. B., 'From "promising report" to "standard procedure": seven stages in the career of a medical innovation', *Milbank Memorial Fund Quarterly*, 1981, vol. 59, pp. 374–411.

McLoughlin, D., 'The politics of childbirth', *North and South*, August 1993, pp. 54–68.

Maher, B., Lamping, D. *et al.*, 'Psychosocial aspects of chronic hemodialysis: The National Cooperative Dialysis Study', *Kidney International*, 1983, vol. 23, Suppl. 13, pp. S-50–7.

Malhauser, I. *et al.*, 'Bicentric evaluation of a teaching and treatment programme for Type I (insulin dependent) diabetic patients: improvement of metabolic control and other measures of diabetic care for up to 22 months', *Diabetologia*, 1983, vol. 25, pp. 470–6.

Malloy, T., Chairman Rural GP Network political issues committee, *New Zealand Doctor*, 2 April 1997.

Mann, F., *Acupuncture: The Ancient Chinese Art of Healing*, London, Heinemann, 1962.

Marks, H. M., *The Progress of Experiment. Science and Therapeutic Reform in the United States, 1900–1990*, Cambridge and New York, Cambridge University Press, 1997.

Marks, L. and Hilder, L., 'Ethnic advantage: infant survival among Jewish and Bangladeshi immigrants in East London, 1870–1990', in L. Marks and M. Worboys (eds), *Migrants, Minorities and Health: Historical and Contemporary Studies*, London, Routledge, 1997, pp. 179–209.

Marks, L. and Worboys, M. (eds), *Migrants, Minorities and Health: Historical and Contemporary Studies*, London, Routledge, 1997.

Marland, H. and Rafferty, A. M. (eds), *Midwives, Society and Childbirth: Debates and Controversies in the Modern Period*, London and New York, Routledge, 1997.

Martin, E., *Flexible Bodies: Tracking Immunity in American Culture from the Days of Polio to the Age of AIDS*, Boston, Beacon, 1994.

Maxwell, J., 'The iron lung: halfway technology or necessary step?', *Milbank Quarterly*, 1986, vol. 64, pp. 3–29.

Mays, N., *Management and Resource Allocation in End Stage Renal Failure Units: A Review of Current Issues*, London, King Edward's Hospital Fund, 1990.

Mecklinger, L., 'Das Gesundheitswesen der DDR – Konzept und Realität', in *Das Gesundheitswesen der DDR – zwischen Konzept und Realität*, Berlin, Wissenschaftliche Arbeitstagung der Interessengemeinschaft Medizin und Gesellschaft e.V. 26.11.1994, pp. 61–7.

Medawar, P. B., *The Threat and the Glory: Reflections on Science and Scientists*, ed. by David Pyke, Oxford, Oxford University Press, 1990.

Mein Smith, P., *Maternity in Dispute: New Zealand 1920–1939*, Wellington, Government Printer/Historical Branch, 1986.

——, *Mothers and King Baby: Infant Survival and Welfare in an Imperial World: Australia 1880–1950*, Basingstoke, Macmillan, 1997.

Miller, L. and Goldstein, J., 'More efficient care of diabetic patients in a county-hospital setting', *New England Journal of Medicine*, 1972, vol. 286, pp. 1388–90.

Mize, R. D., Bucholz, R. W. and Grogan, D P., 'Surgical treatment of displaced, comminuted fractures of the distal end of the femur', *JBJS*, 1982, vol. 64-A, pp. 871–9.

Modell, B., 'Effect of introducing antenatal diagnosis on the reproductive behaviour of families at risk for thalassaemia major', *British Medical Journal*, 1980, vol. I, p. 737.

——, 'Delivering genetic screening to the community', *Annals of Medicine*, 1997, vol. 29, pp. 591–9.

Modell, B. *et al.*, 'A multidisciplinary approach for improving services in primary care: randomised controlled trial of screening for haemoglobin disorders', *British Medical Journal*, 1998a, vol. 317, pp. 788–91.

——, 'Audit of prenatal diagnosis for hemoglobin disorders in the United Kingdom: the first 20 years', in A. Cohen (ed.), 'Cooley's Anemia, Seventh Symposium', *Annals of the New York Academy of Sciences*, 1998b, vol. 850, pp. 420–2.

Mokyr, J., 'Evolution and technological change: a new metaphor for economic history?', in R. Fox (ed.), *Technological Change*, Amsterdam, Harwood Academic Publishers, 1996, pp. 63–83.

Moncrief, J., Popovich, R. and Nolph, K., 'The history and current status of continuous ambulatory peritoneal dialysis', *American Journal of Kidney Diseases*, 1990, vol. 16, pp. 579–84.

Moore, J. R., 'The closed fracture of the long bones', *JBJS*, 1960, vol 42-A, pp. 869–74.

Mörl, F., *Lehrbuch der Unfallchirurgie*, Berlin, VEB Verlag Volk und Gesundheit, 1968.

Morrice, A., 'The medical pundits: doctors and indirect advertising in the lay press, 1922–1927', *Medical History*, 1994, vol. 38, pp. 255–80.

Moss, L., *Acupuncture and You*, London, Paul Alek Books, 1964.

Moulin, A. M., *Le dernier langage de la médecine: histoire de l'immunologie de Pasteur au Sida*, Paris, PUF, 1991.

——, 'Body parts, the modern dilemma', *Transplantation Reviews*, 1993, vol. 25, pp. 33–5.

——, 'AIDS and the history of the right to health', in *AIDS, Health and Human Rights*, Fondation Marcel Mérieux, Les Pensières, 1993, pp. 67–73.

——, 'The crisis of organ transplantation. The quest for "cultural compatibility"', *Diogenes*, 1995, vol. 172, pp. 76–97.

——, 'The foundations of the right to be grafted', in J. L. Touraine *et al.* (eds), *Organ Shortage: the Solutions*, Dordrecht, Kluwer, 1995, pp. 223–34.

——, *L'aventure de la vaccination*, Paris, Fayard, 1995.

——, 'Reversible history: blood transfusion and the spread of AIDS in France', in C. Hannaway, V. Harden and J. Paracandola (eds), *AIDS and the Public Debate*, Amsterdam, IOS Press, 1995, pp. 170–86.

——, 'Immunology or the science of boundaries: A "science dans le siècle"', in J. Krige and D. Pestre (eds), *Science in the Twentieth Century*, Amsterdam, Harwood Academic Publishers, 1997, pp. 479–95.

——, 'L'équivoque médicale: interprète ou agent double', *Sciences Sociales et Santé*, 1998, vol. 16, pp. 97–106.

——, 'Les sociétés et leurs vaccins', *Comptes Rendus de l'Académie des Sciences de Paris*, 1999, vol. 322, pp. 983–7.

Müller, K.-D., 'Die Ärzteschaft im staatlichen Gesundheitswesen der SBZ und der DDR 1945–1989', in R. Jütte (ed.), *Geschichte der deutschen Ärzteschaft. Organisierte Berufs- und Gesundheitspolitik im 19. und 20. Jahrhundert*, Cologne, Deutscher Ärzte-Verlag, 1997, pp. 243–73.

Naiman, P. T, Schein, A. J. and Siffert, R. S., 'Use of ASIF compression plates in selected shaft fractures of the upper extremity: a preliminary report', *Clinical Orthopaedics and Related Research*, 1970, vol. 71, pp. 208–16.

Najarian, J. S., Chavers, B. M., McHugh, L. E. and Matas, A. J., '20 years or more of follow-up of living kidney donors', *Lancet*, 1992, vol. 340, pp. 807–10.

National Association of Health Authorities and Trusts, *Complementary Therapies in the NHS*, Report Number 10, 1993.

National Health Committee, *Review of Maternity Services in New Zealand*, Wellington, National Health Committee, 1999.

Neer, C. S., Grantham, S. A. and Shelton, M. L., 'Supracondylar fracture of the adult femur. A study of one hundred and ten cases', *JBJS*, 1967, vol. 49-A, pp. 591–613.

Nelkin, D., *Selling Science: How the Press Covers Science and Technology*, New York, W. H. Freeman, 1995.

Newson-Davis, J. and Weatherall, D. J. (eds), *Health Policy and Technological Innovation*, London, Chapman and Hall, 1994.

Nicholson, M., 'Heterogeneity, emergence and resistance: recent work in the sociology of laboratory science', in G. Lawrence (ed.), *Technologies of Modern Medicine*, London, Science Museum, 1994, pp. 111–19.

Nicoll, E. A., 'Closed and open treatment of tibial fractures', *Clinical Orthopaedics and Related Research*, 1974, vol. 105, pp. 144–53.

Nolan, M., *Breadwinning: New Zealand Women and the State*, Christchurch, Canterbury University Press, 2000.

O'Connor, B., *Healing Traditions: Alternative Medicine and the Health Professions*, Philadelphia, University of Pennsylvania Press, 1995.

Ohnuki Tierney, E., 'The reduction of personhood to brain and personality: Japanese contestation of medical high technology', in A. Cunningham and B. Andrews (eds), *Western Medicine as Contested Knowledge*, Manchester, Manchester University Press, 1997.

Olerud, S., 'Operative treatment of supracondylar-condylar fractures of the femur. Technique and results in fifteen cases', *JBJS*, 1972, vol. 54-A, pp. 1015–32.

Olerud, S. and Karlström, G., 'Secondary intramedullary nailing of tibial fractures', *JBJS*, 1972, vol. 54-A, pp. 1419–28.

Page, L., 'On the other side of the world: impressions of midwifery in New Zealand and Australia', *Midwives*, 1996, vol.109, pp. 88–9.

Papps, E. and Olssen, M., *Doctoring Childbirth and Regulating Midwifery in New Zealand: A Foucauldian Perspective*, Palmerston North, Dunmore Press, 1997.

Parkin, D., 'Chronic renal failure: the economics of treatment', *Community Health*, 1978, vol. 9, pp. 134–41.

Parliamentary Debates (Commons) Official Report, Fifth Series (1957–1958), vol. 583, pp. 588–700, 1577–8.

Pasveer, B., 'Knowledge of shadows: the introduction of x-ray images in medicine', *Sociology of Health and Illness*, 1990, vol. 11, pp. 360–81.

——, *Shadows of Knowledge, Making a Representing Practice in Medicine: X-ray Pictures and Pulmonary Tuberculosis, 1895–1930*, Den Haag, Amsterdam, CIP-Gegevens Koninklijke Bibliotheek, 1992.

Peitzman, S., 'From dropsy to Bright's Disease to end-stage renal disease', *Milbank Quarterly*, 1989, vol. 67, Suppl.1, pp. 16–32.

Peppard, N., 'General Review', in G. Wolstenholme and M. O'Connor (eds), *Immigration: Medical and Social Aspects*, London, CIBA Foundation, 1966, pp. 1–8.

Pernick, M., 'Back from the grave: recurring controversies over defining and diagnosing death', in R. Zaner (ed.), *Death: Beyond the Whole-Brain Criteria*, Dordrecht, Kluwer, 1988, pp. 17–74.

Petrou, M. and Modell, B., 'Prenatal screening for haemoglobin disorders', *Prenatal Diagnosis*, 1995, vol. 13, pp. 1275–85.

Petrou, M. *et al.*, 'Antenatal diagnosis: how to deliver a comprehensive service in the United Kingdom' in A. Bank (ed.), 'Cooley's Anemia, Sixth Symposium', *Annals of the New York Academy of Sciences*, 1990, vol. 612, pp. 251–63.

Pickering, A., *The Mangle of Practice: Time, Agency and Science*, Chicago, Chicago University Press, 1995.

Pickstone, J. V. (ed.), *Medical Innovations in Historical Perspective*, Basingstoke, Macmillan, 1992.

——, 'The biographical and the analytical, towards a historical model of science and practice in modern medicine', in I. Löwy (ed.), *Medicine and Change: Historical and Sociological Studies of Medical Innovation*, Paris, INSERM Editions, 1993, pp. 23–47.

Pinch, T., 'The social construction of technology: a review', in R. Fox (ed.), *Technological Change: Methods and Themes in the History of Technology*, Reading UK, Harwood Academic, 1998, pp. 17–35.

Pinch, T. J. and Bijker, W. E., 'The social construction of facts and artifacts; or how the sociology of science and the sociology of technology might benefit each other', *Social Studies of Science*, 1984, vol. 14, pp. 399–441.

Pinch T. and Bijker, W. E., 'Science, technology and the new sociology of technology: reply to Russell', *Social Studies of Science*, 1986, vol. 16, pp. 347–60.

Pinell, P., 'Cancer policy and the health system in France: "Big Medicine" challenges to the concept and organization of medical practice', *Social History of Medicine*, 1991, vol. 4, pp. 75–101.

Pouchelle, M. C., 'Transports hospitaliers, extravagances de l'âme', in F. Lautman and J. Maitre (eds), *Gestion Religieuse de la santé*, Paris, L'Harmattan, 1995, pp. 247–99.

Power, H., 'A model of how the sickle cell gene produces malaria resistance', *Journal of Theoretical Biology*, 1975, vol. 50, pp. 121–7.

Prelinger, C. M., 'The female deaconate in the Anglican church: what kind of ministry for women?', in G. Malmgreen (ed.), *Religion in the Lives of English Women, 1760–1930*, London, Croom Helm, 1986, pp. 161–92.

Pritzel, K., *Gesundheitswesen und Gesundheitspolitik der Deutschen Demokratischen Republik*, Berlin, Osteuropa-Institut, 1977.

Prochaska, F. K., 'Body and soul: Bible nurses and the poor in Victorian London', *Historical Research*, vol. 60, 1987, pp. 336–48.

Prottas, J., *The Most Useful Gift. Altruism and the Public Policy of Organ Transplant*, San Francisco, Jossey-Bass, 1994.

Rafferty, A. M., 'Travel and travail: founders of international nursing', in *Past is Present*, The Canadian Association for the History of Nursing Keynote Presentations, 1988–96, Vancouver, 1997, pp. 189–214.

Rahn, B. A. *et al.*, 'Primary bone healing', *JBJS*, 1971, vol. 53-A, pp. 783–6.

Ramsay, M., 'Anaesthesia by acupuncture', *BMJ*, 1972, vol. 3, p. 703.

——, 'Anaesthesia by acupuncture', *BMJ*, 1973, vol. 1, p. 233.

Rand, J. A. *et al.*, 'A comparison of the effect of open intramedullary nailing and compression-plate fixation on fracture-site blood flow and fracture union', *JBJS*, 1981, vol. 63-A, pp. 427–41.

Raper, A., 'Sickle-cell disease in Africa and America – a comparison', *Journal of Tropical Medicine and Hygiene*, 1950, vol. 53, pp. 49–53.

Registrar General for Scotland, *Annual Report of the Registrar General for Scotland, 1978*, Edinburgh, General Register Office, 1979.

——, *Annual Report of the Registrar General for Scotland, 1990*, Edinburgh, General Register Office, 1991.

Reiser, S. J., *Medicine and the Reign of Technology*, Cambridge, Cambridge University Press, 1978.

Richardson, J., *Complementary Therapy in the NHS: A Service Evaluation of the First Year of an Outpatient Service in a Local District Hospital*, Lewisham, Lewisham Hospital NHS Trust, 1995.

——, *CTC Annual Report*, Lewisham Hospital NHS Trust, 1995.

Richardson, J. and Brennan, A., 'Complementary therapy in the NHS: service development in a local district general hospital', *Complementary Therapies in Nursing and Midwifery*, 1995, vol. 1, pp. 89–92.

Richardson, R., *Death, Dissection and the Destitute*, London, Routledge, 1988.

Rivett, G., *From Cradle to Grave: Fifty Years of the NHS*, London, King's Fund, 1997.

Roberts, J. I. and Group, T. M., *Feminism and Nursing: An Historical Perspective on Power, Status, and Political Activism in the Nursing Profession*, Connecticut, Praeger, 1995.

Rockefeller Foundation, *Rockefeller Foundation Annual Report*, New York, 1922.

Rockwood, C.A. and Green, D. P., *Fractures*, 2 vols, Philadelphia and Toronto, J.B. Lippincott Company, 1975.

Rogers, E., *Diffusion of Innovations*, 4th edition, New York and London, Free Press, 1995.

Rohland, L. and Spaar, H., *Die medizinisch-wissenschaftlichen Gesellschaften der DDR. Geschichte – Funktionen und Aufgaben*, Berlin, VEB Verlag Volk und Gesundheit, 1973.

Romano, C., 'Diffusion of technology innovation', *Advances in Nursing Science*, 1990, vol. 13, pp. 11–21.

Rosen, P., 'The social construction of mountain bikes: technology and postmodernity in the cycle industry', *Social Studies of Science*, 1993, vol. 23, pp. 479–513.

Rosenberg, C., *The Care of Strangers: The Rise of America's Hospital System*, New York, Basic Books, 1987.

——, 'Disease in history: frames and framers', *Milbank Quarterly*, 1989, vol. 67, pp. 1–15.

Roth, J. and Ruzek, S. (eds), *The Adoption and Social Consequences of Medical Technologies*, Greenwich, CT, JAI Press, 1986.

Royal College of Obstetricians and Gynaecologists, *Report of the RCOG Working Party on Routine Ultrasound Examination in Pregnancy*, London, Chameleon Press, 1984.

Royal College of Physicians Committee on Renal Disease and the Renal Association, *Manpower and Workload in Adult Renal Medicine*, typescript report, London, Royal College of Physicians, 1983.

Royal College of Physicians Medical Services Study Group, 'Deaths from chronic renal failure under the age of 50', *British Medical Journal*, 1981, vol. 283, pp. 283–7.

Royal College of Physicians of London and British Diabetic Association, *Provision of Medical Care for Adult Diabetic Patients in the United Kingdom*, London, RCP/BDA, 1985.

Ruban, M. E., *Gesundheitswesen in der DDR*, Berlin, Verlag Gebr. Holzapfel, 1981.

Russell, L. B., *Technology in Hospitals: Medical Advances and their Diffusion*, Washington, DC, Brookings Institution, 1979.

Russell, S., 'The social construction of artefacts: a response to Pinch and Bijker', *Social Studies of Science*, 1986, vol. 16, pp. 331–46.

Saks, M., 'The paradox of incorporation: acupuncture and the medical profession in modern Britain', in M. Saks (ed.), *Alternative Medicine in Britain*, Oxford, Clarendon Press, 1992, pp. 183–98.

Sauerteig, L., 'Vergleich: Ein Königsweg auch für die Medizingeschichte? Methodologische Fragen komparativen Forschens', in N. Paul and T. Schlich (eds), *Medizingeschichte: Aufgaben, Probleme, Perspektiven*, Frankfurt/Main, Campus, 1998, pp. 266–91.

Savatier, J., 'Les prélèvements sur le corps humain au profit d'autrui', *Les Petites affiches*, 1994, vol. 149, pp. 8–13.

Schatzker, J., Horne, G. and Waddell, J., 'The Toronto experience with the supracondylar fracture of the femur 1966–72', *Injury*, 1974, vol. 6, pp. 113–28.

Schatzker, J. and Lambert, D. C., 'Supracondylar fractures of the femur', *Clinical Orthopaedics and Related Research*, 1979, vol. 138, pp. 77–83.

Schlich, T., 'Osteosynthese: Geschichte einer schwierigen Therapiemethode', *Jahrbuch des Deutschen Orthopädischen Geschichts- und Forschungsmuseums*, 2000, vol. 2, pp. 55–72.

——, *Surgery, Science and Industry: A Revolution in Fracture Care, 1950s-1990s*, Basingstoke, Palgrave, 2002.

Schneider, R., *10 Jahre AO. Jubiläumsbericht herausgegeben aus Anlaß des zehnjährigen Bestehens der 'Schweizerischen Arbeitsgemeinschaft für Osteosynthesefragen'*, AO-Dokumentationszentrale, Bern, AO, 1969.

——, *25 Jahre AO-Schweiz. Arbeitsgemeinschaft für Osteoynthesefragen 1958–83*, Biel, 1983.

Scottish Home and Health Department/Scottish Health Service Planning Council, *Obstetric Ultrasound in Scotland: Report of the Ad Hoc Group appointed by the Specialty subcommittee for Obstetrics and Gynaecology of the National Medical Consultative Committee*, Edinburgh, Her Majesty's Stationery Office, 1988.

Scribner, B., 'A personalized history of chronic hemodialysis', *American Journal of Kidney Diseases*, 1990, vol. 16, pp. 511–19.

Serres, M., 'Foreword' to Jacques Testard, *L'Œuf transparent*, Paris, Flammarion, 1986, pp. 5–19.

Sharland, D., 'Anaesthesia by acupuncture', *BMJ*, 1972, vol. 4, p. 612.

Sharma, U., *Complementary Medicine Today: Practitioners and Patients*, London, Routledge, 1992.

Shimizu, K., *Shōwa senzenki nihon kōshūeiseishi*, Tokyo, Fuji shuppan, 1991.

Shires, T. G., 'Care of the injured in America: organizational and physiological considerations', in R. Maulitz (ed.), *Unnatural Causes: The Three Leading Killer Diseases in America*, New Brunswick, NJ, Rutgers University Press, 1989, pp. 20–7.

Siddons, H., 'Diabetes specialist nurse', *Diabetic Medicine*, 1992, vol. 9, pp. 790–1.

Skocpol, T., *Protecting Soldiers and Mothers: The Political Origins of Social Policy in the United States*, Cambridge, MA, Belknap Press of Harvard University Press, 1992.

Skrabunck, P., 'Acupuncture in an age of unreason' *Lancet*, 1984, vol. 1, pp. 116–17.

Smaje, C., *Health, Race and Ethnicity: Making Sense of the Evidence*, London, King's Fund Institute, 1995.

Sozialismus, wissenschaftlich-technische Revolution und Medizin. Rat für Planung und Koordinierung der medizinischen Wissenschaft beim Ministerium für Gesundheitswesen, Berlin VEB Verlag Volk und Gesundheit, 1968.

Stanton, J., 'Making sense of technologies in medicine', *Social History of Medicine*, 1999, vol. 12, pp. 437–48.

——, 'The cost of living: kidney dialysis, rationing and health economics in Britain, 1965–1996', *Social Science and Medicine*, 1999, vol. 49, pp. 1169–82.

——, 'Supported lives', in R. Cooter and J. Pickstone (eds), *Medicine in the Twentieth Century*, Amsterdam, Harwood Academic Publishers, 2000, pp. 601–15.

Starr, P., *The Social Transformation of American Medicine. The Rise of a Sovereign Profession and the Making of a Vast Industry*, New York, Basic Books, 1982.

Starzl, T., *Memoirs of a Transplant Surgeon: The Puzzle People*, Pittsburgh, University of Pittsburgh Press, 1992.

Stephens, W., 'Personal view', *BMJ*, vol. 287, p. 906.

Stern, P. J. *et al.*, 'Intramedullary fixation of humeral shaft fractures', *JBJS*, 1984, vol. 66-A, pp. 639–46.

Stewart, A. *et al.*, 'Malignant disease in childhood and diagnostic irradiation in utero', *Lancet*, 1956, vol. 2, p. 447.

Stewart, M. J., Sisk, D. T. and Wallace, S. L., 'Fractures of the distal third of the femur', *JBJS*, 1966, vol. 48-A, pp. 784–807.

Stewart, T., 'Diabetes mellitus', in J. Hasler and T. Schofield (eds), *Continuing Care: The Management of Chronic Disease*, 2nd edn, Oxford, Oxford University Press, 1990, pp. 130–49.

Stocking, B., *Initiative and Inertia: Case Studies in the NHS*, London, Nuffield Provincial Hospitals Trust, 1985.

——, *Expensive Health Technologies. Regulatory and Administrative Mechanisms in Europe*, Oxford, New York Tokyo, Oxford University Press, 1988.

——, 'Influences on the diffusion process: government and national funding agencies', in S. Kirchberger, P. Durieux and B. Stocking, *The Diffusion of Two Technologies for Renal Stone Treatments across Europe*, London, King's Fund, 1991, pp. 121–32.

Summers, A., *Angels and Citizens: British Women as Military Nurses, 1854–1914*, London, Routledge and Kegan Paul, 1988.

——, 'Nurses and ancillaries in the Christian era', in I. Loudon (ed.), *Western Medicine: An Illustrated History*, Oxford, Oxford University Press, 1997, pp. 192–205.

Takahashi, A., 'Western influences on the development of the nursing profession in Japan, 1868–1938', PhD thesis, University of London, 1999.

Tann, J., 'Space, time and innovation characteristics: the contribution of diffusion process theory to the history of technology', *History of Technology*, 1995, vol. 17, pp. 143–63.

Tapper, M., 'An "anthropathology" of the "American Negro": anthropology, genetics and the new racial science, 1940–52', *Social History of Medicine*, 1997, vol. 10, pp. 263–89.

Taube, D., Winder, E. and Ogg, C., 'Successful treatment of middle aged and elderly patients with end stage renal disease', *British Medical Journal*, 1983, vol. 286, pp. 2018–20.

Ten Rhyne, W., *Dissertatio de Arthritide: Mantissa Schematica: De Acupunctura: Et Orationes Tres*, London, Royal Society, 1683.

Thomas, L., 'Notes of a biology-watcher: the technology of medicine', *New England Journal of Medicine*, 1971, vol. 285, pp. 1366–8.

Thorn, P. and Russell, P. 'Diabetic clinics today and tomorrow: mini-clinics in general practice', *British Medical Journal*, 1973, vol. 2, pp. 534–6.

Tilly, C., 'Social movements and (all sorts of) other political interactions – local, national, and international – including identities', *Theory and Society*, 1998, vol. 27, pp. 453–80.

Tittmuss, R., *The Gift Relationship*, New York, Pantheon Books, 1991.

Tomlinson, S., 'Diabetes mellitus – the pissing evile: science and medicine, molluscs and man', *Mediscope*, 1988, vol. 66, pp. 58–60.

Tomlinson, S. and Hawthorne, K. 'One-to-one teaching with pictures – flashcard health education for British Asians with diabetes', *British Journal of General Practice*, 1997, vol. 47, pp. 301–4.

——, 'Pakistani Moslems with Type-II diabetes mellitus: effect of sex, literacy skills, known diabetic complications and place of care on diabetic knowledge, reported self-monitoring management and glycaemic control', *Diabetic Medicine*, 1999, vol. 16, pp. 591–7.

Trunkey, D. D., 'Trauma', *Scientific American*, 1983, vol. 249, no. 2, pp. 20–7.

Tulloch, J., 'Managing the press in a medium-sized European power', in M. Bromley and H. Stephenson (eds), *Sex, Lies and Democracy: The Press and the Public*, London, Longman, 1998.

Tuttle, C. R., 'Experiences of perinatal care and childbirth in New Zealand: a model in transition', *IJCE*, 1997, vol. 12, pp. 30–2.

Uebermuth, H., 'Wandlungen der Knochenbruchbehandlung im 20. Jahrhundert', *Beiträge zur Orthopädie und Traumatologie*, 1975, vol. 22, pp. 202–8.

Valier, H., 'The politics of scientific medicine in Manchester 1900–60', PhD thesis, Manchester University, 2001.

Vaughan, P., *Doctors Commons: a Short History of the British Medical Association*, London, Heinemann, 1959.

von Hippel, E., 'The dominant role of users in the scientific instrument innovation process', *Research Policy*, 1976, vol. 5, pp. 28–39.

Vyas, A., 'Knowledge awareness and self management among South Asians with diabetes in Manchester; a pilot randomised trial to investigate a primary care based education package', MPhil thesis in Medicine, University of Manchester, 1999.

Wade, P. A., 'ASIF compression has a problem', *The Journal of Trauma*, 1979, vol. 10, pp. 513–15.

Wailoo, K., 'A "disease sui generis": the origins of sickle cell anemia and the emergence of modern clinical research, 1904–24', *Bulletin of the History of Medicine*, 1991, vol. 65, pp. 185–208.

——, 'Genetic marker of segregation: sickle cell anemia, thalassemia and racial ideology in American medical writing 1920–1950', *History and Philosophy of the Life Sciences*, 1996, vol. 18, pp. 305–20.

——, *Drawing Blood: Technology and Disease Identity in Twentieth Century America*, Baltimore, Johns Hopkins University Press, 1997.

Waissman, R., *Le Don d'organes*, Paris, PUF, 2001.

Ward, E., *Timbo: A Struggle for Survival*, London, Sidgwick and Jackson, 1986.

Watts, J., 'Tests of acupuncture', *BMJ*, 1973 vol. 3, p. 780.

Weatherall, D., 'Towards an understanding of the molecular biology of some common inherited anemias: the story of thalassemia' in M. Wintrobe, *Blood, Pure and Eloquent*, New York, McGraw-Hill, 1980, pp. 372–414.

Webster, C., *The National Health Service: A Political History*, Oxford and New York, Oxford University Press, 1998.

Weindling, P., 'Public health and political stabilisation: the Rockefeller Foundation in central and eastern Europe between the two World Wars', *Minerva*, vol. 31, 1993, pp. 253–67.

Wheeler, K., 'Maternity Services (1996 Advice Notice) – where to from here?' *Health Manager*, 1997, vol. 4, no. 4, pp. 5–8.

Wickstrom, J., Hamilton, L. and Rodriguez, R. P., 'Evaluation of the AO compression apparatus', *The Journal of Trauma*, 1967, vol. 7, pp. 210–27.

Wildy, T., 'From MOI to the COI – publicity and propaganda in Britain, 1945–1951: the National Health and Insurance campaigns of 1948', *Historical Journal of Film, Radio and Television*, 1986, vol. 6, pp. 3–16.

Williams, A. S., *Women and Childbirth in the Twentieth Century: A History of the National Birthday Trust Fund 1928–93*, Stroud, Sutton Publishing, 1997.

Willocks, J., 'The use of ultrasonic cephalometry', *Proceedings of the Royal Society of Medicine*, 1962, vol. 55, p. 640.

Willocks J. *et al.*, 'Intrauterine growth assessed by foetal cephalometry', *Journal of Obstetrics and Gynaecology of the British Commonwealth*, 1967, vol. 74, pp. 639–76.

Wing, A., 'Why don't the British treat more patients with kidney failure?', *British Medical Journal*, 1983, vol. 287, pp. 1157–8.

——, 'Treatment of renal failure in the light of increasingly limited resources', *Contributions to Nephrology*, 1985, vol. 44, pp. 260–75.

Winter, A., *Mesmerized: Powers of Mind in Victorian Britain*, Chicago, Chicago University Press, 1998.

Winter, K., *Das Gesundheitswesen in der Deutschen Demokratischen Republik*, Berlin, VEB Verlag Volk und Gesundheit, 1974.

Wolbarst, A. B., *Looking Within: How X-Ray, CT, MRI, Ultrasound, and Other Medical Images are Created and How they Help Physicians Save Lives*, London, University of California Press, 1999.

Wolfe, K., *The Churches and the British Broadcasting Corporation, 1922–1956*, London, SCM, 1984.

Wood, A., *Magnetic Ventures: The Story of Oxford Instruments*, Oxford, Oxford University Press, 2001.

Working Party of the British Transplantation Society and the Renal Association, *United Kingdom Guidelines for Living Donor Kidney Transplantation*. Access online at: http://www.jr2.ox.ac.uk/bts/index.htm, January 2000.

Working Party of the Standing Medical Advisory Committee, *Report on Sickle Cell, Thalassaemia and other Haemoglobinopathies*, London, HMSO, 1993.

Wujastyk, D., 'Medicine in India', in J. van Alphen and A. Aris (eds), *Oriental Medicine: An Illustrated Guide to the Asian Arts of Healing*, London, Serindia Publications, 1995, pp. 19–37.

Young, J., 'The Development of the Office of Alternative Medicine in the National Institutes of Health, 1991–1996', *Bulletin of the History of Medicine*, 1999, vol. 72, pp. 279–98.

Your Life in Their Hands: An Enquiry into the Effects of the Television Series Broadcast in the Spring of 1958, Part II, Additional Tables and Appendices, London, BBC, 1958.

Yoxen, E., 'Seeing with sound: a study of the development of medical images', in W. E. Bijker, T. P. Hughes and T. J. Pinch (eds), *The Social Construction of Technological Systems*, Cambridge, MA, MIT Press, 1987, pp. 281–301.

Index